W9-AQT-082

THE AMERICAN TRADITION IN THE ARTS

WITHDRAWN

Also by Richard McLanathan

Images of the Universe. Leonardo da Vinci: The Artist as Scientist

The Pageant of Medieval Art and Life

Leonard Baskin: *Eagle*, 1960, ink, 15⅞₁₆ x 11 (Munson-Williams-Proctor Institute, Utica, N.Y.)

N
6505
.M28

Richard McLanathan

THE
AMERICAN
TRADITION
IN
THE
ARTS

Harcourt, Brace & World, Inc. New York

235168

Copyright © 1968 by Richard McLanathan

*All rights reserved. No part of this publication may be reproduced
or transmitted in any form or by any means, electronic or mechanical,
including photocopy, recording, or any information storage and
retrieval system, without permission in writing from the publisher.
First edition
Library of Congress Catalog Card Number: 65-21032
Printed in the United States of America*

The lines on p. 427 from Hart Crane's "The Bridge" are from *Complete Poems
and Selected Letters* by Hart Crane © 1933, 1966 by Liveright Publishing Corp.,
reprinted by permission of Liveright, Publishers, New York.
"The Great Figure," on p. 427, is from *The Collected Earlier Poems* of William Carlos Williams,
copyright 1938 by William Carlos Williams,
reprinted by permission of New Directions Publishing Corporation.

For Jane and also for Phip

8/28/74

FOREWORD

American art is a branch of the great tree of Western European art, with its roots deep in the Near East, the classic lands of the Mediterranean, and the North. Its growth has been influenced by other arts, of the Asiatic desert and of North Africa, of the Middle and the Far East, but despite differences between the various major branches, there is an organic relationship of the whole. The characteristics of American art are, therefore, not to be found in differences in kind, but, rather, in differences of emphasis and in the combination of elements often common to the whole. America has been truly called a melting pot, and the cultural bouillabaisse that has resulted is made up of rich and varied ingredients. The prevailing flavor, however, except in the Spanish dominated Southwest and in French Canada, as in a few smaller areas subject to strong Dutch, Scandinavian, and German influence, has been British. And yet there was a sea change that took place as the ideas and ideals, the styles and forms of the Old World were transported to the New, and much of the change must be attributed to the radically different environment of the New World as well as to the traditions, preferences, and necessities of those who had settled or been born on these shores.

Especially in recent years, when American art has undergone another period of rediscovery, much of value has been written, both monographs and broader surveys. This study naturally and gratefully rests on the solid contributions of all those who have worked and are working in the same field. Its purpose is not to be one more monograph or survey, but by selecting examples of the various arts in America from the beginning of settlement to our own times—considering architecture, painting, sculpture, and the decorative arts, with some emphasis on the popular arts, seen as the productions of individual personalities and in the context of their times—to show the singular mixture of qualities and modes that constitute the characteristic style and tradition in American art.

Reproductions of works of art, whether in color or in black and white, are but shadows of the originals. Because of the drastic distortion which results from the reduction necessary for purposes of book illustration, and because color, always prob-

ix

lematical, adds greatly to expense, it was decided to use only black-and-white illustrations, but to use as many as possible while keeping the cost of the book within reasonable limits.

No author can illustrate all the works he would like to, and each individual would inevitably, from personal preference and special interest, make a different choice. Furthermore, any choice is governed by such practical considerations as whether or not a work is sufficiently meaningful in black and white and at reduced scale to make it worth including. The illustration program of this book was arrived at with all these considerations in mind.

There has been no attempt to create a visual encyclopedia of American art through more than three centuries. The field is too large and too rich for that to be possible. If, however, the illustrations suggest something of the scope and the variety of American art through these years, with perhaps something also of the vitality and quality of the American creative mind, they will have fulfilled their essential purpose. And since there can be no substitute for the experience of an original object, if the illustrations inspire readers to look at those many works of American art to be found in the ever-increasing number of museums across the country, and to seek out those examples of historic architecture which have been preserved, they will have fulfilled an even more important function as well.

In the captions for the illustrations, all paintings are in oil on canvas unless specified otherwise. Media and materials are noted where pertinent. In giving dimensions of pictures, height precedes width; for sculpture, only the major dimension is supplied; while in the case of most decorative arts objects, architecture, and such small objects as miniatures, no dimensions have been considered necessary. Credits and courtesy lines have been included in the captions. The locations of works of art which are illustrated are noted in the captions but not in the text. Locations of works not illustrated are given in the text in an abbreviated reference so as to present as little interruption to the reader as possible. The complete names of the museums and other institutions owning the works of art are listed in the back of the book, with a brief note on the nature of their collections.

No author of a book which is the product of close association with American art for many years can properly express his gratitude to all of those whose advice and interest have enabled him to achieve such insight as his abilities may have allowed. Teachers, students, colleagues, curators, dealers—all have made important contributions to his knowledge and understanding, as have those authors of the basic books in the American field, the greater number of which are included in the bibliography at the back of this volume. Two individuals especially, however, provided an invaluable opportunity for a unique experience of American art. One was Edwin J. Hipkiss, first Curator of Decorative Arts at the Museum of Fine Arts in Boston, whose pioneering work in the field not only led to the acquisition of the collections now in the Museum, but also helped to win the recognition and respect which American art now enjoys. The other was Maxim Karolik, through whose foresight, enthusiasm, and generosity the three collections which bear his and his wife's names were formed to become a part of the permanent treasures of the Boston Museum. It was a privilege to work closely with both for a number of years, and an honor to succeed the former as the second Curator of the Department. It is a deep satisfaction to acknowledge my gratitude to them both here.

No such book can be produced without the co-operation and assistance of the many individuals, too numerous to mention here, who have supplied information and photographs from which the illustrations have been chosen, who have granted permission for their reproduction, who have allowed the quotation from copyright material in the text, and who have given unselfishly of their time to check data, to read sections of the manuscript, and to answer from their special knowledge the innumerable questions which arose. To each of them goes the author's heartfelt thanks. My greatest indebtedness, however, is to my wife, whose enthusiasm, assistance, and patience made the whole project possible.

RICHARD McLANATHAN

New York City

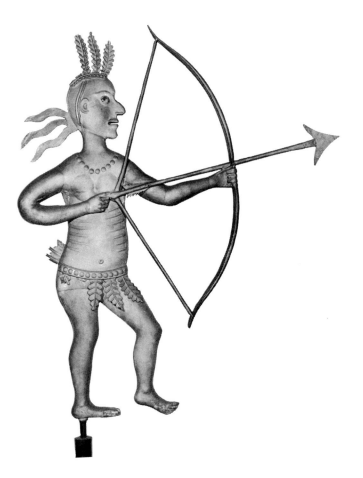

Shem Drowne: Weathervane of Province House, Boston, 1716-76, h. 48
(Massachusetts Historical Society)

CONTENTS

Contents

Contents

THE AMERICAN TRADITION IN THE ARTS

Mission San Xavier del Bac, near Tucson, Ariz., 1784-97
(Photograph, Wayne Andrews)

INTRODUCTION: SPAIN AND FRANCE IN THE NEW WORLD

America was founded in adventure. The first explorers—Spanish conquistadors, Portuguese seamen, French fishermen, English sea rovers—were adventurers in search of gold and glory. And the settlers were adventurers also, both those who came to get rich quick and were so soon disillusioned, and the rest who had the stamina to stick it out. All sought something better than they had known before, land of their own or freedom to worship as they would; some fled an unbearable past. Whether driven by hope or despair, all who came, whether in the *Mayflower*, the *Arbella*, the *Godspeed*, or the *Susan Constant*, dared to cut their ties with the life they had known and to venture forth into a New World. In an age of jet now and pay later, it is hard to conceive what an awesome and difficult barrier the Atlantic presented for the first centuries of the history of America, and how irrevocable for most was the choice to brave it. The majority who came were less prepared for what awaited them than will be the first astronauts to explore interplanetary space.

It took courage to come, for the New World was partly dream and partly nightmare. Since the beginning of time men had envisioned an idyllic land somewhere far to the westward, beyond the Pillars of Hercules, an Atlantis, Hesperides, or Hy-Brasil, where there were peace and plenty and riches for the taking. While some propagandists described the New World as such an Eden, the reports of others made it plain that, if it was an earthly paradise, the devil himself was loose in it. What else could explain the monstrous behavior of natives who tortured and ate their captives, the sweltering jungles and swamps swarming with mosquitoes, the tropical fevers, the burning deserts and the floating islands of ice perpetually enveloped in dense fogs, the poisonous serpents and ferocious beasts, the tidal waves, earthquakes, floods, and hurricanes? Constant change and violence seemed to rule the lives of men as well as of nature here. And always there was the vast continent, stretching to a limitless horizon.

The skills and experience gained in the Old World often proved of little value in the New as men were forced to experiment to meet the demands of existence. Social distinctions, so important in Europe, and differences in wealth, education, and background tended to become less pronounced as men's capacities were tried by the compelling conditions of survival. Older patterns of life and of society, no matter how much the settlers clung to them, were gradually transformed by the pressures of the new land. Ideas as well as aspirations changed, and out of the experience grew a profound sense of individualism and a self-reliance equal to the rigors overcome. The demands of life caused men to turn their hands and minds to a great variety of activities. They improvised to solve new problems, and came to judge the results functionally. If an idea worked, it was right; and if it did not, no matter how good a notion it might seem, it was abandoned. It is with good reason that pragmatism has been called the American philosophy.

The shortage of labor increased the sense of individual worth and fostered a spirit of independence. European ties remained, and inherited traditions were strong and various, but the common experience of the wilderness, the endless extent of the New World, of frequent hardship and death, and of the conquest of a continent provided a unity amid the diversity of national origin, of religion, and of class. In his varying reactions to this shared experience the immigrant adventurer became, in Crèvecœur's familiar phrase, that new man, the American.

Only gradually did settlement take place. First were corporate trading posts and plantations established under royal charters in the West Indies and along the Atlantic coast from the Caribbean northward, in much the same pattern and for the same purpose as in the East Indies, Africa, and Muscovy. But America was more than an outpost for trade in an exotic land. It was a way to release some of the pressures built up in a disturbed Europe, pressures engendered by hatred, war, and persecution. It provided a fine place to dump the unwanted, the debtors, the remittance men, the beggars, the criminals, the unemployed, and the unemployable. But for others it gave a chance to try for utopia. No matter that man had never yet achieved it. There were always those who wanted to try again, and out of their trials, unsuccessful though all such attempts are bound to be, eventually came what seemed for many the hope of the world. But for all who came it was an avenue into a new life, stranger and more unexpected than any could know.

The Spaniards were the first by more than a century. In a series of conquests more spectacular than any in history, they overthrew the empires of the Aztecs, the Incas, and the Chibchas, and the sudden, limitless wealth of their pillaged temples

Pueblo de Taos, N.M.,
photograph taken by
William Henry Jackson, c. 1884
(George Eastman House Collection)

4

and treasuries served to maintain the most inefficient and reactionary government in Europe in power for generations beyond its time. Spanish explorers fought their way through jungles, mountains, and deserts with unbelievable hardship and relentless cruelty, followed by the friars, who were just as indomitable in their missionary zeal. The king's viceroys were ruling Spanish America in regal splendor and living in cities adorned with palaces and cathedrals before a single permanent settlement had been made in the New World by another nation. The University of Mexico had flourished for nearly three quarters of a century, and three generations of grandees had lived and died in many of the stately mansions of the ancient cities of New Spain when the first boat, loaded with Pilgrim settlers, grated on the shore at Plymouth. The first printing press in the Western Hemisphere was set up in Mexico in 1539, exactly a century before Stephen Daye established the first press in any of the English colonies, in the Harvard Yard, to produce the *Bay Psalm Book, The New England Primer,* and John Eliot's monumental *Indian Bible.*

Palaces and churches remain as symbols of Spain's dominion over vast territories and numbers of the native population, but the Spanish colonial system, a ponderous autocracy, tempered, as an eminent historian has pointed out, only by corruption, was an anachronism that stifled human development and stood in the way of growth and progress.

The major artistic heritage of Spain in the New World owes little to the empty splendors of the viceregal court and much to the faith of the Jesuits and the Franciscans who established the chain of missions across what is now Texas, the Southwest, and up the West Coast. As later in New France, the artistic abilities of the native population were enlisted in the service of the church. The passion of Spanish Christianity found a new power in the *santos* and the *bultos,* painted and carved by native craftsmen. The sorrowing Virgin and the suffering Christ, the emaciated saints and the fearful skeletal figure of *Death in His Car* combine Spanish realism with the expressiveness of attenuated, sinewy form that recalls the dark-shadowed pagan past of their creators. None of the missions within the boundaries of the United States has the Baroque richness of so many of those in Mexico. Yet in their translation of familiar forms into a vernacular fitted to the skills of the natives, they are buildings of dignity and austere beauty appropriate to the rigors of the new land, and are monuments to the heroism of their founders and to the dedication of the anonymous craftsmen who raised them.

Bulto, *Death in His Car*
(Collection of the Taylor Museum
of the Colorado Springs Fine
Arts Center)

As the trading posts established by Breton fishermen along the Gulf of St. Lawrence and up the river gradually turned into settlements, the French, like the Spaniards, brought the Baroque style of contemporary Europe to America. Shortly after 1600 the greatest of early Canadian bishops, François de Laval-Montmorency, established the first art school in North America at Cap Tourment. French and Indian youths were taught all the skills necessary to build, furnish, and adorn a church, from carpentry, joinery, and masonry to painting and sculpture. The results were less spectacular than those achieved in New Spain, and the work less powerful. But the numbers involved were very few and the native tradition as different as the climate. The few steep-roofed churches that remain unspoiled by later improvement, and the wood sculptures and painted altarpieces, the embroidered vestments, and the metalwork have a simplicity and awkward vigor that give them a character of their own.

Intrepid Frenchmen enlarged the empire of New France until it spread down the Mississippi to the Gulf, and across the North Country far to the west and up to the bleak shores of Hudson Bay. They established forts and trading posts, but few settlements, and today little evidence remains of the once colossal extent of the French possessions in the New World. The oldest existing house in the Midwest, however, is a restored French Colonial building dating from about 1737 and now known as the Cahokia, Illinois, Courthouse from its use in that capacity for some years after 1793. Of upright hewn logs narrowly spaced on horizontal sills, in the construction known as *poteaux-sur-sole,* it is a larger and more luxurious example of a type common in French frontier territory from Canada to the Gulf. The interstices between the logs of such French Colonial buildings as this were filled with whatever was locally available, from soft brick to clay with Spanish moss or hair as a binder. The hipped roof of double pitch, surrounding *galerie,* casement windows with interior shutters, and end chimneys are common to a number of Louisiana plantation houses as well as to *habitant* dwellings that once existed from the Gulf to the far north, though the *galerie* often was limited to the front of the house, which was sometimes of two stories rather than one.

Of a number of great plantation houses in the French Colonial style but a handful are left. Perhaps the most distinguished is Parlange, named from an early owner in whose family it has descended, in Pointe Coupée Parish, Louisiana. Built by the Marquis Vincent de Ternant in 1750, it is of two stories with surrounding *galeries* and tall hipped roof. Standing among an-

Cahokia Courthouse,
Cahokia, Ill., c. 1737
(Photograph, Library of Congress)

6

Parlange Plantation,
Pointe Coupée Parish, La., 1750
(Photograph, Library of Congress)

cient live oaks looking toward the river, it is reached by a drive
lined with cedars and defined with a pair of octagonal *pigeon-
niers*. Luxurious in scale and generous in proportion, it has almost no decorative detail inside or out, merely simple wooden
trim, cypress floors, and plastered and papered walls.

Patrick Connelly's Tavern, built in Natchez, Mississippi,
shortly before 1800 is a smaller example of the same type.
Though similar in many respects to some of the Spanish Colonial houses of the West Coast, these few remaining buildings
in French Colonial style nevertheless represent a French tradition, once strong throughout large areas of the United States,
which otherwise exists only in romantic place names, in the legal system of the State of Louisiana, named by La Salle for the
grand monarque, and in the Creole customs that are still retained there by Americans conscious of an historic past.

Absolutism of either church or state, both of which prevailed in the Spain and the France of the seventeenth century,
did not encourage the independence of mind or allow the freedom of action necessary for success in the New World. So the
future of North America lay neither with heroic Spaniards nor
with gallant Frenchmen, but with the stubborn British and the
various nationalities which helped to populate the British colonies along the Atlantic shores. Though the purpose for the colonization was the same—to make a profit—the necessities of the
new land demanded a commitment lacking among those who

wanted to find a fortune by whatever means and return to Europe to enjoy it. The British colonies were founded with the idea of permanence. North of what became Latin America, the wealth that attracted settlers was the land itself. Though the colonial proprietors tried to retain title and thus build great feudal estates, they soon found that to exploit their opportunities they had to offer land in freehold, for, once on this side of the Atlantic, the immigrants could be kept by no one from moving on to another settlement or striking off into the wilderness if they did not care for the conditions of life in the colony. Thus, whatever the primary purpose, whether to provide a refuge for freedom of worship for various Protestant sects, as in the case of Pennsylvania, or for Catholics, as in Maryland, or an opportunity for a new life for debtors, as in North Carolina, there was a sense of destiny among the British colonials lacking among the others. And nowhere was that sense of destiny more apparent than in the "errand into the wilderness" of the founders of the Massachusetts Bay Colony.

Many differing national and regional traditions were brought to the New World where they coexisted, often influencing one another, and were influenced in turn by groups of newcomers and by ideas from Europe. But all were gradually altered by the conditions of life on the edge of a vast and wild continent.

The Cabildo, Jackson Square,
New Orleans, La., 1795
(Courtesy of Louisiana State Museum)

8

In the American arts of the seventeenth and eighteenth centuries, many of these strands may be differentiated, and the stubbornness with which men clung to the ways of their fathers, as well as the inescapable changes wrought by the new environment, may be seen in the houses and other buildings they constructed and in the things with which they furnished them, as in their patterns of life and thought. Many, especially in the longer-established centers on the coast, retained Old World habits and ideas, but men who had known the wilderness tended toward a stripped-down notion of what was important and what was not, which often paid slight regard to the attitudes and customs of the inhabitants of the older settlements. Increasingly, the power came into the hands of those who shared both the fundamentalism and the radicalism bred by the New World experience, and who felt that the future lay within their grasp. Just as the language with which they expressed their hopes and determinations was familiar, but the ideas they expressed were new, their styles in architecture, painting, and the other arts were based primarily on those of England, but the ideals which these arts embodied were somehow not the same.

As the eighteenth century progressed, the patterns of an American tradition began to emerge. The major elements were British, and Britain continued to provide the single strongest influence throughout the century, especially in the coastal regions. But there were other and conflicting elements as well, and on the frontier and in the back country curious mixtures often prevailed. The growing American tradition contained many of the discordant forces of its various components, but its basic assumptions about the nature of man, his relation to his fellow man and to nature, and his belief in a limitless potential in the New World provided a unity to match the inherent diversity in a dynamic and constantly shifting balance which has prevailed until today.

I

Colonial Enterprise: The Seventeenth Century

Detail from the gravestone of Joseph Tapping, 1678,
King's Chapel, Boston, Mass. (Photograph, Allan I. Ludwig)

THE TRADITION AND THE ARTS OF THE PURITANS

The Massachusetts Bay Colony was intended by its leaders to be "a City upon a Hill." It was both a holy experiment to prove that men could live according to the Bible and prosper, and a Puritan stronghold and refuge in the New World from which to advance the religious cause, both in the New and the Old. The Bay Colony by its charter included the area already settled by the Pilgrims at Plymouth. The Pilgrims, too, wanted to purge the church of all the man-made elements, ritual, sculptures, paintings, stained-glass windows, and the other things which they felt came between man and God. But their small group had left England, and had been given sanctuary in Holland for a time before coming to the New World in 1620. The founders of the Bay Colony, however, had stayed in England, hoping to reform the church from within. When it appeared that Archbishop Laud with the approval of the king was determined to lead the established church back toward catholicism, the Puritan leaders, with the support of London merchants, decided also to emigrate to New England, and, in 1630, the Great Migration began.

Within a period of six months, more than a dozen ships carrying more than a thousand men, women, and children, with all the supplies and belongings they could take aboard, landed on Massachusetts shores. The charter they brought with them granted great power to the magistrates of the new colony, and the result was a theocracy, as intolerant of deviation in Protestant dogma as either New France or New Spain in Catholic. Yet because they believed the early church to have been organized along democratic lines, they so formed the Congregational Church in the New World, thus creating a significant precedent for the future.

The Pilgrims' difficult experience of exile had welded their little group into close community. The Mayflower Compact, which John Quincy Adams called the "genesis of American Democracy," was drawn up and signed "at Cap-Codd the 11. of November . . . Ano: Dom. 1620," to create a "Civill body politick" and to ensure the rule of law and the rights of individuals under governors of their own election. To the south, the first settlers suffered tribulations so severe that, according to Captain John Smith's account in his *Generall Historie of Virginia*, 1624, "one amongst the rest did kill his wife, powdered her, and had eaten part of her before it was known; for which hee was executed, as hee well deserved: now whether shee was better roasted, boyld, or carbonado'd, I know not; but of such a dish as powdered wife I have never heard of." Nevertheless, Virginians won the same legal rights and privileges, for, as Smith remarked, "No man wil go from hence to have lesse freedome there than here." English common law, due process, individual property rights, and government through a representative assembly were early established in the British colonies. It was the exercise of these rights during long periods of healthy neglect by the mother country that laid the foundations and brought about the necessity for independence before the end of the following century.

Many of the Puritans settled in what became Boston, where they found a certain Mr. William Blackstone enjoying the pleasures of a considerable library of the classics in a rural retreat among apple trees atop Beacon Hill. Others founded Ipswich, Salem, and other towns along the North Shore. With hard work and London connections, they soon established trade with the West Indies as well as with England, learned the useful alchemy that turns West Indian molasses into rum, and prospered. Serious of purpose, they worked hard to make their New Canaan flourish. "An hour's idleness is as sinful as an hour's drunkenness," one stern Puritan pastor admonished his flock, and with this spirit, and the conviction that the Lord rewarded the godly with prosperity in this world as well as with salvation in the next, success became an outward sign of grace. "From Rags to Riches," the great American success story, was thus written early. Cotton Mather in his ponderous epic of the great Puritan experiment, the *Magnalia Christi Americana,* made this clear in his bowdlerized account of the career of William Phipps, from a frontier cabin to knighthood and the royal governorship of the Province of Massachusetts, via a diving operation which retrieved a king's ransom of gold from a sunken Spanish plate ship off Hispaniola. According to Mather, the bluff ex-lumberjack and mariner, addicted to what might be described as shore-leave behavior on a full-time basis, was a spotless instrument of the Lord's will and a shining example of virtue's reward, which included a rich wife, a fleet of ships, and a handsome brick mansion on Boston's fashionable Green Lane furnished with the latest from London and supplied with a well-stocked wine cellar.

There may have been few whose rise was as spectacular, but many a man who had arrived penniless ended up a prosperous citizen with a considerable estate. Wages were high because there was always more work than workers, and labor itself was a virtue. No one frowned on trade, since it was the source of wealth. Even the Southern planters, who had not yet heard that they were gallant cavaliers who were supposed to spend all their time wooing the fair, fighting duels in their honor, riding blooded horses, and gambling fortunes, did all the business they could. Like their neighbors to the north, they were intent on making a success so that they could enjoy a position of power and prestige of which their antecedents had never dreamed.

Those who knew a craft or set out to learn one did especially well. Some combined half a dozen activities. John Hull, for instance, was a farmer, a blacksmith, a breeder of horses and cattle, and a merchant whose ships traded with the West Indies, England, and Spain. Not only the first and one of the best of colonial silversmiths, he also served as treasurer of the Bay Colony and, as mintmaster, produced the famous pine-tree shillings. There was always work for turners, joiners, carpenters, millers, housewrights and shipwrights, blacksmiths and white-smiths, shoemakers, saddlers, and coopers, and rarely did a man limit himself to just one category, but turned his hand to whatever was needed. And especially in the earlier days, so many of the basic necessities had to be supplied that there was little time for any but the most useful arts. Yet the spirit of pride in the new homes recently established in what had been a wilderness expressed itself in ways that went beyond the purely functional. Blankets and coverlets were woven in decorative patterns, chests were carved and painted in variations of designs handed down for generations and were often inscribed with initials and dates, bed hangings were embroidered, and curtains were hung at windows. Ingeniously made treen tankards and salvers were gradually replaced with pewter, and finally perhaps by silver, all usually of colonial manufacture.

Puritanism, with its abhorrence of frivolity and show, seems barren ground from which to expect a flowering of the arts, yet its ideals were as important for the arts as for other aspects of American culture. The Puritans shared with their times the idea that the arts were largely practical, and, as was general until the end of the eighteenth century, they used the term in the sense inherited from the Middle Ages and long expressed in the articles of apprenticeship in which the master agreed to instruct the youth in the "art and mystery" of his craft, whatever that

craft might be. But even more than their contemporaries, they believed that the arts, in the limited use of them that the Puritan faith allowed, were a part of life rather than merely an adornment, and were supposed to fulfill a serious purpose. Just as they cultivated the "plain style" in their speech and writing, an expository manner appropriate to the clear interpretation of the Scriptures in their sermons, they demanded a similarly straightforward style in their arts.

The faith of the Puritans heightened their respect for the individual, since it regarded each person as a separate soul, destined either for salvation or damnation, a fate preordained in heaven. They knew that there were saints among them—the elect—and the likeness, the identity, of each became a matter of moment. The smallest details of life took on significance because each episode, no matter how minor, was an expression of the will of God and a part of His grand plan. Thus the features of the Puritan worthies were recorded by their compatriots with an unsparing realism in the same spirit in which William Bradford faithfully recorded *The History of Plimoth Plantation*, John Winthrop kept his famous *Journal*, and Cotton Mather compiled his weighty *Magnalia Christi Americana*. Like the writer, the limner was acting as "a Lord's remembrancer" of "God's divine Providence" which pervaded every aspect of existence. The Puritans' belief in the divine order encouraged an orderly clarity in their lives and works as well as in their towns and villages. It led to the acuteness of vision seen in their portraits. Everything was scrutinized and noted with that sense of fact which has continued as a characteristic of American art.

The plain style informed their architecture and other arts equally with painting and letters. It represented a higher utilitarianism and was essentially functional. The arts of the Puritans were not, however, dehumanized, since they were dedicated not only to the service of God, but also to that of man. Their houses were more livable than many of the period on either side of the ocean, though notably unadorned, and their meetinghouses were impressively dignified, since they were the symbols of their faith and of the central pattern of their lives, the community dedicated to the service of God. For them, the aesthetic could not exist apart from the humanly useful. As a result, art for art's sake has never been widely accepted in America, and art has generally been associated with a higher and often directly moral purpose.

There was little work in the Puritan community for the artist as we know him today. But there was much for the craftsmen,

Detail from the gravestone
of Samuel Green,
1759, Lexington, Mass.
(Photograph, Allan I. Ludwig)

some of whom on occasion turned from painting houses or vessels to painting signs, hatchments, coaches, and perhaps even portraits, while others tried their hand at carving death's-heads and angels, hourglasses, and extinguished torches on tombstones, a number of which are preserved in New England graveyards, to form the first regional style in sculpture in America. Usually of slate, the tombstones are in a totally different tradition from those sculptured in England during the period, being based on flat patterns derived from woodcuts and engravings, such as the broadside elegy decorated with a still medieval skeleton or other *memento mori*. On the Joseph Tapping stone of 1678, in the burying ground of King's Chapel in Boston, is carved a vigorous allegory of grisly death and bearded time borrowed from Francis Quarles's *Hieroglyphiques of the Life of Man,* published in London forty years earlier. By 1709 Nathaniel Lamson of Charlestown, Massachusetts, dared to try his hand at a portrait effigy on the stone of the Reverend Jonathan Pierpont in Wakefield, Massachusetts, creating an image of strange intensity and power. Families like the Soules of Plympton and the Worcesters of Harvard, Massachusetts, continued the old tradition into the second half of the eighteenth century with increasing geometric stylization. Their soul symbols, rising heavenward, are so abstract that some have incongruously thought them influenced by African images. Though the local tradition that these stones represent was soon to disappear entirely among tons of marble urns and classically draped mourning females, the few examples that remain are expressive reminders of the faith with which the Puritans celebrated the soul's passage from a sinful world into the shining light of a new Jerusalem.

Puritan emphasis on the individual and disapproval of mundane scenes or religious images limited the artist to portraiture. The richer of the Puritans, like the more successful of the Southern planters of the seventeenth and earlier eighteenth centuries, had their portraits painted when they went back to England. That of *Governor John Winthrop* (Massachusetts Historical) of 1649, for example, is a solid piece of conservative painting strongly influenced, as was so much of English art and fashion of the day, by the Dutch. That hardy soldier, Sir Richard Saltonstall, brought over a group of family portraits with him when he came to settle Watertown, Massachusetts. The portraits painted on this side of the Atlantic were that much more provincial, but they were, in general, in the same style, totally unlike the Flemish elegance that ruled at court, where Van Dyck and the far greater Rubens were the gods of art. But the Baroque rich-

Nathaniel Lamson:
Detail from the gravestone
of Rev. Jonathan Pierpont, 1709,
Wakefield, Mass.
(Photograph, Allan I. Ludwig)

17

ness of courtly art was associated in the minds of the middle-class Puritans with licentiousness and papistry. More preoccupied with inner life than with outward show, they created powerful and impressive characterizations.

A self-portrait of a sea captain who arrived in New England in about 1650 is a revealing document and character study. Captain Thomas Smith stares out of the vigorously and far from expertly painted *Self-Portrait* with an intensity that suggests the scrutiny of the mirror image that was his model. The softness of the hair emphasizes the sternness of the expression, as does the unexpected delicacy of the lace stock. In the background is a glimpse of a fortress and an engagement at sea beyond, a detail

Thomas Smith: *Self-Portrait*, c. 1690, 24½ x 23¾ (Worcester Art Museum)

whose significance has vanished with the years. His right hand holds a skull resting on a scrap of paper, painted with painstaking care so that we may read the Captain's verses inscribed on it in a very definite hand:

> Why why should I the World be minding
> therin a World of Evils Finding.
>   Then Farwell World: Farwell thy Jarres
>   thy Joies thy Toies thy Wiles thy Warrs
> Truth Sounds Retreat: I am not Sorye.
>   The Eternall Drawes to him my heart
>   By Faith (which can thy Force Subvert)
> To Crown me (after Grace) with Glory.
>   T. S.

As Edgar Richardson has noted, it is "as if some lichen-covered tombstone in a Puritan burying ground by the sea were speaking to us."

Sturdy and stern, with a faith founded upon a rock, such were the Puritan founders of New England. Anne Bradstreet (*The Tenth Muse Lately Sprung Up in America,* to quote the title of her book of verses published in London in 1650) observed with sensitivity and pleasure the beauty of the New England countryside, listened to the songs of birds and the chirping of crickets, and enjoyed the turning of the leaves in autumn. No one has ever described the spider and its web in more perceptive detail than Jonathan Edwards, America's greatest Puritan theologian. But for them, as for every good Puritan, the tangible world was at best a distraction and too often a lure to lead the minds of the faithful away from "the mystery of God's grace and man's corruption."

Yet there is a sensitive appreciation of the charm of childhood in the full-length portrait by an unknown limner of little *Alice Mason.* Painted in 1670, probably in Boston, it is one of the earliest of American paintings and remains one of the freshest. Still medieval in its flatness, despite the starkly simple design of the whole, it reveals an unexpected gentleness in the delicate detailing of the figure of the two-year-old girl, dressed in her best finery and clutching an apple. And there is a fragile beauty in the pair of portraits of Mr. and Mrs. John Freake, painted four years later by another unknown limner in a closely related style. The serious young merchant and shipowner, who was to be "killed by ye blowing up ye deck of a ship by ye Carelessnes of some aboard" shortly after, is soberly but richly dressed. The dark-brown coat with silver braid and buttons and the white gloves and Venetian lace collar make a subtle pattern of the time-darkened canvas.

Anonymous: *Alice Mason,* 1670,
38¼ x 24⅞
(Courtesy of the Adams National Historic
Site, National Park Service,
United States Department of the Interior)

Anonymous: *John Freake*, c. 1674, 42½ x 36¾
(Worcester Art Museum, Sarah C. Garver Fund)

20

Anonymous: *Mrs. Elizabeth Freake and Baby Mary*, c. 1674, 42½ x 36¾
(Worcester Art Museum, gift of Mr. and Mrs. Albert W. Rice)

Mrs. Freake and her little daughter Mary are portrayed with even greater delicacy. The lace at the mother's neck and gold and white embroidery on her red petticoat appearing beneath her gray-green skirt, and the sleeves tied with red and black bows, contrast with the pale yellow dress and cap of the little girl. The creamy white of the lace on apron and pinafore, the light blond hair, and the pale flesh tones complete a delightful color scheme. The paint is firmly and evenly applied and shows all the qualities of the knowing artisan. Unlike Captain Smith, who used modeling in tones of light and shade to achieve his effects, the Freake and Mason limners interpreted their subjects in terms of flat, linear design, according to a tradition that harks back to Elizabethan painting in England. The areas of soft color and delicate pattern are carefully brushed in detailed strokes. Craftsmanship rose to art through perception and intensity, to produce the finest paintings to be done in the colonies during the century.

Thus did traditions overlap in the New World. The vigorous provincial Baroque of Captain Smith could precede in time the Freake and Mason limners' return at a later date to a yet earlier manner. But whatever the stylistic influence on the largely untrained men who painted these early portraits, their unifying characteristic is an intense expression of the individuality of the sitter.

EARLY ARCHITECTURE IN THE COLONIES

Among the most memorable of the personalities the limners have recorded for us is *Anne Pollard,* whose likeness dates from 1721, when she was, according to her own reckoning, a hundred years old. Since she had long outlived the rest of her generation, there was no one to gainsay her account of being the first one to jump ashore, as a young girl, from the first boat to land John Winthrop's followers at Salem. Looking at the mask of age that the unknown painter has depicted for us—a face on which time has written its record of experience, but with an indomitable light in the penetrating eyes that observe us not without a gleam of humor—one finds it unlikely that anyone would have had the temerity to deny Mrs. Pollard's story, if, in the presence of such an ancient beldam, he could have been so rude.

One would have given much to have heard Mrs. Pollard's reminiscences of the beginnings of settlement, of the pressing needs of people weakened by disease and the hardship of voyage in tiny crowded vessels that rolled and pitched as they lumbered through stormy seas, and, after the landing, of hunting and fishing to provide fresh food, and of the shelters constructed as quickly as possible with whatever materials were at hand. Some of these were dugouts roofed with poles and bark. Others were huts made of stakes driven into the ground with wattles woven between them and then daubed with clay, while the roof, resting on a ridge supported on forked posts, was of thatch or turf. But the most practical form was the wigwam, borrowed from the Indians. Made with an oblong framework of poles driven into the ground with their upper ends bent together to form a rounded roof, it was covered with bark, woven mats, or skins. The colonists soon improved on the hole in the roof for smoke by building fireplaces with wooden, clay-daubed chimneys at one end and a wooden door at the other. The re-creations at Jamestown and at the Pioneer Village in Salem give a good idea of the various makeshifts that were hurriedly adopted in all the early settlements, north or south.

As soon as possible, each householder built a frame house of the general type re-created at Plimoth Plantation. By 1627, when the emissary of the merchants of New Amsterdam, Isaac de Rasières, made an official visit to Governor Bradford, "honor-

Anonymous: *Anne Pollard,* 1721,
28 x 23
(Massachusetts Historical Society)

ably attended," according to a contemporary account, "with a noise of trumpeters," he reported that "New Plymouth," lying "on the slope of a hill, stretching east, toward the sea-coast," had "a broad street about a cannon-shot of eight hundred [yards] long leading down the hill; with a street crossing in the middle southward to the rivulet and northward to the land. The houses are constructed of hewn planks, with gardens, also enclosed behind and at the sides with hewn planks; so that their houses and courtyards are arranged in very good order, with a stockade against a sudden attack; and at the ends of the streets there are three wooden gates. In the center, on the cross-street, stands the Governor's house. . . . Upon the hill they have a large, square house, with a flat roof, made of thick sawn planks, stayed with oak beams, upon the top of which they have six cannon, which shoot iron balls of four and five pounds, and command the surrounding country. The lower part they use for their church, where they preach on Sundays and the usual holidays."

Iron was scarce and precious, so the usual fasteners were pegs or treenails—"trunnels," they called them—instead. Walls were boarded or covered with hand-split clapboards, and the roof was often thatched, though hand-riven shakes were increasingly used as less likely to catch fire and more satisfactory in the climate of the New World. Chimneys were at first made of planks lined with clay, or of sticks laid log-cabin fashion and daubed liberally with clay, but these were replaced as soon as possible with the safer fieldstone or brick. Except in extraordinary cases, windows had only shutters and were left unglazed during the first decades, and for generations after on the frontier, where similarly primitive conditions repeated themselves as settlers moved ever westward into the wilderness.

Little remains today of the great forests that once covered so much of the British Isles. It is fortunate that many of the early settlers came from East Anglia and other districts where wood was still plentiful enough to be used for building, and brought with them a tradition of wood construction. The houses they built in the New World were as nearly like those they left behind as the strange new conditions would allow. By the middle of the century Edward Johnson, in his *Wonder-Working Providence of Sions Saviour in New England* (1654), observed that, in all the settlements of the Bay Colony, "the Lord hath been pleased to turn all the wigwams, huts, and hovels the English dwelt in at their first coming, into orderly, fair, and well-built houses, well furnished . . . together with orchards filled with goodly fruit trees, and gardens with variety of flowers . . ." as

Plimoth Plantation, a re-creation of the Pilgrims' settlement as it was about 1630, Plymouth, Mass. (Photograph, Plimoth Plantation)

complete a re-creation as the colonists could make of the towns and villages they remembered in England.

They were not the New England towns that we think of today, with white painted dwellings facing on a green dominated by a church with a tall steeple. Steep-roofed houses—the larger, with overhanging second stories, weathered and low-studded, often with thatched roofs, and with small windows heavily shuttered— were scattered along the road, their narrow lots extending to the rear. A foursquare meetinghouse was prominently located, since it served both for religious services and for meetings of the town, where public business was transacted. The minister's house, perhaps a little larger than the rest, was usually nearby. There was a town pound for stray animals, and a mill on a neighboring stream. Sudbury, Massachusetts, was such a village, founded in 1638 among the lush meadows of the Musketaquid River, its houses clustered around one of the large irregular areas of common ground used for pasturage "for working cattel." But it was unlike the English towns that Sudbury's in-habitants had left in that here every adult male was a landowner who took full part in the affairs of the town government and was eligible for public office. This was the profound difference.

There were no log cabins in the early settlements except on Delaware Bay, where Swedes and Finns established New Sweden in 1638. Generations later, the Scots borrowed the form from Delaware and introduced it throughout the frontier areas, where it proved so practical that it was universally adopted wherever there were trees available. Its use became so general that for a later age it became the symbol of a simpler, earlier America, with its rugged vigor and homespun virtue.

There was another type of log construction, however, that was in general use from the earliest times for building defensible structures such as blockhouses and the garrison houses to which everyone in the neighborhood flocked for safety in case of attack. Logs were hewn square with the broad ax and notched together at the corners in half-dovetail or lapped joints which were then pegged. Though its windows have been enlarged, the McIntire Garrison House in Scotland, Maine, still stands, basically un-altered, as an example of the time-defying solidity of the massive timbers beneath the outer covering of clapboards. With small windows protected by plank shutters and alert defenders at the loopholes, such buildings withstood many an attack from howling warriors during the long time of troubles that have been called Queen Anne's War and the French and Indian War, and the other remote colonial phases of Europe's dynastic and political upheavals.

There was comparatively little difference in architecture up and down the coast during the earlier years. Most of the early houses in the colonies were of wood, the universal American material, though brick soon began to be used in increasing quan-tities in the South. Dating from about 1655, Bacon's Castle in Surrey County, Virginia, with its curved Flemish gables and immense, clustered Tudor chimneys, set diagonally and joined only at the caps, is the most remarkable early example remain-ing. Virginia had some half-timbered houses within a short time of settlement, and there were probably some in the North also, but it soon proved practical to cover the plaster, too vulnerable to American weather, with clapboards. Houses were sheathed inside with boards set either horizontally or vertically. All sorts of material was used for insulation between the inner and outer walls—unbaked bricks, eelgrass, sawdust, and wattle and daub.

The Fairbanks House in Dedham, Massachusetts, is reputed to be the earliest frame house still in existence in America. The oldest part, about half the main block, probably dates back to 1636. As was the case with a number of such houses, it began with a small building of a single room and a loft with a chimney at one end. Then it was doubled in ground plan with an addition next to the chimney, whose flue was doubled also. Then it was increased in height, and, finally, ells were added. The low sweep of the roof, the dark, clapboarded surfaces, and the small windows, since replaced, recall houses of similar date still to be found in the southeastern counties of England whence so many of the early New Englanders came. The various enlargements and additions made through the years are clearly seen in the picturesque and organic massing, determined in true medieval fashion by function rather than by any preconceived notions of design or such abstract principles as symmetry, which were to transform the architecture of the next century in America from its ancient traditions into the Renaissance style of contemporary Georgian England.

Fairbanks House, Dedham, Mass., begun in 1636
(Photograph, The Fairbanks Family in America, Inc.)

27

Adam Thoroughgood House, Norfolk, Va.,
1636-40 (Photograph, Norfolk Museum of
Arts and Sciences)

Another aspect of the medieval tradition is represented by the brick house that Adam Thoroughgood built between 1636 and 1640 in Princess Anne County near Norfolk, Virginia. Thoroughgood came to America as an indentured servant in 1621, earned his freedom, and prospered. In its original form, his house, like the Fairbanks House, was steep-roofed and a story and a half high, but it had two rooms to a floor. There were end chimneys, which became common in Southern houses, and medieval cross-mullioned windows with fixed transoms beneath segmental arches. It is an example of a type of house that was also built in wood throughout much of the South in the seventeenth century and—with the substitution of sash windows for casements, the addition of dormers to light the upper story, and but a few minor changes—on into the eighteenth. The massive chimneys, constructed wholly outside the house, and rising in stages, became a standard feature in the region.

At almost exactly the same time the Reverend Henry Whitfield and his followers founded the town of Guilford on the shores of Long Island Sound in Connecticut. They bought the site from the Indians in 1639 and apparently started immediately to build the massive stone house that still stands, a unique remaining example of stone construction of very early date, intended not only as a home for the minister, but also as a garrison and meetinghouse. The hall has a hinged wooden partition to divide it so that during the winter the entire space, large enough for religious services and town meetings, need not be heated when not in use. In almost all the early houses the cooking was done in the great fireplace in the hall, or keeping room, as it was also called. It served as dining and living room as well, and often had a bedstead in one corner. In the case of the Whitfield House, however, a separate kitchen was soon added, giving the building an L-shaped plan, with a stair tower built in the angle, so that the whole has a thoroughly medieval look.

The combination of the wood-building tradition of many of the colonists and the scarcity of lime for mortar combined to keep masonry construction at a minimum. It markedly increased, however, as the eighteenth century approached, especially in the growing cities, where wood proved a fire hazard, and after 1700 most of the more substantial buildings, public or private, were built of brick. Late in the seventeenth century Philadelphia was described as a city of stately houses "of brick, generally three stories high, after the mode of London . . . several families in each." William Penn's prosperous capital thus had a Georgian look even before the turn of the century.

Whitfield House, Guilford, Conn., c. 1640
(Photograph, William Bixby, Jr., Killingworth, Conn.)

By the end of the seventeenth century, most of the houses in the towns had windows of diamond panes, brick or stone chimneys, and the kind of comfort earlier enjoyed only by the governors and elders. The most classic example remaining of a seventeenth-century dwelling is the Parson Capen House in Topsfield, Massachusetts. It was not built until 1683, yet its style is that of a century earlier in England. Beautifully proportioned, generous in scale, it suggests the importance of the position of the minister in the community. The second story has a framed overhang in the front, while the attic has an overhang at the sides. Both are bracketed and have pendants at the corners, "pendills," as they are called in early records. Its paneled chimney is a perfect specimen of its kind.

The interior of the Capen House has spacious rooms, with low ceilings and cavernous fireplaces. As was usual in New England during this period and for a century later, the central chimney has tremendous bulk. It contains the flues for a fireplace in every room, and during constant use in the colder months the massive brickwork stored up warmth for the whole house. Opening the heavy front door, made of several thicknesses of planks fastened

Parson Capen House, Topsfield, Mass., 1683 (Photograph, Richard McLanathan)

together with nails whose heads form a simple pattern, one enters a narrow hall. Directly opposite the front door is the steep, boxed stair, winding upward against the face of the chimney, to the left is the hall or keeping room, and to the right, the parlor or great chamber. The interiors are entirely of wood, embellished only by the molded edges of the boards that sheathe them, and the doors are simply made of boards cleated together. The structure of the house is revealed throughout to express the austerity and the dignity of the Puritan ideal.

While the settlers of Virginia, where Anglicanism was established, built churches of brick in a Gothic style that was anathema to the Puritans, the latter created a new architectural form, the meetinghouse, as their place of worship. Suspicious of cruciform plans, stained glass, sculptured ornament, and other "theatrical gaudiness," in Cotton Mather's phrase, they raised buildings as bare and simple as barns. Often square or nearly so, meetinghouses had central aisles to separate the rows of painfully hard benches for the men on one side and the women on the other.

The focus of the interior was not the altar but the pulpit, for the sermon was the most important element in the service. Sometimes there was a gallery for additional members of the congregation, and the roofs were often hipped, or sometimes pyramidal, rising to a small platform which carried a belfry. The outstanding example is the Old Ship Meetinghouse in Hingham, Massachusetts, the oldest remaining church in what used to be the British colonies. It was built in 1681 at a cost of £430, paid for by the congregation, who voted that its dimensions be 45 by 55 feet, with posts 20 feet high. Though it was later enlarged, its original leaded windows were replaced by sliding sash, and Georgian porches were added to it, it still preserves its original three monumental king-post trusses spanning the shorter dimension, whose curved struts suggested to earlier observers the construction of an inverted ship and thus gave the building its name. In the eighteenth century pews replaced the narrow oak benches, and a gallery was added, but the appearance of the lofty interior is otherwise unchanged. The exposed framing has the medieval dignity of a Gothic hall, and properly invites the comparison, not only because of its system of construction, but also because its trusses have a longer span than the width of the nave of any English Gothic cathedral. Its clapboarded, painted exterior has a similar forthright logic, and the whole presents the functional Puritan aesthetic with laconic directness.

Other such meetinghouses were built during the later seventeenth century and on into the eighteenth. Notable among them was Boston's Old Brick Meetinghouse of 1713, the most important building of its kind in the colonies until it was surpassed within a decade by Christ Church on Salem Street in the North End of Boston, better known as Old North, from whose soaring steeple the sexton, Robert Newman, flashed the two signal lanterns to send his friend Paul Revere on his momentous ride. Christ Church was designed by a print seller named William Price, who was obviously inspired by the churches built by Sir Christopher Wren after the Great Fire of London in 1666, and thereafter Wren's influence gradually transformed the colonial meetinghouse into the church.

The older tradition continued for some time, however, as a few spare, steepleless structures continued to be built. One of the best preserved is that in Alna, Maine, dating from as late as 1789. The starkness of its clearly ordered, white-painted interior is relieved only by the balustered divisions that replace the earlier box pews, and by the slightly curving profiles of the supports of the gallery. The Alna Meetinghouse stands alone in an open field on a wind-swept hilltop, a reminder of the stubborn continuity of Puritan tradition.

17th-cent. room, with turned armchair, a joined bench and table with treenware,
inlaid chest of drawers with a Bible box on it, and turned candle stand
(Courtesy, Henry Francis du Pont Winterthur Museum)

EARLY COLONIAL FURNITURE AND FURNISHINGS

There is little record of what the Puritans were able to bring across the Atlantic with them, but it could not have been much. And because the resources of the Pilgrims were far slenderer and their vessel tiny and badly overcrowded, they must have brought even less. Undoubtedly a few things came, yet if all the objects of various kinds reputed to have been in the *Mayflower*'s cargo were gathered together, they would "freight an Indiaman of good tonnage" as a nineteenth-century writer observed. Enough examples of early furniture remain, however, to give an idea of what seventeenth-century American interiors must have looked like, and to make it possible to trace the growing variety and comparative luxury of types of furnishings and a gradually increasing use of Renaissance styles in anticipation of the greater wealth and ease of colonial life which were to appear in the eighteenth century.

Some of the Pilgrims' possessions, dating from the years soon after settlement, are known, many of which may be seen in the Historical Society at Plymouth. Among such early pieces is the sturdy cradle, framed in oak with pine panels and having a galleried hood with small turned balusters, that dates from the middle years of the seventeenth century and descended in the family of Samuel Fuller, who was a Mayflower passenger.

There is a chair that belonged to William Bradford, the respected governor of the Plymouth colony for over thirty years. Despite its connection with Bradford, it is of a type called a Brewster chair because later generations associated the style with Bradford's equally famous contemporary, Elder William Brewster, who was also a Pilgrim leader. Made of ash in about 1640, it has heavy round posts and turned spindles both above and below the seat. Originally, there were round finials atop the front posts. Usage through the centuries has worn off the lower ends of the posts up to the level of the stretcher. When the Governor sat in it, perhaps to write part of his famous history of the Plymouth Plantation, it undoubtedly had the cushion for which the seat is designed.

Another type of what was always called a "great chair" in the early inventories is the Carver chair, named from the example in Plymouth that belonged to John Carver, the first governor of

Fuller cradle, c. 1650
(Nutting Collection,
Wadsworth Atheneum, Hartford, Conn.)

33

Gov. Edward Winslow's armchair,
made in Cheapside, London, 1614
(The Pilgrim Society, Plymouth, Mass.)

the Plymouth colony. Unlike the Brewster chair, it has no turnings below the seat.

Slat-back armchairs are another type of great chair, made from the earliest times. Because the curved slats in the back are more comfortable than the turnings of the Brewster and Carver chairs, slat-back chairs continue to be made down to our own day.

The fourth kind of great chair is the wainscot chair, framed and paneled according to the same principle of construction as the Fuller cradle. In England, where there was a differentiation between the crafts, wainscot chairs were made by a joiner, while the others were made by a turner, since their parts were turned on the lathe. In the colonies, however, one man was likely to do both jobs.

The most important piece of furniture in the seventeenth-century house was a cupboard, either a "court cubbard," as it was listed in 1657 in Governor Bradford's inventory, which has an open shelf for the display of ornaments along with a closed section, or else a press cupboard, in which drawers replace the open shelf. The Wadsworth Atheneum, in Hartford, Connecticut, has a handsome Southern example of the court cupboard, dating from about 1640, made of oak, with yellow pine as the secondary wood, and found near the border of Virginia and Maryland. The bulbous turnings are typical, but there were often split turnings used as additional decorative elements, as in a press cupboard from Salem, Massachusetts, dating from later in the century, which is now in the Henry Ford Museum in Dearborn, Michigan. The turnings were painted black to simulate ebony, for a touch of added elegance.

These pieces of furniture, though often described as of the "Pilgrim style," actually are Jacobean, because their prototypes were introduced into England by Flemish craftsmen during the reign of James I. The style is a watered-down form of Italian Renaissance, then beginning to penetrate northern Europe. As in the case of other styles transported into the New World, it continued in vogue after it had become outmoded in Europe.

While the houses of the better-established communities along the coast might boast imposing furnishings, for most of the seventeenth century the average colonial householder was content with the simplest form of bed, a trestle table, benches, and a stool or two, perhaps of the three- or four-legged variety, such as are commonly called milking stools today, or perhaps a form or joint stool, so called because it was a product of the joiner's craft. Stretcher tables were similarly constructed, with legs ornamented with simple turnings.

The general storage piece was the six-board chest, one of the most completely functional furniture forms ever devised, which could be made by anyone with the commonest of materials and a modicum of skill. Earlier examples were put together with pegs and later ones with nails. More elaborate were the joined chests, like those associated with the name of Thomas Dennis of Ipswich, Massachusetts, to be followed by chests with drawers as well as with hinged tops. Most of the commoner furniture, almost completely medieval in style, was simply worn out by much use and then discarded, and the remaining examples are thus extremely rare, while some of the more pretentious pieces were more highly valued and have lasted to our own time.

Among such prized possessions were Bible or desk boxes, often with slanting tops and decorated with shallow carving, like one in the Brooklyn Museum which has chip-carved rosettes and other motives suggesting Netherlandish prototypes. Another example, in Detroit, has a front decorated with a bold tulip pattern suggesting a relation to the famous sunflower chests, which were joined case pieces developed in Connecticut in the second half of the seventeenth century, several of which were perhaps made by Peter Blin of Wethersfield. The tulip pattern originally came to England from Holland with the Restoration, while the sunflower is probably a New World variety of the old Tudor rose.

The Connecticut Valley also saw the origin of the Hadley chest, whose creation has been ascribed to one Nicholas Disbrowe, one of the founders of Hartford, Connecticut, in 1636. Whether the work of Disbrowe, or of Samuel Belding or John Allis of Hatfield, Massachusetts, these chests are all solidly constructed. Their shallow, carved decorations were originally painted red, brown, or green like the Bible boxes, since the early colonists, whether Puritans or not, liked color in their furniture

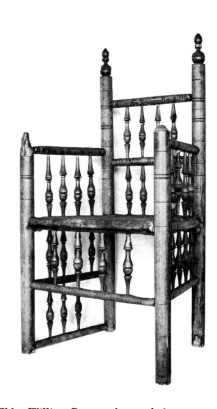

Elder William Brewster's armchair, 17th cent.
(The Pilgrim Society, Plymouth, Mass.)

Press cupboard, Massachusetts, 1680–1700
(Owned by the Henry Ford Museum & Greenfield Village)

35

as in other household objects and in costume. A painted chest of drawers made in New England in the late seventeenth century emulates expensive japanned furniture in its exuberant decoration of gardens with trees and flowers and formal façades, motives borrowed from textiles, embroideries, and other sources, in red and white against a black ground.

As the century progressed, many new forms of furniture came to the colonies. The Restoration brought caned chairs and settees from the Continent into England, and these made their way across the Atlantic, bringing to America the Charles II style of tall proportion, crested backs, and turned legs that often ended in Spanish feet. The East India Company started to import tea into England about 1650, but its high cost caused its use to remain medicinal until increasing importation lowered prices. The addiction of Catherine of Braganza, Charles II's Portuguese queen, to tea drinking created a craze that made tea tables, pots, caddies, and cups a necessity in a well-appointed home late in the century. At least partly for this reason, gateleg tables were increasingly common, and the butterfly table became almost an American specialty.

Banister-back chairs, of similar proportion and style, were popular, while chairs with padded seats and backs, often called Spanish chairs, were upholstered in leather or flame-stitch embroidery like the squabs on the day beds, which were another new furniture type. Slant-top desks became more common with the increase in letter writing. The advent of the wing chair in the latter part of the century was a real step ahead in comfort, and the vigorous forms it assumed were a measure of the skill and the individuality of their makers.

By 1700 the houses of the more prosperous colonists had assumed an air of comfort and, in some cases, of comparative luxury which seems out of accord with the Puritan ideal. The Jacobean style, with the usual time lag, was modified by and merged with the William and Mary. Walnut gradually replaced oak as the dominant wood. High chests, or highboys, as they are generally called in America, replaced the more ponderous court and press cupboards, vase turnings replaced the heavier bulbous balusters, and ornately carved surfaces with applied split turnings gave way to effects of pattern and color gained by veneering and inlaying with exotic, richly grained woods to prepare the way for the greater formality and elegance of the eighteenth century.

Toward the end of the seventeenth century the influences of current British styles became stronger and reached a height in the following period. The colonies were growing fast, and with increased wealth came the urge among the merchants, planters, and shipowners to import the latest from London and to emulate British fashions, from cut of costume to style of architecture. The more rapid their rise, the more they sought to re-create in the colonies the elegance of a life they had never known. Some of their houses with their furnishings were models of the best design of the period on either side of the Atlantic, and yet those who lived in them were, whether they were aware of it or not, different men with different experience, different ideas, and different ideals. And as the eighteenth century progressed, those differences became ever clearer until they erupted into transforming political expression.

Trestle table, New England, c. 1650, l. 146½
(The Metropolitan Museum of Art, gift of Mrs. Russell Sage, 1909)

37

Graeme Park, Horsham, Montgomery Co., Pa., 1721
(Photo by Pennsylvania Historical and Museum Commission, Harrisburg, Pa.)

THE MIXTURE OF TRADITIONS AND THE ARTS

OF

THE

DUTCH

Many besides Englishmen were involved in the American experiment. French Huguenots, and, later, some Royalist refugees settled in South Carolina, Virginia, Pennsylvania, and New York in considerable numbers, bringing with them their language, their music, and a sense of manners no doubt sorely needed in the New World. Several of our most gifted craftsmen, such as the distinguished furniture makers Charles-Honoré Lannuier of New York, Anthony Quervelle of Philadelphia, and Prudent Mallard and François Seignouret of New Orleans, and, most notably, the goldsmith and patriot Paul Revere, were of French ancestry. There were even a few Protestant Walloons, refugees from persecution in the Spanish Netherlands, who left traces of their local traditions in the flaring, curved roof-overhang, erroneously credited to the Dutch, which is to be found in the domestic architecture of eastern Long Island, southern New York, and northern New Jersey.

The Swedes and the Finns who settled in Delaware introduced not only the log cabin to the New World, but also the use of corner chimneys and fireplaces, once common in smaller houses throughout the Middle Colonies, and a distinctive form of the gambrel roof. Though the contract was signed by a mason named John Kirk, both Swedish planning and roof line are handsomely displayed in Graeme Park, the interesting house built at Horsham, in Montgomery County, in 1721, by Sir William Keith, royal governor of Pennsylvania. Only one room deep, the house is an utterly simple stone building of unusually high proportion, with tall, narrow windows, heavy chimneys, and steep pitch to the lower roof surfaces. It appears almost medieval in its tall, unsymmetrical austerity, yet the interiors are paneled in a most advanced Georgian style with great richness, reflecting the state that went with formal banquets, liveried servants, and travel in a "large glass coach" and six with footmen and outriders.

Many groups of German Protestants flocked to the hospitable territories of William Penn. Among them were The Society of the Solitary, the Pietist followers of Johann Konrad Beissel, Seventh-Day Baptists who built the picturesque medieval community still standing at Ephrata, in Lancaster County, Pennsylvania. Its stone Cloister, with plastered walls decorated with paintings in Gothic style, again rings to the lovely choral singing

John Frederick Amelung: Goblet, 1793
(The Corning Museum of Glass;
photograph, The Smithsonian Institution)

39

Ephrata Cloister, Ephrata, Pa., 1740's (Photo by Pennsylvania Historical and Museum Commission, Harrisburg, Pa.)

that was their chief mode of religious expression. The *Saal,* where the brothers lived, was built in 1740, and the Sister House, the home of the Roses of Sharon, was completed three years later, yet the whole is a composition straight out of the Middle Ages. As utterly remote from today as it was from its contemporary world, the plain and substantial buildings, with their tiny windows and shed dormers, have a hushed atmosphere of quiet peace that expresses the spirit of those who built them and there lived their exemplary and dedicated lives.

Other groups established similar settlements elsewhere. The Moravians, who had originally come with Oglethorpe to Georgia, moved north to Pennsylvania, where they built self-sufficient communities. Their sturdy independence is expressed in such buildings as the Moravian Seminary at Bethlehem, whose high-roofed stone Sisters' House dates from 1773. Earlier, in 1766, they founded Salem, North Carolina, the first planned town on the frontier, where many houses have recently been carefully restored, including the Single Brothers' House, the older part of which is half-timbered, built in 1769. Working together, all the United Brethren in the area put up the massive frame in two unseasonably sweltering days in May "without injury to any workman, though a piece of timber fell, and when the work was ended the musicians blew their trumpets from the top of the house." Other such communities sprang up at Lititz, north of Lancaster, Pennsylvania, where David Tannenberger was the

40

foremost piano and organ builder in America, and at Nazareth, north of Bethlehem. There the Hall, intended as the manor house of Count Zinzendorf, the idealistic Moravian leader, still stands, its stone bulk topped with a tall, steep roof lined with rows of small dormers in a design of unmistakably Germanic flavor.

There was not a colony without people of German stock. They brought useful skills from a dozen areas of their homeland, including the colorful arts of the Pennsylvania Dutch, as some of them came to be called. Germans were not only the first organ builders in the colonies but also the makers of many other musical instruments. They were famous ironworkers and glassmakers, and produced the Conestoga wagon which carried the pioneers westward. Perhaps even more important, German gunsmiths from Lancaster developed the deadly long rifle, and German blacksmiths were among those who forged the American ax—the dual instruments for the conquest of a continent.

And no group employed these instruments more effectively than the Scots, the greater number of whom seemed, like the Germans, naturally attracted to the frontier. They practiced the crofter's crafts of spinning and weaving; and their passion for education, rivaled only by the New England Puritans and the Moravians (famous for their choral music), built churches and schoolhouses, "lighthouses of religion and learning," in the most

Sketch of the Moravian Settlement of Salem, N.C., in 1787
(Old Salem, Inc.)

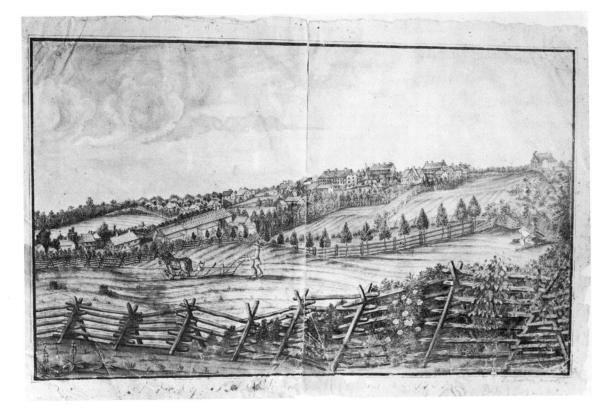

Single Brothers' House,
Salem, N.C., 1769 and 1786
(Old Salem, Inc.)

remote settlements. The Scots were also expert distillers who made whiskey the liquor of the frontier, just as rum was that of the coast. A favorite medium of exchange, invaluable in the fur trade, whiskey could be swapped for all sorts of goods and services, and often made up part of the pay of the schoolmaster. The circuit-riding Presbyterian minister, who traveled with works in Greek and Latin along with the Bible in his pack, and who was as quick with the long rifle as with a classic tag or an apposite quotation from Scripture, was also often paid in this most acceptable liquid currency.

The interest of the Dutch in the New World started with the voyage of an Englishman in the employ of the Dutch East India Company. Henry Hudson sailed up the river that has since borne his name in 1609, the year in which Santa Fe was established as the capital of Spanish New Mexico, and two years after the settlement of Jamestown. Hudson did not discover the Northwest Passage as he had hoped, but he did find the richest fur country on the continent, second only to the valley of the St. Lawrence, which lay in the firm grasp of the French. Dutch merchants were not slow to follow up the fur trade, but only gradually did trading posts such as Fort Orange, later Albany, and New Amsterdam, later New York, become settlements as well. Because Dutch citizens were happy at home, comparatively few wished to emigrate, so other nationalities, including Frenchmen, Germans, Danes, Poles, Portuguese, Spaniards, and Italians, both Christian and Jew, were encouraged to swell the numbers of settlers. By the middle of the eighteenth century Peter Kalm, the Swedish botanist, reported that he heard eighteen languages spoken in New York City, which thus early took on the polyglot and lively commercial character for which it has been known ever since. Life in convivial Manhattan, where every other house was reputed to be a tavern, was in marked contrast, however, to the rural quiet that prevailed along the shores of the Hudson. There one could see Dutch farmhouses, sometimes of brick, as in Holland, and sometimes of stone, but mostly in the prevalent American material of wood, finished with clapboarding, and having long, low roofs covered with hand-riven shakes. Even the form of the covers on poles to protect the haystacks from the rain was unmistakably Dutch.

The Netherlanders were the worst ruled of all the colonials. Their situation improved somewhat after the English captured New Amsterdam and named it New York after the new proprietor, the Duke of York, the future James II, and brother of the recently restored Charles. Thereafter such British names as

Conestoga wagon, c. 1800
(Owned by the Henry Ford Museum
& Greenfield Village)

Livingston, Pell, and Gardiner began to appear among patroons, along with the familiar Dutch names of Van Cortlandt, Philipse, Schuyler, and Van Rensselaer. These great landowners had grants that carried feudal privileges similar to those of the seigneuries in French Canada. Their rights were not to be modified until the rent wars of the 1840's, and the prevalence of this ancient system, with the wealth that it produced, helped to make New York the most aristocratic of the British colonies and, at the time of the Revolution, the most Tory.

Early views of New York and Albany show typically Dutch houses, many of brick, with crow-stepped gables set to the street. On his visit to the latter city in 1744, Dr. Alexander Hamilton, a Scottish physician who settled in Maryland, observed that "the Dutch keep their homes very neat and clean, both without and within. . . . Their chambers and rooms are large and handsome. They have their beds generally in alcoves so that you may

Hardenbergh bedroom, 1760's. A Hudson River Valley interior with an armchair and a side chair typical of the region, a small joined table, a bed with hangings, oriental rugs, and a Dutch *kas* painted in trompe l'oeil (Courtesy, Henry Francis du Pont Winterthur Museum)

go through all the rooms of a great house and never see a bed. They affect pictures much, particularly those showing Bible history, with which they adorn their rooms. They set their tables much with china. Their kitchens are likewise very clean, and there they hang . . . plates and dishes all around the walls . . . having a hole drilled through the edge of the plate or dish and a loop of ribbon put into it to hang it by." He complained that "they live in their houses in Albany as if they were in prisons, all their doors and windows being perpetually shut," because "the excessive cold winters here obliges them in that season to keep all snug and close, and they have not summer enough to revive heat in their veins so as to make them want to air themselves." Though he observed them to be "a healthy, long lived people," he ungallantly described "their women in general, both old and young," as "the hardest favored ever I beheld . . . so homely that a man must never have seen any other . . . else they would never entrap him."

The Albany Institute of Art has an outstanding collection of the arts of the Hudson Valley, including a group of religious paintings which are probably examples of the pictures "showing Bible history" noted by Dr. Hamilton, and which are interesting relics of life in Dutch America in the first half of the eighteenth century. Much of their charm is the result of the contrast between the developed Baroque compositions of the engravings from which they were derived and the homely idiom with which they were interpreted by the unknown and untrained artists who produced them. At the Albany Institute one can also see the handsome delftware prized by the Dutch housewife and the sturdy tables with heavy, turned legs, solid armchairs, pewter plates and mugs, embroidered coverlets, Turkey carpets, and blue-and-white tiled fireplaces that appeared in so many Dutch houses. At the Van Cortlandt Museum are several examples of the typical Hudson Valley side chair of the early years of the century, with yoke cresting on a vase-form back splat and turned back posts, fat, trumpet-turned front legs connected by a bulbous stretcher, and rush seat. The H. F. du Pont Museum at Winterthur, Delaware, has an outstanding example of the ponderous type of Dutch cupboard known as a *kas*, with heavy cornice molding, turnip feet, and a design in grisaille of pendent fruit painted in trompe l'oeil.

It is easy, after seeing these, to agree with Dr. Hamilton's admiration for the comfort and neatness of Dutch houses. In the case of the manors of the great landholders there was considerable elegance as well. Among the most interesting of the few

Red earthenware pie plate, signed by David Spinner, c. 1800 (The Brooklyn Museum, gift of Mrs. Huldah Cail Lorimer)

44

that remain is the Van Cortlandt Manor at Croton-on-Hudson, dating from the 1660's, which still has the loopholed shutters then necessary for defense, and which has recently been expertly restored. Its low eaves and long roof line are strongly Dutch in character, as is its heavy masonry construction. With its mill, stables, barns, workshops, and other houses and outbuildings, it was the center of an independent little settlement on the shores of the river that then was the great highway. Here, as in other such houses, furniture and furnishings of Dutch and English style were happily mixed. A strong Dutch influence in England, dating from the days of the Commonwealth, was strengthened after the Glorious Revolution of 1688 threw out the Catholic James and put Queen Mary and her Dutch husband on the British throne, so that there was a distinct and continuing relation between the styles of the two countries. It was largely from Netherlandish cabinetmakers that Englishmen learned the arts of veneering and inlaying which became so important in eighteenth-century furniture, both in the colonies and in Britain itself.

The Philipse Manor at Yonkers, New York, though for the most part nearly a century later in date, shows the persistence of a Dutch flavor in the proportion and simplicity of detail of its exterior, while the richness of the architecture of its grand drawing room, entirely British in character, is an expression of the taste and increased luxury of a later day. Perhaps the most distinguished of the manor interiors, however, is that from the Van Rensselaer House in Albany, preserved in the Metropolitan Museum of Art, which suggests much of the courtliness and conservatism of the life of the leading families of the Hudson River Valley.

What has been called the first native school of American painting developed at the very beginning of the eighteenth century in the Valley, with a group of portraits that reflect the remoteness and rustic dignity of life there at that early date. Probably the first and among the most impressive works by any of the Patroon Painters, as they have been called, is the full-length heroic figure of *Pieter Schuyler*, probably dating before 1710, and belonging to the City of Albany. The directness and vigor of the unknown painter's style emphasizes the command-presence of his subject, who was a notable and successful battler against the French and the Indians, and who became the first mayor of Albany, a position which doubtless demanded similar qualities of firmness and decision.

Another full-length portrait, that of *Ariaanje Coeymans*

45

Anonymous: *Pau de Wandelaer*, c. 1725,
45 x 35⅜
(Courtesy Albany Institute of History and Art)

(Albany), was probably painted by that same forthright hand
in 1723. As in the Schuyler portrait, the painter has borrowed
the composition from a European engraving, but again the
Baroque flourish has been frozen into a flat pattern of rude
strength. The subject was the heiress to considerable property,
which she administered with a strong and capable hand, but
the painter presents her, dressed in a formal gown and standing
on a balustraded terrace, incongruously holding a rose. Looking at her features, one can see ample corroborative evidence
for Dr. Hamilton's opinion of Dutch women. But her lack of
beauty is more than compensated by the extraordinary sense of
character the picture conveys, and the contrast of the courtly,
standardized pose and costume with the gaunt and forceful figure, which one critic has likened to an Indian warrior, is impressive and somehow moving.

The portrait of *John van Cortlandt*, who grew up in the
handsome manor at Croton, is now in the Brooklyn Museum.

46

GEORGIAN ARCHITECTURE IN THE COLONIES

In 1699 the village of Middle Plantation became the capital of Virginia, the most populous and prosperous of the colonies in America during much of the eighteenth century. The College of William and Mary had been founded there six years before and the community had been growing in population and importance. So when the State House in Jamestown was burned, the Assembly voted to move to Middle Plantation and there build a new town to be named Williamsburg in honor of King William III.

There had been other planned towns in America. Charleston was laid out in its neat gridiron in 1680; Philadelphia, with its system of green squares, in 1682; and in 1694 Anne Arundel Town was rebuilt, according to a radial plan derived from Wren's projected rebuilding of London, and renamed Annapolis to replace St. Mary's City as the capital of neighboring Maryland. The Virginia Assembly had the same Renaissance approach of a grid system with carefully calculated vistas and points of view, and Theodorick Bland surveyed the site in accordance with its explicit instructions. The 99-foot-wide Duke of Gloucester Street stretched three-quarters of a mile from the College at its western end to the Capitol at its eastern. This main axis was intersected by a minor one formed by the twin roadways enclosing the Green, which ended in a sweeping curve before the tall gates of the Governor's Palace to the north. Open land was kept free of encroachment around both Capitol and Palace, as well as in Courthouse Green and Market Square, and there were restrictions governing the building to be done on the half-acre lots into which the rest of the area was divided.

After Thomas Jefferson transferred the capital to the newer city of Richmond in 1779, Williamsburg became a sleepy town, forgotten except for the College. Because there was no growth, remnants of its former grandeur remained, despite fire, neglect, and decay, until the most ambitious restoration ever undertaken in America was started in 1927. Remaining buildings were restored and others, including the Palace and Capitol, were recreated according to historical and archaeological evidence. Though the precedent set by this example has been detrimental to the cause of historic preservation in America by encouraging a confusion between restoration of existing structures and the

51

Drayton Hall, near Charleston, S.C., 1738
(Photograph, Library of Congress)

construction of wholly new buildings according to old models, Williamsburg today uniquely presents the appearance of an early eighteenth-century capital. Its public buildings, streets, shops, and taverns as well as its houses, kitchens, barns, stables, smokehouses, carriage houses, slave quarters, and gardens, have all been treated inside and out with the utmost historical accuracy, based upon careful scholarship, to produce a whole of extraordinary completeness.

The College, the first building at William and Mary, was "modelled by Sir *Christopher Wren*," according to a contemporary account, and "adapted to the Nature of the Country by the *Gentlemen* there." The royal charter was granted in 1693, and the cornerstone was laid two years later. Although intended to form the traditional quadrangle, the fourth side was never completed, and within ten years it suffered the first of several disastrous fires which destroyed so much of the fabric of the building that it had to be virtually rebuilt, according to evidence derived from documents, descriptions, and old prints. The result is, however, convincingly Wren-like in its broad simplicity, its restrained use of decorative detail, and the vertical emphasis supplied by the proportions of the windows, the gabled dormers, and tall cupola.

Today the reconstructed Capitol, similar to the College in style and symmetry, stands at the other end of Duke of Gloucester Street, while halfway between, at the end of the Green, the Governor's Palace again rises behind its brick wall with wrought-iron gates between posts surmounted by the lion and the unicorn. The most palatial residence in the colonies when it was originally built, in 1706, it has the haughty splendor appropriate to the monarch's representative, who governed his colony of Virginia with as firm a hand as distances, poor communications, and the sometimes doubtful co-operation of the local gentry who made up his Council and House of Burgesses allowed.

Virginia was a colony with few towns and no cities, whose royal governor ruled through a system of offices controlled by the families which had become rich through landholding and tobacco. Waterways were the highways, and the great plantations, each like a small village, since each had to be virtually self-sufficient, were strung out along the rivers and coastline. Each had its dock and storehouses where goods were received direct from Bristol, London, or other British ports. Williamsburg, though tiny compared to other colonial capitals, was a lively center of gaiety and of social as well as political activity during the "Publick Times," when the Assembly was in session

Governor's Palace, reconstructed
as originally completed, 1706-20
(Courtesy of Colonial Williamsburg, Inc.)

52

and the General Court convened. As late as 1776 the year-round population of Williamsburg was only 1,600, while Philadelphia boasted 40,000 and even Charleston counted 12,000. The wealth as well as the distribution of the population was based on land-holding, and the Carters, Byrds, Burwells, Lees, and other leading families owed their position to the vast estates they had assembled, often with greater acquisitive zeal than strict legal principle. The ruinous method of raising tobacco by mining the land with a succession of the single crop, so that every few years virgin land was needed, gave the advantage to the most successful land speculator, who spent most of his time on his plantation and traveling through his estates to direct the multifarious activities that made up its economy.

The Governor's Palace in Williamsburg is an English building inside and out even though constructed in the colonies. Its furnishings are English in origin because the various governors brought their furniture with them when they came to Virginia. In similar fashion, whether of Dutch, French, or other ancestry or origin, most wealthier colonials followed British taste when they built and furnished the houses that established them as among the leading citizens.

"From England," a French visitor observed, "the Virginians take every article for Convenience or ornament which they use, their own manufactures not being worth mentioning." And except for Charleston, the same was true throughout the South until the Revolution cut off the source of supply, and other Southern cities, such as Baltimore, began to take their places as craft centers. Though there were a few independent cabinetmakers and an occasional silversmith to be found, as at Williamsburg, and there were itinerants who did a better sort of work, the village and plantation craftsmen who produced the rougher and more utilitarian necessities tended to be slaves. In general, the white artisan was driven to seek his living in farming or else to move on.

Only in the back country in the South, where immigrants brought with them the traditions and patterns of life that had developed in Pennsylvania and elsewhere in the North, did the free craftsman flourish. In the remote valley of the Yadkin in North Carolina, for example, the Moravian settlements of Betha-bara, Bethania, and Wachovia, now Winston-Salem, with their well-built houses, comfortably furnished with the products of their own workmanship and design, not only were famous for the attractive and useful pottery sold throughout the Piedmont area, but also, from mid-century on, drew youths as apprentices

53

from far and near to learn a variety of skilled crafts. But all through the plantation and tidewater South even the more skilled craftsman was usually lumped by the planters with "the *profanum vulgus*," as "Mechanicks and ignorant wretches," and because of the preference for imported goods even the shoemakers had a hard time of it. Thoughtful men recognized the serious weaknesses in the situation, and in Virginia efforts were made to rectify it, but the combination of the economic system and Britain's discouragement of manufactures in the colonies seemed to make it inevitable throughout the greater part of the South.

The one activity that involved the skilled crafts was the construction of plantation houses, courthouses, and churches, when the owner or the person responsible—such as Henry Cary, who was supervisor of the construction of the Capitol and Governor's Palace at Williamsburg—gathered the trained men necessary, often importing them from England. Before the Revolution, except in cases where drawings were sent from England, most houses were planned by their owners with the help of what architectural books might be at hand and the services of as skilled a housewright as could be found. Expert artisans were scarce and only the richest could afford the cost of construction of houses of any size or pretension, like the larger plantation houses that are so admired today. The average planter's dwelling was a simple and modest structure, often of the general style of the Thoroughgood House, such as could be put up by the owner and his family, with the possible assistance of neighbors, and the labor of servants and slaves.

The most elaborate of the remaining early Georgian houses in the colonies is Drayton Hall, built on the Ashley River ten miles or so from Charleston in 1738 by John Drayton, a member of the King's Council. Perhaps the most advanced example of architecture in America in its day, it shows a professional command of the Palladianism that was to become the fashion in the second half of the century. It also has a scale and monumentality unequaled elsewhere in America at this date. Raised on a high basement, with double-pitched hip roof, it has a two-storied portico (Doric below and Ionic above) on the landward façade, with a recessed central bay, and a balcony above for the drawing room on the second floor. The pedimented river front has similarly grand double stairs which lead into the great two-storied entrance hall recalling the best work of Inigo Jones in its superb double stairs, unequaled in the colonies and rarely matched in England. Interiors are fully paneled through-

54

out, ceilings are richly plastered, and fireplaces are appropriately elaborate. Though many of the features of the design were available in architectural books of the day, the whole displays the grasp and sureness of a professionally experienced architect who was aware of the latest and the best of British design. There is no clue as to who he might have been, but, fortunately, we have the evidence of the house, rescued from decay and destruction, and restored by an appreciative owner. The foundations of the matching twin dependencies remain to suggest the grandeur of the over-all composition.

With two notable exceptions, Southern mansions, such as Drayton Hall and the larger houses elsewhere in the colonies, were patterned as closely as possible after those of the country gentleman in England. The exceptions are Mulberry Plantation, built by Thomas Broughton on the west branch of the Cooper River not far from Charleston, in 1714, and Stratford Hall, built by Thomas Lee near Lee's Landing on the Potomac in about 1725. Broughton's fanciful creation defies stylistic classification. At first glance, the main block, with gambrel roof and narrow dormers, appears to have a flavor of Virginia, but its end gables are clipped to form what is called a jerkin-head roof, common to thatched houses and barns in Kent and Surrey, but rare in America, except in nearby Charleston. The eaves flare in the bell cast typical of Flemish houses in northeastern New Jersey and western Long Island, while the gables display the decorative S form of iron beam anchors, a typically Dutch feature seen in the colonies most often in the Hudson Valley. Most remarkable of all are the four corner pavilions, their hipped roofs topped with bell-shaped turrets, finials, and handsome iron weathervanes pierced with the date of the construction of the house. Standing in the midst of gardens with clipped hedges, Mulberry presents an unforgettably lively and picturesque appearance.

Broughton may have come by his architectural taste quite naturally, since a few years after he built Mulberry, Sir John Vanbrugh, the great English Baroque architect, was commissioned to build Seaton Delavel, one of his most impressive houses, as the Broughton family seat in Yorkshire. Mulberry is one of the earlier evidences of the tremendous flood of prosperity that came with the introduction of rice planting late in the seventeenth century in South Carolina. On the pediment of the entrance porch is carved a sprig of the tree which gave the house its name, a reminder of the vain hope of South Carolinians of the time to become even wealthier through the introduction of

Mulberry Plantation,
near Charleston, S.C., 1714
(Photograph, Library of Congress)

silkworm culture. But it proved to be not the silkworm but the indigo plant that made Charleston one of the richest communities in the New World and the only true urban center in the South.

Stratford, in Virginia, could scarcely be a greater contrast to Thomas Broughton's Mulberry. Built of brick made on the site, its fortresslike bulk, topped by heavy pyramidal roofs crowned by the most massive chimneys in American domestic architecture, is uncompromisingly solid and stern. The basement story seems compressed beneath the weight of the house above, and the heavy stone steps are splayed as awkwardly as a cow run, but the brickwork is superb, and shows off to great advantage, since the house is virtually without ornament, except for the molded water table marking the separation between the stories, the cornice, and the chimney caps. The blunt forcefulness of its design is a great rarity in the Georgian period, and again evokes echoes of Vanbrugh, the only architect of the century who used masonry masses with such expressive power, and who also employed the same curious motive of connecting with arches each group of four chimney stacks, surrounding balustraded outlooks from which the owner could watch for his ships coming up the distant Potomac.

The house is constructed on an H plan, rare in America and perhaps borrowed from the Capitol at Williamsburg, and the interiors are fine and large. Curiously, there is no main stairway, merely a steep, winding flight tucked into a small space in the east wing. But the Great Hall, 28 feet square and rising to a tray ceiling 18 feet high, is equaled only by that at Carter's Grove of a quarter of a century later. Paneled to full height, it has Corinthian pilasters carrying a complete entablature with an academic correctness and formality unique in the colonies in the early Georgian period. Thomas Lee, an ambi-

Stratford Hall, Stratford,
Westmoreland Co., Va., c. 1725
(Robert E. Lee Memorial Foundation, Inc.)

The Great Hall, Stratford, Va.,
c. 1725
(Robert E. Lee Memorial
Foundation, Inc.)

tious merchant, shipowner, and land speculator, built for the future at Stratford, which is today carefully maintained by the Memorial Foundation that bears the name of Robert E. Lee, only one of the number of his distinguished descendants for whom this extraordinary house was home.

William Salmon's *Palladio Londonensis*, first published in London in 1734, seems to have provided designs for much of the detailing of a notable group of Virginia houses of the second quarter of the eighteenth century. Among these are William Byrd's handsome Westover on the James River in Charles City County, with its high pitched roof, tall chimneys, and gabled dormers reminiscent of the Governor's Palace in Williamsburg, and Carter's Grove, built by Carter Burwell, grandson of the rich and arrogant "King" Carter, a few miles below Williamsburg. Westover dates from about 1730-34, and Carter's Grove from 1750. With a small group of other houses of the period in the vicinity, they show stylistic affinities to houses in Shrewsbury, England, and seem to have been designed, with his Salmon in hand, by one Richard Taliaferro (pronounced "Tolliver") of Williamsburg, who is thought to have had connections with Shropshire. All have undergone changes, however, except the Wythe House in Williamsburg, which has been restored to its original condition.

Westover, Charles City Co., Va., c. 1730-34
(Photograph, Virginia State Chamber
of Commerce)

Richard Taliaferro: George Wythe House,
from the garden, 1755
(Courtesy of Colonial Williamsburg, Inc.)

George Wythe was the architect's son-in-law, the lifelong friend of Jefferson, a signer of the Declaration of Independence, and the law instructor of John Marshall. The house which Taliaferro built for him in 1755 stands facing the Palace Green and next to the Bruton Parish Church. Vegetable and flower gardens, a rear lawn that doubtless served as a bowling green on occasion, and all the necessary buildings made it the same sort of self-sufficient unit on a small scale that the plantation was on a large. The warm brick façade has the almost austere simplicity and elegance of proportion of Carter's Grove. Unlike the latter, however, the Wythe House has an interior carried out with the same simplicity as the exterior, a simplicity that nonetheless shows the taste and ability of the planter turned architect. Its atmosphere of serenity and quiet good living makes it an unlikely setting for a cold-blooded murder plot, through which Wythe's great-nephew, overeager to inherit his share of the estate, is reputed to have speeded the jurist's death by adding massive doses of arsenic to his meals.

Magnates from Charleston to the Province of Maine built houses in the prevalent Georgian style. Though there was often an understandable time lag, in general, the earlier of them reflected the more exuberant Baroque of Wren in detail and retained a trace of Gothic verticality in proportion, as may be seen in the College, Capitol, and Palace at Williamsburg. After about the middle of the century they expressed the more correct Palladianism, anticipated at Drayton Hall, of Lord Burlington and William Kent, whose more academic style was spread through the architectural books that became the bibles of the colonial designers.

In Boston, Thomas Hancock, bookseller turned successful merchant, ordered from London figured wallpapers for his new house on Beacon Hill, the building of which took a decade before it was finished in 1740. He asked for hangings decorated with squirrels, fruit, flowers, peacocks, and other birds. For the grounds he requested flowering plum trees, yews, and tulip bulbs, because, he wrote his London agent, "it's allowed on all hands the Kingdom of England don't afford so fine a prospect as I have both of land and water. Neither do I intend to spare any cost or pains in making my garden beautiful or profitable." The house, of Braintree granite with Connecticut freestone trim, constructed by the master mason Joshua Blanchard, was demolished in the nineteenth century.

Governor William Shirley's country retreat of about 1747 at Roxbury, near Boston, boasted a giant order of pilasters, and a balustraded hip roof topped with a gigantic cupola. Its colossal entrance hall was paved in squares of dark blue and white marble. Double doors on axis led into the Grand Saloon, two stories high, with a coved ceiling and musicians' gallery, and, through an immense Palladian window, the Governor and his guests could look out across terraces and a formal garden with a maze to the Old Harbor in the far distance.

In Medford, Massachusetts, the splendid house of Isaac Royall, a West Indian merchant, completed in 1750, presents in its different façades two skillful variations on the Georgian theme. Its interiors understandably equal Thomas Hancock's in richness, since they, too, were the work of the same joiner, William Moore, and are surpassed in the North only by the Wentworth-Gardner House in Portsmouth, New Hampshire, a model of the height of the Palladian style of its day, built in 1760 as a wedding present from Madame Mark Hunking Wentworth to her son Thomas.

After the middle of the century Philadelphia and Charleston houses tended toward a rococo richness in their interior architecture and furnishings. Rooms from the house once occupied

Isaac Royall House, east front, Medford, Mass., completed 1750
(Photograph, Russell Blake)

by Samuel Powell, Philadelphia's much-traveled mayor, remain outstanding examples of the Chinese taste, carried out with delicate fantasy. Dating from 1768, they are now preserved in the Philadelphia and the Metropolitan museums. The richly carved mantelpieces closely resemble plates in Abraham Swan's *Designs in Architecture* of 1757, very popular among American builders. Throughout the Middle Colonies and the South many other examples of variations on the Georgian theme might be cited. Though only a small proportion of them has been preserved, the considerable number which remains suggests the wealth and power of the leading citizens of the colonies and the closeness of their ties with Britain.

As in the first half of the century and earlier, most of the houses were executed by anonymous designers with the aid of such useful handbooks as Swan's. An exception is the group of houses by William Buckland, an English-born indentured servant brought over in 1755 by Thompson Mason to oversee the building and decoration of Gunston Hall, still preserved in Fairfax County, Virginia. The finest of Buckland's designs is the Annapolis house of Matthias Hammond, a rich young attorney, built in 1773-74. The front doorway with arched fanlight, carved with festoons of roses and with ribbons of laurel, is a fitting introduction to rooms whose plain plaster walls and ceilings accent the distinction of the scroll-topped window frames and doorways and the detailing of chair rail and cornice—all carved with perfection of scale—and emphasize a restraint which anticipates the coming simplicity of the Federal period. Buckland was evidently proud of his work, because he had his portrait painted by Charles Willson Peale with the plans and elevations of the Hammond House in hand. From indentured servant he had become the leading architect of Maryland, but he died at the untimely age of forty in the year the Hammond House was completed.

The work of Buckland, like that of Taliaferro and the other earlier architectural designers, known and unknown, was essentially in the current British mode, and, at best, equaled anything of similar scale executed in England during the period. It remained for another architect, Peter Harrison of Newport, to bring colonial architecture to its climax, with buildings which not merely followed the prevailing fashion but also looked forward to the Classical Revival, the style, initiated by Jefferson in his designs for the Capitol at Richmond in 1797, which served to express the national aspirations of the new republic during the first half of the nineteenth century.

PETER HARRISON AND THE CLIMAX OF COLONIAL ARCHITECTURE

Eighteenth-century Newport rivaled Boston in wealth and pride. Though its harbor was lined with docks, wharves, warehouses, and shipyards, in 1739 its ambitious citizens built Long Wharf, 50 feet wide and more than 2,000 feet long, with twenty-seven shops and warehouses on it. From its western end one could look up Queen Street, lined with handsome houses and shaded with rows of arching trees, to the brand-new Colony House, built at the same time. Like Trinity Church (1725-26), famous for its raised pulpit with suspended sounding board, where the fashionable Malbones, Wantons, Cranstons, and other leading families worshiped, the Colony House was designed by Richard Munday, an innkeeper and carpenter, who was responsible for many of the best buildings in town during the first half of the century.

His Colony House is one of a small group of outstanding public buildings of the period, including the Capitol at Williamsburg, Boston's Town House of 1712-13 (later known as the Old State House, and famous for the lion and unicorn that decorate its gable end), and the old Philadelphia State House of 1731-36 (with later additions), better known as Independence Hall, designed by the Speaker of the Assembly, Andrew Hamilton. Only Williamsburg provided a setting to rival the mile-long approach from the waterfront to Munday's Colony House. Like the others, it is built of brick, but with rusticated sandstone trim and a granite basement. Its roof is flattened at the top to form a balustraded deck and also to produce the unusual truncated gable of the façade. The central feature, a broad doorway with balcony above, resembles that of the Hancock House in Boston, begun two years earlier. The tall, two-storied cupola adds vertical emphasis to a vigorous and distinctive design. Unfortunately, Munday died in 1739, before the Colony House was finished.

In the same year a young Yorkshire Quaker turned Anglican, who was to become the most distinguished architect in the colonies before the Revolution, made his first visit to Newport. Peter Harrison was seventeen when he first saw Newport. By the time he was twenty-three he was captain of one of the largest British merchantmen in the American trade, and at

Richard Munday: Colony House, Newport, R.I., 1739-42 (Photograph, Rhode Island Development Council)

61

thirty he settled in Newport. He became a successful merchant, farmer, shipbuilder, surveyor, and engineer, and also mastered navigation and seamanship, drafting, cartography, and woodcarving. In 1746, after what a former employer described as "a scandalous affair of Peter Harrison, who finally got Betty Pelham with child," he married the girl, who happened to be one of the richest heiresses in the colony, and found himself in a position to indulge his hobby of architecture. In the following year the generosity of Abraham Redwood, a former Antigua planter, who gave the Newport Philosophical Society the sum of £500 toward the purchase of books, led to the subscription by other citizens of £5,000 for the construction of a proper library to house them, and Peter Harrison contributed a design based on the latest Palladian models in England. Referring to the library of architectural books that he had recently acquired, he turned out the first example of the monumental temple front in America.

The Redwood Library immediately became a showpiece and led to the adoption of the Palladian style in the colonies. Harrison's academic method of using elements from books was that of his British contemporaries, and the results were sufficiently admired to inspire the Anglican congregation of Boston to ask him to design their new church. So in 1749 he presented a bundle of drawings for King's Chapel to the Reverend Henry Caner and the committee, headed by Peter Faneuil, which had raised funds for the project. The results bore out their judgment that "Mr. Harrison, of Rhode Island," was indeed "a gentleman of good judgment in architecture," because the interior has been correctly considered the finest example of Georgian church architecture in the colonies.

The handsome fenestration and paired giant Corinthian columns displaying the full grammatical use of the order, though based on James Gibbs's *Book of Architecture*, are handled with a sureness and freedom that is a long step beyond the Redwood Library. The Unitarian congregation that has owned the church since 1785 has preserved it in perfect condition, so that, upon entering, one steps back into the middle of the eighteenth century in its most vigorous and stylish expression. Unfortunately, the exterior of King's Chapel was never finished. The portico of tall Ionic columns was added only after the Revolution, and without the crowning balustrade Harrison's plans called for; and the "Elegant and lofty steeple of two square stories and an octagonal spire . . . to be finished in the richest manner" and embellished with "highly finished and

REDWOOD LIBRARY
NEWPORT R.I.

The Redwood Library, Newport, R.I., as originally completed by Peter Harrison in 1748 (Redwood Library and Athenaeum, Newport, R.I.)

ornamental urns," was never carried out, even though Ralph Allen of Bath, England, the original Squire Allworthy of Fielding's *Tom Jones,* offered to ship over enough Bath stone and the skilled stoneworkers necessary for its construction. Harrison's design has been lost, so that one can only conjecture on the appearance of the completed church, but if the quality of his concept was consistent throughout, it would surely have been among the outstanding Georgian churches of the period on either side of the Atlantic.

St. Michael's Church in Charleston, South Carolina, dating from 1751, has a handsome steeple and the first giant portico after the Redwood Library, probably based on James Gibbs's St. Martin's-in-the-Fields on Trafalgar Square. It has been tentatively ascribed to Harrison on stylistic grounds and because he had many friends and business associates in Charleston and was a frequent visitor there. The spire is unusually stout in proportion to the rest of the building, and the result is vigorous and impressive. The source of its design may be a plate in Gibbs's *Book of Architecture,* but, as in the rest of the building, the Georgian vocabulary has been handled with the free assurance of a knowing architect. Its interior, good though it is, cannot, however, match King's Chapel. St. Paul's Chapel, founded by Trinity Church on Broadway between Vesey and Fulton Streets in New York, is its only possible rival.

Built in 1764-66 for the convenience of those who lived too far uptown easily to attend services in the mother church, St. Paul's Chapel is the ambitious and elaborate design of Thomas McBean, a Scottish pupil of Gibbs, who borrowed freely from the latter's St. Martin's-in-the-Fields. The spire, almost a duplicate of St. Martin's, and the giant Ionic portico were added after the Revolution, between 1794 and 1796, completing the original concept, probably under the direction of Major L'Enfant, the planner of the city of Washington, who designed the handsome sculptured glory over the altar. The nave has the same distinction of proportion of Harrison's chapel in Boston, but the richness of the Corinthian order, the skillful interpenetrations of the elliptically vaulted ceiling, and the sparkle of the series of Waterford chandeliers produce an effect of Anglican High-Church elegance appropriate to the place of worship of the royal governor of the colony. Once damned for being built too far uptown, "in a place so remote and sequestered, so difficult of access, and to which the population could never extend," St. Paul's has survived its parent church and remains the only ecclesiastical structure dating from colonial times left in the city. Surrounded by skyscrapers, it is an impressive statement of Georgian grace and colonial dignity in the midst of the crowds and noise of modern Manhattan.

Peter Harrison never surpassed his design for King's Chapel. Christ Church in Cambridge, built about 1760, has great spaciousness for its comparatively small scale, and retains its charm even though two additional bays were inserted in 1857. The Brick Market of 1761-72, with its arcaded ground floor and giant order of Ionic pilasters, still lends dignity to downtown Newport. Two years earlier, Harrison had donated the drawings for Touro Synagogue to the little Congregation Jeshuat Israel of Newport, made up of perhaps twenty families of Sephardic Jews originally from Spain, Portugal, and Holland. Congregations in New York, London, Amsterdam, Jamaica, Curaçao, and Surinam gave financial assistance. Rabbi Isaac Touro outlined the ritual requirements of the building, which was started in the summer of 1759 and not completed until late in 1763. A look inside shows why its construction took so long. Though the exterior is austerely simple, the interior rivals that of King's Chapel in richness and in brilliant and facile control of the full vocabulary of the Palladian style.

Placed cater-cornered to the street so that the Ark of the Covenant could be toward the east, the Synagogue has the required gallery for women on three sides and a central pulpit for the reading of the Law, but all is transformed into the brightness and almost gaiety of the height of contemporary Georgian style. Every element is detailed with elegance and verve, from the Corinthian colonnade of the gallery superposed on the Ionic below, to the throne for the elders on the north side and the elaborate two-story composition for the Ark which dominates the east wall. Though the building has not been used for many years, it was always, like the graveyard nearby, with its "sepulchral stones, so old and brown," described in Longfellow's poem, kept in perfect condition through a bequest of Abraham Touro in 1822, until it recently and fittingly became a national monument. It is not only the oldest synagogue in the United States and an outstanding example of the architecture of its period, but also the site of President Washington's famous address in the summer of 1790, when he told the assembled congregation that "it is now no more that toleration is spoken of, as if it was by the indulgence of one class of people that another enjoyed the exercise of their inherent natural rights. For happily the Government of the United States . . . gives to bigotry no sanction, to persecution no assistance."

Life became more difficult for Harrison as the cause of independence gained strength. In the 1770's he moved to New Haven to become collector of the port. A Tory and an Anglican, he had no sympathy with the rebels. He stood stoutly by his guns, though he suffered increasingly from the insults and gibes that were the lot of the Loyalists. When in April of 1775 he heard that active rebellion had broken out, he died of a stroke. That autumn a mob broke into his house and destroyed his library of architectural books and all his records and drawings. His colonial world had been shattered by the musket fire at Concord and Lexington.

Peter Harrison: Touro Synagogue, Newport, R.I., 1759-63
(Photograph, Society of Friends of Touro Synagogue)

Port Royal parlor, with Chippendale high chest, armchairs, side chairs, and sofa, 1760-85 (Courtesy, Henry Francis du Pont Winterthur Museum)

CRAFTSMEN AND PATRIOTS

The eighteenth century was the great age of the craftsman in America as in Europe. Among all the artisans, goldsmiths and cabinetmakers led the rest in prestige and in the respect accorded them by the community. The owners of the great houses scattered up and down the Atlantic coast looked to London for the models for their furniture and plate, just as for their fashions in clothes. In Charleston and in all the major centers in the Middle Colonies and to the north there were craftsmen who could work in the latest styles. In furniture they developed their own interpretations of the plates in Thomas Chippendale's *The Gentleman and Cabinet-Maker's Director* and Robert Manwaring's *The Cabinet and Chair-Maker's Real Friend and Companion,* which resulted in a recognizable regional accent. Except for Connecticut, which turned out its own exuberant versions of what was being done in Rhode Island, Massachusetts, and New York, and for the work of certain rugged individualists in the Connecticut River Valley, in New Hampshire north of Portsmouth, and in the more primitive back country, none of these regional styles was provincial; they were merely separate and distinct in character.

In England in the eighteenth century there was only one style, that of London, which produced virtually all the fine furniture, and whatever was made elsewhere was a country cousin; unlike England, the American colonial centers produced styles that became distinct. A general Queen Anne style prevailed until after the middle of the century, and walnut was the favorite wood until it was replaced by the heavy, dark mahogany of Santo Domingo. Butternut was also used, as were cherry in New England and in upstate New York, maple in New England and in Pennsylvania, and other woods as well. The Massachusetts makers clung to spare and rather narrow proportions with slender legs, while New York craftsmen preferred broader, bigger forms with stouter legs and larger and heavier detail. Philadelphia consistently produced the most graceful and elaborately decorated pieces in the colonies, reflecting a scarcely Quakerish sense of luxury in their increasing tendency toward the rococo after the middle of the century.

From about 1755 the style of Chippendale prevailed, but with a more consistently Georgian character than in England, where the Chinese and Gothic taste led to greater variety and elaboration. In the colonies Queen Anne forms were often retained and combined with Chippendale. Thomas Elfe, who came to Charleston in about 1747, was a leader among that city's cabinetmakers, whose case pieces are distinguished by a delicate fret-carved frieze, and who took to mahogany early because it was easily imported from the West Indies, Cuba, and Honduras. Philadelphia, the leading city in the colonies and the second largest in the British Empire by shortly after mid-century, attracted many foreign craftsmen, and fortunes won through Quaker thrift and enterprise kept a regiment of cabinetmakers busy. Thomas Afflick, William Savery, James Gillingham, and Benjamin Gostelowe are but a few of the more prominent among the many who worked in a manner more strongly influenced by French taste than elsewhere in America, as seen in their rococo-accented works. New York preferred the huskier and more robust forms produced by such makers as Thomas Burling and Gilbert Ashe, while Thomas Cogswell and Major Benjamin Frothingham, Washington's friend, made *bombé* desks and secretaries, high chests with corkscrew finials, and plain tables of trim proportion for their fellow Bostonians. There was hardly a town from Pennsylvania north that did not have at least one cabinetmaker who could turn out furniture of admirable quality in both design and craftsmanship.

Nowhere did there emerge such distinctive achievements, however, as were produced in Rhode Island by John Goddard and the Quaker family of Townsend. From their shops on Easton's Point, overlooking the harbor crowded with merchantmen and privateers, the source of many a Newport fortune, came furniture which shows them to have been the creators of what has been properly called "the most original style in America." These gifted joiners designed and made furniture in which the cockleshell was the dominant motive, appropriate for a seaport town and for patrons whose wealth came from maritime trade. The shells appear, both concave and convex, on the fronts of blockfront case pieces, chests of drawers, and secretary bookcases, combined with scroll feet, which, having a touch of the fashionable Chinese taste, also befitted a seagoing community. Newport designs are always simple and architectonic, based on a tripartite scheme of blocking in bold relief. The plain surfaces show off the gleaming richness of the Santo Domingan mahogany, with the vigorously carved shells providing the major

Secretary bookcase,
attributed to John Goddard,
Newport, 1760-75
(Courtesy, Museum of Fine Arts, Boston,
M. and M. Karolik Collection)

68

decoration. The Rhode Island cabinetmakers also made many pieces of simpler design but of similarly impeccable craftsmanship for the export trade to the West Indies and more distant ports.

Though the craft of the furniture maker reached a height in the eighteenth century, that of the goldsmith was the first of the arts to flourish in the New World, and goldsmiths were among the leading citizens from earliest times. In 1620 Thomas Howard was recorded as plying the craft at Jamestown, and in 1634 John Mansfield was active at Charlestown, Massachusetts, though the work of neither has come down to us. Unlike Europe, and especially England, where the craft was strictly controlled, the colonies had no guild to regulate the practice and to ensure the quality of both metal and workmanship, and no law that required the inspection and marking of each piece as in the Old World. American smiths were expected to maintain the proper standard, and the considerable amount of their surviving work shows how well they fulfilled their trust. The rigor with which they continued the apprentice system resulted in consistent excellence of craftsmanship.

Inventories of colonial estates of the seventeenth and eighteenth centuries prove that silver was highly prized, and that, in the days before banks, plate—as all solid silver is properly termed—was capital. In 1777, the crucial year of the Revolutionary War, John Langdon, later governor of New Hampshire, sprang to support the cause with "a thousand dollars in hard money; I will pledge my plate for three thousand more; I have seventy hogsheads of Tobago rum, which will be sold for the most that they will bring. They are at the service of the State. If we succeed in defending our homes and firesides, I may be remunerated; if we do not, then the property will be of no value to me." Even as active and as wealthy a businessman as Langdon had three times as much in plate as in cash. The goldsmith, since he dealt in precious materials, was the equivalent of the banker as well as being a highly skilled artisan. He fashioned useful and beautiful objects out of ingots made by melting down outmoded or damaged pieces or coin—English, Dutch, Portuguese, or Spanish in origin—acquired through the far-flung commercial enterprises carried on by the colonials. Plate was a hedge against inflation, and could be used as security and even occasionally as a medium of exchange.

Many goldsmiths were merchants and traders as well as craftsmen, and a few became rich. John Edwards of Boston in

Jacob Gerritse Lansing: Silver teapot, first half of 18th cent., h. 7⅜ (Courtesy Albany Institute of History and Art)

1746 left an estate of nearly £5,000, a vast fortune in those days; and his fellow townsman John Burt left more than £6,000 when he died the year before. Especially successful was John Hull (1624-83), one of the earliest colonial goldsmiths as well as one of the most versatile of individuals of his time. His London-trained half brother brought him to Boston at the age of ten and taught him the craft. "I fell to learning and to practicing the trade of goldsmith," he wrote in his partly retrospective diary, "and through God's help obtained that ability in it as I was able to get my living by it." In 1652 he noted that "upon the occasion of much counterfeit coin brought into the country . . . the General Court, ordered a mint to be set up," and Hull was appointed mintmaster. As a partner he took on Robert Sanderson (1608-93), who had served his apprenticeship in London. The quality of the work they produced is attested by a number of remaining pieces, most outstanding among them being the tall cups for the First Church in Boston. In addition to being mintmaster, Hull was also treasurer of the colony and captain of the Ancient and Honorable Artillery Company.

In 1659 he wrote in his diary, "I received into my house Jeremie Dummer and Samuel Paddy to serve me as apprentices eight years. The Lord make me faithful in discharge of this new trust committed to me, and let his blessing be to me and to them." Despite Hull's pious hopes, Paddy did not make the grade, but Jeremiah Dummer (1645–1718) definitely did. He was one of the first generation of native craftsmen. Born in Newbury, Massachusetts, where the school his son established on the family farm still associates the name with his birthplace, Dummer not only was an expert goldsmith, but also, as Hull proudly predicted, turned out to be "very useful in his generation" as a judge of the Inferior Court, a justice of the peace, and treasurer of Suffolk County. His most remarkable work is a pair of impressive candlesticks (Garvan Collection, Yale) in the form of rectangular shafts of eight clustered columns with circular stems flaring into square molded bases. Over ten inches high, they were "Made," according to the inscription on one of them, "to commemorate the marriage of David Jeffries and Elizabeth Usher 1686."

John Coney (1655/6–1722), who also served his apprenticeship with Hull and Sanderson, was not only one of the most prolific of goldsmiths, judging from the quantity of his work remaining, but also one of the best of the period, who received orders from New York, Connecticut, and Rhode Island as well as Massachusetts. A leading citizen of Boston, he was an origi-

John Coney: Grace cup with cover, engraved with Stoughton arms, 1701, h. 10¼
(Courtesy of Harvard University)

70

nal subscriber toward the building of King's Chapel. For Lieutenant Governor William Stoughton he made the tall grace cup, a large cup filled with wine so that each diner could pledge the health of the rest after grace at the end of a meal. This particular example, almost a foot high, with bold gadrooning on the lower body, vigorous moldings of base and cover, and springing curves of the handles, is perhaps the finest piece of Colonial silver in existence. Because the elderly Lieutenant Governor was ill, he could not attend the Harvard commencement of 1701 as he had hoped, and asked his friend Judge Samuel Sewall to present it to the college in his stead. "After dinner and singing," Sewall wrote in his diary, "I took it, and had it fill'd up, and drunk to the president, saying that by reason of the absence of him who was the Firmament and Ornament of the Province, and that Society, I presented that Grace-Cup *pro more Academiarum in Anglia.*"

It is interesting to compare the sugar box (Boston) made by Coney between 1680 and 1690 with that of 1701 (collection of Mrs. Edsel B. Ford) by Edward Winslow (1669–1753), who had been an apprentice of Dummer's. Both pieces are variations of a common type, a broad, oval, footed bowl with a domed cover and a coiled serpent handle. But where Coney's is decorated with elliptical bosses on body and cover, and with a cutout acanthus design, Winslow used his favorite device of gadrooning to enrich the moldings of base and cover, to express the volume of the curving body, and to define the strongly executed coat of arms on the hasp. Though the two boxes differ widely in design, they are alike in expressing the strong individuality of style and the high quality of craftsmanship of their makers.

John Coney: Sugar box, c. 1680-90, h. 4 13/16 (Courtesy, Museum of Fine Arts, Boston, Tyler Collection)

Edward Winslow: Standing salt, after 1674, h. 5½ (Courtesy, Museum of Fine Arts, Boston, gift of Philip Leffingwell Spalding, 1938)

71

Winslow also produced a superb standing salt, one of the three known in Colonial silver. It was made after 1674, since it bears the initials and crest of John and Mary Edes, who were married in that year. Winslow was a descendant of a founder of the Bay Colony, and carried on an active public career in addition to his productive work as a goldsmith, serving as constable, tithingman, surveyor, overseer of the poor, selectman, sheriff of Suffolk County, captain of the Artillery Company and of militia, colonel of the Boston Regiment, and judge of the Inferior Court of Common Pleas. A portrait by John Smibert records his distinguished appearance in the prime of a long, admirable life.

Though New Amsterdam had become New York when the first known silver was produced there, both the style and the names of the craftsmen were still predominantly Dutch. Tankards are of appropriately broad dimension and generous bulk, often engraved with coats of arms in very large and elaborate cartouches, like that in the Yale College collection, made by Peter van Dyck (1684–1750/51) in about 1704 for a member of the Wendell family. The Dutch also favored pear-shaped teakettles which tend to bulge broadly at the bottom and rise through molded stages to a high, domed cover.

The most unusual pieces of Colonial silver are the *rimonim*, elaborate sets of ritual objects, which the famous New York smith Myer Myers (1723-95) made for the Congregation Mikveh Israel in Philadelphia, for Shearith Israel in New York, and, perhaps most interesting because of their inscriptions, for the Touro Synagogue in Newport, where they find a fitting setting in Peter Harrison's handsome interior.

There were many families of goldsmiths in the colonies, such as the Syngs of Philadelphia. The first of the Syngs, Philip, was born and trained in Cork, Ireland, and came to America in 1714. His son, also Philip (1703-89), was a junior warden of the Masons and served on the vestry of fashionable Christ Church. A friend of Benjamin Franklin, he was a founder and first treasurer of the American Philosophical Society. There were other goldsmithing brothers and nephews as well, but Philip junior's inkstand of 1752 in Independence Hall not only is of great historical interest because it was used for the signing of the Declaration of Independence and the Constitution, but is also a particularly fine example of the craft. Syng's style is characterized by handsome proportions and a simplicity which is scarcely typical of Philadelphia, where taste ran rather to rich decoration in molded and hammered relief in a manner suggesting the influence of French taste.

Jacob Hurd (1702/3-58) was the leading Boston goldsmith in the generation after Coney. Among the most spectacular of his many excellent remaining pieces is the mid-century grace cup in the collection of the Boston Museum of Fine Arts. More than a foot high, it is forceful in design and bears the arms of the Rowe family, beautifully engraved. The famous Admiralty Oar (Massachusetts Historical), the symbol of authority of the Court of Vice Admiralty, was also made by Jacob Hurd. Almost two feet long, it bears the British royal arms on one side of the blade and the Admiralty anchor on the other.

Hurd's contemporary Apollos Rivoire (1702-54) was Boston's leading Huguenot craftsman and Coney's last pupil. He was better known, however, through the anglicized form of his name that he passed on to his far more famous son, Paul Revere. Paul was a goldsmith, a bronze founder, and an engraver, and turned his ingenious hand to all sorts of other things, even to making false teeth for his friend Dr. Joseph Warren, which provided the only means of identification when the young doctor's body was finally found months after he had died at Bunker Hill. A friend of James Otis, Samuel Adams, and John Han-

A View of Part of the Town of Boston in New England and British Ships of War Landing Their Troops, 1768, engraving by Paul Revere
(Courtesy, Museum of Fine Arts, Boston, gift of Pauline Revere Thayer)

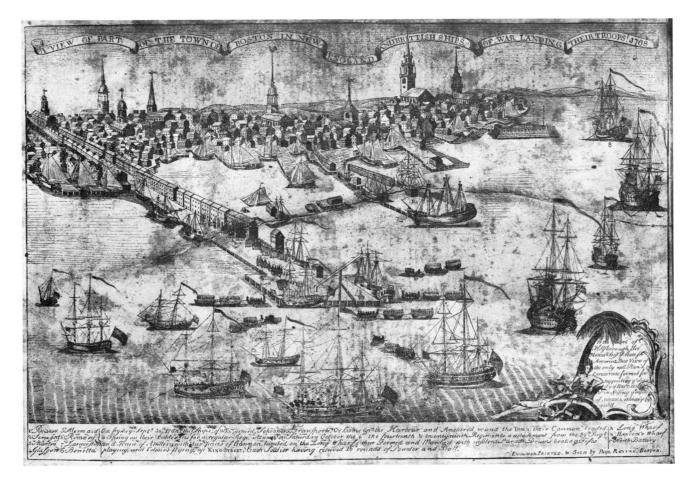

cock, Revere expressed his patriotism not only in his famous ride, but also in joining the Sons of Liberty, in being a Tea Party "Indian," and in making the Liberty Bowl (Boston).

Based upon a form common to Chinese export porcelain, the Liberty Bowl was commissioned by fifteen fellow members of the Sons of Liberty, whose names are inscribed around the rim, in 1768. Early in that year, the House of Representatives of the Massachusetts Bay Colony had sent a circular letter to the assemblies of the other colonies urging a united stand against the hated Townshend Act, which levied duties on various British imports such as paper, glass, and the East India Company's tea. The letter urged "united and dutiful supplications" to King George for redress, since there was a depression and money was short, and the added taxes were a genuine financial burden as well as being distasteful in principle to the independent-minded colonials. Parliament, however, decided to make a test case and sent off an abrupt demand to the Massachusetts Representatives to rescind the circular letter, ordering Governor Bernard to dismiss the Assembly if they refused, and threatening dire reprisals. The Representatives voted 92 to 17 not to comply, and the Liberty Bowl commemorates their spirit. Its rousing inscription reads: "To the Memory of the glorious NINETY TWO: Members of the Hon'bl House of Representatives of the Massachusetts-Bay, who, undaunted by the insolent Menaces of Villains in Power, from a strict Regard to Conscience, and the LIBERTIES of their Constituents, on the 30th of June 1768, voted NOT TO RESCIND." The bowl was used at meetings of the Sons of Liberty at the Bunch of Grapes, the tavern "near the Town House" which was the gathering place of the patriots and where the Tea Party and other events leading up to the Revolution were planned.

Revere was thirty-three when he made the bowl, and already a leader among the craftsmen and artisans who were the backbone of the independence movement. They were represented on the Committees of Correspondence, marched in celebration of the anniversary of the repeal of the Stamp Act, and took their places in the ranks when the war came. Benjamin Frothingham of Boston and Jonathan Gostelowe of Philadelphia, both cabinetmakers, were also majors of artillery, and the famous painter Charles Willson Peale, who started out as a cordwainer, either painted portraits of fellow officers or mended shoes during lulls in the fighting while he commanded a company of militia. And when the Declaration of Independence was signed, the names of Benjamin Franklin, a printer, Roger Sherman, a shoemaker, and George Walton, a carpenter, were among the rest.

JOHN SMIBERT, ROBERT FEKE, AND OTHER PAINTERS

For the greater part of the eighteenth century, painters in America were craftsmen rather than artists, while the sculptor in any modern sense of the term did not appear for a hundred years. Even when it was possible for a man to make a living, or the greater part of it, through painting portraits, the artisan's approach remained, and throughout the eighteenth century and well on into the nineteenth, most American painters were willing to turn their hands to as great a variety of tasks as the most versatile of their fellow craftsmen. Gustavus Hesselius (1682–1755), for example, a relative of Emanuel Swedenborg, after thirty years of experience in America advertised in *The Pennsylvania Gazette* during the winter of 1740 that he and his partner were ready for anything in the painting line, including "Ship and House Painting, Gilding of all Sorts . . . old Pictures Clean'd and mended, &c." His most recent commission had been to paint the greater part of the interior of Philadelphia's new State House, now Independence Hall, but he was the leading portrait painter of Philadelphia and Maryland until, about the time his advertisement appeared, he turned his fashionable practice over to his son John, and spent the last years of his life making spinets and building organs for the various German settlements on or close to the frontier. Yet his work includes one of the earliest religious paintings in colonial America, a *Last Supper*, since lost, done in 1721 for St. Barnabas' Church in Prince George's County, Maryland, and a *Bacchus and Ariadne* (Detroit) and a *Bacchanal,* in which the sexes are as carefully separated as at a Quaker meeting. The first such subjects in Colonial art, they represent deities from Classical mythology accompanied by nymphs and fauns curiously resembling, as Edgar P. Richardson has pointed out, American Indians. In 1735 he painted memorable portraits of actual Indians *Tishcohan* and *Lapowinsa* (Historical Society of Pennsylvania), the chiefs of the Delaware who two years later were to be victimized by the greedy colonials when they turned the famous Walking Purchase into a marathon. A commission for the proprietor John Penn, the portraits display the sober reserve of the Indian recorded with objective directness, yet beneath their stoicism smolders the suspicious perplexity and vague awareness of the

Anonymous: *Elizabeth Rebecca Brodnax,* 1720's, 30 x 25
(Property of W. F. Brodnax III, on loan to the Virginia Museum)

75

inevitable results for them and their people of the encroach-
ments of the white man.

The "&c." at the end of Hesselius' advertisement could cover
a great deal of ground, as can be seen from various painters'
announcements appearing in the newspapers of the period. In
addition to "painting in general"—which often included decorating carriages, furniture, and fire buckets as well as producing shop signs, standards, overmantels, fireboards, "landskips,"
and portraits—many offered instruction in drawing, while some
gave lessons in music and dancing. Painters also sold prints
and artists' supplies, made frames, and decorated clock faces
and tinware. They did graining and marbleizing, and painted
oriental rug designs on wooden floors, as in the Grand Saloon
of Governor Shirley's magnificent mansion in Roxbury, Massachusetts. Or they undertook mural decoration in simulation of
fashionable scenic wallpapers, as in the distinguished Portsmouth house built by Captain Archibald McPhedris between
1718 and 1723, where the awkward but impressive life-sized
Indians flanking the arched window of the stair landing and
Sir William Pepperell, mounted on a mettlesome horse, victorious at Louisburg, are traditionally ascribed to Langdon
Towne, the hero of Kenneth Roberts' novel *Northwest Passage*.

In 1729 a far better painter than Gustavus Hesselius and the
other earlier migrants appeared upon the American scene, a

Anonymous: *The Potter Family*, overmantel, 18th cent., oil on wood
(Newport Historical Society)

Scot named John Smibert (1688–1751), who happened to come
to the New World through the idealistic vision of an Irish cleric,
George Berkeley, Dean of Derry. A friend of Swift, Addison,
and Steele, Berkeley was credited "with every virtue under
heaven" by Alexander Pope. In Rome he saw the groups of
young seminarians walking through the Piazza di Spagna and,
struck by a sudden idea, drew up *A Proposal for the better supplying of Churches in our Foreign Plantations, and for Convert-
ing the Savage Americans to Christianity, By a College to be
erected in the Summer Islands, otherwise called the Isles of Bermuda.* So persuasive a promoter was he that Sir Robert Walpole promised a parliamentary grant of £20,000. Berkeley set
about getting together the beginning of a faculty, and sailed for
the New World late in 1728 with his wife and young son and
several others, including John Smibert.

Smibert, whom Berkeley had met in Italy, had started out
as a house painter in his native Edinburgh, though his family
had hoped he would enter the ministry. He had moved on to
London, where he painted coaches and made copies of old
masters for picture dealers. By 1717 he was in Florence, where,
according to George Vertue, the engraver who became the Va-
sari of English art, "from ye great Duke's pictures he copyd
several particularly the Card. Bentivoglio of Vandycke & many
other heads making his whole study after Titian Raphael Rubens &c. At Rome he painted several persons from life . . ."
and then went on to Naples and elsewhere. Cosimo III of Tus-
cany, "ye great Duke," was so pleased with Smibert's work that
he had given him a picture of the head of St. Peter. After three
years in Italy, Smibert had returned to London and soon was
living in Covent Garden, a successful if not famous portrait
painter. There, in 1728, with the same charm that had enabled
him to wheedle the promise of a grant from Parliament, Dean
Berkeley persuaded Smibert to join him in his venture as professor of drawing, painting, and architecture.

After four months at sea, Berkeley and his entourage landed
at Newport, Rhode Island, to await word of the grant. But with
the Dean's persuasive presence removed from London, the idea
was abandoned, and, after a pleasant four years or so in Newport, Berkeley returned to Britain to become Bishop of Cloyne.
Though he was a leading philosopher of his day, whose *New
Theory of Vision* and *Treatise Concerning the Principles of Human Understanding* represent a substantial development of the
theories of John Locke, Berkeley is rather remembered, when

Anonymous: Wall panel
from Southbridge, Mass., c. 1750,
oil on wood, 41½ x 27⅞
(Old Sturbridge Village, Sturbridge, Mass.)

he is remembered at all, as the author of a much-quoted line from the final stanza of a poem expressing his dream of the future of America, in which he had hoped to have a part:

> Westward the course of empire takes its way;
>   The first four acts already past,
> A fifth shall close the drama with the day:
>   Time's noblest offspring is the last.

In the meantime, with Scots practicality, Smibert set out for Boston, at that time a city of 15,000, about the same size as his native Edinburgh. Since he was the first artist of any standing ever to visit Boston, he immediately received commissions to portray several leading citizens, including Chief Justice Samuel Sewall and Nathaniel Byfield. In 1730 he opened his new studio with a public showing of his collection of copies after old masters, casts from the antique, and, in flattering proximity, the brand-new likenesses of the Boston worthies. It was the first art exhibition to be held in America and aroused the greatest possible public interest. When no less a critic than the Reverend Mather Byles, nephew of Cotton Mather, who was Boston's self-appointed and generally accepted keeper of the public conscience, was moved to commemorate the event in creaking verses of genuine enthusiasm, published in local and London papers, the community's seal of approval was set on Smibert's work, and his success was assured.

> Thy Fame, O *Smibert*, shall the Muse rehearse,
> And sing your Sister-Art in softer Verse.
> 'Tis yours, Great Master, in just Lines to trace
> The Rising Prospect, or the lovely Face . . .
> In hoary majesty, see *Sewall* here;
> Fixed strong in thought there Byfield's Lines appear . . .

The poet goes on to mention "Roman ruins" that "nod their awful Head," and "gloting monks" debating their "am'rous rights," the latter a subject that must have been something of a shock to Boston propriety, though it may well have passed muster in the still Puritan stronghold as a fitting commentary on the evils of papistry. The "Vandycke" which Byles later mentions is surely the copy of the head of Bentivoglio, now in the collection of Harvard College. This single painting became a sort of school of art and a source of revelation and inspiration, mediocre though it may appear today, for dozens of aspiring young American artists, a fact to be interpreted equally as a tribute to the imagination and determination of the young Americans and as an index of the artistic poverty of the New World in

John Smibert: *The Bermuda Group*, 1729, 69½ x 93
(Yale University Art Gallery, gift of Isaac Lothrop of Plymouth, Mass., 1808)

colonial and early republican times. The great name of Rubens and references to several Classical subjects are also scattered throughout the verses, so there may have been copies of other works to suggest in diluted fashion something of the glories of the great masters, but they have not come down to us.

The initial exhibition contained the most ambitious picture Smibert painted in America, though he had done at least one other similar canvas before he came. It is the life-sized portrait of the Dean and the others of the hopeful group of would-be faculty members and their families, usually called *The Bermuda Group*. Berkeley stands at the right, dictating to Richard Dalton, who has pen in hand. The Dean's wife is seated with their little son Henry in her lap. To the far left the painter

looks out of the canvas, just as he studied himself in the mirror while painting this self-portrait. Next to him stands his nephew, Dr. Thomas Moffat of Edinburgh, who imported Gilbert Stuart's father to run a snuff mill in Rhode Island. John James leans on the back of the chair of Mrs. Berkeley's sister. The portraits are convincing, the arrangement a bit self-conscious but not without grace, the color is rich, and the whole has dignity and elegance in the British baroque manner of Sir Godfrey Kneller and his studio-factory, dominant in London during the early years of the century.

In the same year as the successful exhibition, Smibert married a Boston girl and settled in a comfortable house in Queen Street on Scollay Square, then a substantial residential district. He combined portrait painting with business when he opened the first color shop in town, where he sold artists' supplies, prints, and picture frames, a venture announced in the Boston *News-Letter* and the *Gazette*. The atmosphere of New England was congenial to him, for he refused an invitation from Bishop Berkeley to move to Cork. His style became firmer, his reading and expression of character more precise, and his later sitters have a vitality lacking in the more generalized earlier works. In 1742 Boston's new market, the gift of Peter Faneuil, was "completed in a most substantial and elegant manner . . . after a design by Mr. Smibert," as recorded by Charles Bulfinch, who so sympathetically retained the character of the original design in his necessary enlargement of it in 1805.

Faneuil Hall was located near the entrance of Damnation Alley between Dock Square and the waterfront, which has now retreated some distance through generations of filling. Two stories high, 40 feet wide, and 100 feet long, it was one of the few important public buildings in the colonies. From the beginning, the market stalls below and the large meeting room above were intimately connected with the history of Boston and with the larger history of the beginnings of the nation. The gigantic weathervane in the form of a grasshopper with large green glass eyes, a motive copied from the vane of the Royal Exchange in London, was hammered out of copper by Deacon Shem Drowne in his shop nearby in Ann Street. Smibert painted a portrait of the donor to hang in the meeting hall, but it was burned in a fire that gutted the structure in 1761; however, the building was immediately restored and Henry Sargent's copy of Smibert's *Peter Faneuil* still hangs there.

In 1745 the successful siege of Louisburg brought Smibert the commission to paint a full-length, life-sized portrait of *Sir*

John Smibert: *Sir William Pepperell,*
1745, 96 x 56
(Courtesy of the Essex Institute,
Salem, Mass.)

80

William Pepperell, the military commander. The artist shows him with the baton of command firmly held in his right hand and pointing with his left to the burning fortress into which shells are still being lobbed. Pepperell stands silhouetted against a sky clouded with the smoke of battle. The details of his elegant costume—a long coat with wide cuffs, the long embroidered waistcoat then in fashion, and the lace at the wrists and cascading down the chest—are effectively handled, but not allowed to interfere with the substance of the stocky body. The painting has an awkward dignity and a strong individuality that are completely convincing.

Smibert has left us many such forthright representations of the men and women of New England in the 1730's and '40's. Boston gave him what he needed to develop his gifts to their fullest extent. Bostonians were more interested in "the preservation of the likeness," as Copley later observed, than in anything else. They valued character and respected individuality. Smibert had no real pupils, but his studio, with its collection of copies and casts, was kept intact for thirty years after his death by his nephew John Moffat, and individual works, like the *Bentivoglio,* were studied by generations of later American painters. But more than he could have known, he brought to the colonies an idea of what art could be, and opened the eyes of Americans to the richness of the tradition they shared.

When Smibert died in 1751, two Massachusetts-born painters who had arrived on the scene a decade earlier were active in Boston. Joseph Badger (1708-65) was a house painter and glazier who developed a curious remoteness in his stiff treatment of his adult sitters that turned out to be particularly appropriate in such portraits as that of the Puritan philosopher *Jonathan Edwards* (Yale). John Greenwood (1727-92) had much more personality. His portraits are equally wooden, but his earthy humor makes his *Sea Captains Carousing at Surinam* (St. Louis) his most interesting picture. Dating from 1757-58, about five years after he had left Boston for what is now Dutch Guiana, it is a caricature, probably done for a tavern club as a joke. Painted with satirical vigor in a cool palette on a six-foot length of bed ticking, it is the first American genre painting, and sets a standard for raciness which later artists working in this mode seldom lived up to.

According to tradition, the seated figure just right of center, who has fallen into a drunken stupor, is Joseph Wanton, one of Newport's most prominent merchants. Captain Ambrose Page vomits into the unsuspecting Wanton's pocket while he care-

John Greenwood:
Abigail Gerrish and Her Grandmother,
c. 1750, 28½ x 27½
(Courtesy of the Essex Institute,
Salem, Mass.)

lessly sets his own coattails alight by reeling against a lighted candle. To the right, Godfrey Malbone dances with Captain Nicholas Powers, while Captain Esek Hopkins, the future commander-in-chief of the Continental Navy, admiringly raises an unsteady wine glass. At the round table Captain Nicholas Cook, future governor of Rhode Island, holds a long pipe and converses with various companions, most of whom are too stupefied by the punch or too eagerly imbibing to pay much attention. The artist himself has been identified with the unhappy figure in the doorway. The breezy assurance of the handling suits the coarse liveliness of the subject, which is a vivid reminder of the more robust qualities of eighteenth-century life. Greenwood stayed on in Surinam for a few years before settling in London, where he gave up painting for the far more remunerative business of art dealing, in which he was considerably successful.

Smibert's *Bermuda Group* served as an example for a number of other paintings, by far the most interesting of which is the portrait of the family of Isaac Royall, who owned the extremely handsome house in Medford, Massachusetts. It is the first dated work by a mysterious and gifted painter named Robert Feke, about whom the most careful scholarly detective work has discovered tantalizingly little. He seems to have been born in Oyster Bay, Long Island, in about 1705, the son of a preacher and one of a large family with close Newport connections. He is referred to as a mariner after his death, and it is entirely likely that he did go to sea, because somewhere he picked up a knowledge of the latest style in London as practiced by Highmore, Hudson, Ramsay, and other portraitists fashionable before the period of Reynolds and Gainsborough. From his paintings it is clear that his formal training was sketchy, but that he was a born artist. *Isaac Royall and Family*—which includes, besides Isaac, his wife and child, his wife's sister, and his own sister—is a most ambitious undertaking. The composition is obviously based on Smibert's, perhaps at the suggestion of Royall himself, but it is carried out with none of the formulated assurance derived from academic training. There is an intense formal presence to each of the figures, however, an effect that Smibert rarely achieved. Feke was not a psychologist, but an observer of great keenness. Poses are stiff and anatomy often not understood, but what he saw he recorded with solidity and with lightness of touch and cool objectivity. Colors are lighter and brighter, textures studied with obvious pleasure, and forms arranged with instinctive taste.

Robert Feke: *Isaac Royall and Family*, 1741, 56³⁄₁₆ x 77¾
(Harvard Law School)

In 1742 Feke settled in Newport, where he married Eleanor Cozzens. The town records list them as "both of Newport," and they are said to have "lived in a large old house on Touro street, facing School street," near the synagogue designed by Peter Harrison. That peripatetic physician Dr. Alexander Hamilton of Charleston, South Carolina, recorded in his diary that on July 16, 1744, his friend Dr. Moffat showed him about the town and "carried me to one Feake, a painter, the most extraordinary genius ever I knew, for he does pictures tolerably well by the force of genius, having never had any teaching. . . ." Hamilton was so intrigued by the artist that he went on to describe his appearance. "This man had exactly the phiz of a painter," he noted, "having a long pale face, sharp nose, large eyes,—with which he looked upon you steadfastly,—and long curled black hair, a delicate white hand, and long fingers. . . ." An early self-portrait, probably inspired by Smibert's in the Berkeley picture, which exactly bears out Hamilton's description, probably dates from 1729. Though no earlier pictures are known, its quality proves that he must have been painting for a time before this, for it is not the work of a beginner. Further, he must have had an established reputation to have received a commission from Isaac Royall, one of the richest men in the New World, and to have had such other sitters as Mr. and Mrs. Charles Apthorpe in 1748 and James Bowdoin II, whose likeness now appropriately hangs at Bowdoin College, in Brunswick, Maine.

Feke's portrait of *Brigadier General Samuel Waldo* is his masterpiece. Like Smibert's *Sir William Pepperell,* the *Waldo* is life-sized. The general stands in a landscape painted with subtlety and atmosphere. He rests his spyglass on a rock and assumes a courtly pose, left hand on hip to hold back the long coat in a graceful sweep revealing a richly bordered long waistcoat. There is none of the heavy burliness of Smibert's *Pepperell,* yet this figure is as solid and far more sophisticated. In the distance, the citadel of Louisburg is under bombardment, and the landscape falls away to provide a setting that is more than merely a backdrop, for the dramatic depth emphasizes the substance of the isolated figure. There is elegance without the usual Colonial pomposity. The painting has character and verve, precision and control.

Signed and dated portraits and other contemporary evidence prove that Feke was in Philadelphia in 1746 and again in 1750. Between 1741 and the latter year he produced some seventy portraits, and after that he dropped from sight. Nothing like the *Waldo* portrait was to be painted again until Copley, some thirty years Feke's junior, hit his stride a decade and more later. A reputed family tradition has it that "his health declining, he sought the milder climate of Bermuda, where he died at about the age of 44." Yet there is no record of Feke in Bermuda, Barbados (which was often visited by Americans of the period), or Newport. The *Waldo* portrait shows him to have been worthy to be Copley's rival, and the only other painter of first rank the colonies produced. Yet he disappeared without a trace.

Robert Feke: *Brig. Gen. Samuel Waldo,* c. 1748, $96\frac{3}{4}$ x $60\frac{1}{4}$ (Bowdoin College Museum of Art, Brunswick, Me.)

John Singleton Copley: *Mrs. John Winthrop*, 1773, 35½ x 28¾
(The Metropolitan Museum of Art, Morris K. Jesup Fund, 1931)

JOHN SINGLETON COPLEY AND THE CLIMAX OF COLONIAL PAINTING

In 1748 the *Boston Gazette* carried the announcement that "Mrs. Mary Pelham (formerly the Widow Copley, on the Long Wharf, tobacconist) is removed to Lindel's Row, against the Quaker Meeting House, near the upper end of King Street, Boston, where she continues to sell the best Virginia tobacco, cut, pigtail, & spun, of all sorts, by wholesale and retail at the cheapest prices." For Mrs. Pelham's ten-year-old son, John Singleton Copley, it meant a great change. Long Wharf was the extension of King Street from the brick Town House out into the harbor, the center of Boston's busy waterfront.

There was much going on to fascinate a boy—the landing and departure of ships, the lading and unlading, the curious cargoes, the sailors of all nationalities, and even occasionally pirates, captured at sea and brought back in chains for trial. But it could be a rough and frightening place, too, with street fights and the brawling of drunken sailors sometimes ending in cracked skulls and fatal stabbings. And there must have been some wild tales told by sailors coming into the Widow Copley's little tobacco shop to buy a twist. The half mile from the end of the wharf to the brick Town House, now known as the Old State House, was the main entrance to the city, since most visitors came by water instead of across the narrow neck that was the only link to the mainland. The new house, away from the waterfront in Lindel's Row, now Exchange Place, must have been different, too, because Peter Pelham was a London-trained engraver of mezzotints who was also a painter, though none of his pictures has been identified. He sold paints, brushes, and other artists' supplies, advertised as a teacher of "Dancing, Writing, Painting upon Glass, and all kinds of needlework," and was an enthusiastic musician as well. He had been in Boston for twenty-two years, and made engravings after paintings of Smibert, Greenwood, and others, so his house must have been a hive of varied artistic activities. When his stepfather died three years later, young John knew he wanted to be a painter, and by the time he was fifteen he had embarked upon his career.

Copley's earliest works are stiff but competent exercises in the manner of Greenwood and Badger. In 1754 a visiting artist

John Wollaston: *John Page*, mid-18th cent., 50 x 40
(The College of William and Mary in Virginia)

Joseph Blackburn: *Mary (Polly) Warner*, 1761, 50⅛ x 40⅛ (Courtesy of Warner House Association, Portsmouth, N.H.; photo by Armsden)

came to town whose influence on colonial painting was to be great. Joseph Blackburn (in America 1753-63) was apparently an Englishman who had been trained in the British rococo manner of Hudson and Highmore. He seems to have brought with him a supply of mezzotints after fashionable British portraits from which he copied compositions and costumes, turning New England matrons into stiff clotheshorses with shiny fluttering draperies, and posing their merchant husbands like mincing dancing masters. Blackburn is at his best with attractive girls like *Polly Warner*, who was lucky enough to grow up in the handsome McPhedris-Warner House in Portsmouth, New Hampshire, where her picture still hangs. Painted in 1761, it shows her dressed in shining satin, with roses in her hair, and her pet bird perched on the back of her hand. For a decade, until he returned to England, Blackburn painted the gentry of New England, all looking similarly empty-headed but dazzlingly dressed. In the same way John Wollaston (in America 1749-58 and again briefly in 1767), another British journeyman painter, spent ten years producing portraits of countless almond-eyed and overdressed subjects from New York south to Virginia before entering on a new career with the British East India Company in Calcutta.

In the meantime Copley was studying all the pictures he could find, those in Smibert's studio, the Fekes, Greenwoods, Badgers, Blackburns, and the engravings that had belonged to his stepfather. It took him only a little more than a year before he could beat Blackburn at his own game in rendering the glossy sheen of satins and silks, the frilly whiteness of lace, and the more sober richness of the darker reds, plums, browns, and blues of the men's coats and the crisp curliness of their wigs.

In 1756 he painted plain *Ann Tyng* (Boston) in a gray gown trimmed with blue ribbons and white lace, and holding a shepherd's crook while feeding a white lamb. About two years later he painted two little daughters of Isaac Royall, Mary in a blue dress with a hummingbird on the tip of one finger, and Elizabeth in white with a puppy in her lap, seated on a couch draped in gold and wine red. The material falls in rich folds to make an effect of the greatest luxury, but the little girls are so di-

John Singleton Copley:
Mary and Elizabeth Royall,
c. 1758, 57½ x 48
(Courtesy, Museum of Fine Arts,
Boston, Julia Knight Fox Fund)

89

John Singleton Copley:
Col. Jacob Fowle,
c. 1763, 50 x 40
(In the collection of
The Corcoran Gallery of Art,
gift of Mary H. Daingerfield)

rectly and understandingly painted that the picture rises far above the level of decorative elegance of most rococo portraits. The personalities of the two lively, natural children come through with a directness that brings the picture into its proper human focus, while it remains the most complete statement of an aristocratic ideal that America was to produce until the appearance of John Singer Sargent late in the nineteenth century.

Probably before 1765 Copley portrayed *Mrs. Jerathmael Bowers* (Metropolitan) in a white satin dress and a purple sacque, her dark hair trimmed with roses and pearls, and with an immense pink rose at her bosom. She holds a black-and-white King Charles spaniel. The whole composition is from a mezzotint after Sir Joshua Reynolds' portrait of *Lady Caroline Russell*, but it displays a sureness of handling and control that is beyond anything seen so far in America and places him among the leading painters of fashionable portraits of the period on either side of the Atlantic.

By about 1760 Copley had acquired the ability to draw with the brush, and about five years later he had, in one critic's phrase, "learned to think in paint." From 1760 on came a memorable series of characterizations. The mathematician and classical scholar *Edward Holyoke* (Harvard), the set of his chin corroborating a contemporary's judgment that he "was as orthodox a Calvinist as any man I know, but too much of a gentleman and of too catholic a temper, to cram his principle down another man's throat," sits solidly in Harvard's presidential chair, which he occupied with distinction for more than thirty years. The merchant and shipowner *Epes Sargent* (National Gallery), a vigorous seventy, leans on a column base, one expressive hand, strong but marked by age, against his gray coat, while he looks out of the canvas with level gaze.

Thomas Hancock (Boston) smugly stands as large as life in a grand-manner setting complete with crimson drapery and curving portico, obviously satisfied with a surrounding splendor which even outdid that of his palatial house on Beacon Hill. *Mercy Otis Warren* (Boston), sister of James Otis, the firebrand patriot orator, wife of the Revolutionary leader who became paymaster general of the Continental Army, poses in a blue dress trimmed in silver with white lace, and a silvery white cap. The sharpness of the eye and the firmness of the mouth suggest something of the personality of the charming bluestocking who was acclaimed the poetess laureate of the Revolution. Her three-volume history of the Revolutionary War is full of amusing anecdotes, but her letters exchanged with her dear friends

Abigail Adams (as Portia) and Hannah Winthrop (as Honoria), which she signed Philomela, best show her lively spirit. Copley also revealed the humor and intelligence of *Mrs. John Winthrop*, the Honoria of the letters, though her pose is prim and the elegance of her costume conventional.

Copley developed an approach to portraiture that anticipates a device later used by photographers of revealing personality by representing his subject in a distinctive and individual gesture. *Dr. Sylvester Gardiner* (private collection) leans forward in his chair about to make a witty remark. *Ezekiel Goldthwaite* (Boston), the canny moderator of Boston's town meetings, looks up from his work, pen in hand, while his wife offers us a peach as plump as herself. It is in this way that Copley gave us the extraordinary series of likenesses of the leaders of the Revolution. *Samuel Adams* (City of Boston) is shown as he confronted Governor Hutchinson the day after the Boston Massacre. He points to a document labeled "Charter of William and Mary to Massachusetts," and the paper in his hand is inscribed "Instructions of the Town of Boston." It is the moment about which he wrote his friend James Warren: "It was then, if fancy deceived me not, I saw his knees to tremble. I thought I saw his face grow pale (and I enjoyed the sight) at the appearance of the determined citizens peremptorily demanding the redress of grievances." *John Hancock* (City of Boston) sits, tensely elegant in a royal blue suit laced with gold, about to enter a transaction in the large ledger on the table. Through something in the pose and expression one can feel the slightly equivocal character of the ambitious and vain young millionaire whom Sam Adams astutely involved in his revolutionary schemes. And *Joseph Warren* (1772-74, Boston), the "very clean young doctor," dressed in a black suit with immaculate white shirt and hose, pauses momentarily to look directly out of the picture, his eyes keen and his mouth with a suggestion of a smile. At his left hand are anatomical diagrams of the human skull symbolizing his skill in medicine, whose practice he continued even during those crucial months when he was the brilliant spokesman for the patriot cause.

From the 1760's come two portraits which are profoundly revealing of the temper of the times just before the Revolution. Both are of craftsmen. One is of *Nathaniel Hurd* (Cleveland), the goldsmith son of the more famous Jacob Hurd, who also engraved bookplates for Harvard College. With a black turban and mole-colored banyan lined in pink, he wears a dark blue-green waistcoat and a shirt, open at the throat. He leans for-

John Singleton Copley: *Dr. Joseph Warren*, 1772-74, 50 x 40 (Courtesy, Museum of Fine Arts, Boston, gift of Dr. Buckminster Brown)

ward slightly, strong hands clasped on the table. The mouth is wide, the lips full, there is a shadow of beard, and the glance of the dark eyes is direct. There is no background or setting except for the books on the green-covered table, one of which is Guillim's *Display of Heraldry,* a standard reference work of the day for the correct engraving of arms and crests.

The other portrait is of Copley's friend *Paul Revere,* who made many a frame in silver or gold for miniatures that the artist painted. As in the painting of Hurd, there is no background and the setting is reduced to only the most significant elements. Revere sits behind a table with a shiny mahogany top on which are scattered the engraving tools with which he is about to embellish the pear-form teapot he holds in his left hand, resting it on an engraver's sand cushion. He is without a wig and his brown hair is unpowdered. The folds of the loose white shirt are as carefully studied as are the details of the teapot and the reflection of the craftsman's capable fingers on its gleaming surface. Yet attention is compellingly drawn by the animation in the glance, the slight tilt of the right eyebrow, the generous firmness of the mouth. The stocky body suggests the power and energy to carry out the will of the quick intelligence lurking behind the dark eyes. This is doubtless the way Revere, "cool in thought, ardent in action," looked during the exciting times of the agitation about the Stamp Act, of secret meetings and marches of the Sons of Liberty, the tense days of the Boston Massacre and the Tea Party, during which he made the Liberty Bowl with its proud and independent inscription.

At a time when craftsmen were looked down upon in the South, and, though more respected, relegated to the lower orders of society in England, Revere was content to be painted in his working clothes and holding an object of his own making, as if to be judged by the quality of the work itself. There is no parade of dress or uniform, though the goldsmith was among the leaders in his profession, a Mason in high standing, and a companion of Sam Adams, the eloquent James Otis, and the elegant John Hancock, and was closest of all to Joseph Warren, in whose memory he named a son. The painting stands as a landmark in American art not only because it expresses the self-confident individualism of those who were the major participants in the cause of independence, but also because it shows Copley at the height of his powers. Its impact depends upon the intensity of vision resulting from the extraordinary discipline that enabled him to achieve and to command a style of such power that he painted pictures better than any he had

John Singleton Copley: *Paul Revere*, 1765-70, 35 x 28½
(Courtesy, Museum of Fine Arts, Boston, gift of Joseph W., William B., and Edward H. R. Revere)

ever seen. The series of portraits produced during the decade and a half before the Revolution represents Copley's first triumph by establishing him as the greatest American artist of the century, and his country's greatest portraitist until Thomas Eakins appeared in Philadelphia a century later as a contender for that honor. Copley's second triumph was to be shared with a rival, and occurred only after he had left America for England.

In 1769 he married Susanna Clarke—Suky, he called her—the daughter of a rich Tory merchant. He had as many commissions as he could undertake and was well paid, receiving fourteen guineas for a half-length. "I am now in as good business as the poverty of this place will admit," he wrote shortly before his marriage. "I make as much money as if I were Raphael or Correggio, and 300 guineas a year, my present income, is equal to 900 a year in London." He bought a farm on Beacon Hill next to Thomas Hancock's handsome mansion, and in the comfortable house there, with its view, of which Hancock boasted, across the Common to the harbor, the first of his four children was born. At the invitation of a group of prominent citizens who wanted portraits, he and Suky spent six months in New York, making side trips to Long Island and to Philadelphia, where he was delighted by the "flowery luxsuriance" of a copy of a Titian *Venus* he saw there.

When the Copleys returned early in 1772, the painter's mind was almost made up. For more than ten years he had been increasingly chafing at the restrictions he felt the colonial environment placed upon him. "Was it not for preserving the resemblance of particular persons," he wrote, "painting would not be known in the place." Copley's friend Captain Bruce took the portrait of the artist's half brother, *Henry Pelham* (private collection), to London and showed it to Sir Joshua Reynolds, president of the Royal Academy, who thought so highly of it that he remarked that no young artist he knew, with all the advantages of academic training in Europe, could equal such a performance. He did, however, criticize "a little hardness in the drawing, coldness in the shades," and urged Copley to come to Europe to study "before it was too late in life, and before your manner and taste were corrupted or fixed by working in your little way in Boston."

Copley then painted the portrait of little *Mary Warner with Her Dog* (Toledo) in which he tried to correct the faults that Reynolds had pointed out, and to realize the richness of color and tone that he imagined existed in the works of the old masters. But, to his crushing disappointment, Reynolds liked the second picture less than the first. Looking at them today, one can see how they did not conform to the current style against which Reynolds was judging them, but it is also possible to judge them on their own terms, and see them as more than portraits, excellent though they are as such. For both are expressions of aspects of childhood that transcend time and place, the little girl enjoying the companionship of her dog as only a child can, the boy lost in the dreams of youth, wistful and wondering.

Copley felt his own powers within him. He was desperate to break out of the confinement of portrait painting into the great and noble world of history painting, then universally recognized as the height of art. "It would give me inexpressible pleasure to make a trip to Europe," he wrote, "where I should see those fair examples of art that have stood so long the admiration of all the world." He was sure that this experience would enable him to realize Reynolds' judgment that he could become "a valuable acquisition to the art and one of the first painters in the world." Yet he was a craftsman with a growing family to support, so he hesitated to make the break.

The rising tension in Boston with the imposition of the Stamp Act and the civil disruption leading up to the Tea Party made up his mind for him. He was a friend of Warren, Revere, and Adams, yet his father-in-law was Richard Clarke, to whom a major portion of the tea was consigned. From his house on Beacon Hill he could see the regiments of British regulars, intended to intimidate the colonials, drilling on the Common, and could hear the drum and fife and the shouts of command. At night there were cries and echoes of running feet, the sounds of violence in the dark streets and crooked alleys. When the arrival of the tea split the town wide open, despite his painful shyness, he drove himself to act as mediator. Richard Clarke's house and warehouse were attacked by howling mobs, and he and the other merchants fled to Castle Island for safety. Copley conferred with Adams, Hancock, and Warren, urging moderation, and even addressed the town meeting. He talked compromise with the merchants, but they, safe behind the guns of Castle William, were hard to convince. He seems, nevertheless, to have achieved a kind of stalemate, and during the next few days the tension eased.

The disruption had put an end to portrait commissions, so he determined to take the time to go abroad to study. He sailed for London and the Continent, armed with letters of introduction from many friends. There he saw all that he had longed to see, visited the legendary cities he had so long envisioned, and wrote homesick letters to Suky. But the Tea Party had made the Revolution inevitable. It was a matter of time, and the time came sooner than anyone but Sam Adams and the Liberty Boys expected. Suky hurriedly packed up what little she could and fled, and Copley returned from his Grand Tour through Italy and France to meet her and the children in London.

In London he also found, not only an increasing number of Tory refugees from the colonies, but his exact contemporary Benjamin West, who in the decade and a half since he had left the Pennsylvania frontier, had made a place for himself as one of the leading painters in England, and had become the favorite artist of the king. As a Quaker, West did not believe in violence, but there was no question that his sympathies were with the colonists, as were those of Pitt and Burke and many others. Copley found himself forced by the war to remain in England whether he wanted to or not. Even if he could return there was no work at home. So the family settled down in a house at 25 George Street, Hanover Square, which, though they did not know it, was to be their permanent home.

III

The
New
Republic

John Singleton Copley: *The Copley Family*, 1776–77, 72½ x 90⅜
(National Gallery of Art, Washington, D.C., Andrew Mellon Fund)

JOHN SINGLETON COPLEY AND BENJAMIN WEST

AND THE BEGINNINGS OF ROMANTICISM

Up to the eve of the Revolution, life in the colonies followed, as far as possible, the patterns of Georgian England. In the mother country, however, there had already been more than faint stirrings of the coming Romantic movement, in the development of which the two young colonials were to play a considerable part. The works of Copley and of West anticipated by decades, and provided germinal impulse to, the flowering of Romantic painting in Europe.

The two men were as unlike as could be. Copley, intense, unsure, endowed with unusual gifts of intellect and imagination, wracked with doubts yet determined, was driven by lofty ideals to high artistic achievement and personal defeat. West, serene, idealistic, uninvolved in anything but his art, created a career through good organization and hard work which was to carry a man of limited imagination and moderate gifts to the heights of fame in his own day, but to be unjustly neglected by the next. The reputation of Copley has gained the greater luster with the passage of time. Because of their lack of a European background, each had been thrown on his own considerable resources and was thus freer to realize his own aims, unlimited by social patterns, hierarchies, or academies, his hopes and vision enlarged to match the broader horizons of the New World. Thus the very circumstances which made their lives more difficult were a source of strength for their art, and made them, all unaware, artistic pioneers.

It seems unfortunately inevitable that the two should have been rivals. Both were colonials, essentially strangers to the world of art and fashion in which they found themselves, having won their way there by extraordinary determination. Both had considered themselves good American Englishmen, lacking the experience to understand the profound differences in attitude and background which separated their lives from those among whom they were to live. West adjusted to the strains by maintaining his Quaker simplicity of approach to everything, and sticking to his painting. The dozens of young Americans who thronged his studio gave him those contacts with people of similar background that he needed, and his naturally optimistic and uncomplicated view of life gave him peace. But for the more sensitive and lonely Copley, the discovery, which seems to have come upon him gradually, of his position as an alien in a foreign land, when he had thought of himself as a son returning home from afar, was a traumatic experience. He reacted by working yet harder, perfecting his art ever more, realizing ever more ambitious projects, until, as also seems inevitable, this lonely, gifted man, whose valiant spirit had achieved so much, was to be finally overwhelmed by the world against which he had been driven to pit himself. In the playing out of this drama, however, the two men made their significant and generous contribution to art.

West was an innovator in his treatment of the events of his own times as an imaginative re-creation of them, as in his *Death of General Wolfe* (1770), when, for the first time in a major work, the actors in that tragic episode were clothed in the uniforms they actually wore instead of the togas of fashionable antiquity. As he quite reasonably pointed out to Sir Joshua Reynolds, "the event intended to be commemorated took place on the 13th of September, 1758, in a region of the world un-

Benjamin West: *The Death of General Wolfe*, 1770, 59½ x 84
(The National Gallery of Canada, Ottawa)

known to the Greeks and Romans, and at a period of time when no such nations, nor heroes in their costume, any longer existed . . . if instead of the facts of the transaction, I represent classical fictions, how shall I be understood by posterity?" Further, he included an Indian as a silent spectator, a reminder of the remoteness of the scene and an effective symbol of the New World.

West's Romantic manner was well developed before 1800, and appeared even in portraiture, as in the painting of the colorful *Colonel Guy Johnson,* superintendent of Indian affairs in the colonies, with the rich reds of his uniform contrasting with the silent, shadowed figure of the standing Indian warrior. The latter may be the famous Joseph Brant, who served as his secretary, but seems rather to represent the stoic native dignity which West so admired. The Colonel rests upon his rifle, but the Indian points to the elaborate peace pipe which he holds and, past it, to the scene in the background of an idyllic Indian family group. With his feathered headdress and fringed robe, he is the very ideal of the noble savage. In vibrance of color and contrast of dark and light, the portrait has an impressive and pervasive mood.

West's *Saul and the Witch of Endor* (1777, Hartford) is a tensely dramatic expression of the supernatural achieved through haunting effects of light. His later, Wagnerian *Death on a Pale Horse,* best seen in a small version in the Minneapolis Institute or in the 1802 oil study in the Philadelphia Museum, was greeted, when woodenly executed at great scale by his son Raphael in 1817, as a major artistic achievement. It is an interesting demonstration of Edmund Burke's ideas of "the terrible sublime" as set forth in his famous essay *On the Sublime and the Beautiful,* and is based on Milton's description of Death which that author quoted:

. . . as black . . . as night; fierce as ten furies; terrible as hell; and shook a deadly dart. What seemed his head the likeness of a kingly crown had on.

West's little-known designs to decorate Fonthill Abbey (several of which are in the Smith College collection, Northampton)—the colossal fake-Gothic country house built by William Beckford, an eccentric millionaire who stalked its stage-set battlements at midnight like the ghost of Hamlet's father—were as wildly romantic as the famous Gothic novel, *Vathek, An Arabian Tale,* of which Beckford was the author.

Benjamin West: *Col. Guy Johnson,* 1776, 79¾ x 54½
(National Gallery of Art, Washington, D.C., Andrew Mellon Collection)

101

Earlier, he had also pioneered in those vast figure pieces, based on classic or Biblical themes so attractive to the bourgeois tastes of his friend and patron George III, which led to the Romantic Classicism of the French School. His *Agrippina and Her Children Landing at Brundisium with the Ashes of Germanicus* (Yale), for example, with poses carefully studied from Roman reliefs of the period of Augustus, anticipates Jacques Louis David's famous *Oath of the Horatii* by nineteen years. His *Christ Healing the Sick in the Temple* (1811) is so huge that a special gallery had to be constructed to show it when he sent it back home as a gift to the Pennsylvania Hospital. Like his other such works, it was extravagantly admired in its day. Difficult as such paintings are for our generation to look at, they were without question significant forerunners of greater works to come.

Copley also shared in this leadership. His *Una and the Red Cross Knight* (1793, National Gallery), its subject taken from Spenser's *Faerie Queene*, a source for West and later for Washington Allston as well, is strongly in the Romantic vein. Sad though Copley's personal life may have been, during his English career he nonetheless produced important works of far higher quality than West could achieve in all but a very few instances. The first major picture he painted, after his arrival in London on the eve of the Revolution, was the famous *Watson and the Shark*, later much admired and widely known. At the time it was held up to question by some, because it dealt, not with Classic or national heroes, but with a group of waterfront characters in an actual episode in the life of one of them, Brook Watson, who seems to have been for a time during the Revolution a Loyalist informer. Copley re-created the event, which occurred in Havana Harbor, in all its horror. Watson, swimming, is attacked by the shark, its sharp-toothed mouth open, rising from the shadowy waters, an horrendous symbol of the dangers of the deep, while companions in the boat try to fend off the monster and rescue their friend. Watson lost a leg in the adventure, which did not prevent his later becoming a rich merchant and eventually lord mayor of London. It is a tense and frightening scene, and in it Copley has introduced the theme of man's battle against the forces of nature, which was to be a dominant theme in American art thereafter. The picture was far in advance of its times. Today we can appreciate it as an impressive achievement and recognize it as a significant harbinger. Since it was painted in 1778, and engravings of it received wide circulation, its influence was considerable in the development of the Romantic movement. It has an intensity and impact which cannot be measured in terms of its carefully controlled composition and the realization of each significant detail. It has a power and a conviction which West could never achieve. Nothing like it was to be seen until Théodore Géricault's *The Raft of the Medusa* (1819) and Eugène Delacroix's *Death of Sardanapalus*, which was exhibited in the Paris Salon of 1827, nearly half a century later, and has often been considered the starting point of French Romantic painting.

As the acknowledged leader in England in the field of monumental history painting then so fashionable in Europe, West showed his works in Paris. His paintings, as well as Copley's and the landscapes of Constable, were sought out by the French artists, a number of whom visited England during these important years around the turn of century. Thus the two American colonials share an advance position in the development of European Romantic painting with the great landscapist and a now forgotten Scot, Gavin Hamilton, whose classic episodes were painted mainly in Italy, where almost all artists of the day went to study.

John Singleton Copley: *Watson and the Shark*, 1778, 72½ x 90¼
(Courtesy, Museum of Fine Arts, Boston, gift of Mrs. George von Lengerke Meyer)

Between 1779 and 1780 Copley carried out a yet more ambitious project, *The Death of the Earl of Chatham in the House of Lords* (Tate Gallery, London), with more than fifty portraits, each carefully studied, when possible, from life. It is a theatrical tour de force unified by a strong design in light and shade to record the last act of Pitt in denouncing the crown's policy toward the colonies. In the following year Copley exhibited it, not in the Royal Academy's annual exhibition, but at a special showing, charging admission. *The Morning Post* estimated that it realized £5,000 and perhaps made him five thousand enemies because the receipts of the Royal Academy's exhibition fell a third below the previous year, though it contained seven Gainsboroughs and fifteen paintings by Sir Joshua Reynolds. The merchants of London had deeply admired Chatham. They flocked to see the impressive rendering of the dramatic circumstances of his death, and commissioned many portraits of the intense young artist who had memorialized their hero. Shortly after this he completed his *Death of Major Pierson* (Tate Gallery, London), the subject being a young British officer of twenty-four who refused to surrender to a superior French force in an engagement on the Isle of Jersey, and who died at the moment of victory. It was Copley's greatest accomplishment in history painting. The civilian onlookers, for which his wife and children posed, act as a kind of Greek chorus to express his horror of war.

All his life he had striven for mastery and control, and in such works as this he achieved it, but it was a hard-won victory. He felt keenly the condescending attitude of British artists toward him as a colonial, and sickened at hearing his countrymen called traitors. Intensely loyal himself, he lacked the official position of West to ease the difficulties of his situation. In 1782 he painted a portrait of the American businessman *Elkanah Watson* (Princeton), then in London, with a merchant vessel in the background. Together they sat in the gallery of the House of Lords to hear the King acknowledge on December 5 of that year the independence of the American colonies. Together they returned to Copley's studio, and, as Watson recorded in his diary, the painter, "with a bold hand, a master's touch, and I believe an American heart . . . attached to the ship the Stars and Stripes. This, I imagine, was the first American flag hoisted in England."

There was no returning. Copley had to remain in England, though he was homesick for Boston. He had never dreamed that the troubles which he had tried so hard to mediate following the Tea Party would have led to a complete break. He had his wife and family to support, so he stayed and worked. The portraits of these years are excellent, such as that of his own family, completed in 1785 and now in the National Gallery in Washington, the gift of a descendant. It shows his infant son, the future chancellor, Lord Lyndhurst, with his little sisters (two of whom had died by the time the painting was finished), the artist's wife and her father, and himself, handsome, keen-eyed, and reserved; but from his letters and from what we know of the times we can guess at some of the tumultuous feelings hidden behind that iron restraint. He went on to do other outstanding pictures, among them the *Portrait of the Sitwell Family* (private collection) of which, as Sir Osbert recalled, John Singer Sargent exclaimed on first seeing it, "I can never equal that!" The Corporation of London commissioned a colossal picture, 25 by 20 feet, of *The Repulse of the Floating Batteries at Gibraltar* (1791) for which Copley went to Germany to sketch the likenesses of four of the Hanoverians who were involved in the action. It was shown to crowds of people in a tent especially erected in Green Park, but the Duke of Bolton protested, so it had to be moved, then moved again. Finally the King offered a place near Buckingham Palace. "*My* wife," he is reported to have said, "won't complain." Its showing ruined the success of the Royal Academy's exhibition that year also.

All this represented a success that he could scarcely have hoped for, but at a price. When his young wife had fled Boston she had left behind a dead child he had never seen. He felt increasingly lonely, his health gave way, and his later years were clouded by a growing melancholy which corroded his remarkable talents until he could paint no more. After years of increasing despondency he died of a stroke in 1815 at the age of seventy-seven. He had come a long way from the fatherless boy who had grown up on Long Wharf in Boston, and who had set out on a painting career when still in his teens, and from his own character and determination had forged a style of such quality and power that the impact of even his earliest works remains undiminished by time. At the outbreak of the Revolution he had written home: "Poor America . . . Yet certain I am she will finally emerge from her present calamity and become a mighty empire. And it is a pleasing reflection that I shall stand amongst the first of the artists that shall have led the country to the knowledge and cultivation of the Fine Arts, happy in the pleasing reflection that they will one day shine with a luster not inferior to what they have done in Greece and Rome." He lived to see only the smallest beginning of that hopeful prophecy, but time has confirmed the value of his contribution.

Copley's temperament, which was in marked contrast to West's outgoing optimism, seems to have doomed him to frustrations. He knew himself to be a better painter, and keenly felt their rivalry. His life was a record of steady achievement, won at the expense of heroic effort, but ending in sadness. West was just as patriotic; as a Quaker he could not be involved in conflict, but he made no bones about his loyalties, and his friend the King respected his feelings. The same scruples caused him to refuse a knighthood. Highly regarded and honored throughout his long career, when he died at eighty-two in 1820, he was buried in Westminster Abbey, next to his friend Sir Joshua Reynolds, his predecessor as president of the Royal Academy. His had also been a long road from the Pennsylvania frontier. His works, so admired in his day, are uneven in quality, ranging from the lamentable to the excellent, but never, at their highest moments, approaching the intensity of expression and the disciplined control of Copley. A man of great goodness of heart and unquestioning seriousness of purpose, his house was the refuge for innumerable aspiring young artists. His instruction at his studio and at the Royal Academy was helpful and practical, and his role in history was to share with his more gifted but less fortunate countryman a position in the forefront of the growing Romantic movement both in Europe and in America.

Matthew Pratt: *The American School* (Benjamin West instructing his pupils), 1765, 36 x 50¼ (The Metropolitan Museum of Art, gift of Samuel P. Avery, 1897)

WASHINGTON ALLSTON AND THE TRAGEDY OF *BELSHAZZAR*

Washington Allston (1779–1843) was born on a plantation on the Waccamaw River near Charleston, South Carolina. Like Edgar Allan Poe, he was deeply impressed as a child by the ghost stories and curious folklore of the Negroes, which left a lifelong mark on his imagination. His youth was spent in Newport, Rhode Island, a favorite summer resort for a number of Charlestonians, where he and Edward Malbone, later to become the leading American miniature painter, became great friends, and went to Harvard together. From childhood he had been interested in art, and in Newport had studied with a part-time painter named Samuel King. At Harvard he saw Smibert's copy of Van Dyck's head of *Cardinal Bentivoglio*, probably the only painting on this side of the Atlantic at the time which could in any way suggest the qualities and style of the great tradition of European painting.

While an undergraduate, Allston painted a number of pictures illustrating subjects from Thompson's *Seasons* and from Mrs. Radcliffe's highly popular *The Mysteries of Udolpho*, a Gothic novel abounding in secret passages, remote castles, ghosts, abductions, bandits, and other sinister Italians. After graduation he and Malbone went to London and enrolled as pupils of Benjamin West at the Royal Academy. During his earlier years he delighted in the wild landscape style of Salvator Rosa as well as the brooding melancholy and flashes of violence of Gothic fiction, a taste which led him to appreciate the mannered work of the minor English painters Fuseli and Opie, and later to attempt a novel of his own in the Gothic vein, *Monaldi*, whose hero was a painter like himself. But he also discovered Turner and other artists, and his interests gradually widened. "Up to this time," he wrote, shortly after he was settled in London, "my favorite subjects, with occasional comic intermissions, were banditti, and I did not get over the mania until I had been more than a year in England." His account went gleefully on to tell his satisfaction in successfully painting a picture including a man with his throat cut! It is difficult today to recapture the charm of this extravagant part of the movement, generally more indulged in England and on the Continent than in the United States, though the writing of Poe is very much in this vein; and in Charles Brockden Brown, now forgotten, America produced a Gothic novelist of her own, whose works, along with Schiller's *Robbers* and Goethe's *Faust*, Shelley considered most influential in his own development. Keats praised his *Wieland* (1798) as a work of "powerful genius—accomplish'd horror." Brown added another dimension to the usual trappings of the Gothic novel by his intense preoccupation with the inner life of his characters, thus leading the way to Melville and Hawthorne. Similarly, Allston transmuted the childish shudders of Mrs. Radcliffe into the enriched emotional expression of his most important works.

Allston's major paintings began to appear within a few years of his starting to study with West. "With his huge, imposing Landscapes," such as *The Rising of a Thunderstorm at Sea* (1804, Boston) and *Diana in the Chase* (1805, Boston), came, as his biographer, Edgar P. Richardson, has pointed out, "the first true landscapes of mood in American art." During these years of study he visited Paris with another American pupil of West's, John Vanderlyn, and spent days at a time in the Louvre. Four years in Italy followed, where he saw much of Washington Irving, who was so impressed by his ability and charmed by his conversation that he almost decided to take up an artistic career himself. Irving's considerable artistic gifts are shown by the sketches he made wherever he went, and his continuing interest led him to title his best-known work *The Sketch Book*, and to assume the nom de plume of Geoffrey Crayon.

In Rome, Allston haunted the Caffè Greco, the favorite rendezvous of artists and writers in the Via Condotti, where one might find Goethe, Thorwaldsen, Hans Christian Andersen, Shelley, Keats, Turner, Cooper, and many others. He also knew the group that often met with Wilhelm von Humboldt, the Prussian resident minister, whose brother, the famous scientist, had just returned from exploring the Andes; the latter's report of his travels was to inspire the American painter Frederic Church to follow in his footsteps. Madame de Staël was one of this group also. Her book on Germany, *De l'Allemagne*, had fired the imaginations of two young Bostonians, George Herbert Ticknor and Edward Everett, and led them to learn German and depart for a year's study at Göttingen. It also served to bring German scholarship into the American colleges and lead young American artists to study in German academies. Napoleon had disapproved of her book—another reason why many were interested in it—and Madame de Staël was at the moment an exile in Rome, though she had purchased land in northern New York State from Judge Cooper, the author's father, and was contemplating moving to the United States.

Allston, like Irving, Everett, Ticknor, and all the other young American travelers of his day, had extraordinary opportunities to meet the great personages of Europe. The young men came armed with letters from Jefferson, always eager to advance the cause of learning and the arts in the United States, or from others of the older generation of American leaders, all of whom had international connections. Benjamin West's door was always open to any young countryman, and he often advanced his pupils funds and found them patrons. Lafayette was a friend of all Americans, and a visit to La Grange to pay one's respects to the old companion-in-arms of Washington's was almost a patriotic duty. At a time when revolutionary change was in the air, when the whole Western world was in a ferment, this new generation of Americans was regarded by European intellectuals and artists, as Madame de Staël addressed Ticknor and Everett, as "the advance guard of the human race." The American experiment seemed to be working; perhaps it was the pattern of the future. Everett returned to assume the chair of Greek at Harvard at a time when attention and sympathy were fixed upon the Greek struggle for liberty. Ticknor returned to Cambridge to inspire his students in modern languages to appreciate their own inheritance as well, which Irving had already revealed in his tales of the Catskills and the valley of the Hudson.

Allston, however, worked in the dream world of his friend Samuel Taylor Coleridge, whose portrait he painted, along with that of Wordsworth. His own *Self-Portrait* (1805, Boston) shows how he looked during the early years abroad, very youthful and with fashionably wind-rumpled hair. He developed a romantic portrait style which was all his own, though based on Gilbert Stuart's practice, with the concentration on the head, the rest melting away into shadow, as in the case of *Dr. Channing* (Boston), an especially appropriate treatment for the saintly and magnetic Unitarian philosopher. His distinctive use of color, so different from contemporary English practice, caused George Inness, the American Romantic painter of a later generation, to remark of his *Benjamin West:* "How real seems that portrait along side of Stuart's pink fancy of Washington! —and what a piece of bosh, by contrast, is the 'Portrait of Benjamin West, Esq.' by Sir Thomas Lawrence." During these early years he was formulating an approach to painting which he later recalled for William Dunlap:

Titian, Tintoret, and Paul Veronese absolutely enchanted me, for they took away all sense of subject. . . . It was the poetry of color which I felt; procreative in its nature, giving birth to a thousand things which the eye cannot see, and distinct from their cause. . . . Now I

109

. . . think I understand why so many great colorists . . . gave so little heed to the ostensible *stories* of their compositions. . . . They addressed themselves, not to the senses merely, as some have supposed, but rather through them to that region (if I may so speak) of the imagination which is supposed to be under the exclusive domination of music, and which, by similar excitement, they caused to teem with visions that "lap the soul in Elysium." In other words they leave the subject to be made by the spectator, provided he possessed the imaginative faculty—otherwise they will have little more meaning for him than a calico counterpane.

Here, from the pen of a young American artist studying abroad, in a passage whose bearing upon Allston's own development has been pointed out by Richardson, is an explicit statement of a basic principle of the experimental art of our own day. In its denial of the significance of formal subject matter, and in its emphasis on the idea of communication at an emotional level through the abstract means of pure color, Allston anticipates the art of a century and more later, and at the same time describes the evocative qualities of his own painting, in which he sought, as in a line from his once-famous poem, "The Sylphs of the Seasons," "To catch a Poet's dream." Thus we can see him as a part of an artistic tradition that links his world and ours, and in which his landscapes especially, as exercises in romantic mood, like music, assume a significant place.

His pictures could be lyric and almost Claudian, like the *Diana in the Chase* (Boston) or the *Coast Scene of the Mediterranean* (1811, Boston), with the sails of fishing boats silhouetted against a golden sunset sky, or deeply foreboding, as in *The Rising of a Thunderstorm at Sea.* His *Moonlit Landscape* (1819, Boston), with figures in the moonlight, with a small sailboat drawn up on the shore, could be an illustration of one of Byron's poems, though it has no specific subject. Is it a meeting, or a departure? No one knows. But its real subject is in its mood,

Washington Allston:
Elijah in the Wilderness,
1818, casein on canvas, 49 x 72½
(Courtesy, Museum of Fine Arts, Boston,
gift of Mrs. Samuel and Miss Alice Hooper)

110

Washington Allston: *Moonlit Landscape*, 1819, 24 x 35
(Courtesy, Museum of Fine Arts, Boston, M. and M. Karolik Collection)

mysterious, quietly suspenseful, enigmatic. His *Elijah in the Wilderness* (1818, Boston) is his most powerful and impressive work, a forbidding rocky landscape, with bare mountain crags and a single blasted tree in the foreground, beneath an ominous sky, dwarfing the tiny kneeling figure of the lonely Prophet. Curiously, it was painted in what today would be called casein; Allston, evidently sharing the typically American urge to experiment, used sour milk as a medium most successfully, for the picture is sound and brilliant today.

Unfortunately, however, his greatest experiment was a failure, and a failure which shadowed his entire later life. Apparently inspired by Michelangelo, he early became intent upon doing immense figure-pieces. When first in England, he painted *The Dead Man Restored to Life by Touching the Bones of the Prophet Elisha* (1811), which was awarded a prize by the British Institution and was purchased by the Pennsylvania Academy of the Fine Arts; this was followed by other attempts in this same direction. Charles Leslie, his Philadelphia friend, who found a successful though minor artistic career in England, praised highly the color of his *Uriel in the Sun* (1817, Boston), a very large canvas with a single gigantic figure, painted about this time. Perhaps Allston was experimenting with medium in these paintings also, because today there is no trace left of the richness of Venetian color which Leslie so admired. With glowing color, the effect would have been very different, but such compositions were beyond his powers; the figures are awkward and stiff, the drawing dry and labored. When he returned from Europe in 1818 he was in poor health, but he had a scheme for a masterwork, *Belshazzar's Feast*, of which he had already made "a highly finished sketch." He wrote to his friend Washington Irving in London:

I think the composition the best I ever made. . . . Don't you think it a fine subject? I know not any that so unites the magnificent and the awful. A mighty sovereign, surrounded by his whole court, intoxicated with his own state, in the midst of his revelry, palsied in a moment, under the spell of a preternatural hand suddenly tracing his doom on the wall before him; his powerless limbs, like a wounded spider's, shrunk up to his body, while his heart, compressed to a point, is only kept from vanishing by the terrific suspense that animates it during the interpretation of his mysterious sentence. His less guilty but scarcely less agitated queen, the panic-struck courtiers and concubines, the splendid and deserted banquet table, the half arrogant, half astounded magicians, the holy vessels of the temple (shining as it were in triumph through the gloom), and the calm, solemn contrast of the prophet, standing, like an animated pillar, in the midst, breathing forth the oracular destruction of the empire!

Nothing better illustrates the essentially literary cast of the painting of the Romantic movement. The subject is actually no more melodramatic than Géricault's *Raft of the Medusa*, with its welter of corpses and starving men driven mad by thirst, or of Delacroix's *Death of Sardanapalus*, with its confusion of the dead and the dying, of wildly plunging horses, and of saber-swinging soldiers, and, in the midst, the doomed ruler, immobilized by despair. The Gothic novel is not so remote from all this, and Allston's early and continuing preoccupation with such emotionally charged subjects, so closely related to the ranting style of acting of the day, was not out of line with the direction which European Romanticism was taking. But it was a fatal choice for him. In such endeavors he was isolated in America, where painting was following a different tack. Alone in his studio, he worked away at the colossal canvas (12 by 18 feet), painting and repainting, not letting anyone see the work, but refusing other commissions so that he could continue his fruitless struggle.

Admired for his charm and his brilliant conversation, respected for both his literary and his artistic achievements, he was an international figure who was constantly being sought out by visitors from at home and abroad. During these later years, his studio at Cambridgeport, with all its mementoes of the early times in London and Rome, became increasingly a meeting place for his large circle of friends as well as for out-of-town visitors. There one might find Henry Wadsworth Longfellow, whose *Voices of the Night* seemed so to echo the yearning and nostalgia of the painter's pictures, and the historian Prescott, who was then working on his *Conquest of Mexico,* to be published in the year of Allston's death. Richard Henry Dana (of *Two Years Before the Mast*) and the young James Russell Lowell, who was to succeed to Longfellow's Harvard professorship and had two careers ahead of him, one in letters and another in diplomacy, often stopped by, as did Oliver Wendell Holmes, "the Autocrat of the Breakfast Table," who, with the redoubtable Margaret Fuller, wrote at length on the retrospective exhibition of the artist's works held in 1839. It was discussions of this event at meetings of the Transcendental Club in Concord that led Emerson to write his famous essay *Art.* Allston, always hospitable, received his visitors in a red-lined velvet robe, and kept in touch with his friends across the sea, with Thorwaldsen and "Old Canove," whose mantle had fallen on the shoulders of a young Bostonian named Horatio Greenough (who was proving a better critic than a sculptor), and with Irving and Bryant, with the English Lake Poets, Wordsworth, Coleridge, and Southey, and with his old pupil Samuel F. B. Morse. He died in 1843 in his sixty-fourth year, defeated by the *Belshazzar,* and was buried near the Harvard Yard by the light of torches in a funeral attended by devoted friends.

Allston's personal discoveries about the "poetry of color" in the paintings of the great Venetian Renaissance masters he saw in Europe, and his friendship with the poet Coleridge were not only important for his finding his own style but also for introducing the painting of mood into American art. In 1814, in order to call attention to "the admirable works exhibiting now by Allston," Coleridge wrote three essays which he always considered among his best statements about the arts. In the last essay of the series, which appeared in the unlikely medium of *Felix Farley's Bristol Journal,* he analyzes and praises Allston's "great picture" (*The Dead Man Revived*), which, "with his Hebe, landscape, and sea-piece, would of themselves suffice to elucidate the fundamental doctrines of color, ideal form, and grouping: assist the reasoner in the same way as the diagrams aid the geometrician, but far more and more vividly."

Allston must have been well aware of, if he had not actually contributed to, the theories which Coleridge was formulating and which were most fully stated in his essay *On Poesy of Art* of 1818, where he defined art as "the mediatress between, and reconciler of, nature and man. It is, therefore, the power of humanizing nature, of infusing the thoughts and passions of man into everything which is the object of his contemplation." It was Allston's infusion of an emotional state into his landscapes and seascapes that was his particular contribution. As in the case of Irving and Cooper, his reputation as one of his country's own old masters was established during his lifetime. Although by living in Cambridgeport he was largely deprived of the stimulation he had found in Europe, which had proven helpful, if not essential, for his artistic growth, his very presence in the United States was an encouragement to younger artists, and lent dignity to their efforts and aspirations. His works led to the further development of an introspective, subjective and emotional focus in art, in great part an inheritance from the Puritan past, which still continues.

Washington Allston: *Study for Belshazzar's Feast*, 1817, 25½ x 34¼
(On deposit at the Museum of Fine Arts, Boston, from the Boston Athenaeum)

THE CLASSIC IDEAL AND THE FEDERAL TRANSITION

Thomas Jefferson ushered in the Greek Revival in America with a Roman temple. His Capitol at Richmond, Virginia, finished in 1789, was designed after the Maison Carrée at Nîmes, which he had seen on his trip to the Continent two years earlier. The Revolution and the War of 1812 had made it a bit difficult for even the staunchest Federalists to continue to look to England to supply a model and an ideal for the young republic, deep though its debt might be to British institutions. The excesses of the French Revolution and the asininities of the French ambassador of the Revolutionary government to the United States, Citizen Genêt, markedly diminished public admiration for the nation's first ally, even among those Americans most strongly infected with what Fisher Ames, eloquent spokesman for Massachusetts Federalists, called "the *rabies canina* of Jacobinism." Recovery from the War of 1812, "Mr. Madison's War," so unpopular with merchants and businessmen because of its interference with the far more important matter of trade, led the country into an era of dramatic growth and prosperity. The 1820's were a time of pride and confidence, of a sense of purpose, of a feeling that great things were in the offing. If all this was accompanied by a certain amount of self-assertion, it seems easy to forgive such youthful brashness. One has only to remember that in but a few years—and there were veterans of Bunker Hill and Yorktown still very much alive to give testimony to it—independence had been won, a stable government established, a considerable section of a continent conquered, with cities, growing in wealth and size, and a countryside "tamed to the plow" being steadily extended westward. Surely America was destined for greatness, and she needed aims and models worthy of her destiny.

It was during these years that the struggle for independence of the Greeks attracted deep and sympathetic attention in both Europe and America. Their courageous battle against the Turks not only recalled our own Revolution but also brought back echoes of a past whose grandeur was reaffirmed by the discoveries of archaeologists at Pompeii and Herculaneum. Copies of James "Athenian" Stuart's and Nicholas Revett's *The Antiquities of Athens*, four magnificent volumes issued in London from 1762 to 1816, with a supplementary volume in 1830, were

Artists and
Artisans
of the
Early
Nineteenth
Century

Oval looking glass,
attributed to John Doggett,
Roxbury, Mass., 1800-10
(Courtesy, Museum of Fine Arts,
Boston, M. and M. Karolik Collection)

Heating radiator, cast iron,
New York, c. 1815
(Courtesy of The Cooper Union Museum)

finding their way into American libraries. Many American schoolboys, like the young John Quincy Adams, were weaned on Livy and Tacitus, Plutarch and Cicero; and the first volume of Gibbon's monumental *Decline and Fall of the Roman Empire* appeared in 1776, an auspicious year for Americans. So it was not Greece alone which captured the imagination, but also Rome, republican Rome, with its intimations of the high responsibilities of citizenship. Its symbol was Cincinnatus, who, like the leaders of the American Revolution, was called from his plow to the service of his country. It was by thoughtful design that his name was adopted by Washington's companions-in-arms when, at the end of the Revolution, conscious of extraordinary experience shared, they joined together into the Society of the Cincinnati, dedicated to keep alive the principles for which they had fought to such good effect.

What was at first a Classical Revival soon became increasingly a Greek Revival. Byron's death on the shore at Missolonghi in 1824 was but one of the more dramatic episodes which fired the imagination and captured the admiration of an already sympathetic people. Classic names were soon to be found scattered across the map of America. Romes, Spartas, and Corinths joined the Concords, Salems, and Harmonies, equally to express a utopian future hopefully to be realized in the New World. The feeling was so universal that it did not seem incongruous for President Monroe to include in a message to Congress in 1822 the remark that "the mention of Greece fills the mind with the most exalted sentiments and arouses in our bosoms the best feelings of which mankind is capable," and for Albert Gallatin seriously to petition that the United States government lend the Greeks an American fleet.

The peculiar convenience of Greece as an ideal was that it could mean all things to all people. For Jefferson, it represented the purest democracy with a maximum of individualism. For conservative Federalists, it stood for the timeless and the constant in the face of change, for, as Nicholas Biddle noted in his diary, "the two great truths in the world are the Bible and Grecian architecture." For some, it was the land of myth, of Hawthorne's *Twice-Told Tales,* for others, a realm of art and classic beauty. For New England intellectuals, it epitomized their own ideal of plain living and high thinking, and for the ambitious and the *nouveaux riches,* it provided the most readily recognizable status symbols. Benjamin Latrobe (1764–1820), the fourth architect of the national Capitol, who designed such outstanding monuments as Baltimore Cathedral and the Bank of Pennsylvania (1800), the first Greek design in America, and also, as a skilled engineer, provided Philadelphia with her model water works, summed it up in an address to the Society of Artists of Philadelphia in 1811. "The history of Greece," he stated, "refutes the vulgar opinion that the arts are incompatible with liberty . . . for the Greece of Pericles was free, and only from the time of Alexander lost that freedom, and with it, her perfection in the arts." Once America learns that the home of the fine arts "is in the bosom of a republic, then indeed the days of Greece may be revived in the woods of America, and Philadelphia become the Athens of the Western World." Though one could not expect that a Bostonian, a New Yorker, or a Charlestonian would have agreed to the precise locale, the sentiment was otherwise universally acceptable.

Before the full flush of the Greek Revival, however, came the Federal period, when during the years from the Revolution to about 1820 the age of Chippendale and Palladio ended as the influence of Wren and Gibbs gave way to that of Robert Adam, whose more delicately proportioned manner crossed the Atlantic in the useful volumes of William Pain and Isaac Ware. The Federal style reached its finest flowering in the works of a versatile Yankee, Samuel McIntire (1757–1811), in the New England seaport town of Salem, Massachusetts. According to his friend the Reverend William Bentley, whose gossipy diary is such a gold mine of information, McIntire was not only an architect, sculptor, carver, and cabinetmaker, but accomplished in other fields as well, even in music, where "he was among our best judges and able performers."

McIntire's furniture was among the finest of the period when the country, "growing from the gristle into the bone," in Cooper's words, began increasingly to express its new feelings of nationalism in the forms of the Greek Revival and in growing Romanticism. As architecture was dominated by the designs of Robert Adam, furniture was deeply influenced by those of Hepplewhite and Sheraton before the evolution of the latter's mode, under the influence of the French Empire, into the richer, fuller forms perhaps best seen in the mature style of Duncan Phyfe. McIntire was never more impressive as a cabinetmaker than in the chest-on-chest he designed and carved for Elias Hasket Derby of Salem in 1796. Made by William Lemon, the piece shows a modified Hepplewhite style, the top section with flanking Ionic colonnettes, and the lower serpentine-fronted, with heavy bracket feet. The rich carving, strictly limited to provide a frame to set off the design of the mahogany-veneered drawer-

Chest-on-chest,
attributed to William Lemon,
McIntire carving and design,
Salem, Mass., 1796
(Courtesy, Museum of Fine Arts, Boston,
M. and M. Karolik Collection)

117

fronts (carefully selected from a choice flitch to have just the right decorative effect), is typically McIntire's in style. It displays, in the controlled and crisp manner of which he was a master, the baskets and bowl of fruit, the bunches of grapes, swags, cornucopias, and rosettes which appear throughout his work. Adam-style urns top the corners of the cornice, and a figure of Victory, crowned and bearing an olive wreath, appropriate for the date of the piece, occupies the broken pediment.

Stephen Badlam (1751–1815) of Dorchester was also a very productive maker during these years, turning out many of the shield-backed Hepplewhite and the square-backed Sheraton chairs then so popular, while John Seymour, who arrived in America from Devonshire in 1785, and his son Thomas, who was active through the first quarter of the century, are among the leading Boston furniture makers of the period. Their case pieces with satinwood and bird's-eye maple veneers, ivory key escutcheons, fine dovetailing of the drawers, with interiors painted in the distinctive "Seymour blue," are individual and distinguished interpretations of the contemporary styles, which appear at their best in tambour desks and in sideboards, such as the extraordinary example in the Karolik Collection in the Boston Museum of Fine Arts. A painting by Henry Sargent (1770–1845) of a *Dinner Party* shows an interior of the Federal period, with Sheraton sideboard, Hepplewhite dinner table, and the rather restrained furnishings typical of the time, to be found from New England, as here, to the Savannah of William Jay's Regency-style houses. The Owans House of 1817, now restored and administered by the Telfair Academy, which occupies the house Jay also designed for Alexander Telfair, the son of the Governor, in the following year, is admirably furnished in this fashion.

Sheraton-style sideboard with double tier, attributed to
John Seymour, 1800-10
(Courtesy, Museum of Fine Arts,
Boston, M. and M. Karolik Collection)

Silversmiths also abandoned the more robust forms of the eighteenth century for the elegant refinement of the Adamesque. Teapots were no longer full-bodied and generously rounded, but became chastely straight-sided and generally oval in section, like that made in 1799 by Paul Revere as a part of the set (Boston) presented to Edmund Hartt, in whose yard the *Constitution* was built, for his construction of the frigate *Boston*, "that ornament of the AMERICAN NAVY." Sometimes they were fluted, like the one Revere made for Jonathan Hunnewell for £14 11s. in 1796, with its delicately engraved swags and pine-cone finial. Other silversmiths also spanned the Colonial and the Federal periods, like Richard Humphreys (advertised 1771-96) of Philadelphia, maker of camp cups for George Washington (Yale), and Joseph Richardson, Jr. (1752–1831), who made medals for presentation by the President to friendly Indian chiefs. The younger men generally worked in a somewhat more advanced Classical style. Anthony Rasch (fl. c. 1807-25) of Philadelphia produced in about 1810 an extraordinarily striking pair of sauceboats with arching serpent handles, ram's-head spouts, and winged-lion feet, in French Empire style, now in the Metropolitan Museum. Here, as in cabinetmaking, there is no diminution of quality of either design or craftsmanship.

Henry Sargent: *The Dinner Party*, 1815-20, 59½ x 48
(Courtesy, Museum of Fine Arts, Boston, gift of Mrs. Horatio A. Lamb in memory of Mr. and Mrs. Winthrop Sargent)

It was Charles Bulfinch of Boston who introduced the Adam manner to New England architecture, and who preceded McIntire in the graceful Federal style, so appropriately named because it suited the taste of those who were politically Federalist as well. Bulfinch himself hardly fits into this category, however. His style, increasingly Classic and simple, was spread broadcast across the young nation by edition after edition of Asher Benjamin's invaluable builders' handbooks, and the Federalist style, with its echoes of Adam and Regency, was, in turn, transformed into a national style. For the Greek Revival was more than its name implies. The inhabitants of the outlying villages, those who were founding new settlements in the western reserves or opening the wild country beyond the Alleghenies and along the banks and reaches of the larger rivers, men who of necessity thought more about Indians than about Greeks, and who carried with them traditions of building often harking back to the Middle Ages, found the manuals of Asher Benjamin eminently practical. They gave, along with admirable structural diagrams, sample designs of houses and churches of increasingly spare and austere simplicity, their Greek-derived forms, devoid of almost all ornament, capable of being realized by those to whom the books were particularly addressed by the author.

As Benjamin states in his preface to *The Practice of Architecture*, a copy of which he presented, respectfully inscribed, to Bulfinch, "Those Carpenters in country villages who aspire to eminence in this business, having no Architect to consult, are under the necessity of studying the science thoroughly and without a master. To them, therefore, is this book peculiarly adapted; it contains the principles of many expensive folios, condensed into a narrow space and applied to modern practice." The orders were there, clearly presented in their proper Vitruvian proportions so that they might be employed for some ambitious project, such as a church or a courthouse, for a portico suitable to the dignity of some local worthy or large landowner. But most Americans were satisfied with the familiar boxlike forms already traditional, though many began to build their houses end on to the street, widening the corner trim into flat pilasters, applying a simple cornice to turn the gable into a pediment, and perhaps topping the front door with the flattened triangle which made the whole consistently "Greek." Though there are exceptions, this was generally the extent of the archaeological accuracy, whether the building was large or small, pretentious or modest. Despite the classical correctness which Jefferson endeavored constantly to maintain as a proper example, the same kind of practical and free use of a generally Classical vocabulary, largely Greek in flavor, following the example set by Bulfinch, became the rule.

The interest in painting during the early years of the republic was limited, as before the Revolution, largely to portraiture, though inventories list an occasional "fancy picture," usually a fourth-rate Italianate landscape, such as a Rosa-like scene with banditti, or a shipwreck on a rocky coast. In the country districts and even on the frontier there were itinerant artists who, much like those of a previous generation, were willing to turn their hands to producing likenesses as well as to painting signs or decorating the walls of the front room of the house or the parlor of the local inn with stenciling or with the stylized rendering of motives derived from the locality or from memories of imported wallpaper. In the centers on the Eastern seaboard a more formal style continued, however, and with Copley's departure for England in 1774, Charles Willson Peale (1741–1827) of Philadelphia was left to dominate the field. The son of a well-born English remittance man who had died when Peale was a child, he had learned several trades by himself, and decided at the age of twenty-one to teach himself to paint. He went to Boston to get help from Copley, who was only three years older but who had been an independent professional since his teens, and he made such progress that friends paid his way to London to study with Benjamin West, with whom he stayed two years. On his return he remained unrivaled until Gilbert Stuart came back in 1793. He served with distinction in the Revolutionary War, was a member of the Pennsylvania Assembly, and set about recording for posterity the appearance of the military and civilian leaders of the Revolution in paintings that were eventually to form a part of his Museum, the first of its kind. Curious, enthusiastic, vigorous, imaginative, and warmhearted, he raised a whole family of artists, naming his children after Rubens, Rembrandt, Titian, Raphael and other artists. And there have been painting Peales ever since. The robust charm of his personality perhaps shines through most strongly in his *Peale Family Group*, complete with the family dog, Argus, who was for so many years the faithful custodian of the Peale Museum. The painting is inscribed: "C. W Peale painted these Portraits of his family in 1773. wishing to finish every work he had undertaken—compleated This picture in 1809!"

In 1795 he painted the famous *Staircase Group* (Philadelphia), with his sons Raphaelle and Titian Ramsey Peale going

Charles Willson Peale: *Peale Family Group*, finished in 1809, 56½ x 89½
(Courtesy of The New-York Historical Society, New York City)

Charles Willson Peale:
The Artist in His Museum,
1822, 103½ x 80
(The Pennsylvania Academy of the
Fine Arts)

up a back stair. Originally framed with a real doorframe, and complete with a real bottom step, it is a fascinating piece of illusionism that shows the powerful preoccupation with fact that runs through American art. His *Exhuming the Mastodon* (Peale Museum) records the unique event which provided the first mastodon skeleton to be dug up and assembled and put on display in his Museum. He abandoned art for science for some years, only to take it up again at the age of seventy-four. In his self-portrait, *The Artist in His Museum,* painted at eighty-one, he holds aside a drapery, inviting us to enter to see the work of which he was so proud: America's wild life, each animal type arranged in the first habitat groups known, mounted by him with appropriate flora and painted backgrounds; America's history, with the likenesses of her great leaders; America's past, with Indian relics, fossils, and the mastodon bones; and, as a symbol of the country, the wild turkey which his friend Franklin also felt should be the national emblem. His painting materials and instruments for taxidermy are nearby.

Peale had the character and ability to achieve the countless creative and useful projects conceived by his lively imagination. He was constantly inventing things, and in his old age he shocked his children by careening down the hills near Philadelphia at a breakneck pace on a velocipede of his own manufacture. He died in his eighty-seventh year as a result of a thorough drenching suffered while on his way to court the lady whom he hoped to make his fourth wife.

Gilbert Stuart (1755–1828) was perhaps the only other artist in our history who could hope to compete in personality and charm with Peale. The son of a ne'er-do-well Rhode Island snuff miller, he early showed talent and managed to get to England, where he soon was among the leading artists in a group that included Reynolds, Gainsborough, and Romney. Ebullient and improvident, he was soon hopelessly in debt, despite many commissions. Dunlap reports that he rivaled the Prince of Wales in his fashionable dress, and once when John Trumbull saw him in jail Stuart greeted the extremely stiff and proper former aide-de-camp of Washington's as "Bridewell Jack" and asked him what he was in for.

To escape his debtors, Stuart fled to Ireland, where he immediately became enormously popular and received many commissions, only to repeat the process of getting into debt. So, armed with a sketch for his famous full-length portrait of Washington, he returned to America in 1793, worked for some time in Philadelphia with great success, then settled down to reign supreme in Boston. It was at this time that he developed the distinctive style for which he is famous: portraits with all the concentration on the head, eliminating almost everything of setting or costume, thus creating timeless impressions of his sitters. His unique brushwork flickers with life, creating a result vibrant with his own keen vitality. Of flesh he wrote, "it is like no other substance under heaven. It has all the gaiety of a silk-mercer's shop without its gaudiness of gloss, and all the soberness of old mahogany without its sadness."

His *Athenaeum Portrait of Washington* (Boston) is so convincingly satisfying in its impression of life and truth that it has been said that if Washington were to return to earth and did not look like the portrait he would be summarily judged an impostor. His warm human sympathy shines through his pictures: he was fascinated with people, not parade. When looking at an official court portrait of Napoleon by David he once remarked, "How delicately the lace is drawn! Did one ever see richer satin? The ermine is wonderful . . . and, by Jove, the thing has a head!" As he grew older, his hand developed an increasing tremor. The most vivid memory his pupil Thomas Sully (1783–1872) had of his term of study was the times when Stuart would let him stand behind him while he painted, to see the wizardry of his swift and masterly touch. During the long illness of later years, however, when pain drove him increasingly to the bottle, his devoted and gifted daughter Jane sometimes had to finish his paintings for him. Only once did he have a rival, when the gigantic and genial frontiersman and self-taught artist, Chester Harding (1792–1866), stopped in Boston for a few weeks before taking England by storm. "How rages the Harding fever today?" Stuart would ask humorously. A late portrait of him by Sully's pupil John Neagle (1796–1865) shows him old, in pain, but indomitable, with, as a visitor recorded, "the most keen and penetrating eye that I have ever seen," in which the old extravagant humor still smoldered.

With the death of Stuart and of Peale an era passed. The country had outgrown the Federalism of the early republic, and a new age was at hand, to be expressed, on the one hand, in the Classic forms of Greece, poetically symbolic of a hoped-for ideal, and, on the other, by the increased emotionalism of the Gothic and the other aspects of the Romantic movement.

Gilbert Stuart: *Chief Joseph Brant,*
1786, 30 x 25
(New York State Historical
Association, Cooperstown, N.Y.)

*Thomas
Jefferson's
Models
of
Architecture*

Though Jefferson's Capitol has been grossly disfigured by the addition of wings necessary to accommodate the vastly enlarged machinery of government of more recent times, its essential simplicity and grandeur may still be recognized. It was not only his most important single building, but also his most classic. Despite the accuracy which he endeavored to maintain in his treatment of the exterior, the original interior arrangements showed a good deal of practical resourcefulness, that side of his character now most clearly seen in the ingenious planning and the labor-saving devices and conveniences found in his own house at Monticello, and in his plan for the University of Virginia. He was essentially, like any Englishman of the period, a follower of Palladio, whose *Four Books of Architecture* he owned in at least one edition, along with several other volumes by such British Palladians as James Gibbs and Robert Morris. Gibbs's *Book of Architecture* and *Rules for Drawing the Several Parts of Architecture* and Morris' *Select Architecture* were a part of his library. But he made a significant distinction between "the classic style of antiquity" and contemporary classicism. As he wrote in his autobiography, even before his European trip in 1784, he wished, "by introducing into the state an example of architecture" of this sort, to improve the status of the arts in Virginia, and we know from drawings preserved in the Huntington Library and Art Gallery that he had a temple form in mind. As governor, he introduced in the House of Delegates a bill with the revolutionary idea of providing three separate buildings for the three departments of government, a concept of functional differentiation which anticipates his remarkable creation of the University of Virginia as "an academical village." A contemporary style was appropriate for domestic architecture, he felt, but only the Classic, based on models from the antique, could embody the symbolic dignity and hopes for the future proper for American public buildings. As chairman of the building committee for the Capitol, he set about supplying the plans.

The project matured while he was in France. Though the foundations had already been at least partly constructed, the legislators had decided, probably largely on the very practical grounds of expense, that the state government should be housed in a single building, so he hastened to produce the design. For this he enlisted the assistance of a distinguished French architect, C. L. Clérisseau, a teacher of the gifted Scotsman Robert Adam and author of a handsome work on *The Antiquities of France*. This volume includes detailed engravings of the Maison Carrée at Nîmes, "an ancient Roman temple," as Jefferson wrote home, "being considered as the most perfect model existing of what may be called Cubic architecture," his term for the pure Classic style of antiquity. He "applied to M. Clérisseault . . . to have me a model of the building made in stucco, only changing the order from Corinthian to Ionic, on account of the difficulty of the Corinthian capitals. . . . To adapt the exterior to our use, I drew a plan for the interior, with the apartments necessary for legislative, executive, and judiciary purposes. . . . These were forwarded to the directors in 1786, and were carried into execution."

The Frenchman and the Virginian worked together on the project, and drawings preserved in the collection of the Massachusetts Historical Society show that the design was Jefferson's, with only an occasional detail in the more authoritative draughtsmanship of the professional's hand completing the whole. It is also interesting to note that the man in charge of construction in Richmond, Samuel Dobie, who was an experienced builder with ideas of his own, and who later produced an interesting design for the national Capitol, did not hesitate to add pilasters along the sides which were not there in the original model, and cut a lunette in the pediment. It was an age of individualism. As a result of these and other changes—such as switching the order from Corinthian to Ionic, a practical idea because it later proved necessary to import the more elaborate capitals for the University of Virginia from Italy—the Richmond State House has a slight but definite Palladian flavor. It was, however, the first example of the temple form used in modern times for any building of importance, and remained the solitary specimen until twenty-two years later the Church of the Madeleine was commenced in Paris in 1807. Thus Jefferson's achievement marks the beginning of the Classical Revival movement, not only in America but in Europe as well.

As Secretary of State and as President, Jefferson exerted great influence on the architecture and the plan of Washington. A sketch plan preserved in the Library of Congress shows him pursuing further the ideas embodied in his earlier scheme for the enlargement of Richmond. It envisions spacious blocks interspersed with green areas (for he was always the countryman at heart), with long vistas and tree-shaded streets and walks. The President's House and the Capitol were placed in the same relation to each other which they have now, proving that Major L'Enfant incorporated many of Jefferson's ideas in his famous plan. Jefferson lent the French engineer his extensive collection of city maps collected in Europe, including those of Paris,

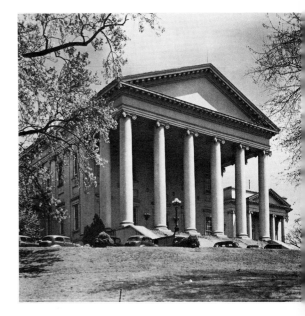

Thomas Jefferson:
Capitol, Richmond, Va., 1798
(Photograph, Library of Congress)

125

Marseilles, Bordeaux, Lyons, Strasbourg, Turin, and Amsterdam, among others, and assisted and backed the Frenchman in every way possible. He was also responsible for the appointment of B. H. Latrobe (1764–1820), an English pupil of Samuel Pepys Cockerell, and an able designer and engineer, as architect of the national Capitol.

Though the Capitol at Richmond has the historical significance of standing as the initial monument of the Classical Revival, Jefferson's most important single architectural achievement is the University of Virginia. His aim was "to make the establishment the most eminent in the United States." The entire concept of the University demonstrates the theoretical aspects of his mind, his powerful idealism, and his intense practicality. On October 6, 1817, with a group of visitors, including Madison and Monroe, the cornerstone of Pavilion VII on the West Lawn

Thomas Jefferson: University of Virginia, 1818-25
(Edwin S. Roseberry, Charlottesville, Va.)

was laid with due ceremony, and five years later he reported the completion of "all the buildings proposed . . . ten distinct houses or pavilions containing each a lecturing room, with generally four other apartments and the accommodation of a professor and his family, and with a garden, and the requisite family offices; six hotels for dieting the students, with a single room in each for a refectory, and two rooms, a garden and offices for the tenant, and a hundred and nine dormitories, sufficient each for the accommodation of two students, arranged in four distinct rows between the pavilions and the hotels, and united with them by covered ways; which buildings are all in readiness for occupation." The Rotunda, suggested by B. H. Latrobe as the appropriate architectural element to stand at the northern end of the Lawn and as a practical form to contain "rooms for religious worship, for public examinations, for a library and other associated purposes," including a planetarium in the domed library ceiling, was substantially completed by 1825.

Today the broad lawn is shaded by tall trees. The flanking pavilions, joined by arcaded walks, still "serve as specimens for the Architectural lecturer," as "models of taste and good architecture, and of a variety of appearance. . . ." Their wooden trim and columns gleam crisply white against warm red brick. The axis of the composition extends outward, at the upper end, from the Rotunda, a round building based on the Pantheon in Rome, to what was once a superb view across a limitless sweep of forested hills rolling uninterrupted to the southern horizon, now blocked by the disgraceful intrusion of Cabell Hall, designed by Stanford White and constructed between 1898 and 1902. To enhance the perspective, the spacing of each pair of pavilions was increased progressively outward from the Rotunda, so that the whole complex—conceived in human terms and designed at human scale, its parts thoughtfully planned in their relation to one another—not only forms a coherent statement of Jefferson's ideals of education, but also gives expression to his own passionately held views of the essentially basic relation of man and nature so necessary for a sane and productive life.

Though other of Jefferson's designs are more architecturally deft and unified, Monticello remains most revealing of himself. Preoccupied with building, he seems never to have been able to bring himself to complete it. "Architecture is my delight," he told a friend late in life, "and putting up, and pulling down, one of my favorite amusements." Monticello proves it. He was only twenty-four when he began to work on the plans for his

127

mountaintop retreat in the form of a Classical villa, a unique idea perhaps derived initially from Palladio's recommendation to build on an elevated site, but certainly inspired by his love for the panoramic views over green Virginia hills, "where," as he wrote his lifelong friend, the charming Maria Cosway, "nature has spread so rich a mantle under the eye. How sublime to look down into the workhouse of nature, to see her clouds, hail, snow, thunder, all fabricated at our feet! And the glorious sun, when rising as if out of a distant water, just gliding the tops of the mountains and giving life to all nature."

The development of his style can be traced in the successive changes of design for the house. It began with a purely Palladian scheme for a central block of superposed columns, forming a two-storied portico rising to a pediment, with flanking wings, a design apparently based on a plate in Morris' *Select Architecture*, which was to reappear in Pavilion VII at the University of Virginia and to become a favorite house plan throughout the Old Dominion. As the construction progressed he added bays at either end, designed two pairs of "outchambers"—separate octagonal buildings to mark the outer corners of the platform, which contains the service rooms and storerooms for the house, such as the rum cellar, the beer cellar, and the wine and meal rooms, which he sank largely below ground level to form a plinth for the villa. The platform extends north and south on the transverse axis of the house, and then, turning at right angles, marked by the outchambers, to the west in parallel arms containing the stables, carriage house, smokehouse, and laundry, the whole forming a broad U in plan. The westernmost ends of the platform so formed were accented with another pair of outchambers, which were to be square in plan.

By autumn of 1770 one of the octagonal buildings was completed, and early the following year he wrote: "I have lately removed to the mountain from whence this is dated. . . . I have here but one room, which like the cobbler's serves me for parlour for kitchen and hall. I may add for bedchamber and study too. . . . I have hope of getting more elbow-room this summer." The room was much needed. It was all very well for a youthful bachelor to camp out in a single room, but on the first day of January, 1772, he married Martha Wayles Skelton, and the young couple settled happily in the now mostly finished main block of the house. Progress on the building continued intermittently through the troubled years of the Revolution, and in 1782 the first version of the house was finished, but it brought him little satisfaction, for early that fall his beloved

Thomas Jefferson: Monticello, completed 1809
(Photograph, Library of Congress, John Collier, copyright 1943)

Martha died. Deeply saddened, he turned to architecture for solace, involving himself in plans for buildings in Williamsburg and elsewhere, and then in the project for the state Capitol, on which he continued to work when he went to Europe two years later. On his return in 1789, after five years' absence, the Palladian villa must have looked rather old-fashioned, compared to the new buildings he had seen in France and to the recent style of domestic architecture—houses smaller in scale, more intimate in feeling, and simpler and subtler in taste.

"All the new and good houses are of a single story," he reported. "That is of the height of 16. or 18. f. generally, and the whole of it given to rooms of entertainment; but in the parts where there are bedrooms they have two tiers of them from 8. to 10. f. high each, with a small private staircase." A new notion had come into domestic architecture, the luxury of privacy, almost unknown in the eighteenth century, a significant index of the changing times. Jefferson doubled the plan of Monticello in depth, moving the eastern portico outward, and topped the central block with a dome beneath which was what he called his "sky room." The new interiors were based largely on Fréart de Chambray's *Parallèle de l'Architecture Antique et Moderne;* Jefferson's own copy of that work is in the Library of Congress, and one can see the plates marked in his own hand, selected as models for the ornamentation of the various rooms. There was also a new emphasis on such conveniences as the "alcove bedrooms to which I am much attached," his own having the alcove open on both sides for better ventilation, the area on one side serving as a study and that on the other as a dressing room. He designed special dumb-waiters from the wine cellar, a device to show the direction and velocity of the wind, folding glass doors which, by means of an arrangement of sprockets, moved simultaneously and equally when either one was opened or closed, and a private toilet with a receptacle which was removed on a cart through the air tunnel without being carried through the house. He planned "roundabouts," paths encircling the mountaintop, with groves of trees designed to frame the views, and romantic natural landscaping in the style of the poet Shenstone's famous estate, The Leasowes, which he had visited in 1786, and of the plans in Whateley's book on modern garden design.

He planned garden houses to illustrate various styles of architecture, including "a specimen of Gothic, and . . . of Chinese." He enjoyed arranging his collection of curios, including Indian relics, fossils, and several mammoth bones. By 1809 the house was almost finished, though the terrace railings were not installed until 1824, and, in fact, there was always something still to be done. He continued designing houses for friends as well as other buildings. On his grateful retirement from public life, which meant that he could spend all his time at Monticello, he was able to resume correspondence with his old political opponent John Adams, also retired, at the ancient Adams family homestead in Quincy, Massachusetts. All partisan passions spent, the two could look back together on extraordinary events of the Revolution and the early days of the republic, in which both had taken such a significant part. "All my wishes end," Jefferson had written in 1787, "where I hope my days will end, at Monticello." And so they did, on the Fourth of July, 1826, on the fiftieth anniversary of the Declaration of Independence. When the world learned that Thomas Jefferson, its author and the third president, and John Adams, the second president, had died on the same day, one in Virginia and the other in Massachusetts, "such an event at such a time," as a contemporary observer noted, "could not fail to strike the soul with awe and wonder . . . it is not in the power of words to express, and no American will ever forget."

Architecture was for Jefferson a passionate avocation; yet it was more than that, also, because it was always an expression of those extraordinary qualities of mind and imagination, of vision and of faith, which made him, in a still broader sense, a leading architect of the republic itself.

Jefferson led the way in a movement which transformed the architecture of the nation, while Samuel McIntire changed the face of a town to make it a model of the style of the early republic. Though one could still find in Salem the beetle-browed, dark old houses with small-paned casement windows and roofs so steep that even the devil himself could not get a foothold, prosperity from the East Indian trade had brought many changes to the scene. But it was McIntire who very largely transformed the town's appearance. Hardly a street in Salem lacked its evidence of his taste and skill, and hardly a house of merchant or magnate was without examples of his superbly designed and carved furniture in a style popularized by Hepplewhite's *Guide* and Sheraton's *Drawing Book*, yet distinctively his own. His early Pierce-Nichols House on Federal Street still has Palladian accents in the heavier proportions of

Samuel
McIntire's
Salem

131

its white clapboarded façade, mottled with the shadows of the arching elms, and has fence posts bearing the flame-topped urns which were to become almost a McIntire trade-mark. He designed Federal Hall, a few moments' walk down the same street. Its dance floor was famous for springiness and was a favorite place for the fashionable balls and assemblies which many of the men attended attired in Chinese robes and at which one danced the hornpipe as well as the latest steps from London, Paris, or Boston. For this was the Salem of the Crowninshields and the Derbys, the great East India merchants, and of Nathaniel Bowditch, who retired from the sea at the age of thirty, having made his fortune, and who, disgusted with the inaccuracies of the available books on navigation, published his *First American Practical Navigator*, printed at Newburyport, in 1802, thus revolutionizing the subject and making Yankee seamanship the best in the world.

Elias Hasket Derby was a proof of the riches to be won by the canny and the resolute from the seaways. It was appropriate that he should have commissioned McIntire to build his magnificent house overlooking the long wharf projecting out into the harbor, where the vessels of the Derby fleet landed goods from all over the world. Their freight often included booty captured from the British during the war, for during those troubled days many a Salem craft left the harbor cargoless, but, manned with a crew of fire-eating young adventurers well armed with both weapons and determination, later returned heavy-laden with what a more recent day might call liberated merchandise. Though his friend Charles Bulfinch may have had a hand in certain elements of the façade, the house that Derby ordered was pure McIntire in style and in detail, as one of the architect's own drawings, preserved in the collection of the Es-

Samuel McIntire:
Drawing for the Derby Mansion,
Salem, Mass., 1795
(Courtesy of the Essex Institute, Salem, Mass.)

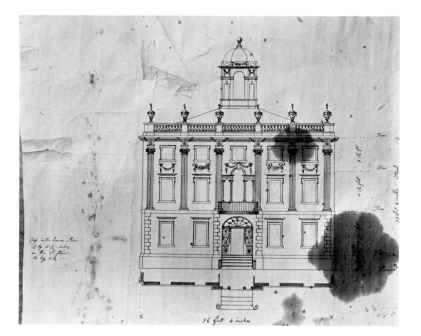

sex Institute, confirms. A colossal order of Corinthian pilasters rises through the second and third stories to support a cornice crowned by a balustrade whose posts are topped with garlanded urns of bold scale. Above, in the center of the low hipped roof, was a domed lantern through whose Palladian openings the owner could scan the harbor for approaching ships. The interiors, designed and executed to the last crisply carved detail by McIntire and his assistants, were cool and spacious, furnished with things brought from all parts of the world. One could look out from the oval parlor across the terrace, which was planted with rare fruit trees and shrubs, to the garden with its elegant summer house, also designed by McIntire and adorned with four chic and frivolous figures carved in wood by John and Simeon Skillin of Boston, who doubtless carved figureheads for vessels of the Derby fleet. Beyond the white-painted fence on top of a stone retaining wall lay the busy harbor below. Nearby, along the waterfront, was the Custom House, also by McIntire, its pediment enlivened by a magnificent eagle whose fierceness and air of resolution effectively expressed the character of the town in its days of bustling prosperity; it was here, in a later, quieter time, that Nathaniel Hawthorne, as inspector of customs, amidst dusty volumes of records and files of invoices, was visited by visions of an earlier, ghost-haunted age. Fortunately, this and many of McIntire's other buildings are still there, though Elias Derby's palace has long since disappeared and its handsome furnishings have been dispersed.

When the architect died in 1811 at fifty-four, his friend Dr. Bentley noted in his diary that "this day Salem was deprived of one of the most ingenious men it had in it." Jefferson, fourteen years older, was to outlive him by fifteen years, and his friend Bulfinch by thirty-three. The design which McIntire submitted in competition for the national Capitol was superbly accomplished, large in spirit as in scale, sure in its grasp of essential form and proportion, and a direct expression of great dignity in the thoroughly understood vocabulary of the Georgian Baroque. It was his greatest concept, but, unlike that of Bulfinch for Boston's State House and Thornton's accepted design for Washington, it was contemporary in character, not forward-looking, since, as Talbot Hamlin has pointed out, the Classic was the modern of that day. But it shows the abilities and qualities of mind and imagination of a man trained as a New England cabinetmaker and wood carver, and suggests something of the even greater achievement which time denied him.

The McIntire style remains, however, as an expression of the vital period of the early republic. It is a style of elegance and

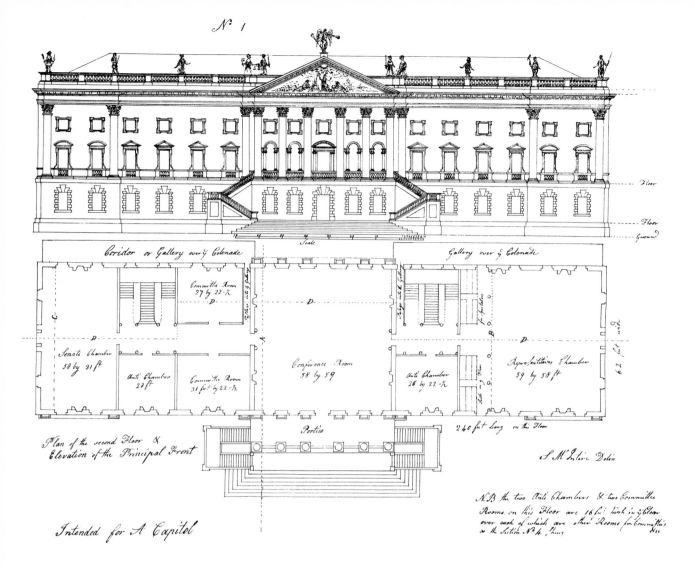

Samuel McIntire: Competition drawing for the U.S. Capitol, 1792
(Maryland Historical Society, Baltimore, Md.)

urbanity as befitted a society which lived as familiarly with
the products of Hong Kong and Canton, of Bombay and Calcutta, as of London, Paris, or Boston. As Lucy Larcom, recalling her girlhood in the New England seacoast town of Bev-
erly, Massachusetts, wrote: "The sea . . . penetrated to every
fireside, claiming close intimacy with every home and heart. The
farmers up and down the shore were as much fishermen as
farmers, . . . as familiar with the Grand Banks of Newfoundland as with their own potato-fields. . . . Men talked about a
voyage to Calcutta or Hong-Kong, or 'up the Straits'—meaning Gibraltar and the Mediterranean, —as if it were not much
more than going to the next village. It seemed as if our nearest
neighbors lived over there across the water; we breathed the

air of foreign countries, curiously interblended with our own. The women of well-to-do families had Canton crepe shawls, and Smyrna silks and Turk satins, for Sabbath-day wear . . . and children had foreign curiosities and treasures of the sea for playthings. . . . Green parrots went scolding and laughing down the thimbleberry hedges that bordered the cornfields, as much at home out of doors as within. Java sparrows and canaries . . . poured their music out of sunny windows into the street . . . long before the robins came. . . . The pathos of the sea haunted the town, made audible to every ear when a coming northeaster brought the rote of the waves in from the islands across the harbor-bar, with a moan like that we heard when we listened for it in the shell. Almost every house had its sea-tragedy. Somebody belonging to it had been shipwrecked, or had sailed away one day, and had never returned."

For all of tidewater America, the sea was the highroad, and lives were lived according to its patterns and disciplines. Many reaped its rich rewards for initiative and daring. Like the Puritans of the Massachusetts Bay Colony of a century before, these later inhabitants of the towns and villages within reach of the Atlantic knew the great world and were a part of it, and were far less provincial in outlook than many parts of Europe or, indeed, of their own frontier, where a different sort of society was even then developing.

Charles Bulfinch (1763–1844) of Boston started out in architecture as a gifted and serious amateur, but he mastered the craft, devoted a lifetime to its practice, and became the first American professional in the field. Born in his grandfather's house on Bowdoin Square, with its marble walk shaded by immense Lombardy poplars, and with its garden of gnarled fruit trees and ancient grapevines, he could remember being taken as a child up to the roof to watch the bombardment and burning of Charlestown by the British fleet and the battle of Bunker Hill. After graduation from Harvard in the class of 1781, he entered the countinghouse of Joseph Barrell, a leading merchant, instead of following his father and grandfather into the practice of medicine. When he came of age in 1784 the legacy of an English uncle made it possible for him to take the Grand Tour, not as unusual a part of a young American's education at that time as it may seem to us today. He spent seven months in England, visiting friends and relatives, and, as he wrote

Charles

Bulfinch,

Citizen

as

Architect

135

home, "gratifying my curiosity with the sight of buildings," before setting out for Paris, where he called upon Jefferson and Lafayette, both of whom took him sight-seeing and gave him additional letters of introduction for his further travels in France and Italy.

"From Paris," he recalled, in the fragment of autobiography he wrote late in life for his grandchildren, "I proceeded in the spring of 1786 through Nantz and Bordeaux and by the canal of Languedoc to Marseilles, and then to Antibes." From there, perhaps fired by Jefferson's enthusiasms as much as from his own natural inclination, and without telling his family, because he was afraid they would worry over his change of plan, he "crossed in an open felucca to Genoa, thence to Leghorn and Pisa, by Viterbo and Siena to Rome." Rome was still the city of opposites, which Piranesi, who had died eight years before, so superbly recorded, of shacks and palaces, of princes and beggars, of Baroque perspectives, and of cattle grazing, as in a Claudian pastoral, among vine-covered ruins, a dramatic contrast to the bustling modern world with which the young Bostonian was familiar. After three weeks in Rome, he traveled northward by way of Florence, Bologna, Parma, and Milan, crossed the Alps at Mont Cenis, then to Lyons, and again to Paris. Later, he lingered on in London, where at his family's earnest request he had his portrait painted by a former Bostonian, Mather Brown, in the "very rough . . . but modish style of painting introduced by Sir Joshua Reynolds. Mr. Copley indeed paints in another manner, his pictures are finished to the utmost nicety, but then—they are *very dear*."

For a bright young man with both seriousness and curiosity this *Wanderjahr* must have been a stimulating and enlightening experience, and must have done much to eliminate such lingering provincialisms of mind and attitude as had withstood the onslaughts of learning and logic to which he was subjected during four years at Harvard College. "This tour," he later wrote, "was highly gratifying . . . but did not confirm me in any business habits of buying and selling." He returned to a Boston that was still in many ways a small provincial town. Even within the narrow confines of its peninsula, there were fields and farms. The tidal waters of the lower Charles River washed the marshy edge of the Common, where proper Boston cows were led out to graze. Except for John Hancock's handsome stone mansion and a few others strung along Beacon Street, Beacon Hill was pasture land. The spires of Christ Church (Longfellow's "Old North"), of the Old South, and of the Brattle Street Church rose above streets which were even narrower then. One could still find food, drink, and a night's lodging at the Bunch of Grapes, the inn famous as the headquarters of Paul Revere and the Liberty Boys, or at the Green Dragon on Union Street, meeting place of the Tea Party Indians. The Old State House was still in use, and on top of Province House, the former palace of the royal governors, Deacon Shem Drowne's Indian hunter still told the direction of the wind to the nautical-minded Bostonians. Except for the bridge to Charlestown, the only way one could enter or leave the town was by boat or by way of the road across the Neck, which was so narrow that at high tide passers-by were often showered with cold salt spray driven by the east wind blowing across the harbor.

For the young man just returning, architecture had been an avocation; soon it was to become his profession. As in the case of Jefferson, it was but one aspect of a life devoted to public service, in the course of which, very largely through his efforts, the quaint and rather untidy town of Boston was, in the next thirty years, transformed into the model city that so aroused Dickens' admiration by the tastefulness of its architecture and the neatness of its appearance.

In 1787 a group of businessmen met at Bulfinch's house to plan the voyage of the ship *Columbia*, which was to trade for furs on the northwest coast to exchange for Chinese goods in Canton. This venture was of great importance in the development of the China trade, since it took the American flag around the world for the first time. In the same year the Great and General Court of Massachusetts decided to build a new State House. A committee was appointed, and four months later Bulfinch submitted his plan, with detailed estimates of cost—a remarkable undertaking for a young man of twenty-four without professional experience. Construction was not started until after the legislature had voted to adopt the design in 1795, and on the Fourth of July of that year the cornerstone was hauled to its place by fifteen white horses representing the fifteen states of the Union, and was laid by Governor Samuel Adams, with the Grand Lodge of Masons, Paul Revere, Grand Master, assisting. Before it was completed, Bulfinch had designed the first Connecticut State House (finished in 1796) in Hartford, and in Boston had built several churches and the Federal Street Theatre (1793). The city's first theater, its Corinthian interior carried out in lilac, blue, and gold, with the boxes hung in scarlet, it opened in February, 1794, with "the tragedy of Gustavus Vasa Ericson, the deliverer of Sweden."

At the same time Bulfinch embarked on the first example of group planning in the country, the project called the Tontine

Buildings from the manner of its financing, but better known as Franklin Place. He designed a crescent-shaped range of houses whose central pavilion was the Franklin Library, facing another, straight range across a little segmental green which was fenced and planted with trees. His brother-in-law defaulted unnecessarily on a debt, and forced him into bankruptcy, despite the fact that shortly all the houses were sold and the area came to be considered the most desirable residential section in the city. After this, architecture became his livelihood. He designed many houses, but the most famous are the three for Harrison Gray Otis, the famous Federalist statesman and orator: the first (on Cambridge Street) built in 1796, the second (now 85 Mt. Vernon Street) in 1800, and the third (now 45 Beacon Street) in 1806, the shift in their location reflecting the changing geographical center of fashionable Boston. All were examples of that free handling of interior space in which Bulfinch was a pioneer, and were designed for Otis' famous lavish hospitality, symbolized by the ten-gallon punch bowl on the stair landing, which was constantly replenished. For Joseph Barrell he designed a country house in Somerville, whose lawns sloped down to the water, where a liveried boatman was in constant attendance to ferry guests back and forth across the Charles.

All of Boston was changing. The focus of the town was the new State House on Beacon Hill, whose golden dome, Dr. Holmes's "hub of the solar system," now dwarfed by tall surrounding buildings, could then be seen from afar. Arrayed on the slopes of the Hill, formerly "Mr. Copley's pasture," were handsome houses, largely in his style, if not all of his actual design. Bulfinch designed most of Boston's churches, including the Gothic Federal Street Church (1809) for the great Dr. Channing. Today only New North Church, now St. Stephen's,

Charles Bulfinch: Drawing for the first Harrison Gray Otis House, 1796 (Massachusetts Historical Society)

Charles Bulfinch: Boston State House, 1795-98, Pendleton lithograph (The Boston Athenaeum)

remains, which was somewhat altered when Hanover Street was widened, and has recently been admirably restored through the initiative of Richard Cardinal Cushing, Boston's archbishop. Among the other churches designed by Bulfinch was Holy Cross, the Catholic cathedral, financed by public subscription, with John Adams' name at the head of the list. Bulfinch gave his friend the much admired Bishop Cheverus the complete plans for it as his contribution, and saw to its proper construction. In gratitude, the members of the diocese presented him with a handsome silver tea urn, appropriately inscribed. Bulfinch's finest church, however, was not built in Boston; it is the Meeting House in Lancaster, Massachusetts, dedicated in 1817, which, fortunately, still survives. The perfection of its proportions and the masterly use of red brick with white painted trim have never been surpassed. The interior contains the finest of his pulpits, carried out with impeccable workmanship by one of the parishioners, a cabinetmaker named Jacob Fisher. The structure remains one of the best buildings of the period in America.

Bulfinch's other works include a half-dozen banks, several insurance company buildings, customs houses, school and college buildings for Andover, Harvard, and elsewhere, and the Court House and the City Hall in Boston, the latter particularly effective in its use of hammered granite. He built Boston's first Public Library, new market houses, and almshouses. He enlarged Faneuil Hall without doing violence to that even then historic shrine already christened "the cradle of liberty" by James Otis. He designed Massachusetts General Hospital, the original granite hospital now called the Bulfinch Building, under whose famous Ether Dome the first operation was performed with the use of that anesthetic. He planned prisons and docks, set the general pattern for the future development of the Back Bay, and was responsible for the lighting and cleaning of Boston's streets and for the regulation of its traffic. Even in those days the streets were so crowded that visitors were amazed to see the heavy drays, with sometimes as many as five horses, hitched in tandem because of the narrowness of the streets, "obeying with amazing sagacity the word of command of the driver, who stands in the plank or bar close behind the shaft horse." Even today Bulfinch's spirit pervades the Boston scene, expressed in the mellow brick façades, tree-shaded streets, and rational and civilized planning, always simple and conceived at a human scale; there is probably no other city in America whose appearance is more the result of the work of a single individual.

Charles Bulfinch: First Meeting House,
Lancaster, Mass., 1816
(Photograph, Library of Congress)

These are but the outward evidences of his contribution to the city, however, because in addition to being her leading architect, he was for twenty-two years a selectman of the town, for the last nineteen of which he was chairman of the board and superintendent of police—"a record," according to Josiah Quincy (who, as Boston's official historian and one-time mayor, should know), which "is probably unique in American municipal history for variety, faithfulness, and promotion of the public welfare." They were years of trial during the depressions caused by Jefferson's embargo and the war, when Bulfinch, like many others, twice faced bankruptcy, and once even suffered the humiliation of being jailed for debt, at a time when he was the chief administrative official of Boston and one of the country's leading citizens. They were also years of dramatic change which saw the town of about 15,000 grow into a city three times the size, whose cultural and intellectual pre-eminence challenged Philadelphia. When in 1818 he was appointed architect of the public buildings by President Monroe, a significant chapter in the history of Boston as well as in his own life was ended, and a new one begun.

Bulfinch moved to Washington in the first week of January, 1818, and found, as he wrote home, that "nothing announces a metropolis until we approach an assemblage of brick houses, forming a village, and . . . two stone edifices of richly ornamented architecture. These are the wings of the Congress hall; they were burnt as far as they were combustible, and are now undergoing repair. . . . From this place, called Capitol Hill, the ground suddenly falls, and expands into an expansive vale, beautifully surrounded by high grounds, and washed on one side by a majestic river. . . . One is immediately convinced that a great city must grow up here, and in anticipation we think we see it before us . . ." Such was his impression of "This embryo capital, where Fancy sees/Squares in morasses, obelisks in trees." But unlike the scornful poet Tom Moore, the architect was undeterred by the acres of scrubby wasteland, the mud, and the marshes of Goose Creek, and not only could he envision Major L'Enfant's grand plan carried out, but he was also prepared energetically to contribute toward its realization, a project of a magnitude which had been attempted before only by kings or emperors, begun in America when the faltering new republic was scarcely launched.

A more appropriate appointment for the Washington position could not have been imagined. The national Capitol had been through the hands of Thornton, Hallet, Hadfield, and Latrobe, and though none had been able to finish it, each had left his mark on it, and each had had disputes with the Commissioner of Public Buildings and with the numerous congressional committees appointed to superintend various aspects of the work.

Capitol of the United States as completed by Charles Bulfinch in 1830 (Courtesy Kenneth M. Newman, The Old Print Shop, Inc.)

Bulfinch at fifty-five was respected as an acknowledged leader of his profession. His years of experience both as an architect and as chairman of the board of selectmen—virtually mayor—of Boston, combined with his natural tact and courtesy, stood him in good stead. He had deep respect for Latrobe and maintained friendly relations with Dr. William Thornton, the witty and crotchety West Indian Quaker, whose amateurish but brilliant design had been accepted for the Capitol.

"I shall not have credit for invention," he wrote home to Boston after he had made his first inspection of the building and realized the magnitude of the task and the many problems involved, "but must be content to follow in a prescribed path." Yet he actually achieved far more than that. Despite what Colonel John Trumbull called "intrigues which perpetually controlled the good intentions and pure taste of Mr. B.," he made all the improvements that were possible, related and unified the various parts, and completed the work, which he had inherited as a patchwork of false starts, evidences of change in design, and partly repaired damages resulting from its burning by British troops when they captured the city in 1814. He also laid out the grounds, planning and superintending the grading and the planting of the landscape and the approaches, designing gates and fences, walks and steps, and placing sculptures, thereby realizing a grand plan with that extraordinary completeness of which no other American architect of his day except Jefferson was capable. The result was a coherent whole. Even Mrs. Trollope allowed herself to become enthusiastic.

The work on the Capitol demanded his constant attendance, yet he found time to design Washington's Unitarian Church (1822)—of which his son, Greenleaf, later became minister—and a penitentiary, a navy yard in Norfolk, and a number of other buildings for the government, as well as his last and in many ways most distinguished public building, the State House at Augusta, Maine, unfortunately later drastically altered. He provided the plans for this building, begun in 1828 and completed in 1833, at the request of Governor Enoch Lincoln and General William King, the ardent Jeffersonian who had led the separation movement of Maine from Massachusetts in 1820. The Bulfinch house on Sixth Street was much visited by New England friends, among them Horatio Greenough, who wrote home that he "found much pleasure in the society of the Bulfinch family" and thought Mrs. Bulfinch "one of the finest women in the world." He was there to do a bust of the President at the same time that Chester Harding, another friend, was painting his portrait. With two such lively companions John

Quincy Adams must have found the sittings far from dull. In 1822 Morse came to Washington to paint the famous picture of the House of Representatives in session. Bulfinch helped provide him with a room in which to work near his own office and next to the House chamber, so that his sitters, whenever they heard the debate becoming heated, could hurry back. When the painting was finished, Morse gave Bulfinch a cast of his *Dying Hercules*, the only one remaining of the original six, now in the collection at Yale University.

In 1830 the Capitol was finally completed, and Bulfinch moved back to Boston. For the first time in his life there were quiet years, summers spent with relatives in Maine and winters in the same old house on Bowdoin Square where he had been born and where, as the tall clock on the landing struck noon on April 15, 1844, he died in his eighty-first year. The country had gone far since the days when, as a small boy, he had watched from the roof of that same house the crucial events of the Revolution taking place, and he himself had played a not inconsequential part in the country's proud development.

The unique quality of Bulfinch's achievement was largely the result of his idea of the responsibilities of an architect. He has so often been called a follower of Robert Adam that many must think that he was just that and nothing more. An examination of his buildings and his drawings shows that such is not the case. He undoubtedly shared with others, like Samuel McIntire, a liking for the slender, clean-lined ornament, so well adapted to expression in wood, which derives from Adam, but there was also in him, as in Jefferson, a strong Palladian strain, natural in one brought up in the British tradition and undoubtedly reinforced by his travels in England and by the architectural books he studied in learning his profession. For these were the two resources at his disposal: his observations made in Europe —recorded in little sketches to which he seems constantly to have referred throughout his career—and the architectural library which he began forming while on his Grand Tour and kept adding to throughout his life. This collection was, with Jefferson's, the largest of its kind before Ithiel Town, inspired by Bulfinch's example, assembled his extraordinary library, which formed the nucleus of the handsome house he designed around it in New Haven in 1830. It is from these slender sources, based upon his own innate practicality and good sense, and motivated by the highest ideals of the duties of citizenship and of public service, that his extraordinary career was constructed. He used his inherited vocabulary of architectural design freely, governed only by his own feeling for the appropriate, for he addressed himself directly to the demands of each project, the resolution of which dictated the architectural result, which was, in the words of Horatio Greenough, "the external expression of the inward function of the building . . . the adaptation of its features and their gradation to its dignity and importance. . . ."

Bulfinch always maintained a traditionally New England preference for simplicity, with a strong feeling for structure, for abstract form, and for native materials—wood, brick, and granite—which he used with great distinction. Because of the directness of his approach, his houses are models of versatile and adaptable arrangement, and his hospitals and prisons were far ahead of their times in the humanitarian respect for the individuals who were to occupy them. Just as Jefferson used the century-old language of Locke to express in the Declaration of Independence the new political concepts which had grown up in America, so Bulfinch used the architectural vocabulary of eighteenth-century Europe to design the buildings to house and to symbolize the new political institutions of America. In his Boston State House, in Thornton's national Capitol design (1793) as modified by Latrobe (1803), and in Bulfinch's final work, the Maine State House, a form evolved that was so appropriate that we scarcely recognize its novelty.

Influenced by Chambers' Somerset House (the Strand block of which was finished in 1780 and the rest nearing completion when Bulfinch was in London), with suggestions of the Garde Meuble on the Place de la Concorde and echoes of Campbell's *Vitruvius Britannicus* and of the brothers Adam, these designs have provided models for similar buildings all over the world, so satisfactorily do they express the nature of the institution contained within their walls, the two wings, united by a pedimented façade and crowned by a dome, forming an organic whole. "Architecture," Talbot Hamlin wrote of the national Capitol, "is not a matter of details or of refinement alone; it is not merely a matter of superficial form. In large public buildings it is the expression of more than a personal attitude. It is the erection in concrete and tangible form of a people's dream. . . . Here one gets the real birth of an American architecture . . . which out of so many diverse influences—from France and England, from Rome and Greece—but equally out of American conditions, out of American materials and ways of work, out of the very texture of American democracy, created a living architecture."

ARCHITECTURE OF THE GREEK REVIVAL

When Charles Bulfinch returned to Boston in 1830 after twelve years in Washington, he was a man of sixty-seven who was ready to enjoy a greater leisure than a busy life, full of projects and responsibilities, had up to that time allowed. Boston had grown from a town of 40,000 people to one of some 75,000; its government, over which he had so long and ably presided as chairman of the board of selectmen, had changed from that of a town to a city, complete with mayor, city council, and a real police force to cope with the unruly element frequenting the waterfront and to keep an eye on "the nymphs of Ann Street." The job of filling the Mill Pond with gravel from the top of Beacon Hill had been finished and a whole new quarter thus added to the city, which entered a period of vigorous development under the able leadership of Josiah Quincy, mayor from 1823 to 1828. The mills that had lined the Mill Pond and the waterfront had moved to the new factory towns which were rising at the waterfalls of the New England rivers, among them Lowell and Lawrence in Massachusetts and Manchester in New Hampshire, on the Merrimack. The Boston and Lowell Railroad was incorporated in the year of Bulfinch's return, to be followed by three others in quick succession.

There was renewed talk of filling in the Back Bay, a project for which Bulfinch had drawn up admirable plans years before; rows of brick bow-fronted houses were rising where before had been broad tree-shaded lawns and a country atmosphere. A great era of shipbuilding and commercial prosperity had begun; the tempo of life was quickening; growth and change were everywhere. Two years before Bulfinch returned, Gilbert Stuart, the great portrait painter, had died in his brick house on Essex Street, having outlived most of his sitters, among them so many of the architect's friends and contemporaries. Bulfinch undoubtedly continued in architecture, but as far as we know he had no important commissions. Those were left to the younger men, his pupils and followers, now well embarked on their own careers, yet retaining the same friendly system of mutual assistance and professional co-operation which had characterized his relations with them.

The oldest of these was Asher Benjamin (1773–1845), who had been his assistant on the Connecticut State House, and who had become, through his design books, a major codifier and disseminator of Bulfinch's style through much of the United States. Benjamin's own style is shown by the West Church (1806), which now contains a branch of the Boston Public Library, and which stands next door to Bulfinch's first Harrison Gray Otis House (1796), the home of the Society for the Preservation of New England Antiquities, on Cambridge Street.

Alexander Parris (1780–1852), who had been Bulfinch's assistant on the Massachusetts General Hospital project (1817), was better known in his own lifetime as an engineer who designed, among many other major projects in this field, the famous dry dock at the Boston Navy Yard. From 1848 until his death he held the post of civil engineer in charge of the navy yard in Portsmouth, New Hampshire, many of whose buildings are his. There, in connection with dredging the harbor, he is credited with being the first in America to detonate underwater charges with electricity. But he also designed many houses and other buildings in Boston and in his native Portland, Maine.

Parris is perhaps best remembered today as the architect of Quincy Market and its surrounding granite warehouses, planned to create a handsome frontispiece for the city on the harbor. It was then located directly on the waterfront which, with successive fillings, has now moved blocks away. Next to, and on axis with, Smibert's Faneuil Hall (1742), which Bulfinch had enlarged so sympathetically in 1806, the complex of buildings

Alexander Parris: Quincy Market, 1825-26 (Bostonian Society, Old State House)

was begun in 1825 as part of an imaginative urban renewal scheme of Mayor Josiah Quincy. Here of a morning, in the days when sailing ships still poked their bowsprits over Commercial Wharf at the lower end of the Market House, one might meet Boston merchants, selecting the fish, oysters, cut of beef, or leg of lamb to be carried home by a servant for the family's dinner, before proceeding to their countinghouses for the business of the day.

Another of Bulfinch's pupils was Solomon Willard (1783–1861), the "ingenious young mechanic" who had assisted him in Washington and probably elsewhere. The son of a builder and cabinetmaker, he came to Boston at the age of twenty, almost penniless but confident in his determination, and immediately was hired as a skilled carpenter. He probably studied briefly with Asher Benjamin, but meanwhile was much in demand for the expert carving of architectural details, in both stone and wood, for various projects of Bulfinch's. He made models of the Parthenon and the Pantheon, which he presented to the Boston Athenaeum, and won fame for his vigorous and stylish figureheads for Boston ships. Independent and curious-minded, he never married, but came and went as he pleased, living often in the household of his lifelong friend Alexander Parris. He once turned up in Baltimore, where his Yankee chisel found no difficulty in carving the rococo detail, very much in the French taste, for the famous Unitarian Church designed by Maximilian Godefroy, a former royal engineer of Louis XVI. He conducted classes in drawing, modeling, physics, and chemistry, and submitted the prize-winning design for the Bunker Hill Monument, which was dedicated in 1825 in a ceremony honored by the presence of Lafayette and including appropriate flights of oratory by Daniel Webster, who had succeeded Harrison Gray Otis as the New England Demosthenes.

Willard was not only a very capable architect, as his Town Hall and Academy in Quincy, Massachusetts, prove, but also an imaginative engineer who invented a system of hot air heating, became an expert in this field, and was consulted by Bulfinch on the heating of the White House and also probably of the Maine State House. With the assistance of the Boston port captain, Adoniram Holmes, he invented machines for the handling of larger pieces of stone than had been available for use since the times of ancient Egypt and Baalbek. He designed and constructed special railways for conveying them from the quarries at Quincy, Massachusetts, which he himself discovered, to a deep-water landing, so that they could be transported by ship.

Thus blocks of immense weight and dimension could be cut and taken wherever needed with a small crew of trained men, and granite—the most monumental of materials and one so sympathetic to the ideals of the American architect of this period—was supplied by quarries in Massachusetts and in Maine for buildings constructed in Boston, New York, Washington, Philadelphia, and elsewhere, even as far as the West Coast and South America.

The arrangements for building the Bunker Hill Monument gave Willard an ideal opportunity to show his system of handling the stone and his methods of construction. He wrote a book on the subject, and people came from afar to study the lifting devices, the railway, the heavy-duty scaffolds with ramps, and the minutely timed operation which he had worked out, and which served as a model for others here and abroad. As a result of his inventions, granite was used more freely and importantly during the middle years of the nineteenth century than ever before. Schooners were especially designed to carry the heavy cargoes wherever needed, and some of the best quarries were opened on remote Maine islands, which in our day of steel and concrete have been abandoned to the sea gulls and the terns, but which supplied columns for a courthouse in St. Louis and material for a store in Chicago, a bank in New Orleans, and a post office in Dallas.

It is to Willard's ingenuity that we owe the distinguished sidewalks, still remaining in some parts of older American cities, made of immense granite slabs, often channeled to provide a sure footing. Most of them, however, have since been broken up as too heavy to move or to repair, and have been replaced with concrete, with its inevitable cracking and deterioration within a decade, as contrasted with the century or more of use already provided by the natural material. After years of a successful and productive career as an architect and engineer, Willard suddenly decided to retire to Quincy to practice experimental farming, which he did, as he did everything else, with vigor, imagination, and success. He died there at the age of seventy-seven.

Meanwhile Isaiah Rogers (1800-69), the son of a Marshfield shipbuilder and a close friend of Willard, after whom he named his eldest son, was working on his first important commission. This was the design for the Tremont House, a hotel completed in 1829 on Tremont Street at the corner of Beacon Street, opposite where one Harvey Parker was running a boardinghouse which eventually became a hotel in its own right,

Isaiah Rogers: Tremont House, 1829, water color by George Harvey (The Boston Athenaeum)

famous for its rolls. But the fame of Tremont House was far greater. Charles Dickens noted that it had "more galleries, colonnades, piazzas, and passages than I can remember, or the reader would believe." Notable visitors stayed in it and admired its sumptuous public rooms; fashionable parties and civic functions took place in its chandeliered banqueting halls and ballrooms. Davy Crockett, a self-appointed universal authority, admitted that even he had never before seen such splendor. Its simple granite façade with finely proportioned Doric portico and handsomely appointed interiors do not alone give it its importance as the first modern hotel, but its plan does. The arrangement of reception rooms so that they could be opened together for large, or closed off for small, functions; the kitchens with the storage rooms and serving arrangements carefully worked out; the strategically placed and adequate toilet facilities, including bathrooms with running water; and the privacy for the guests, with locks on every door and free soap in every room, were all unique in their day, and the whole demonstrated on a larger scale the free treatment of interior space in which Bulfinch had been a pioneer.

The success of the Tremont House was so immediate that the twenty-nine-year-old Rogers was swamped with commissions. He went on to New York to outdo himself in the Astor House (1836), which was followed by other hotel designs all over the country. These included the Bangor House (1832) in Bangor, Maine; the Corinthian-colonnaded Charleston Hotel (1839); the colossal second St. Charles Hotel in New Orleans, with the richness of its deeply shadowed, columnar façade and the luxury of the scale of its interiors expressive of Creole traditions of hospitality and good living. Rogers also designed the later Maxwell House, of coffee fame, in Nashville, with its 600 rooms, and the famous Burnet House (1850), with a dome reminiscent of that of Bulfinch's Boston State House, in Cincinnati, the city to which he eventually retired.

He left, however, one other famous example of his work in Boston, the city where he had started his distinguished career—the granite theater in the Gothic style known as the Howard Athenaeum (1847) in its heyday, when it saw the triumphs of Jenny Lind, of Charles Kemble and his lovely daughter Fanny, and of the beautiful Fanny Elssler. During more recent times, when Scollay Square had become the favorite haunt of sailors—a gaudy mixture of bars, tattooing parlors, and dance halls—the Athenaeum achieved perhaps an even greater fame as the "Old Howard," the palace of burlesque, until at last it suc-

149

cumbed to the forces of civic virtue and progress, and disappeared, along with all the rest of that historic and redolent neighborhood of Boston, to make way for a modern government center.

Other outstanding members of the Boston group included a young English cabinetmaker turned architect named Richard Upjohn (1802-78), who had just appeared on the Boston scene, and a Parris pupil, Ammi B. Young (1798–1874), from Montpelier, Vermont, where he had designed the State Capitol with more than one look in the direction of Bulfinch's Boston State House. Upjohn worked in Parris' office from 1834 to 1839 before embarking on an independent career during which he was to create, along with Alexander Jackson Davis, the finest of our Gothic Revival architecture. Young was shortly to produce the massive Doric Customhouse (1837-47), since crowned with the tower which was, after Willard's Bunker Hill Monument, Boston's first skyscraper; and thereafter succeeded Robert Mills

Charles Bulfinch: India Wharf, 1806
(Bostonian Society, Old State House)

as architect to the United States Treasury Department from 1852 to 1860, during which time he produced literally dozens of Federal buildings all over the United States, which not only maintained a very high standard of design in a period of marked deterioration in style, but which also pioneered in fireproof construction methods, relying increasingly on an imaginative use of cast iron.

Thus Boston had the most flourishing school of architects in the country, all carrying on Bulfinch's tradition of versatility. They turned from such formal commissions as Parris' St. Paul's

150

on Tremont Street (whose pediment was to have been embellished with sculptures, but his friend Solomon Willard was always too busy to carry them out) to the imposing granite waterfront warehouses, which are today recognized as the true heirs of Bulfinch's monumental India Wharf. India Wharf was probably the first of its kind on such a scale, and in its austere dignity of treatment of a utilitarian structure it set a standard to which his followers faithfully adhered. It has long since been demolished, but its successors are, so far, scheduled for preservation under the city's renewal scheme. Of this Boston group, Parris, Willard, and Rogers dominate the scene. Their work combines a stripped simplicity of design, imaginative and daringly experimental concepts, and a preference for basic geometry of form expressed in the uncompromising material of granite, used so massively as to sometimes appear, especially in the case of Willard, almost megalithic in character.

There was one other architect who was more briefly associated with Boston, but through whom that experience had far-reaching consequences. Ithiel Town (1774–1844) was a Connecticut Yankee who spent his early life in Cambridge, where he went to school in the shadow of the "factories of learning" in the Harvard Yard. His interest in architecture led him to study with Asher Benjamin, who had then just produced the second of his many architectural guides, *The American Builder's Companion.* It was published in Boston in 1806, the year that saw the foundation of the Boston Athenaeum, modeled after that in Liverpool. The Athenaeum was established by a group led by Joseph Buckminster, the preacher revered for his eloquence as the "Chrysostom of America," who spent a large part of his small fortune in purchasing and donating to it 3,000 volumes acquired in Europe. These included works on the topography and sights of Greece and Rome, which would have been of especial interest to Town. Bulfinch's own library, rivaling Jefferson's as the most extensive of its kind on this side of the Atlantic, was undoubtedly available to him as to any other aspiring young architect or scholar, and not only enabled him to study various editions of Palladio, Colin Campbell's *Vitruvius Britannicus,* Stuart and Revett's famous and sumptuous *Antiquities of Athens,* and Major's *Ruins of Paestum,* but also stimulated Town's ambition to form such a library for himself.

Town started out in practice in New Haven, where his first major work, the Center Church of 1814, an outstandingly accomplished design in the English Baroque of James Gibbs, still graces the Green. However, like all the Bulfinch followers, he was much interested in engineering; he built several covered bridges over the Connecticut River, and, as a result of this experience, in 1820 he designed and patented the famous lattice truss which bears his name. It proved to have the qualities which his friend Eli Whitney, the inventor of the cotton gin, recognized, on inspecting a model which Town had made of it, as "the simplicity, lightness, strength, cheapness, and durability . . . such as to render it highly worthy of attention." Eliminating the necessity of supporting arches, and capable of construction with wood, the material always available in America, without the need for special skills, it was used to bridge countless streams and rivers throughout the United States, with spans up to 220 feet between piers. Most of Town's bridges were covered, since this made them last, in his estimation, "seven or eight times as long as those not covered." Some built during his lifetime still remain in country districts where progress has not decreed their destruction. The principle of their design anticipated that of the steel-girder bridges which often replaced them after sometimes a century or more of use. Doubling or tripling the lattice made them capable of carrying railroad traffic; the fees and royalties from his remarkably useful invention made Town a comparatively rich man, and few have used their wealth more imaginatively.

In 1825 Town moved to New York, where he was already one of the group of those interested in the arts which surrounded the renowned conversationalist Dr. David Hosack, professor of botany at Columbia. He frequently met with John Trumbull, William Dunlap, Samuel F. B. Morse, the portrait painter Samuel Waldo, De Witt Clinton, and others, including also Robert Livingston, who as Jefferson's minister to France carried out the Louisiana Purchase, and who sent back from Paris the first casts after the antique to come to the New World, as his gift to the newly formed Academy of Arts. Town was one of the three architects to be among the founders of the National Academy of Design in 1826, so by this time he must have been regarded as a leader in the field. It was at the Academy that he met his future partner, a very gifted young draftsman named Alexander Jackson Davis, later to become even more famous as a Gothic Revival architect than Town. Leaving his large practice in the capable hands of Davis, Town set out for Europe in the company of Morse and the painter Nathaniel Jocelyn. He visited the British Isles and the Continent, and brought home quantities of

Alexander Jackson Davis: Premium drawing for the U.S. Customs House for New York, 1833-42,
pencil, pen, and water color (Courtesy, Museum of Fine Arts, Boston,
M. and M. Karolik Collection)

Alexander Jackson Davis: Cross section of U.S. Customs House for New York, 1833-42,
pencil, pen, and water color (Courtesy Avery Library, Columbia University)

carefully selected architectural books and engravings. Four thousand works on architecture and engineering were kept in his New York office, while the rest were housed in the handsome Grecian villa he had built on Hillhouse Avenue in New Haven in 1830.

In the *Ladies' Companion* for January, 1839, Mrs. Sigourney, "the Hartford Sappho," described the room on the second floor, which was the heart of Town's house, as "a spacious apartment 45'l. x 22'h., with two skylights 6' sq.—three windows at one end and three sash doors opening on the balcony. There and in the lobbies are arranged in *Egyptian, Grecian,* and *Gothic* cases . . . between 9,000 and 10,000 volumes. Many of these are rare . . . and valuable . . . more than three-fourths are folios. . . . There are some 20,000 to 25,000 separate engravings. . . . There are also 170 oil paintings besides mosaics and other works of art and objects of curiosity." All this was housed in a fireproof building. His entire collection, both in New York and in New Haven, was available to any serious student with the same generosity that Bulfinch had shown him so many years earlier. It was Town's hope that his example would lead the way "to present to our country the means of educating artists," and to enable the public to understand and "to appreciate the arts." In 1835 he published a pamphlet containing an "Outline for a Plan for an Academy and Institution of the Fine Arts," which became the model for the donation of Augustus Street's Fine Arts Building to Yale nineteen years later.

Town designed the second Connecticut Capitol (1827-31), in the form of the Parthenon, in New Haven, and many other buildings including the Customhouse (1833-42), now the Sub-Treasury Building, in New York, and such outstanding houses as the Grecian villa (1830) for Aaron Skinner (near Town's own house in New Haven) and the splendid Bowers House, with its gracious Ionic portico, in Northampton, Massachusetts. The firm's New York offices were a meeting place for architects from both at home and abroad, and many of their schemes, in the beautiful renderings in which Davis was unrivaled, were exhibited regularly at the National Academy of Design and the Mechanics' Institute of New York. These designs undoubtedly were most influential on the course of Classic architecture in America, forecasting as they do the porticoed grace and dignity of the innumerable houses and other buildings which rose throughout the country up until the eve of the Civil War.

Among Davis' drawings is one showing an interior of a Grecian house of 1830. Its uncluttered clarity is entirely appropriate to the serene and simple exterior style: front and back drawing rooms are separated by a screen of Ionic columns that enhances the sense of scale, as does the simple frieze and cornice, enriched with an acanthus molding next to the ceiling, which has a central rosette. The furniture is of strictly Classic design, derived directly from Greek or Roman sources, much like some of the pieces made by Duncan Phyfe during these years; the richness of gilding on dark wood, the strict geometry of the overmantel mirror and the matching picture frames, the crimson upholstery, and the blue and gold carpet give it character and distinction.

On Ithiel Town's death at the age of sixty, he left a flourishing architectural practice for his firm and a record of selfless service to the cause of education and the arts in the United States. As a small boy he had been sent to a neighbor's to borrow a book from which his older sisters could copy an alphabet to embroider on household linen. It was called *The Young Man's Best Companion*, and it took him, as he remembered in later years, a very long time to get home with it because he was so fascinated with the "various copyslips, mathematical diagrams, dials for different latitudes, mariner's compass, etc., neatly engraved on copper plates," which he examined with wonderment, and which awakened in his mind the "great propensity and love for mathematics, drawings, paintings, engravings, etc.," to which he dedicated his life. His professional achievement stands among the best of its period.

William Strickland (1788–1854), the bright young son of a carpenter and builder, early showed evidence of unusual abilities. When still a boy he contributed engravings to periodicals such as the *Analectic Magazine* and became an expert theatrical scene painter who could also turn his hand to landscape and portraiture. Wishing to give him a proper architectural training, his father apprenticed him to B. H. Latrobe in Philadelphia, Bulfinch's predecessor as architect of the national Capitol. Strickland enjoyed the benefit of the association for only about two years before being fired at the age of seventeen for displaying an understandably boyish preference for fishing over the more serious and far duller tasks assigned to him. Like the others of the small group who had the advantage of working with a man of Latrobe's unusual breadth of experience, however, he inherited an enthusiasm for Greek forms and an interest in engineering which lasted throughout his career.

In 1818, when he was thirty, his drawings for the Second

Bank of the United States were adopted by the directors. Completed in 1824, this austerely handsome building was a model of the Doric order, eminently suitable to house the weighty financial affairs of the monolithic bank, so ably controlled by the firm hand of Nicholas Biddle, whose monopoly was to be challenged only by Old Hickory himself.

Fortunately, Strickland's bank still stands in downtown Philadelphia, shaming by its admirably proportioned grandeur the later and larger buildings, many now demolished, with which it had been surrounded. Today it contains the offices of those directing the restoration of this historic part of the city. The immediate success of the bank's design led to other commissions, as various as Washington's tomb at Mount Vernon, laying out the route of the Wilmington and Susquehanna Railroad, and, his crowning achievement, the Capitol of Tennessee at Nashville, which was started in 1845 but not completed until 1859, five years after his death. It is a fitting monument, a design full of the echoes of Greece, with elements appreciatively studied from the Erectheum on the Acropolis and the Choragic Monument of Lysicrates, but imaginatively interpreted and daringly combined to form a new whole, properly expressive of American aspiration toward a Greek ideal.

Robert Mills (1781–1855) of Charleston, South Carolina, was another apprentice trained by Latrobe who made a name for himself through his buildings in Washington, Baltimore, and elsewhere in the South. He had started out as a draftsman for Jefferson, and as a young man made a pilgrimage to Boston, armed with a letter of introduction from his employer to Bulfinch, who encouraged him and lent him books from his library. Mills designed the Washington Monument and the Treasury Building (an excellent engraving of which appears on ten-dollar bills) in the national capital, the colossal column honoring the first president in Baltimore, and much besides, though his style appears perhaps nowhere more attractively than in the early John Wickham House, still retaining a Regency flavor, built in Richmond in 1812, which is now the Valentine Museum.

Two gifted pupils of Strickland's were also active in the same area. Gideon Shryock (1802-80) showed his loyalty to the Grecian mode by his picturesque concept for the Capitol of Kentucky, completed in Frankfort in 1830. Thomas U. Walter (1804-87), famous for the cast-iron dome of the enlarged Capitol of the United States, collaborated with Nicholas Biddle, who was as enthusiastic a proponent of Grecian architecture as he was an opponent of Andrew Jackson, in producing for Girard

College, in 1833, a building which satisfied all Biddle's aspirations. He felt it was "a perfect model of the simple, chaste, and pure architecture of the ancients," for, as he wrote, he was convinced that "in every mind . . . there is a keener sympathy with the forms of the external world, a stronger sensibility to the harmonies, both of art and nature, than shallow thinkers imagine, and the cultivation of that sentiment, the diffusion of a love for the beautiful and the graceful, contributes to make men wiser and gentler and happier than much that is taught in the schools and is called knowledge."

Walter also provided the handsome Classical portico for Biddle's palatial house at Andalusia, still standing serenely among lawns sweeping down to the banks of the Delaware, unique in the North, but having many Southern relatives among the plantation houses of the first half of the nineteenth century. Many of these fell victim to the misfortunes of war and the changing times, a few—among them Windsor Plantation near Natchez—remain as romantic ruins, but some are preserved as reminders of a spacious way of life enjoyed by the fortunate few. Outstanding among these are Greenwood (c. 1830) in St. Francis-

Greenwood,
St. Francisville, La., c. 1830
(National Trust for Historic Preservation;
photograph, Library of Congress)

157

ville, Louisiana, whose immaculate encircling colonnade is reflected in the green waters of a pond strategically placed for the purpose, and Oak Alley (1837) at Donaldsonville, Louisiana, with its colossal columns gleaming through the shadows of the avenue of tremendous, moss-laden live oaks, which form its approach and provide its setting.

Far more important for most Americans, however, was the opportunity provided for them to have tasteful and livable houses in a mode which remained fashionable till the outbreak of the Civil War, by following the builders' manuals of Asher Benjamin, of the upstate New York carpenter Minard Lafever (1797–1854), architect of the Whaler's Church (1844) in Sag Harbor, New York (an extraordinarily subtle piece of Egyptianizing in wood), and of the English-born John Haviland (1792–1852), whose most famous building was the New York Halls of Justice, better known as The Tombs (1836-38), massively designed in the Egyptian style.

To leaf through any of the editions of the works of these architects is to experience the essential practicality of their approach and to sense their knowledge and understanding of the abilities and needs of those for whom they wrote—the carpenters and builders across the country. Except in the deeper South, where skilled artisans had to be imported, these were men of experience and ingenuity but without training as designers. As a result, the countryside of America from Maine to the Gulf, and from the Atlantic coast to mid-continent and farther, was graced with examples of simple but dignified churches, courthouses, mansions, farms, and cottages, all displaying a similar consistency of Classic origin, yet also expressing a wide range of regional idioms resulting from the interpretation of their builders and the occasional use of stone, brick, or stucco instead of wood. Because of the remarkable flexibility inherent in the Greek Revival style as illustrated by these authors, it could become a genuine national style; it provided a vocabulary of proportion and of ornament which was subject to the widest variety of application, and was both practical and, in its symbolic suggestion of national cultural aspiration, ideal. Furthermore, its adaptability invited the exercise of that individualism which was so strong a component—even to a point which critics have considered pure cussedness—of the American character.

IV

From
the
Greek
Revival
to
the
Gothic

RESIDENCE OF N. P. WILLIS AT IDLEWILD, ON THE HUDSON.

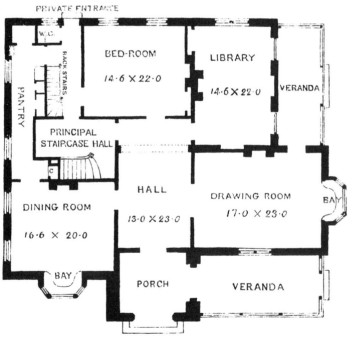

PLAN OF PRINCIPAL FLOOR.

From *Villas and Cottages: A Series of Designs
Prepared for Execution in the United States*, by Calvert Vaux
(New York: Harper & Brothers, 1857)

ANDREW JACKSON DOWNING AND THE TRADITION OF LANDSCAPE DESIGN

"To assist us in determining what to build," Andrew Jackson Downing (1815-52) wrote, "the character of the scenery itself should be considered . . .; a wooden castle, in a flat meadow, is as much out of place as a knight in armor would be running a tilt in the Jersey pine barrens." Downing early displayed a pronounced predilection for association with polite society, and through assiduous attention he developed a manner of a gentility appropriate to a higher station than that of the son of a nurseryman. Though his formal education was somewhat sketchy, he applied the same study to correcting this deficiency also, and cultivated his wealthier neighbors in and about Newburgh, whose estates, overlooking the Hudson, were once supplied by his father with plants, trees, and shrubs. There he met courtly Baron de Leiderer, the Austrian consul general, and several visiting Englishmen, including a landscape painter, who encouraged his already strong Anglophilia and started him on his short but significant career as a major "tastemaker," in the expression given currency by Russell Lynes.

Downing published a work on landscape gardening in 1841, followed within a year by the first of several editions of his best-selling *Cottage Residences*. His success was immediate and dramatic. He built himself a Gothic villa in Newburgh, and at the age of twenty-seven found himself the arbiter of America's taste in architecture and landscape design. His reign was to last but ten years, because he died at thirty-seven, after heroically rescuing several others in the explosion of the Hudson River steamer *Henry Clay*, whose boilers blew up during a race with the *Armenia*. But in that short period a series of books, articles, and designs issued from his pen, which eloquently but firmly informed Americans from Maine to the Gulf exactly *"What to Build,"* and, in addition, how to decorate and to furnish the houses he decreed for them according to "correct architectural taste." Post-Jacksonian America, growing prodigiously, welcomed his dictates. He was reassuringly definite and practical, and threw in enough theory, such as discussions of "the beauty of utility, the beauty of propriety, and the beauty of form and sentiment," to give a properly authoritative impression.

161

Despite the somewhat self-conscious tone of much of his writings, which he seasoned with appropriate quotations from the fashionable poets, they contain a great deal of good sense and sound advice, which were badly needed. In a period when the vast majority of buildings was constructed without benefit of an architect, he argued the case for professional consultation on practical and economic as well as aesthetic grounds. He pointed out that a good house need not cost any more than a bad one, and might well, in avoiding changes and extras, and through more knowing solutions of the problems of planning, amount to less. For him, a house had to be practical to be successful. He insisted on "proper drains" and gave diagrams to show how they should be installed. "No dwelling can be considered complete," he wrote, "which has not a water-closet under its roof," and he supplied a detailed drawing to show how one was to be correctly constructed; his house plans include not only these but such other conveniences as dumb-waiters and "bathing rooms" discreetly located.

The most significant aspect of his approach, however, was his recognition of the different requirements which domestic architecture must satisfy, and, despite his admiration for things aristocratic and British, the definitely democratic purpose of his works. He recommended practical arrangement and labor-saving devices in place of servants, since, "in a country like ours, where the population is comparatively sparse, civil rights equal, and wages high, good . . . domestics are comparatively rare, and not likely to retain their places for a long time." He insisted that the smallest cottage should be properly designed and could share architectural distinction with the most pretentious houses, and he admonished the *nouveaux riches* against building immense houses in the form of castles and châteaux as being both tasteless and inappropriate to the American scene. "Attempts at great establishments are always and inevitably failures in America," he announced. A house, he believed, should look like a house, and, furthermore, it should suit the person for whom it is built.

He deplored the fashion for building Greek temples for dwellings as examples of "the false taste lately so prevalent among us," which was also guilty of painting so many houses "a glaring white . . . 'like the eternal grin of a fool.' " Instead, one should use "a mellow shade of color, in exquisite keeping with the surrounding objects," like that of the buildings introduced into their landscapes "by the great masters." Instead of constructing whitewashed wooden temples, "let us rather," he urged, "be more sensible in our architectural utterance, and express a pleasant, every-day language, in an Old English mansion, a Rural Gothic cottage, or an Italian villa." But, above all, there must be a "happy union between the locality or site, and the style chosen . . .; nature has done so much . . . that it would appear that man had only to borrow a few hints from the genius of the place, and the home features would all be rendered equally delightful."

Downing also established himself as an authority in horticulture. His treatise on American fruit trees was a classic of its kind; it and his other works won the approval of Queen Victoria and Prince Albert, while the Queen of Denmark gave him a handsome ring as a token of her admiration. He was invited to membership in several European learned societies, of which his association with the Royal Botanic Society of London undoubtedly gave him the greatest satisfaction. In 1850 he sailed for England to enjoy for some months the gracious amenities of upper-class British country life. An early admirer of John Ruskin, whose *Seven Lamps of Architecture* had appeared the previous year, Downing believed that the English had brought the standards of rural architecture to the highest degree of perfection, so he sought a partner to share the increasing burdens of his fast-growing practice. In Calvert Vaux (1824-95), Downing found the ideal person.

Well trained in London, Vaux was an ingenious and practical young man who had been brought up in the English tradition of naturalistic landscape design, in a direct line of descent from Humphrey Repton. That eighteenth-century Englishman first composed landscape in terms of developing and enhancing its natural appearance so successfully and over such vast tracts of English parkland that much of what we admire today in the English countryside is actually due to the planning of Repton and his many followers. Downing knew and studied Repton's work and based much of his own practice upon it. He also was fond of quoting Sir Uvedale Price, an English country squire of the late eighteenth century, who was a major creator of the concept of the Picturesque, the idea of looking at landscape as well as planning it in terms before limited to the practice of the landscape painter.

Edmund Burke, the eloquent spokesman in Parliament for the rights of the American colonials during the Revolutionary period, wrote his extremely influential essay on "the Sublime and the Beautiful" in 1756. In it he analyzed aesthetic qualities in terms of our emotional reactions to what we see: if our fears are aroused, it is sublime; if our sensations are those of pleasure, then it is beautiful. Those qualities that tend to be finite, such as smoothness, gentle variation, smallness, and formal grace result in beauty, while those that tend toward the infinite —obscurity, vastness, solitude, darkness, and power—involve our astonishment and terror and result in the sublime. Price decided, however, that there were things which fell between these two opposing categories, qualities revealed in nature by the landscape painter. He analyzed scenery in terms of the charm of the rough and irregular; the stimulation of sudden contrast, of variety and intricacy, which excite curiosity, of suspense and partial concealment, which titillate the imagination; and the shock of the accidental, the unexpected, the unforeseeable. He found these qualities in the broken rocks and eroded cliffs of a stormy shore, in the mystery of shadowy caverns and dense woods, in the disparity between the delicate flowers and mosses and the rugged cliff on which they grow.

The cult of the Picturesque in the late eighteenth and early nineteenth centuries brought on a spate of books on picturesque travel, as people for the first time sought out woods and wastelands, formerly shunned as "barbarous deserts" but suddenly rediscovered by the fashion of looking at things through the eye of a Romantic landscape painter. From then on, people began to admire a sunset as a "perfect Claude" and a rough mountainside "as if from the pencil of Salvator Rosa," needing only colorfully costumed banditti to complete the picture. The cult of the Picturesque was the early phase of the Romantic movement. It was expressed in literature equally in Wordsworth and in the Gothic novel; in painting, in the windswept skies of Constable, the Alpine heights and mysterious lights and atmospheres of Turner, the blasted tree and sinister rocky desert of Allston's *Elijah in the Wilderness,* and in the pictures of Thomas Cole and others of the Hudson River School; and in architecture, in a growing preference for exotic styles—Gothic, Tudor, or even Near Eastern—with emphasis on the unclassically irregular and asymmetrical.

Downing felt very strongly about the character of any given place. At once visual and idealistic in his attitude, like Thomas Cole, he felt a personal affinity with nature, and saw in the natural scenery of America a projection of his own democratic ideals and his hopes for the future. He felt that the arts should be "so understood and cultivated as to elevate and dignify the character," and that "a young country and progressive people" should "develop ideas of beauty, harmony, and moral significance in their daily lives." For him, "the national taste is not a matter of little moment," and it all begins with the environment in which one leads one's life, with man's relation to nature. He deplored the arbitrary placement, so common in America, of a foursquare, boxlike block, flat on the ground, with no attempt by means of planting, artful grading, or the adjustment of mass, line, and color to unite the building with the land. He considered it his responsibility as an architect to study and analyze the character of a place before cutting down a tree, much less building anything; not only to draw a design for the house, but for the whole lot, whether it be a large estate or a small cottage. Thus, like Frank Lloyd Wright half a century later, he designed houses inside and out—the outbuildings, the gardens, and the surrounding landscape—to form a harmonious and suitable whole for both the situation and the owner.

Americans listened to him eagerly. Already prosperous and ambitious, their prideful attention had been called to American scenery by the writings of Irving and Cooper and the paintings of Thomas Cole, and others of the Hudson River School. As a result, they not only were generally most receptive to Downing's ideas, but also were as badly bitten by the bug of picturesque travel as were their British cousins. They trooped off to shudder deliciously at the height and force of Niagara Falls. They poetized over the perfect reflection of Chocorua in its mountain lake and pondered the handiwork of nature in the Great Stone Face. They thrilled at the thunder of the waves breaking on the rocky shore at Newport and admired the rough slopes, the boulder-filled streams, and the wild and lonely grandeur of the Catskills. This mountain area, not too much earlier rediscovered through Cole's romantic vision, was already offering a variety of resort hotels, such as the once famous Catskill House, the colossal columns of whose broad veranda were crowned with elaborate Corinthian capitals brought from New Orleans. At the Trenton Falls House, a haunt for artists and writers, the genial Michael Moore was always glad to accept a painting in payment of a bill. Artists recorded and interpreted the charms of Watkin's Glen (now known chiefly by sports-car buffs), of Bash-Bish Falls in the Berkshires, and of many another now forgotten spot, as well as of Lake George and the rugged coast of Maine. Resorts in the White Mountains vied with spas such as Saratoga for a fashionable and culture-conscious clientele. The railroads ran special excursions exclusively for artists, stopping the train wherever the muse struck, while steamship companies competed with cruises. Annual fall pilgrimages were made by lemming-like hordes to see the autumn foliage and compare the view to the landscapes of a favorite Hudson River painter, while reciting Mr. Bryant's verses. There was hardly a locality so culturally impoverished as not to boast some rocky glen, waterfall, loon-haunted lake, or meandering stream to which might be added such fancies and associations as the imagination could conceive under the stimulus of the sentimental literature that was all the rage, perhaps of unhappy lovers or that ubiquitous forsaken Indian maiden who once turned up with such monotonous regularity.

The valley of the Hudson, hallowed by Irving, Cooper, and Cole, with its romantic highlands and the tumbled masses of the Catskills as a background, was a perfect site for the kind of architecture that Downing liked to design. His own house in Newburgh, Highland Gardens, with its five acres carefully and imaginatively landscaped to enhance the character of the site, was a perfect example of his theories. Its Rural Gothic style harmonized with a terrain planted with artful irregularity and containing specimens of rare trees and shrubs and free-form beds of flowers near the house, in the informal manner he advocated as being in the correct taste.

In 1845 Downing was called to Washington to plan the landscaping of the grounds of the Capitol. Unimpressed by the protests of politicians that the sum of $20,000 was outrageous for such a purpose and that a salary of $2,500 was unthinkable, Downing informed the President that he wished him to call a meeting of his Cabinet so that he might explain the project to them, and also stated that he would do nothing more on it until the undignified harassment ceased. Amazingly, the President did so, and the annoyance stopped. In the meantime, Downing agreed with his friend William Cullen Bryant that the City of New York was sprawling formlessly, and that a section of Manhattan still unencumbered by shanties or speculative building should be set aside forever for the citizens. Thus the idea for Central Park was born. Downing drew plans for it, the results of which we can still see today, as interpreted by Calvert Vaux and by Frederick Law Olmsted (1822–1903), the gifted young landscape designer whom Vaux took on as a partner several years after Downing's death. Each was in turn a perfect disciple: Vaux shared Downing's enthusiasms and point of view, and carried on his work with the same spirit of public responsibility and good citizenship that had motivated the all too short career of his elder partner. Similarly, without Olmsted's untiring fight against political greed and graft, and his imaginative projection

166

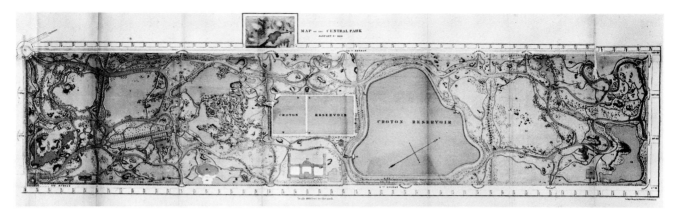

Frederick L. Olmsted and Calvert Vaux: Central Park, a print of 1870
(Courtesy, Department of Parks, New York City)

of Downing's and Vaux's ideals, the great project of Central Park would never have been realized.

Downing's own house, his numerous writings, and his work in Washington and elsewhere won him great fame, but his cause was also furthered by the villa that Vaux designed just after Downing's death for a mutual friend and neighbor, Nathaniel Parker Willis. Idlewild, built on the Hudson overlooking Newburgh Bay, was planned so that no existing tree of any importance had to be cut down; instead, the house was made to conform to the place, with windows and verandas situated to make the most of the views, which were framed by the branches of trees carefully trained and judiciously clipped to give an entirely natural appearance. Each was a living landscape properly composed in the style of the Hudson River School, of which both Vaux and Willis were, like Downing, enthusiastic admirers.

Since Willis was a popular poet, a major contributor to and an editor of many of the gift books and annuals then flooding the country and serving as a most important means of influencing taste and fashion, there could not have been a more effective press agent, and the "Hudson River Bracketed," the style that Downing devised and Vaux demonstrated in Willis' house, spread far and wide. While Downing had cultivated a becoming reserve, Willis suffered from no such shyness. Something of an exquisite, he delighted in being in the public eye, dressed romantically as a poet should, welcomed visitors to Idlewild, and gloried at the world of fashion, whether on the verandas at Saratoga or in the ballrooms of Manhattan. Like Downing he was a born tastemaker, though he lacked the same seriousness of dedication. There is no doubt of his effectiveness, however:

167

reams of his facile verses appeared in countless journals, along with essays on literary and artistic subjects addressed primarily to the growing host of feminine readers from the urban centers of the East to the Western frontier.

Vaux was a competent designer, though he lacked Downing's flair and could not compare in imagination and grasp with their friend and contemporary Alexander Jackson Davis, whose work they both admired. While the firm of Vaux and Olmsted had a wide architectural practice, its major contribution was in the field of landscape design and regional planning. Central Park was followed by others, like the Fenway and Franklin parks in Boston, and the laying out of whole communities, such as Riverside, outside of Chicago, Illinois. In the latter project, the firm carried on in 1869 Downing's principle of enhancing the spirit of the place, and of sharing among all the citizens an equal opportunity to enjoy its beauty, much as Wright later planned in his famous but unrealized Broadacre City. As Willis wrote in a sentiment borrowed directly from Downing and Vaux, but expressed in his own fanciful style, "to fence out a genial eye from any corner of the earth, which Nature has lovingly touched with her pencil, which never repeats itself—to shut up a glen or a waterfall for one man's exclusive knowing or enjoying—to lock up trees and glades, shady paths and haunts among rivulets, would be an embezzlement by one man of God's gift to all. A capitalist might as well curtain off a star, or have the monopoly of an hour. Doors may lock, but outdoors is a freehold to feet and eyes."

"The great charm in the forms of natural landscape lies in its well-balanced irregularity," Vaux stated in his widely read *Villas and Cottages,* which contained his design for Downing's memorial urn to be erected in Washington, and which was appropriately dedicated to Downing's widow. "This is also the secret of success in every picturesque village, and in every picturesque countryhouse, or cottage. Human nature, when allowed a free, healthy scope, loves heartily this well-balanced irregularity, and longs for it in life, in character, and in almost everything," he stated. These were the principles of design that Olmsted followed, and are continued by the firm which still bears his name, as well as by countless other landscape designers. The feeling for the character of the place, and the careful study subtly to enhance and to compose it, not arbitrarily to change it, but to relate it to the land—like "the old, bald, neutral-toned Yankee farm house," admired by Horatio Greenough as seeming "to belong to the ground whereon it stands, as the caterpillar to the leaf that feeds him"—has never been more understandingly and sympathetically demonstrated than in two houses of our own period. Frank Lloyd Wright's Falling Water, built in 1936 on ledges and among boulders across a waterfall in a woodland stream in Bear Run, Pennsylvania, and Philip Johnson's glass house, which he designed for himself on a hillside in New Canaan, Connecticut, in 1949, show a similarly sensitive awareness of the natural character of their sites. Both houses, though utterly different in style, display Downing's delight in a poetic situation, Vaux's admiration for ingenuity of design, and Olmsted's desire for intimate association with unspoiled nature.

Today we may smile at the somewhat moralizing tone of much that Downing wrote, but he and his followers would have shared Wright's scorn for the soul-crippling monotony of the suburbia of our day, and we are deeply in their debt for their having created a tradition of American landscape design which, though still flouted by the speculators, remains a major ingredient in much of the most successful and imaginative of contemporary architectural planning.

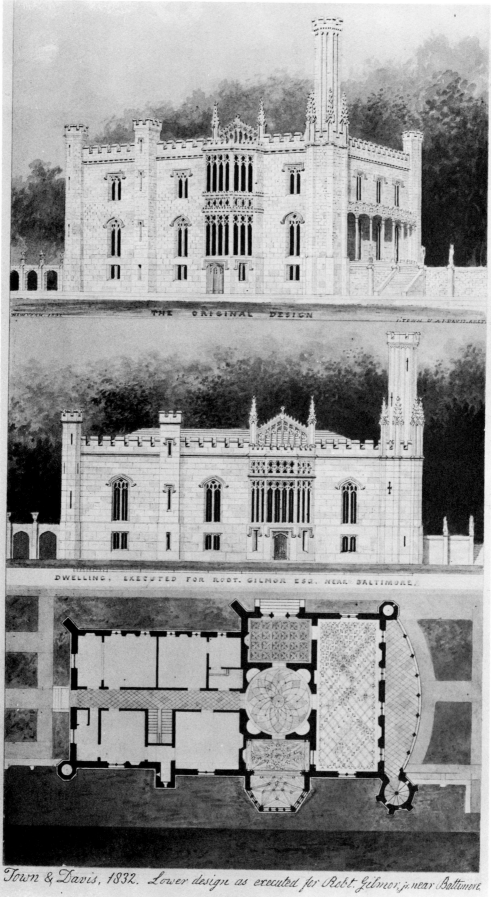

THE ORIGINAL DESIGN

NEW YORK 1832   I. TOWN & A. J. DAVIS, ARCH.

DWELLING, EXECUTED FOR ROBT. GILMOR ESQ. NEAR BALTIMORE.

Town & Davis, 1832. Lower design as executed for Robt. Gilmor, j. near Baltimore.

ALEXANDER JACKSON DAVIS AND THE HEIGHT OF THE GOTHIC REVIVAL

Alexander Jackson Davis (1803-92) had more in common with his friend Andrew Jackson Downing than the same middle name and set of initials. A brilliant and imaginative designer, he always referred to himself as an "architectural composer," as an expression of the essentially picturesque attitude shared by both. Davis was brought up, like Washington Allston, on Gothic novels, and spent his boyhood working out the plans of imaginary castles in great detail, and acting out with his friends favorite episodes from the highly colored romantic fiction to which they were addicted. In later years the works of Sir Walter Scott nourished an enthusiasm for the Middle Ages that remained undiminished, despite his occasional and always expert essays in the Classic mode. After a flirtation with the stage and a fling at painting, at twenty he studied architecture briefly at the Antiques School, predecessor of the National Academy of Design, with John Trumbull, whose own architectural works were limited to little more than a brick church in a Connecticut village, a Yale dormitory, and drawings for the simple classic block of the gallery that was to house the collection of the paintings he presented to the college.

Davis had a more practical apprenticeship during the year or so spent with Josiah Brady, an experienced New York builder and writer of contracts and specifications. Davis had always had a flair for drawing, and he turned out to be a brilliant draftsman, opening his own office on Wall Street in 1826 to furnish "proprietors and builders with plans, elevations, and perspective views for public and private edifices, both in town and country." One of the first members of the newly formed National Academy of Design, he there came to know Samuel F. B. Morse, the sculptor John Frazee, William Dunlap, the first historian of the arts in America, Irving, Cooper, Bryant, the young Thomas Cole, Dr. David Hosack, and others of the artistic and literary group in the city, including his future partner, Ithiel Town. Town was nineteen years his senior, and already famous both for the invention of the lattice truss as well as for Classic architectural design. Letters of introduction from Town, Trumbull, and Hosack opened doors for Davis in Boston, where he stayed some weeks, exploring the library of the Athenaeum and drawing

171

Alexander Jackson Davis: Study for Glen Ellen for Robert Gilmor, Baltimore, 1832, water color (The Metropolitan Museum of Art, Dick Fund, 1924)

views of buildings, for Pendleton and other lithographers, in Boston, Cambridge, Providence, New Haven, and elsewhere. On his return to New York in 1828, Town evidently considered Davis' training complete, because he offered him a partnership. Though architects had frequently joined forces on special projects or for short periods of time, the firm of Town & Davis was the first permanent business association of its kind in the country.

Davis was delighted. Accustomed to being busy, he found himself flooded with work, as the energetic Town traveled about the country to check on the progress of buildings for which he had supplied designs, and to oversee the construction of bridges from Nova Scotia to the far South. The office at 32 Merchants' Exchange, with Town's superb library available to any serious student, became a favorite meeting place for architects and those interested in the arts. Here long and convivial evening discussions took place, and Davis' handsome renderings, for which he was already famous, were admired by friends and visitors from other parts of the country. Davis showed work at every exhibition at the National Academy, and the firm's designs were thus of incalculable influence on the development of American architecture from 1830 until after Town's death in 1844 and well past mid-century. They provided models for the Classic houses, with high columned porticoes and strong Greek detail derived from Stuart and Revett's monumental *Antiquities of Athens*, which were built from New England to the Gulf during these decades, as well as for romantic designs in Gothic and more picturesque idioms.

Davis took hold so satisfactorily that Town felt free to take the lengthy European trip he had so long looked forward to, and in 1829 he sailed with Morse and Nathaniel Jocelyn, an engraver and portrait painter who was a lifelong friend of both. While Town toured England and the Continent, studying buildings everywhere, and collecting books, engravings, and works of art for his library, Davis carried on the firm's practice and even broadened its scope through a virtual mail-order business of plans and elevations for other architects, builders, and clients across the country. For a man of his enthusiastic and volatile temperament, Davis was extraordinarily methodical. The amount of work he turned out was enormous, yet there is no trace of haste in the beautiful renderings, made with such speed and gusto, which regularly won diplomas and medals and were outstanding in every exhibition.

The Gothic style had never entirely disappeared in England

during the years when the Renaissance manner of Inigo Jones and Sir Christopher Wren developed into the theatrical Baroque of the soldier-playwright Sir John Vanbrugh, so well demonstrated at Blenheim, the grateful nation's gift to the victorious Duke of Marlborough. It had lasted through the robust Palladianism of the Georgians and the increasing Classicism of the brothers Adam to emerge strongly with the growing Romantic movement. There were no true Gothic buildings of any moment erected during these centuries, but antiquarian interest and fashion combined to employ Gothic motives, applied picturesquely, as at Horace Walpole's Strawberry Hill or William Beckford's Fonthill Abbey, and more often in furniture and interiors, such as those for which Thomas Chippendale became famous.

Under influence of the cult of the Picturesque it became fashionable to construct often elaborate Gothic ruins, sometimes inhabited by hired hermits appropriately bearded and sandaled and monastically garbed. There was sufficient interest in the Gothic to inspire an architect with the charming name of Batty Langly to write and illustrate a very useful book on the subject, which found its way into the libraries of Bulfinch, Town, and a number of other American architects. All this was a surface Gothic, not a structural Gothic: Batty Langly's basic proportions and relations of elements are essentially Georgian and Palladian, just as were those of Sir Charles Barry, the Classic architect who was commissioned to design the Gothic Houses of Parliament in 1835. And until archaeology set in like *rigor mortis* in the second half of the century, the Gothic Revival in the United States remained a matter of style and atmosphere, and invited the imaginative and expressive variations on a medieval theme so delightfully played by Downing and Davis, and, in the next generation, by Richard Upjohn and James Renwick, Jr. A similar inventiveness was also shown by countless little-known and anonymous builders across the country, who freely translated into native wood the crockets and finials symbolic of the universal enthusiasm for the medievalism for which the Waverley novels were the primary inspiration.

Robert Gilmor of Baltimore, the generous patron of so many American artists of the period, provided Davis with an ideal opportunity to show his mastery of the Gothic idiom in Glen Ellen, named after Gilmor's bride. Built in 1832, it was the perfect dwelling for a man who treasured memories of a visit to Abbotsford and liked to show his guests the cane that its laird had given him. The house was beautifully situated on a gentle slope in the midst of a large tract of rolling farmland. The land was carefully landscaped in the spirit of Downing to enhance its natural character, and accented with five small Greek temples carefully and irregularly disposed to afford pleasing compositions from the house and its approaches. The working farm, its buildings seen in the distance, added to the landscape the further charm of grazing sheep and prize cattle, orchards, and cultivated fields. Visitors entered the grounds through a gate in the form of two arches of a Gothic ruin, one of which contained the gate-keeper's cottage; the whole effect was ingeniously staged to give the impression of medieval remains of considerable extent, with broken, ivied walls and fallen blocks of ancient masonry. The drive crossed a rustic bridge and wound through the park, with views of the temples and the distant farm, and approached the house at the level of the long garden terrace on the edge of which it stood. The façade opposite the carriage entrance was higher, its basement fully exposed, thus presenting a more imposing elevation to the main view. The whole complex was not large, but so perfectly was the scale maintained throughout that the effect was one of dignity without heaviness, because the delicacy of the tracery of the oriel windows accenting each façade and of details of battlemented parapet and octagonal tower were set in effective contrast to the plain surfaces of ashlar masonry. As in all of Davis' Romantic designs, it was based on a scheme of great regularity which constantly approached symmetry but arrived at the controlled balance of mass that expressed freedom from the tyranny of the Classic tradition. Yet Davis' design retained sufficient of its qualities to ensure visual satisfaction and rational planning, entirely lacking the whimsical irregularities and caprices of many later Romantic designs.

The interior was laid out with crossing axes. The halls and major rooms had intricately groined vaults rising high above tessellated marble pavements. The walls were paneled and wainscoted, and the crisply detailed cornices were picked out in color to set off the recurrent motives of the Tudor rose and the Gothic ball-flower. These motives also appeared in the stained glass of the vertical windows, so typical of Davis' style, which flooded the interiors with colored light. The furnishings were consistent with the design of the house, with Gothic chairs and tables and Romantic sculptures, while the walls were hung with paintings by such American artists as Doughty and Cole as well as with the works of British and Italian masters. The completeness of the concept and the consistency of its realization gave Glen Ellen a rare distinction and made it a landmark in American Romantic architecture. Unfortunately, it later burned and long stood, still beautiful, as a picturesque ruin, before being bulldozed in recent years to make way for the Loch Raven Dam.

The indefatigable Davis went on to innumerable other Romantic designs, ranging from cottages to mansions, all displaying his inventiveness and his feeling for mass and proportion. His remodeling of Sunnyside proved far from a hindrance to his career. Starting as a simple, salt-box cottage with a heavy central chimney, the Wolfert's Roost of Jacobus Van Tassel, Washington Irving's famous house on the Hudson is a symbol of the intermingling of the arts in the Romantic period. George Harvey, a landscape painter, planned the general architectural concept which Davis carried out in 1836 and again a decade later to produce the "little, old-fashioned stone mansion, all made up of gable ends, and as full of angles and corners as an old cocked hat." Complete with crow-step gables and clustered chimneys, it became a pilgrimage spot for visitors from the world over, very like Abbotsford, where Irving stayed with such pleasure, and whose owner he so deeply admired.

Of Davis' great houses, Lyndhurst, built for William Paulding, former mayor of New York, and his son Philip as a summer retreat at Tarrytown in 1838, is the most ambitious. The design, inspired by Lowther Castle, is, as Wayne Andrews has observed, "a masterpiece; its graceful asymmetry, its complex massing have been rarely equalled in America, and never surpassed." George Merritt, who bought the house in 1864, engaged Davis to enlarge it in the same style, and the result has been judged "the finest domestic monument to the Gothic Revival in America." Richard Byrnes carried out Davis' designs for the interiors—with moldings and mantels taken from Pugin's newly published *Examples* (which had measured drawings from Windsor, Vicar's Close, and Chatfield) and with superb suites of Gothic furniture—with such skill and craftsmanship that it led to his lifelong professional association with the architect. Byrnes also carved the bosses and finials, inside and out, and executed the woodwork, with built-in bookcases and niches for sculptures and bibelots. The interior planning displays all of Davis' capacities for flexible and logical arrangement. It was ideal for the leisurely and hospitable life that, with a good fortune denied most such houses, continued to go on there from the Pauldings' time until 1965, when the house was taken over by the National Trust for Historic Preservation.

Among other Gothic designs was a suburban villa built in 1844 "upon an eminence, since removed," Davis tells us in a late edition of his popular *Rural Residences*, published in the 1880's, "south of the Croton reservoir on the west side of Fifth Avenue between 37 and 38 Streets overlooking the greater part of New York island." The house had a "prospect tower" for the enjoyment of a view "commanding the Bay, Staten Island, Long Island, and the Jersey shore of the Hudson River." It was built for William Coventry H. Waddell, who was, according to Davis, "U.S. Marshall of the District of New York under President Jackson," and also, Davis remarks, "twice married and each time to *great pecuniary advantage.*" Of stuccoed brick, it stood on a generous lot planted with century-old trees and irregular beds of flowers in the manner prescribed by Downing. Its picturesque tower could be seen from afar. So that there should be no doubt as to the identity of the proud owner, the name "Waddell" was spelled out as a part of the design of the wrought-iron fence on the Fifth Avenue front.

Complete with greenhouse, gardener's cottage, stables, and carriage house with sleek horses and the finest of Brewster's coach work, it so represented the height of fashion of its day that it provided the scene for a lush and sentimental tale entitled *Fashion and Famine*—the very title reveals its inevitably moralizing tone—by "the celebrated novelist" Anne Sophia Winterbotham Stephens; the book was published in 1854 and appropriately dedicated to Lydia Huntley Sigourney, the equally celebrated and sentimental poetess whose verses thronged the pages of gift books and annuals of the day. Roger Hale Newton, Davis' biographer, plunged into the tangle of Mrs. Stephens' luxuriant verbiage to discover descriptions of the house, and emerged with references to "rich and faultless furniture," "statues of Parian marble, rich bronzes, antique carvings in wood, and the most sumptuous upholstery," marble floors "checked black and white," "a high staircase, covered from top to bottom with a carpet that seemed made of roses and wood moss," "windows . . . covered deep with silk curtains," and "sleeping chambers that might have sheltered the repose of an Eastern princess," furniture of "carved ivory and azure damask," and "lace curtains that hung like floating frost-work." There were several reception rooms for the fashionable parties Mrs. Waddell loved to give for such celebrities as Irving and Thackeray, "some of them palatial in dimensions, others bijoux of elegance," and all "so delicately managed," according to our author, that "gorgeousness was avoided." The house was torn down in 1856 to make way for the march of progress up Fifth Avenue, and Davis rescued the handsomely paneled Gothic doors, traceried windows, and "a wonderful spiral staircase," and installed them in his own house, Wildmont, in Llewellyn Park, West Orange, New Jersey, which was destroyed by fire in 1884.

At Tarrytown, also, was the vaguely Romanesque bulk of Ericstan, with its massive round tower. Perched on the edge of a cliff high above the Hudson, it was built in 1855 for the New York merchant John J. Herrick. For exhibition in the Crystal Palace, Davis made one of his most attractive renderings of the house, as seen in the moonlight, silhouetted against the night sky, with a white banner floating lazily from the tower. For William J. Rotch, a New Bedford millowner, he devised a simple and successful design that was widely copied. In Bridgeport, Connecticut, he built a house for the leather merchant H. K. Harral which was until recently preserved in all its original Gothic splendor of cusped cornices, elaborate grand staircase, and multiple parlor mirrors reflecting the sugary-white marble allegories and graces of the American Neoclassic sculptor Chauncey Ives. And in the South, for the enthusiastic patron Philip St. George Cocke, Davis planned Belmead in Powhatan County, Virginia, overlooking the James.

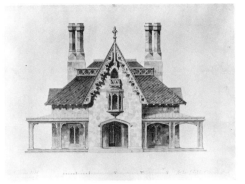

Alexander Jackson Davis:
Study for the Rotch House,
New Bedford, Mass., 1836, water color
(The Metropolitan Museum of Art,
Dick Fund, 1924)

Almost all of Davis' designs were published and exhibited widely, and consequently were of great influence, but none had the impact of the small bargeboarded dwelling, with a single high-peaked gable above a Gothic window in the center of the façade, that has so often been credited to Downing. Actually, it was first published by Davis in 1834, when Downing was only nineteen and had not yet embarked on his short but significant career, although Downing's enthusiasm for the design undoubtedly gave it its great popularity. A particularly attractive example of it was the Charles B. Sedgwick House, which, until its recent destruction, lent a welcome air of distinction to James Street in Syracuse, New York. With its façade three windows wide, and with the delicate pierced trim of gable and porch, it represented the type of "Gothic Cottage" that was built all over the country, translated into stone, brick, flush-boarding, board-and-batten work, clapboarding, and even adobe, according to the owner's preference and the structural requirements of the region.

It was very largely the result of Davis' practice that Gothic became the collegiate style, as it has persisted in being even to our own day. His New York University, completed in 1837 on Washington Square in New York City, with the tremendous window (adapted from that of King's College, Cambridge) of its magnificent chapel in the center of the façade, was a much admired building made of Sing Sing marble, quarried and dressed by the inmates of that famous penal institution. Davis moved his offices to the new University building, into quarters more spacious than those in the Merchants' Exchange, next door to the rooms occupied by his friend Samuel F. B. Morse, where he was invited with others by Morse on January 22 of the following year "to witness the operation of his Electro Magnetic Telegraph." The projected complex of academic buildings designed for the University of Michigan in Ann Arbor was the climax of Davis' Gothic career, though he also did the Yale College Library, now the Dwight Memorial Chapel, in New Haven, the Virginia Military Institute (1848) in Lexington, Virginia, and the Wadsworth Atheneum in Hartford, Connecticut. The latter building has since undergone interior renovation and substantial addition the better to display its distinguished collections.

Davis was also designing in the Tuscan or Italian Villa style, whose popularity took a sharp rise with the construction of Osborne, Queen Victoria's and Prince Albert's summer palace on the Isle of Wight. He redesigned an eighteenth-century house, Locust Grove, on Livingston Manor, just south of Poughkeepsie, with hexagonal music room and Tuscan tower, for his friend Morse in 1851. The house still stands in its large park with vistas of the Hudson. The Italian Villa style flourished until the Civil War, and the Italianate fashion lent itself also to such monumental projects as Davis' State Hospital in Raleigh, North Carolina, and his Pauper Lunatic Asylum on Blackwell's, now Welfare, Island in New York City. A most attractive specimen of it is his design for a villa for Llewellyn Haskell, a wealthy wholesale chemist who conceived in 1851 the idea of a housing development in a beautiful wooded tract in the hills of West Orange, New Jersey. Davis plunged enthusiastically into the project, turning out dozens of designs in all the romantic modes—including his own country house, Wildmont, in Gothic style—to suit the sites being carefully plotted by Downing. Though few remains of the buildings are left, the superb scenery, with planting, now more than a century old, gives testimony to the quality of the planning and the execution of the joint project. It was the first of its kind in America and the prototype of the garden city of which Frank Lloyd Wright was later an ardent proponent.

The outbreak of war put an end to building, and Davis retired to his retreat in Llewellyn Park. Though he lived into the last decade of the century, he did only a few odd jobs in architecture, spending his time arranging his many portfolios of drawings, writing polemics against the wild excesses of postwar architecture, and keeping in touch with his wide circle of friends, especially those remaining of the group that used to congregate in the congenial atmosphere of the offices in the Merchants' Exchange and New York University.

Though Davis turned out innumerable designs in Gothic, he built few churches, perhaps because of the success in this field of a serious-minded young cabinetmaker named Richard Upjohn (1802-78), who arrived from England in 1829 at the age of twenty-seven. On discovering that all one had to do to be an architect in America was to hang out a shingle, Upjohn promptly did so. He worked as a draftsman in New Bedford, Massachusetts, for a while. In 1834 he moved to Boston, where a free and easy exchange between architects existed as a legacy from Charles Bulfinch. When in 1835 Robert Hallowell Gardiner's house in Gardiner, Maine, burned to the ground, Upjohn was engaged to replace it with a picturesque Gothic mansion, which aroused the admiration of Nathaniel Hawthorne. Oaklands still stands in its somewhat overgrown park by the Ken-

Richard Upjohn:
Trinity Church from a Bird's-Eye View,
1847, lithograph after the
architect's drawing
(Courtesy, Museum of the City of New
York, J. Clarence Davies Collection)

179

nebec River, still in the possession of the Gardiner family. Up-john was also adept at the fashionable Italian manner, as the handsome villa for Edward King in Newport, Rhode Island, testifies. Built in 1845, today it serves as the People's Library.

Upjohn was in his element in church design. A devout Angli-can, he was never happier than when occupied with a commis-sion for an Episcopal parish, and he built countless such during a long, busy, and successful career. Intent on emphasizing the dignity and the mystery of the service, he interpreted Gothic forms imaginatively to create buildings of expressive power, even in the simplest of country churches. An example is St. John's in Bangor, Maine, whose vault was made of lath and plaster rather than the more monumental stone he preferred and used so effec-tively, as in Christ Church in Raleigh, North Carolina, and in Grace Church in Utica, New York.

New York City has been lucky enough to have a number of Upjohn's churches, among them the Church of the Holy Commun-ion on Sixth Avenue at Twentieth Street, its cruciform plan emphasized by a corner tower, and the handsome Church of the Ascension on Fifth Avenue at Tenth Street, in which his Gothic vocabulary is used so freely as to become the personal expression of the architect's imagination. But Trinity Church, at the corner of Wall Street and Broadway in New York, is his masterpiece. Fortunately, when the second church of the name to stand on the site developed a badly leaking roof in the winter of 1839, the rector remembered his friend Upjohn and recommended that he be brought in to advise as to the proper solution. Armed with a series of beautifully rendered drawings of a Gothic re-placement, Upjohn did not find it too difficult to convince the vestry to go along with the new scheme. For him, his whole career was a labor of love, and he was never happier than when superintending the construction of Trinity Church. Every detail was his and was executed under his eye—the ornamental bosses and capitals, the sculpture, and the stained-glass windows. The result is a building of such consistency and simplicity that one experiences its effect without being aware of the subtlety of the means used to achieve it. It has an organic completeness, within and without, that allows it to stand, serene and permanent, in its carefully clipped churchyard dotted with gravestones dating back centuries to the first Trinity Church to occupy the site. It is an oasis of human scale and changeless values among the vast sky-scrapers of downtown New York that should dwarf it but some-how look themselves gross and oversized by comparison.

In 1846, the same year that Upjohn was happily ensconced in the little wooden studio-office he had temporarily erected beside Trinity to oversee, like a medieval master builder, the completion of the church's construction, another Episcopal edifice was rising on Broadway at Tenth Street. It was the design of an erratic, gifted, and charming amateur of twenty-eight, James Renwick, Jr. (1818-95). A Columbia graduate with no architectural and slight engineering experience, he had enough money to afford two yachts and enough enthusiasm to allow him to disregard any gaps in his training. The resulting building, Grace Church, is full of lively invention. In 1853, on the strength of his designs for Grace Church, Renwick became the architect to carry out the ambitious scheme of Archbishop John Hughes to build St. Patrick's Cathedral on Fifth Avenue between Fiftieth and Fifty-first Streets. The site was considered far out in the boondocks and the Archbishop's plan was looked upon as a wild dream, but his foresight became increasingly evident as the city steadily crawled northward during the years of the cathedral's construction, begun in 1858. Progress was halted by the Civil War but afterward resumed, to reach completion only in 1888 with the topping out of its spires. It was too vast a project to allow Renwick to approach it with the same youthful *joie de vivre* he showed at Grace Church, and men of a more archaeological turn of mind were responsible for its later phases, but it remains the country's largest monument to the Gothic Revival, and its confrontation with Harrison and Fouilhoux's colossal Rockefeller Center gives a visual excitement of effective contrast otherwise sadly lacking in the present-day city.

This same function is even more strongly performed in the case of his design for the Smithsonian Institution in Washington, D.C., in 1846. The whole story of the Smithsonian is as romantic as it is improbable. It was founded with the fortune that the illegitimate son of a British duke left to a country he had never seen, and it is appropriate that its extraordinary collections, the kind of wonderfully rich miscellany that makes it properly the nation's attic, should be housed in the most outrageously romantic building imaginable. Though there are elements of both Gothic and Romanesque discernible in it, and it has been described as "Anglo-Norman," "Lombard," and "Byzantine," it remains pure Renwick. Although it may present difficulties to the curators of the national historical and artistic collections in matters of display, its value increases every year, as more monolithic, whited mediocrities rise about it, making its pictur-

James Renwick, Jr.:
St. Patrick's Cathedral,
photograph of 1894
(Courtesy, Museum of the City of
New York)

181

esque and variegated red sandstone bulk—with its gesticulating towers, apses, oriels, and battlemented parapets, its outlines softened by the ivy that adds another welcome note of color—a constant assertion of individualism in the monotonous conformity of the nation's capital, and a reminder of a more ebullient and joyous age.

Something of the stylistic exuberance of the period is expressed in the "Classification of Styles" in which Davis' scrapbooks were arranged. He could show a client examples of American Log Cabin, Farm Villa, English Cottage, Manor House, Collegiate, French, Suburban, Switz (*sic*) Chalet, Switz Mansion, Lombard, Italian, Pliny, Tuscan, Palladian, Roman, Etruscan, Palmyran, Suburban Greek, Oriental, Moorish, Round, and Castellated! Davis was too accomplished an "architectural composer" to indulge the excesses suggested by some of these names. For him, as for Upjohn, Renwick, and their contemporaries, the Gothic and other Revival styles carried associations of time's passing and of its continuity, a theme prevalent in the paintings of Thomas Cole. They also provided a rediscovery of the romance missing from the workaday lives of people who had heretofore spent all their time and energies following the sage and practical advice of Poor Richard to achieve places of solid worth in the community and to assist in the unprecedented growth and development of their country. Change was everywhere, and it was matched by a vitality that our age might well envy. Though there were shadows of the coming conflict already creeping across the land during the middle years of the century, most Americans were too busy to see them.

James Renwick, Jr.:
Smithsonian Institution,
Washington, D.C., 1846-55
(Photograph, Library of Congress)

ARCHITECTURAL FANTASY AND FUNCTIONAL EXPERIMENT

As the mid-century approached, America boomed at an ever increasing rate, and with the rush of other developments came a search for novelty and an urge to experiment. It was a time of theory and of trial: Begun in 1848, the Oneida Community, unlike the earlier Brook Farm, later transformed a communistic experiment in "group marriage" and "stirpiculture" (later called eugenics), housed in an Italianate palace in Oneida, New York, into a thriving business of silver manufacture under the astute direction of John Humphrey Noyes. The Latter-Day Saints, in their distant haven in the valley of the Great Salt Lake, constructed granite temples in a romantic style somewhat suggestive of Russia's Stalinist Gothic but without its brutality. Their immense picturesqueness of scale and vigor of outline are proudly forthright as an expression of utopian independence. By means of a book called *A Home for All; or, The Gravel Wall and Octagon Mode of Building*, the first of several editions of which appeared in 1848, Orson Squire Fowler, an enthusiast in the new fad of phrenology, not only introduced a novel and practical material and method of construction, but also started the fashion of the octagonal house. Such centrally planned geometric forms had been used earlier in America and elsewhere, as in William Thornton's inaccurately named Octagon, now the headquarters of the American Institute of Architects in Washington, D.C., in Jefferson's design for Poplar Forest near Lynchburg, Virginia, and in the many early nineteenth-century schoolhouses of eastern Pennsylvania; but after Fowler's book was published a rash of octagons, hexagons, barrel forms, and other geometrical shapes spread across the country.

Fowler's own house at Fishkill, New York, was a fittingly simple example of his dictum that "beauty and utility are as closely united in architecture as they are throughout all Nature." Its gravel walls, hard as concrete, had finally to be dynamited when the house was demolished just before the end of the century. With central heating from a furnace in the basement (the vertical central hall served as an aid to heating in the winters and a means of cooling in the summers), with the rooms piped for illuminating by gas, and with indoor water closets and baths, the house was, according to Clay Lancaster (the witty and

Orson Squire Fowler: Octagon House, Fishkill, N.Y., 1845
(New York State Historical Association, Cooperstown, N.Y.)

learned chronicler of *The Architectural Follies of America*),
"perhaps the most modern house in America in its day." Though
Fowler's own house, a forerunner of twentieth-century function-
alism, no longer exists, there are, fortunately, other examples
which remain, largely in the Northeast and the Midwest. Among
the most interesting of these is the elaborate, domed edifice at
Irvington-on-Hudson presently occupied by Carl Carmer, author of *The Hudson* and of many works of American folklore
and history.

Architectural innovation endeavored to keep up with the pace
of change and the thirst for something new with increasingly
wild flights of fancy. These reached some kind of peak in the
palace built for Phineas T. Barnum near Bridgeport, Connecticut, in 1848, by Leopold Eidlitz, a young graduate of the Vi-
enna Polytechnic Institute. Iranistan was a fitting setting for
the amusing master showman who had made a fortune on the

184

principle that "there's a sucker born every minute," though it looked more appropriate for some oriental potentate, with its bulging domes reminiscent of those of the Prince Regent's picturesque folly at Brighton, its bristle of pinnacles, and its general echoing at great remove of motives and forms of the Taj Mahal. More than a thousand guests were invited to the housewarming, and until it burned in 1858 the house was the site of extravagant receptions, with food brought to tables set on the lawn by servants dressed in turbans and exotic costumes to the music of a brass band. The procession was led by Jumbo, "the world's largest elephant," its rocking howdah occupied by General Tom Thumb, the famous midget, or graced by the charming Jenny Lind, who afterward, by the light of countless Japanese lanterns, might sing from one of the fretted balconies, to be followed by the virtuoso flourishes of Ole Bull's famous violin.

Contemporary descriptions of the house and its interiors, such as that in *Gleason's Pictorial Drawing-Room Companion* of 1851, dwell admiringly on such details as "marble statuary, imported from Florence," "rich rosewood" furniture, ceilings of "rich arabesque mouldings of white and gold," and "curtains, drapery, statuary, mantel ornaments, etc. . . . of unique elegance." The dining room, its walls "painted in dark English oak, the rich panels of which represent the three Fine Arts, Music, Painting, and Poetry," contained a display of "rare and beautiful porcelain, among which is a harlequin dessert-service, every piece of a different pattern, lettered with the initials, P.T.B." Andrew Jackson Downing was highly critical of this kind of uninhibited exhibitionism, remarking tartly that "a villa in the style of a Persian palace (of which there is an example lately erected in Connecticut), with its oriental domes and minarets,"

Leopold Eidlitz:
Iranistan, the house of P. T. Barnum near Bridgeport, Conn., 1848, lithograph by Sarony & Major (Courtesy Kenneth M. Newman, The Old Print Shop, Inc.)

was the expression of a "mere love of novelty," and was "poor and contemptible," and "equally unsuited to our life or climate."

None of polite society, like Downing, approved, but Barnum was delighted. He had astutely placed the house with its main façade and constantly gushing fountain facing the railroad tracks of the main line into New York City, where his famous Museum was located, "the most comfortable, genteel, and cheapest place of amusement in the world." There, for an admission of twenty-five cents, one could inspect "a genuine mermaid," Siamese twins and various freaks, "the very finest in oil paintings and statuary from the hands of the great masters," and musical and dramatic stage presentations. The house in Bridgeport was a landmark and a constant reminder to the railroad passengers of the fascinations of the Museum. Barnum had an elephant hitched to a plow and supplied his Ceylonese trainer with a railroad timetable, instructing him to be plowing whenever a train was due. The results were spectacular. Trains had to slow down to satisfy the curiosity of the passengers, who were agog at the startling possibilities opened by the novel idea of elephant farming; its pros and cons were discussed in the press, and Barnum kept the issue burning by circulating "confidential" reports that the elephant was useless for the purpose, and by simultaneously spreading contradictory rumors that elephants could do practically everything on the farm, from plowing and planting to washing windows and baby-sitting. Barnum's name somehow kept recurring throughout the great debate, and the results became a part of the minor American classic in its genre, of which Barnum was the author, *How I Made a Million; or, The Secret of Success*. His book is the story of a gusty and joyful life dedicated to the only art in which the United States has been universally credited with supreme mastery—that of publicity. His house, like all the rest of his career, was a great publicity stunt, and the mixture of genuine art with the sensational and the grotesque exactly suited the lively spirit of the times.

Appropriately, a rival that has been called "the most luxuriant flower of American-Oriental architecture" arose a few miles below Natchez, the exotic showplace of the newly rich of the cotton kingdom. Dr. Haller Nutt had seen Middle Eastern architecture at first hand when he visited Egypt. He came away with seeds of long-stapled Egyptian cotton, despite the elaborate precautions of the Egyptian government and customs, by the simple expedient of having a packet of the seeds ready in his luggage to be seized, meanwhile sewing a much larger supply of them in his small daughter's favorite doll. The strain of cotton he subsequently raised, added to his perfection of Eli Whitney's cotton gin, supplied him with a fortune that could well afford the Eastern luxury he planned for himself on the tropical banks of the Mississippi, a retreat where he could enjoy at his leisure the pleasures of his large library of classic authors. On the strength of a design suitable for "the banks of some of our noble streams," published by Samuel Sloan of Philadelphia in 1852 in *The Model Architect*, Nutt engaged Sloan to enlarge the octagonal "villa in the oriental style," with its turnip-shaped dome, into an Eastern fantasy. Longwood was started in 1860, with workmen brought in from the North to carry out the more elaborate parts of the construction. Marble fireplaces and paneling were ordered from abroad and the work went on apace. All that remained to be done in 1861 was to fit doors and windows, to finish the installation of woodwork and marble, plastering, and stuccoing, when war was declared. Dr. Nutt managed to complete the ground floor, where he and his family lived, but the rest of the house was never finished. Its central rotunda, illuminated by the plunging light from the domed cupola four stories above, central fountain, multicolored marbles, niches for sculptures, and thirty-odd rooms (including a series of reception rooms thirty-six feet long grouped around the central core) are today just as they were left when the workmen put down their tools—which still remain where they fell—and rushed off to war. Among live oaks festooned with gray streamers of Spanish moss the incomplete house stands empty and desolate, like the ghost of an era so remote from ours that it seems light-years away, though it is but little more than a century.

It is fitting that the octagon craze should have reached a late climax in Texas with two notable examples. In 1889 a house was built on the plan of an ace of clubs to commemorate the winning trump in the card game whose proceeds financed its construction in Texarkana. Hexagon House, a hotel in Mineral Wells, not far from Fort Worth, opened to the public in 1897, complete even to hexagonal dining tables.

Architectural fantasy was not limited to successful showmen, wealthy cotton growers, and rich Texans, however. Houses in towns, villages, and on isolated farms across the country burst out in crockets and finials, with gables and porches trimmed in scroll-sawn bargeboards. Pointed windows appeared in barns and country churches and meetinghouses, and the native "Carpenter Gothic" style, which has added so much flavor to the American scene, was everywhere.

Toward the middle of the century a Maine sea captain encased his foursquare eighteenth-century brick house in Kennebunk in a valentinelike tracery which made it famous as the Wedding-Cake House. Louisiana's old State Capitol at Baton Rouge took the form that Mark Twain described as "a whitewashed castle, with turrets and things, materials all ungenuine within and without, pretending to be what they are not"; and Northampton, Massachusetts, proudly constructed its castellated Town Hall in 1851, next door to a Unitarian church in the form of a Greek temple. A young architect named William Johnston and Thomas U. Walter, able architect of Girard College and the cast-iron dome of the national Capitol, together designed, in a Romantic style, the country's oldest "skyscraper," the eight-storied Jayne Building, in Philadelphia in 1849, for Dr. David Jayne, a manufacturer of patent medicines. Unfortunately, Johnston died before the completion of the building. Its simplified Venetian Gothic, all vertical in emphasis and carried out in granite, is still impressive and anticipates, in its verticality and feeling of upward thrust, the dramatic developments that were to emerge from the Chicago School of Burnham and Root and of Sullivan and Adler, when architecture took to the air, as it has continued to do in cities from Maine to Texas and from coast to coast ever since.

In a country without royalty and claiming, though scarcely practicing, absolute equality, the palaces which human nature demands were more often, in Russell Lynes's phrase, palaces for people "in general than for people in particular." They took the form of the first luxury hotels, such as Boston's Tremont House, the St. Charles in New Orleans, and the hotels in Saratoga, the city which, according to James Silk Buckingham, an English visitor in 1840, "affords the best opportunity that a stranger can enjoy for seeing American society on the largest scale." There, at the Congress Hall or the United States Hotel, Nathaniel Parker Willis loved to pace the broad verandas in season, to observe the fashionable idlers and the pretty girls, all dressed in the latest style, the comings and goings, the flirtations, pursuits, and matchmaking, the shiny carriages drawn by still glossier horses, the constant sound of music, and the nightly balls, with dancing couples whirling in a kaleidoscope of color beneath brilliant chandeliers.

William Johnson and Thomas U. Walter: Jayne Building, Philadelphia, Pa., 1849 (Courtesy Kenneth M. Newman, The Old Print Shop, Inc.)

188

Grand stateroom of the Steamer *Drew*,
chromolithograph by Endicott & Company
(Courtesy Kenneth M. Newman,
The Old Print Shop, Inc.)

The river boats were floating palaces, their appearance well
known through Currier & Ives prints, the paintings of James
Bard, and the writings of Mark Twain. "Huge toppling steamers," Herman Melville called them, "bedizened and lacquered
within like imperial junks. . . . Fine promenades, domed saloons, long galleries, sunny balconies, confidential passages,
bridal chambers, staterooms plenty as pigeon-holes, and out-of-
the-way retreats like secret drawers in an escritoire, present
like facilities for publicity or privacy." Their decorations were
even more elaborate than those of the hotels with which they
shared the luxury of deep-piled carpets covered with immense
roses, of gilt and carved furniture patterned after, if not produced by, the most fashionable makers, of marble-topped tables,
intricate mirrors, oversize oil paintings, and colossal chandeliers,
all enjoyed with the same gusto with which the endless meals
were consumed, to be followed, on the part of the men, by innumerable brandies and other equally effective liquors of native distillation.

Railroad stations also became palaces. Sometimes, in smaller
towns, they were modest casinos, adorned with pierced-tracery
trim and imbricated roofs. And sometimes they were colossal,
like Commodore Vanderbilt's first Grand Central Station, with

John B. Snook, architect,
and Isaac C. Buckhout, engineer:
Grand Central Depot, New York City,
1869-71
(Courtesy Kenneth M. Newman,
The Old Print Shop, Inc.)

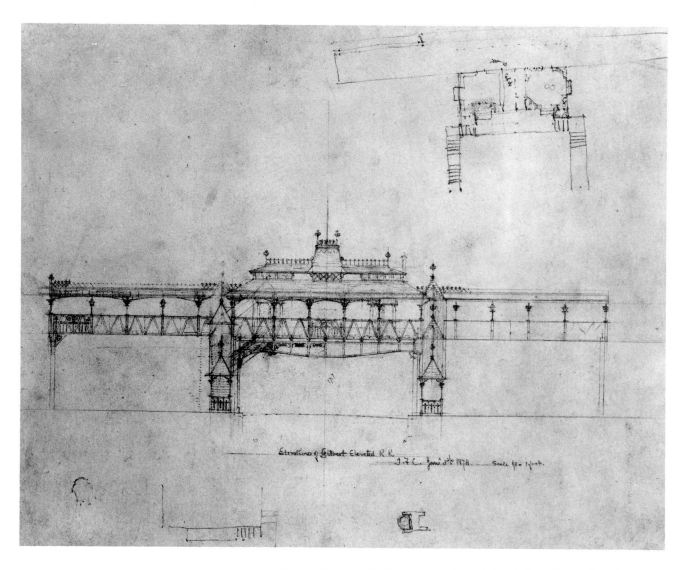

Jasper Cropsey: Design for a station of the Gilbert Elevated Railway, c. 1876, pencil (Courtesy, Museum of Fine Arts, Boston, M. and M. Karolik Collection)

vast covered shed, 600 feet long and 200 feet wide, and lofty waiting rooms. The stations of the Sixth Avenue Elevated Railroad, designed by the painter-architect Jasper F. Cropsey, a follower of Thomas Cole, were airy flights of fancy, with delicate, pierced sawtooth trim, cutout rosettes, and slender scrolled brackets, all forming an expert composition, in angles and diagonals, of stairs, landings, and shallow pitched roofs crowned with pinnacled ventilators, so that each station was a little palace floating on a lacework of iron piers and trusses above the street. Even firehouses, with their fanciful decoration matching the brilliance of the red and gold of the gleaming apparatus, were palaces of sorts, as were the department stores—though

190

somewhat more subdued, to be sure—with façades in a Gothic or Italian manner, broad windows, and an impressive opulence of interior furnishings. But the last word in public palace architecture was provided by the buildings of the great expositions that were modeled on that in London in 1851, with its famous Crystal Palace. Two years later, in the first of many such fairs, New York had its own Crystal Palace, erected in what was then Reservoir Square, but which has been renamed Bryant Park since the New York Public Library replaced the Egyptian-detailed Croton Reservoir on Fifth Avenue. Though New York's Crystal Palace lacked the style and grace of Sir Joseph Paxton's brilliant original in London, it, too, was constructed entirely of iron and glass, and its fate anticipated that of Paxton's, for it caught fire in 1858 and was consumed in a quarter of an hour.

The exuberance of Romantic architecture in America continued into our own century, especially evident in such structures as moving-picture theaters, but beneath the ever more elaborate envelope was a series of structural innovations of great significance which carried on the essentially practical strain of the country's tradition. In 1833 one Augustus Deodat Taylor, a builder-architect, constructed the first Roman Catholic church in Chicago with amazing speed by using a system of thin plates and studs, usually two by four inches, fastened by nails instead of the traditional method of heavy timbers, mortised and tenoned. As in all basic inventions of this sort, there is a question as to whether he was the first to use the simple but revolutionary principle of construction derisively called the "balloon frame," which was based on standardization of parts and on employing light members. With the machine production of nails it was possible, as a contemporary architect observed, for two men with no more technical knowledge or skill than the ability to use a hammer and saw to complete a two-story house in two weeks. By use of the balloon frame cities appeared virtually overnight where gold was discovered in California or oil in Pennsylvania. When, for instance, an oil well was dug on an isolated farm in Pennsylvania during January, 1865, the community of Pithole City, with 10,000 inhabitants, was established by midsummer. As Solon Robinson, a pioneer land speculator, stated in 1855, "if it had not been for the knowledge of balloon-frames, Chicago and San Francisco could never have risen, as they did, from little villages to great cities in a single year." Beneath the gingerbread of the buildings being built across the country was this revolutionary principle that al-

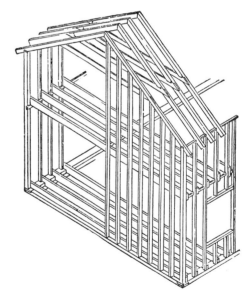

Balloon-frame construction, from *Woodward's Country Homes*, by George E. Woodward (New York, 1865)

191

lowed men to put up their own houses with few tools and little financial outlay, with the help of a son or neighbor. The stylistic guidance of architectural books was furnished by such successors of Asher Benjamin as Minard Lafever, an upstate New Yorker who taught himself to become an outstanding architect, John Haviland, noted for his advanced prison planning, and Richard Upjohn, whose designs for village churches were widely followed.

In 1830 Haviland constructed a front made completely of cast iron for the fireproof Farmers' and Merchants' Bank in Pottsville, Pennsylvania. Cast-iron shop fronts became popular in New York in the 1840's, and in 1848 James Bogardus, a watchmaker from Rochester, New York, erected the first building made entirely of cast iron. Again, it was standardization of parts and simplicity of process that made this further structural development possible. The resulting buildings were mostly in an Italianate style, like the famous A. T. Stewart store, later Wanamaker's, on Broadway at Tenth Street in New York, designed by John Kellum, which was a notable city landmark until, abandoned, it was destroyed by fire in 1956. Cast-iron buildings rose everywhere, and were shipped, knocked down, around the Horn and to far parts of the world, just as prefabricated wooden buildings had been shipped to the East and West Indies from New England in colonial times. And although they are being demolished wholesale through urban renewals—as has happened in the last few years along the St. Louis waterfront—there are still many examples to be seen in any major American city. They represent another great step toward the end prefigured in the thrusting verticality of the slender and virile Gothic of young William Johnston's and Thomas Walter's Jayne Building and in some of the late designs for city buildings of Alexander Jackson Davis.

James Bogardus:
The first cast-iron building, 1848-49, lithograph by Ackerman
(Courtesy, Museum of the City of New York)

There were those who instinctively understood what was going on beneath the surface. The American sculptor Horatio Greenough, writing before the middle of the century, defined "Beauty as the promise of function." Impatient with the popularity of the Greek Revival in architecture, he declared himself "for Greek principles, not Greek things." "The men," he wrote, "who have reduced locomotion to its simplest elements, in the trotting wagon and the yacht *America,* are nearer to Athens at this moment than they who would bend the Greek temple to every use." Yet he also understood something of the reasons for the stylistic extravagance of a period so bursting with energy and drive. He recognized that fashion in architecture as elsewhere "denotes a hope of better things. It betrays a lurking want not clearly expressed, and it gives stones and serpents to stop our craving, only because it has neither bread nor fishes to bestow. Fashion is no positive evil, and has been often a relative good. As etiquette, though a poor makeshift, still professes the existence of propriety, its superstition, with all its darkness, would prove a twilight to the godless; so Fashion may be allowed to protest against finality and be the symbol of yearning yet impotent aspiration." From the vantage point of today, the aspiration seems far from impotent, for we can see what it produced during a period of such restless vitality that it demanded expression at every level, from sham castles to railroads, and from oriental fantasies that might have been planned as stage sets for Poe's "Domain of Arnheim" to skyscrapers.

Duncan Phyfe's shop on Fulton Street, New York, c. 1825, water color
(The Metropolitan Museum of Art; photograph, Museum of the City of New York)

DUNCAN PHYFE AND OTHER CRAFTSMEN

For the same reasons that Classical design long dominated architecture, it persisted in furniture and other objects for the house—such as glass, ceramics, and wallpapers—even after the Gothic and the later French-derived styles, grouped under the general and rather indiscriminate heading of "Victorian," came into vogue. The derivation from European sources is often obvious, but the variety of changes rung on the imported theme is a demonstration of Yankee ingenuity. Certain motives appear again and again, such as the ubiquitous eagle, the official symbol of the republic since 1788. It was stenciled on the fancy chairs made in great quantity by Lambert Hitchcock (1795–1852) at his factory in Hitchcockville, Connecticut, from 1825 on, and widely sold and as widely copied. The eagle motive also provided finials for bull's-eye mirrors and banjo clocks, such as those produced by Simon Willard of Roxbury, Massachusetts, and Eli Terry of Plymouth, Connecticut. It appeared, along with medallions of Washington and Lafayette, on blown-molded whiskey and rum bottles, from Massachusetts to Pittsburgh, on cottons printed in Rhode Island, and on wallpapers, often preserved as covering for hatboxes. It was used as an appropriate major element in the design of such magnificent pieces of commemorative silver as the superb wine cooler (Historical Society of Pennsylvania) made by Thomas Whartenby and Peter Bumm in 1816 for presentation by "The Citizens of Philadelphia to Their Townsman Commodore Decatur Esteemed For His Virtue   Honored For His Valor," and the pair of magnificent urns (New York State Chamber of Commerce) made by Thomas Fletcher and Sidney Gardiner of Philadelphia, decorated with scenes of the Erie Canal, which were presented in 1824 by "The Merchants of Pearl Street, New York, To the Hon. De Witt Clinton Whose claim to the proud title of 'Public Benefactor' is founded on those magnificent works, The Northern and Western CANALS." In spite of the introduction of new techniques of manufacture (such as spinning on a lathe to produce hollow-ware instead of using the laborious method of raising by hammering and frequent annealing) and the increasing popularity of Sheffield plate, the quality of silver remained high and rivals that of the earlier periods, though

Thomas Fletcher and Sidney Gardiner: De Witt Clinton urn, one of a pair, Philadelphia, Pa., 1824, h. 24 (Collection of The Chamber of Commerce of the State of New York; photograph, The Metropolitan Museum of Art)

it has received far less attention from students and collectors, until its decline after the 1840's with the development of electroplating.

It was in Philadelphia, also, that the finest porcelain in the country was produced. William Ellis Tucker founded a factory there in 1825, which remained active until wiped out by the financial panic of 1837. The economy recovered rapidly, but competition with imported wares from England and France was too stiff, and Tucker's venture succumbed. In the meantime, however, it manufactured a variety of simple, Classic designs, in a French taste, which bear comparison with the works of European competitors; the most elaborate have delightfully painted scenes and other motives in cartouches, with accents of gold. The factory's design books, which are in the collection of the Philadelphia Museum of Art, show the range of shapes, from simple white tea sets to richly ornamented urns and vases of impressive scale and quality.

The French influence in America was much strengthened by an influx of refugees after the French Revolution. Many came to New York, others scattered to the south, perhaps as far as New Orleans, and some even found their way to the frontier. The greater number, however, seem to have settled in and around Philadelphia, which, for a supposedly sober Quaker city, developed an extraordinary number of teachers of the French language, dancing, music, and other frivolous but civilized diversions. This influence was reinforced by the work of a group of highly trained French craftsmen who set up shop as makers of fine furniture, and introduced the "architectural and pillared styles of the Empire and the Restoration," so appropriate for the temple houses then being built. Among these was Charles-Honoré Lannuier (1779–1819), who worked in New York from his arrival in 1803 until his early death. He produced refined side tables and other pieces of great style for such discriminating connoisseurs as Stephen Van Rensselaer IV. Another was Anthony G. Quervelle (1789–1856), who came to Philadelphia from Paris before 1817 and made a fortune "by steady industry and strict economy." His fine sense of craftsmanship and vigorous design are especially notable in his elaborate and imposing case pieces, such as that excellent example from about 1835 in the collection of the Museum of Art in Utica, New York.

François Seignouret (1768–c. 1855) came to New Orleans in 1815, and had his own shop from 1822 until he retired in 1853 at the age of eighty-five to his native Bordeaux. He and

William Ellis Tucker factory:
Tuckerware vase, 1832-38, porcelain
(Philadelphia Museum of Art)

Charles-Honoré Lannuier:
Card table, one of a pair,
New York City, c. 1817
(Courtesy Albany Institute of History and Art)

Prudent Mallard (1809-79), also Paris-trained, who probably worked briefly with Duncan Phyfe in New York and opened his own shop in New Orleans in 1838, made handsome, ornate furniture of fine quality appropriate to the high-ceilinged, airy interiors of the gracious Southern houses and representing the Romantic luxury of prevailing Creole taste. Mallard remained active until the war years. New Orleans furniture tended to be large in scale. Among typical examples were the massive armoires, or wardrobes, which took the place of modern closets, and heavy, high-posted beds—pieces in a French taste with carved motives derived from the Rococo and the Italian Renaissance, much modified in the interpretation.

In 1784, soon after Washington had bade farewell to his troops to retire to his beloved Mount Vernon in the troubled times before the ratification of the Constitution, a Scottish widow named Fife brought her children to America, among them her sixteen-year-old son, Duncan. They settled first in Albany, but in 1792 they moved to New York City, where the young man set up a cabinetmaking shop. His fine work was noticed by John Jacob Astor, another immigrant, who was already a millionaire from trade in beaverskins, and the young Scotsman's shop in Partition Street, later called Fulton Street, became the most fashionable and the busiest in the city from 1795 until he retired in his eightieth year, in 1847. The work of Duncan Phyfe (1768–1854), as he chose to spell his name, represented all aspects of the styles of his period, from Hepplewhite and Sheraton to Empire and Victorian, but it always had a personal flavor which was so popular that he had countless imitators, many so expert that today it is impossible to tell their work from his. He advertised that "special attention" was given to orders from the South; and, in fact, his furniture was shipped all over the country, until his style became almost exclusively that of an era.

For the more conservative, he designed and made the simple Sheraton- and Empire-type pieces which are so well known; for those of more Romantic taste he produced pieces of sumptuous dignity, enriched with crisp carving, and with delicate stenciling in gold to accent the dark mahogany, which was sometimes grained to imitate rosewood. Marble columns and tops often appeared on side tables and on the newly fashionable center tables (usually round, though occasionally oval), called by many "loo tables" because they were often used for cards. The center tables had heavy pedestals with short incurved legs ending in claw feet or, more rarely, three legs, a solid stretcher, and

Anthony G. Quervelle:
Secretary bookcase, Philadelphia, c. 1835
(Munson-Williams-Proctor Institute,
Utica, N.Y.)

197

winged paw feet touched in gold to match the stenciling of the apron and the ormolu mounts. His own particular details of design, such as the use of dog-paw feet, splats, incurved or saber legs, and his card tables with clover-leaf tops and pedestal bases are very distinctive. Some of his later pieces, such as Empire side tables of mahogany or rosewood with gilt designs and marble and gilt-bronze mounts, and the beautifully gilt-stenciled mahogany sofas with scrolled arms and winged lion-paw feet, are the most vigorous and splendid examples of their kind to be found. Many of the latter are of the asymmetrical type which is known as a Récamier from the couch on which Madame Récamier reclines in the famous portrait of her by Jacques-Louis David in the Louvre, but which are actually based on the design of the couches called *triclinia*, used in Roman times at banquets.

Phyfe's favorite chair forms were also Classically derived: the *klismos*, or Greek side chair, as seen on ancient grave-reliefs; and the *curule* chair, an interpretation of the Roman magistrate's folding seat. He also designed pier or side tables of simple outline, with columns or scroll-shaped front supports (sometimes with a marble top but more often not), which became a standard feature in American homes, as did the simple veneered pedestal tables for both living room and dining room, the standard scroll-armed sofas, usually covered in haircloth, and sleigh beds, called "French beds" in Phyfe's bills because of their French Empire origin.

Phyfe's forms were so widely known and so popular that they were freely used by furniture makers everywhere in the country and even in factory-made work, such as that of Joseph Meek & Sons, of 43 and 45 Broad Street, New York, who in 1833 were the first to advertise their wares with fully illustrated designs. Here we can already see what happened to line and form when it was adapted to easier and faster manufacture by the machines that were invading the field. Meek, like Phyfe,

Empire sofa,
attributed to Duncan Phyfe, New York,
1815-20
(The Metropolitan Museum of Art,
gift of Mrs. Bayard Verplanck, 1940)

shipped his furniture all over the country. Other manufacturers also appeared, to take advantage, with machine-made merchandise, of the market that was so swiftly growing with westward expansion and the burgeoning industrial revolution. But there remained those—among them Phyfe and the French-trained makers—who clung to the same old-fashioned methods of fine cabinetwork until the Civil War. These included John Henry Belter (1804-63), famous for his use of laminated structure, and the less known but even more distinguished Elijah Galusha (1804-71) of Troy, New York, both of whom worked primarily in the more florid and unclassical Romantic styles, growing in popularity from the 1830's, which were to dominate the second half of the nineteenth century.

John Henry Belter:
Furniture from the Abraham Lincoln parlor suite, New York City, c. 1850, laminated rosewood (Owned by the Henry Ford Museum & Greenfield Village)

The work of many of these men—silversmiths, clockmakers, glass blowers, potters, chairmakers, and cabinetmakers—were sent by canalboat, by ship, by river boat, and, finally, by railroad all over the country. Household objects were taken westward in covered wagons. These may have included a clock, some china and glass, a silver teapot or tea service, a mirror, a portrait, pieces of furniture, and sometimes even a piano, but usually consisted of only a reminder or two of a home left far behind. Occasionally a whole array of furnishings was transported, such as the two pianos, pair of sofas with intricate openwork backs, marble-topped tables, chairs, carpets, cornices, draperies, and even a harp, all of which were hauled a thousand miles or more over plains and mountains, during the years of the mid-century, for the Beehive House in Salt Lake City, from which Brigham Young governed the Territory of Deseret. Furniture from New Orleans and from New York reached the far Southwest, Connecticut clocks went to Texas, Boston bureaus to St. Louis, and a magnificent case piece by Samuel McIntire even turned up in Italy, where it had been taken by a New Englander in the United States consular service in the early years of the nineteenth century. As machine production developed and increasingly predominated after the middle of the century, and as transport became easier, there was a growing tendency toward the standardization of the contents of American houses, despite the great differences of climate and condition, and the handcraft tradition almost entirely disappeared.

Throughout his long career Phyfe maintained a large production at a high standard of both design and craftsmanship. Short in stature, independent, and wryly humorous, he was always on the job to talk to clients and to keep an eye on his assistants and apprentices. In his striped stocking cap and smock, he was a well-known figure on the New York scene, and he stands as a worthy representative of the best type of the American designers-craftsmen, whose works are today justly treasured as outstanding of their kind, worthy of our respect, and significant in our history.

SCULPTURE, CLASSICAL AND OTHERWISE

At the Crystal Palace exhibition in London in 1851, the American section contained, according to one contemporary account, "whole districts . . . solely devoted to the pursuit of agriculture"; yet it also included various objects made by the Goodyear Company of that curious new material, rubber, Samuel Colt's famous pistol (the first in which the chamber, not a set of barrels, revolved), several sulkies, and a model of the floating church for seamen in Gothic style ("painted to represent brownstone" and having "a large stained glass window at the east end with different devices," and "on either side of the chancel . . . a bishop's and priest's chair, all of black walnut"), the original of which, flying a large banner inscribed "Church of the Redeemer," was even then plying the crowded waters of the Delaware for the Churchman's Missionary Association of Philadelphia.

Amidst this dazzling array of wonders, the hit of the American section, and perhaps the hit of the whole show, was the famous *Greek Slave* sculptured by the Yankee Canova, Hiram Powers. According to the official catalogue, "The figure here represented is intended for that of a young and beautiful Greek girl, deprived of her clothing and exposed for sale to some wealthy eastern barbarian, before whom she is supposed to stand, with an expression of scornful dejection mingled with shame and disgust. Her dress, which is the modern Greek costume, appears on the column, and the cross implies her religion and country. The chains on her wrists are not historical, but have been added as necessary accessories." When one looks at the sculpture today in the Corcoran Gallery in Washington (if, indeed, one does bother to look at it), it is difficult to understand the furor that it aroused, and how it could possibly have been so admired that Powers was commissioned to make several replicas for distinguished patrons, ranging from Prince Demidoff to A. T. Stewart, the department store magnate, and to evoke praiseful verses by Elizabeth Barrett Browning:

> Appeal, fair stone,
> From God's pure height of beauty against man's wrong:
>   Catch up in thy divine face not alone
> East's griefs, but West's, and strike and shame the strong,
>   By thunder of white silence overthrown.

Hiram Powers: *The Greek Slave,* 1846, marble, life-sized (In the collection of The Corcoran Gallery of Art)

As the sculptor himself explained, "as there should be a moral in every work of art, I have given to the expression of the Greek slave what trust there could still be in a Divine Providence for a future state of existence, with utter despair for the present, mingled somewhat of scorn for all around her. . . . It is not her person but her spirit that stands exposed." The verdict of a committee of clergymen from Cincinnati that, far from being nude, the slave was "clothed in her own virtue," and the popularity gained from its exhibition at the Crystal Palace led to further appearances in various American cities to admiring multitudes of art lovers and culture seekers. Boston, however, just to be sure, decreed that men and women view the sculpture on alternate days when it was shown at the Athenaeum, since virtue in Boston has always been a delicate matter of grave concern.

A modern observer may see only a wan reflection of the Venus de' Medici, its surfaces honed to an even smoothness, which covers forms uncharacterized by structure of bone or tension of muscle or sinew. The conflicting emotions of trust, despair, and scorn mentioned by the confident sculptor seem most effectively to have canceled each other out, to leave only a vague neo-Greek vacuity. There are no lascivious Turks present, or any suggestion of them, in the figure's face or posture. The mincing hand is meaningless; there is nothing to hide but marble. Yet, swathed in morality and surrounded by sentimental storytelling, largely through the fame of this single sculpture, the nude began again to enter the domain of the arts as a legitimate motive and vehicle of expression, not only in America but in Europe as well. *The Greek Slave* was illustrated in engravings; porcelain factories in Europe and America turned out hundreds of thousands of small reproductions of the sculpture; her head and shoulders were reproduced in marble or cast in plaster as a bust; and no house was really properly and tastefully furnished without at least a little bisque version of the statue—"so undressed, yet so refined," as Henry James remarked—so completely had Powers' work become a very symbol of art and culture of the period.

For most admirers of art during the rest of the century the female nude remained "deprived of her clothing" but heavily draped with the double mantles of morality and sentiment, appearing sometimes as a *Circassian Slave* and sometimes as a *Triumph of Chastity,* an *Andromeda,* an *Eve,* a *Hope,* or a *Startled Nymph,* for the pruderies of the period were as energetic as its pursuit of culture. The situation resulted in tons of mediocre sculptures, a great proportion of which was produced by legions of aspiring and perspiring Americans working mostly in Florence (because of its proximity to the Carrara cliffs from which the faultless white marble was quarried) and in Rome, where Bertel Thorvaldsen, the Danish high priest of Neoclassicism, reigned supreme until his death in 1844. There were dozens and dozens of them chipping away industriously at innumerable figures of "Clytie," "Prynie," or "Proserpine," and also of contemporary worthies—judges, congressmen, professors, and generals—all eager, in the words of John Quincy Adam's apostrophe to Hiram Powers, to "Live in . . . marble through all after-time" through the artistic genius of such sculptors as Harriet Hosmer (1830–1908) of Massachusetts, Chauncey B. Ives (1810-94) of Connecticut, William H. Rinehart (1825-74) of Maryland, and Paul Akers (1825-61) of Maine, or of the three leaders in the field—Powers, Greenough, and Crawford.

Hiram Powers (1805-73) was born near Woodstock, Vermont, and early showed the practical ingenuity that led him later to devise a better method of laying a transatlantic cable than that first attempted, and to plan a railroad for transporting marble from the quarries at Carrara and to organize a joint stock company to carry it out. During his boyhood his family moved to Cincinnati. Young Powers soon found employment at the Western Museum (where Audubon had worked briefly as a taxidermist a few years before), and almost immediately made a name for himself by the creation of life-sized mechanized figures, writhing and moaning in eternal torment in a Dantesque hell with an alarming realism evincing a liveliness of invention that he managed quite successfully to eliminate from his later works. With youthful exuberance he enjoyed showing off his extraordinary imitative talent, as in making at the Museum "a waxen image" that was so lifelike that it "received the tickets of the crowd the whole evening without exciting suspicion."

No quality could have been more appealing to the Americans of the day than his brand of painstaking objective realism, and soon he was receiving commissions for busts of local dignitaries and even visited the great Daniel Webster at Marshfield, Massachusetts, to model his bust. In 1837, after completing plasters of several commissions, and with the assistance of Nicholas Longworth, he took his family to Italy. He settled in Florence, where he turned his careful sketches into marble and won the accolade of Thorvaldsen, who declared him "without a rival in the making of busts" and announced that "the entrance of Powers upon the field constituted an era in art." Powers' success was assured by the fame of *The Greek Slave* six years later. Tuckerman voiced the opinion of the multitude when he described it as "a type of the beautiful, which instantly gained recognition also as the true."

He was a typical Yankee in his practical approach to life. Mrs. Browning found him "a most charming, simple, straight-forward American—as simple as the man of genius he has proved himself to be," while Hawthorne delighted in his raci-ness of expression and has Miriam speak admiringly of his work in *The Marble Faun.* He lived in Florence because marble was near and comparatively cheap, expert assistants plentiful, and life for a man with a number of children less expensive than at home. Also, as Bryant noted, an American artist received more commissions in Rome or Florence than in Boston or New York. Powers did not lack for commissions, and his works sold at high prices, since he was regarded in Europe as well as in America as the leading sculptor of the age. In some measure, however, he had to share this reputation with two other Americans, Hora-tio Greenough, who had come from Boston, and Thomas Craw-ford from New York.

Greenough (1805-52), the elder by nine years, was the first of the Americans to settle in Italy, arriving in Rome in 1824 at the age of twenty with his friend the painter Robert W. Weir, later instructor in drawing at West Point, where he numbered an unlikely cadet named Whistler among his students. The two lived in a house said to have been that occupied by Claude Lor-rain on the Pincio, while Greenough studied a year with Thor-valdsen, with "drawing and modelling from life at the Academy and from the antique at the Vatican."

He had already had an unusual education for a sculptor. Ob-servant and bright, he had started as a child making things, drawing, and showing an incipient sculptural gift by modeling "a lion couchant . . . with a spoon from a pound of butter to astonish his mother's guests at tea." He managed to study with Solomon Willard, the architect of the Bunker Hill Monu-ment and carver of vigorous figureheads as well as works in the obdurate granite from Quincy, which he loved. Greenough also went to Harvard, where he did brilliantly, got a good clas-sical education, learned German and Italian (his favorite lan-guage), and studied anatomy with Dr. Parkman. But he enjoyed most of all his association during these years with Washington Allston, whom he met at the Danas', and who was delighted to

204

have Greenough and other promising undergraduates join the distinguished circle that surrounded him in his studio at Cambridgeport or at the houses of Cambridge or Boston friends. Greenough was no long-haired aesthete, however, but an athletic, lively, and humorous individual whose compact and muscular prose style better expresses his vigorously creative personality than any of the sculptures for which he was so famous in his own day. Eager to get to Italy, he did not wait to receive his diploma, but left with the college's permission in his senior year, settling permanently in Florence after a year's sojourn in Rome and a stay in Paris, where he did a bust of Lafayette.

On his visit to Italy in 1833, Henry T. Tuckerman recalled in his *Book of the Artists*, he found Greenough established in a studio in an old house whose courtyard was full of blocks of marble, and with the already familiar sculptures in the original plaster crowding shelves and corners of the rooms. He saw the *Chanting Cherubs*, which had been commissioned by James Fenimore Cooper, taken from two figures in a painting by Raphael in the Pitti Palace, "the first group in marble to be executed by an American." The busts of Lafayette and of Cooper himself were there, and clay sketches for the colossal statue of Washington, the nation's first such commission to a native sculptor, largely achieved through the efforts of Washington Allston and Edward Everett in 1832. Greenough had found the perfect place to work on it, a former chapel with a lofty interior and a large enough door, and with high windows, "the quiet of the place . . . invaded only by distant rural sounds and the murmur of the nearest foliage in the evening breeze." Emerson spent a few weeks in Florence that same year and delighted in the companionship of "this great man and glorious sculptor." Greenough was honored by appointment as professor of sculpture in the Grand Ducal Academy, and was a familiar and respected figure in the city, robust but reserved, and invariably accompanied by his greyhound Arno, whose portrait in marble long occupied an honored place in Edward Everett's library.

The story of the Washington statue is well known. Seeking, as he wrote, to treat the subject symbolically as most appropriate to its planned disposition in the Rotunda of the national Capitol, Greenough based his concept on the Phidian *Zeus*, using Houdon's famous bust as the source of the head. He worked seven years on the tremendous project before it was complete. Its bulk made transportation extremely difficult, and it was finally shipped from Livorno on a sloop of war, since the hatches

Horatio Greenough: *George Washington*, 1832-39, marble, h. 126 (Courtesy of the Smithsonian Institution National Collection of Fine Arts)

of the *Constitution* proved too small to allow it in the hold. After landing it, the navy had its further troubles getting it to Washington, because its height of over ten feet and its weight of twenty tons presented problems that no railway of the period was prepared easily to solve. It finally reached the Capitol in July of 1841 and was installed in the Rotunda with immense effort. But the lighting was so poor there that it was decided to move the statue outside, not to the western front of the Capitol as Greenough requested, but to the eastern side. Its makeshift shelter soon collapsed, leaving the imperious figure open to the elements and to the gibes of the self-appointed critics of art. Tuckerman called such criticism "one of the most prominent traits of the American character—that indomitable self-confidence which leads each citizen of 'the greatest country on earth,' especially when possessed of legislative functions, to deem himself an adequate judge of all subjects from a system of medicine to a principle in mechanics, and from a dogma in theology to a work of art; the right of private judgment is thus found to trench materially upon the authority of a professional knowledge in all departments; but in none is this charlatanism of universal self-esteem more grotesque in its display than when the higher branches of art, letters, and philosophy are thus made the subjects of complacent and superficial comment."

As Greenough had already discovered when his first work of the kind, the *Chanting Cherubs,* was shown in America a number of years earlier, he was, as he wrote, "rebuked and mortified by loud complaints of their nudity." The same puritanical prejudice "awoke with a roar at the colossal nakedness of Washington's manly breast." A Greek slave "deprived of her clothing" was acceptable, but apparently Washington was insufficiently clothed in his own virtue to meet the necessary standard of public taste. Those who were literal-minded enough to admire Powers' expert imitation of nature in wax as the height of art were blind to Greenough's attempt at a grandeur and monumentality that no American had dared to essay before. For years the huge figure gathered dust in an inadequate room of the Smithsonian Institution, where it was stored after half a century out of doors, until it was finally reinstalled in a place of honor in the new Smithsonian Museum building recently opened on the Mall.

The faults of the sculpture are obvious and they are the faults of its period—overfinishing of detail in comparison to its vast scale, and a frozen theatricality of pose and gesture

206

resulting inevitably in an incomplete realization of the symbolic representation Greenough attempted. Nevertheless, it has a majesty, dignity, and grave repose that no lesser sculptor of the period could have achieved. It is possible to understand the admiration of the more thoughtful critics of the time, who found it, in the words of Alexander Everett, "truly sublime," and recognized that "the design of the artist was . . . to indicate the ascendency of the civic and humane over the military virtues, which distinguished the whole career of Washington, and which form the great glory of his character." Seen at last in a proper setting, it can finally be, as its sculptor hoped, duly respected as an example of "the first struggle of our infant art."

After the *Washington* episode, Greenough returned to Florence, where he and his family soon moved into a new house of his own design, with a gallery, a garden court, and a large studio, which became a meeting place for visiting Americans and for artists, writers, and all those interested in the arts. Americans were flocking to Florence, attracted by the fame of Greenough and of Powers. A rich and culture-conscious nation was assiduously attempting to memorialize itself in marble and bronze, and the hopeful students continued to come, their spirits responding to an atmosphere both beguiling and stimulating. There were convivial international gatherings at Doney's, excursions into the Tuscan countryside for wine festivals, picnics in Fiesole, walks along the Arno, horse races beneath the spreading chestnuts of the Cascine in the autumn, and in winter, skating on the Arno, followed by evenings at the opera or with a group of friends gathered around the tile stove in some studio.

For most, Rome had yet greater attractions, however. With all the faded luster of an imperial past, it was a city of ruins made still more romantic by the paintings of Claude and the verses of Byron. Its tall cypresses grew over heaps of decayed masonry, and towering stone pines cast long shadows across the Forum, which was still a grazing ground as shown in Piranesi's prints. It was the city of Winckelmann and Goethe, of Keats and Shelley, of Irving and Allston, and of Madame de Staël and the exiled Bonapartes. John Gibson, the leading English sculptor there, with whom Harriet Hosmer studied in Canova's old studio, called it "the university of art," with students from all parts of Europe and America, benevolently presided over by Thorvaldsen, by right of succession to the deified Canova, whose work Jefferson had so admired. The leader of the American contingent was Thomas Crawford (1814-57), who had learned basic techniques in the United States with John Frazee before going to Italy in 1835. Crawford entered the picturesque studio of Thorvaldsen "below the Pincio," Van Wyck Brooks tells us, "in Piranesi's old house, with blocks of marble lying about in the great studio garden, overgrown with aloe, mallows and wild roses."

Crawford also received commissions from the United States government, which included figures in the Capitol pediment. He also carved a marble figure of a gigantic dejected Indian chief (1856, New-York Historical). A pair of bronze doors to the Senate wing was assigned to him, while the matching set in the opposite wing was the work of Randolph Rogers. Crawford's colossal bronze *Armed Freedom* crowns Thomas U. Walter's cast-iron dome of the Capitol. It was originally conceived with a liberty cap, which met the objection of the then Secretary of War, Jefferson Davis, as having "an established origin in its use as the badge of the freed slave," so that a helmet was substituted while the work was still in plaster. After the sculptor's untimely death in 1857, the 19-foot figure was cast in bronze and finally raised in place in sections on December 1, 1863, to the salute of the guns emplaced to defend the besieged capital against the forces of the Confederacy of which Jefferson Davis had become the ill-starred president. The sculptures that top the domes of the various state capitols of the country are among the worst in the world, generally to be outdone in total mediocrity only by the official works of Iron Curtain countries. Among this undistinguished throng, Crawford's is far from last, though Oliver Larkin describes it in his admirable *Art and Life in America* as "a formless, bulky female . . . the questionable plumes and odd silhouette rather suggestive of a pregnant squaw three hundred feet in the air."

Crawford's equestrian *Washington* reached Richmond, Virginia, on the same day as the news of his death in London. But he had had a taste of glory. On the successful completion of the casting of the statue in Munich, the sculptor had been greeted with a torchlight reception while "simultaneously burst forth from a hundred voices a song of triumph and jubilee." He had seen the Munich artists prepare his work for shipment to America, suffering "no inferior hands to pack and dispatch it to the seaside," and on the journey "peasants greeted its triumphal progress." On its arrival, "the people of Richmond were emulous to share the task of conveying it from the quay to the Capitol hill," where Jefferson's handsome temple stood; "mute admiration, followed by ecstatic cheers, hailed its unveiling, and the most gracious native eloquence inaugurated its erection."

Crawford died at the age of forty-three, and Greenough at forty-seven, five years earlier. Powers lived on till 1873. But meanwhile sculptors who had stayed at home were making a name for themselves. Henry Kirke Brown (1814-86) soon gave up the sentimental Neoclassicism learned early during four years of study in Italy, financed by his work as a railroad engineer in Illinois. He had studied portraiture briefly with Chester Harding, and had produced his most successful work in the *Washington*, completed in 1856, which stands in Union Square in New York City. This project Greenough had launched before his death, but it was not the first bronze equestrian statue ever wholly executed in this country, as Tuckerman stated. That honor belongs to the *Andrew Jackson*, mounted on a rearing horse, in Lafayette Square, in Washington, D.C., which was dedicated on January 8, 1853. It is the work of Clark Mills (1810-83), an orphan who ran away from an ill-tempered uncle and lived on his own from the age of thirteen, working as an ox driver in a lumbering operation near Syracuse and tending a lock on the Erie Canal. He froze his feet so badly one winter cutting cedar posts in a swamp that he could not wear shoes for several months, and he decided that he would work no more as a common laborer, but would learn a skilled trade. He went from cabinetmaking to being a millwright, and while learning stuccoing in Charleston, South Carolina, he started to model, invented a new and easier way of making life masks, and set himself up as a sculptor of busts. His lifelike accuracy attracted much attention; he soon had a thriving business.

Ambitious to forge ahead, Mills got a block of local stone and, entirely ignorant of technique, started a bust of the state's favorite son, John C. Calhoun, which he completed with painful care, learning as he went along. The result was purchased by the City Council of Charleston as the best likeness of their hero. Mills was awarded a gold medal, and a rich admirer financed his trip to Washington to "take the busts of my friends Webster and Crittenden." On the way he stopped at Richmond to admire Houdon's *Washington*, the first statue he had ever seen. In the Capital he was thrilled to see Greenough's *Washington*, though, hearing the usual criticism that "he didn't look like that," Mills determined to go all out for historic truth. Despite the fact that he had never seen either General Jackson or an equestrian monument, the young self-taught sculptor

Clark Mills: *Andrew Jackson*, 1853, bronze (United States Department of the Interior, National Park Service photograph)

209

was so self-possessed that his quiet confidence impressed the chairman of the Jackson Monument Committee, who proposed that Mills design the statue of Jackson before leaving for Italy on a trip to be financed by a Charleston patron.

In nine months Mills had completed a model "on a new principle, which was to bring the hind legs of the horse exactly under the center of his body, which of course produced a perfect balance, thereby giving the horse more the appearance of life." Thus a concept that Leonardo da Vinci had been unable to realize, and that had been achieved by few later sculptors, was successfully carried out by a young man without formal training or education. It took more than three years of work. Congress was slow in supplying the cannon captured by Old Hickory, cranes broke down, and furnaces blew up. But after six attempts the determined sculptor achieved an unflawed cast in one of the most monumental works of sculpture undertaken in the New World. Learned art historians have found the source of the concept in Pietro Tacca's *Philip IV* in the Plaza de Oriente in Madrid of the first half of the seventeenth century and in Falconet's *Peter the Great* in Leningrad, finished in 1782; it is possible that Mills saw engravings of one or the other of them. In view of the circumstances, however, it seems extraordinarily farfetched to look so far afield when the motive so obviously expresses the forthright and active image of Old Hickory, already something of a folk hero. The statue is undeniably naïve but full of verve and movement, and is the most spirited work of its kind to be produced by an American for a long time.

Mills never did get to Italy. With the $20,000 voted by Congress as his fee, he bought a farm outside Washington and set up a studio and foundry to make another cast of the *Jackson* for the city of New Orleans. The studio blew down in a hurricane and the foundry burned up, but Mills had suffered hardships before and would brook no setback. Both studio and foundry were rebuilt, and he went to work on an equestrian *Washington*, also commissioned by the government. Unveiled in 1860, it revealed the General reining in a prancing horse in another kinetic conception. Three years later, at his foundry on the road to Baltimore, he cast Crawford's *Armed Freedom* for the top of the Capitol's dome. After the successful completion of three more-than-life-sized equestrian figures—tasks of a complexity never before attempted except in a few European foundries of vast experience—producing the sections of Crawford's figure seemed simple enough. Though James Jackson Jarves remarked in his *Art Thoughts* that "Clark Mills' equestrian statues look like some prodigious Congressional jokes on art," they stand out today amid the increasing sameness of the Washington scene as vigorous expressions of the youthful *élan* of a still young and fast-growing country, as yet untried by the tragic and then unthinkable ordeal of a civil war.

Henry Dexter (1806-76), another self-taught sculptor, who had been apprenticed to a blacksmith in Connecticut, was given Horatio Greenough's clay when the latter went to Italy, and he became a successful producer of portrait busts. He had the extraordinary notion of recording the likenesses of the President and of all the state governors in office in 1860. For two years he traveled throughout the Union, and finally exhibited the results in the rotunda of Bulfinch's State House in Boston, where they were seen "by upwards of thirty-thousand people," according to the contemporary account by a friend of the artist, an "embodiment of the spirit of our Government in that eventful year—the last of the Union on the old basis."

Every town and city seemed to want a *Washington*, a *Patrick Henry*, or some other Revolutionary hero or contemporary dignitary of local origin. Thomas Ball's *Washington* in Boston's Public Garden, the result of months of struggle in a drafty barn on Tremont Street, remains one of the best, but Harriet Hosmer's *Thomas Hart Benton* in St. Louis has none of the relentless drive of the famous senator from Missouri, and most of the rest of the countless patriotic images that appeared across the country during the middle years of the century are best considered pious symbols rather than as even minor works of art. But when Erastus Dow Palmer (1817–1904), a cabinet-maker and cameo cutter of Albany, New York, turned to marble in middle life, he produced in *The White Captive* (plaster sketch, Albany; marble, Metropolitan) a figure that puts the more famous *Greek Slave* in its place as the work of a man who, according to Jarves, "fitly represents the mechanical proclivities of the nation." *The White Captive* still has the spurious chains that were "necessary accessories" to so many female figures of the period, for, as Christopher Hobhouse remarks in his account of the Crystal Palace exhibition, "it was a fortunate minority among the objects of statuary who had the free use of their limbs"; however, she is no longer a sugary abstraction, but a figure of supple grace and convincingly realized firmness and plasticity, with the head an immediately observed portrait of the sculptor's daughter. For the first time the cold marble was, in Tuckerman's phrase, beginning to be "warmed into life."

Erastus Dow Palmer: *The White Captive*, 1857, plaster, h. 19¾
(Courtesy Albany Institute of History and Art)

It remained for two men to carry this development forward during the middle decades of the century. One was John Quincy Adams Ward (1830–1910), an Ohio farm boy who was entirely trained in the United States as a pupil of Henry Kirke Brown in Brooklyn, New York, and the other was Dr. William Rimmer of Boston. Ward went west, like the intrepid Harriet Hosmer, to study Indians at first hand before completing his *Indian Hunter* in New York City's Central Park. A supple and virile composition, it is entirely devoid of sentiment and almost without a touch of the storytelling that makes the work of the period seem so tedious today. Throughout a long career Ward maintained a scrupulous integrity with regard to fact; his work rises above the pedestrian because of the intensity with which he pursued his aim of grasping the truth of his subject. His *African Freedman* (Capitol, Washington, D.C.) is not only a document of abolitionism but also a statement on behalf of human dignity. There is a grave presence in his bronze *Washington*, which stands in front of the portico of the Sub-Treasury Building on Wall Street in New York, looking out over the heads of the scurrying crowds; and there is authority in the *Henry Ward Beecher* in Brooklyn, whose layers of coats somehow add gravity to an awkward yet convincing stance.

Next to the painter Ralph Blakelock, William Rimmer (1816-79) was perhaps the most tragic figure in the history of art in America, and among the most gifted. He belongs—with Hawthorne and Melville, and with Quidor, Inness, and Ryder—to the group of solitary and inward-looking spirits who share such a significant place in our art. Born in England in mysterious circumstances, which led him to believe that he was the son of the lost Dauphin, he early came to America, where he suffered from extreme poverty for almost all of a life doomed to loneliness, hardship, illness, and personal loss. With little education, he set out to teach himself painting, sculpture, etching, lithography, music, medicine, anatomy, and drawing, all of which he mastered through a determination as great as his abilities. In the 1840's he dissected corpses at the Massachusetts Medical College, and by the 1860's he had become one of the foremost anatomists of the century, whose lectures in Boston were attended not only by medical students but by artists as well, among whom were John La Farge, William Morris Hunt, and Daniel Chester French. A dedicated teacher, like Thomas Eakins later, he had a rare capacity to communicate his insights and enthusiasms. He would stand at the blackboard and illustrate his points with chalk drawings of dazzling swift-

William Rimmer: *Falling Gladiator*, bronze, h. 63¼
(The Metropolitan Museum of Art, Rimmer Memorial Society Committee
and Rogers Fund, 1907)

ness—of fighting warriors, charging horsemen, winged angels and demons—swirls of figures in violent motion as if in a Dantesque vision. In 1866 he was appointed director of the art school of Cooper Union in New York, where he set up a curriculum unique for its time in its imaginative approach. But, also like Eakins, he was too independent for the school's trustees, and after four years he returned to Boston.

A small figure he carved in chalk while still in his teens early showed both his sculptural ability and the tragic tenor of his life. Entitled *Despair* (Boston), it communicates an emotional tension few sculptors of the time approached. His *St. Stephen* (Boston), a life-sized head hewn from obdurate granite, is similarly moving. His paintings are charged with an almost demoniacal emotion achieved through strange and subtle color as well as by compositions often turbulent with motion. His drawings, a collection of which was published in 1877 as *Art Anatomy*, are full of energy, and are among the most tautly controlled and most forceful American works of the century. The *Dying Centaur* anticipates Rodin in its doomed heroism stated through formal and physical rather than narrative means. The plaster of his *Falling Gladiator* was exhibited in the Paris Salon of 1861, where critics asked, as they were later to question Rodin's *Age of Bronze*, if it had been cast from a human body, so complete was Rimmer's mastery of anatomical form. It is obvious to anyone today that its passionate intensity could never have been achieved by any such mechanical means. In it he transformed the frustrations and defeat of his own life into a symbol of the nation's tragedy, so eloquently and powerfully does it express the agonizing impact of the conflict then just begun.

William Rimmer: *Flight and Pursuit*, 1872, 18 x 26¼
(Courtesy, Museum of Fine Arts, Boston, Miss Edith Nichols Fund)

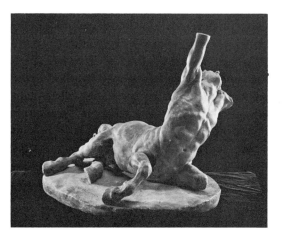

William Rimmer: *Dying Centaur*, 1871, original plaster, h. about 24
(Courtesy, Museum of Fine Arts, Boston, bequest of Miss Caroline H. Rimmer)

V

America Rediscovered: Nineteenth-Century Painting before the Civil War

THE ARTIST AS NATURALIST

On the banks of the Schuylkill, in Philadelphia, there still stands the curious stone house which once belonged to John Bartram (1699–1777) and his son William (1739–1823), and whose garden, now a part of the city's park system, once contained one of the most famous horticultural collections in the world. As a young man, John Bartram was a hard-working Quaker farmer, without money or much education, yet "one day," as he told Crèvecœur, author of *Letters from an American Farmer*, "I was very busy in holding my plough (for thee see'st that I am but a ploughman), and being weary, I ran under the shade of a tree to repose myself. I cast my eyes on a daisy; I plucked it mechanically and viewed it with more curiosity than common country farmers are wont to do, and observed therein very many distinct parts, some perpendicular, some horizontal. 'What a shame,' said my mind, or something that inspired my mind, 'that thee shouldest have employed so many years in tilling the earth and destroying so many flowers and plants without being acquainted with their structures and their uses!' " So he walked to Philadelphia and bought a copy of Linnaeus' great work on plants and a Latin grammar which he studied for three months with a neighboring schoolmaster so that he could read it.

As a result, Bartram became one of the most famous botanists of the age, maintaining correspondence with scholars the world over, and supplying rare plants, shrubs, and trees for botanical gardens, parks, and estates in both Europe and America. He and his son traveled far and wide—beyond the frontier, into the swamps of the Deep South, northward into Canada. The younger Bartram's account of their experiences not only inspired Coleridge and Southey to dreams of founding a utopian settlement on the Susquehanna, but also provided imagery and material for their poetry.

John Bartram had been a friend of Franklin, who gave him one of his new stoves for his house, and of the great scientist Dr. Joseph Priestley, of Benjamin Rush, the famous physician, of Charles Brockden Brown, the novelist, and of Tom Paine, author of *Common Sense* and chief propagandist of the Revolution. From boyhood, William had accompanied his father on the trips during which he collected specimens to send to Lin-

217

John James Audubon: *Snowy Egret*, 1832, pencil, water color, and lacquer, 29¼ x 21¼
(Courtesy of The New-York Historical Society, New York City)

naeus and to various noblemen and scientists from London to St. Petersburg. The son had early learned to make beautiful drawings of flowers and plants, accurate and clear, and also full of a feeling for the beauty of the natural world. The stone house on the Schuylkill became a favorite meeting place for everyone interested in nature and in science. There all received the same warm welcome; they walked through the fields to admire the orchards and plantations of rare trees, and lingered in the famous greenhouse above whose door was the couplet from Pope which summed up their Deist philosophy:

Alexander Wilson: *The Little Owl,*
1805-10,
pen and water color, natural size
(Museum of Comparative Zoology,
Harvard University;
photograph, Houghton Library)

> Slave to no sect, who takes no private road,
> But looks through Nature up to Nature's God.

It was natural that in 1802, when Alexander Wilson (1766–1813) became teacher of the school at nearby Kingsessing, he should have visited the Bartrams, led by his lifelong passion for nature, and that William Bartram's sympathetic interest should have encouraged his studies of ornithology. Wilson, a Paisley weaver, was a poet as well as a self-trained naturalist, and had sought the freedom in America that had been denied him in his native Scotland to express his democratic opinions. Bartram invited him to stay on in the stone house, gave him lessons in drawing and coloring, and introduced him to Alexander Lawson, who later engraved many of the plates for his famous ornithology. In the fall of 1804 Wilson walked to Niagara and back and recorded his adventures in "The Foresters," a poem which appeared in *Port Folio* with his own illustrations. He sent two drawings to Jefferson, who encouraged him to undertake his *American Ornithology.* Wilson thereupon set out on foot to Pittsburgh, and then went alone in a skiff down the Ohio River, stopping at settlements or camping on the bank. From New Orleans he went on horseback to Florida, his only companion besides his horse being a pet parakeet who listened to the Scottish airs he played on his flute.

Wilson collected specimens and made drawings everywhere, and wherever he went his work provided an open-sesame for him. Hearing of his project, bird lovers from the Maritime Provinces to the Gulf sent him information and specimens. Meriwether Lewis told him of his adventures in the West, and learned professors and leading citizens subscribed to his work. He made most of his drawings by candlelight after a day's teaching, for he had to support himself and finance the work, too; yet from 1808 to 1813 he produced eight volumes of his *American Ornithology,* both illustrations and text (the ninth

218

volume was published after his death from his manuscripts in 1814). He wanted to make it the most beautiful book ever published in America, and it remains one of the finest produced anywhere during the period. The plates are crisp and clear, while the text shows a poet's feeling both for language and for nature.

Wilson's was an extraordinary achievement for a solitary man with no resources but his own ability and determination, yet it was overshadowed by the work of another and far greater artist, John James Audubon (1785–1851). The son of a French sea captain who had served under the Count de Grasse during the American Revolution, he was born on his father's estate in Haiti, the child of his father's Creole mistress. He was brought up from the age of six by an indulgent stepmother at Nantes, and then at Couëron in the Loire Valley, where his father retired ten years later. Such education as he received was acquired at Nantes and Rochefort, and he may have studied briefly in Paris with the great Classical painter Jacques-Louis David. To ensure his future, his father sent him as an undisciplined youth of seventeen to America, where he lived on a farm on Perkiomen Creek, not far from Valley Forge, which the older Audubon had bought at the time of the Revolution. There he met Lucy Bakewell, whom he married in 1808.

The young couple moved to Kentucky, where he went into business as a frontier merchant. But the charms of the wild country were far stronger than the demands of business. During boyhood days in France he had spent his time exploring the countryside, collecting birds' nests, and making drawings of birds. He found the wonders of the American wilderness yet more fascinating. After the inevitable financial failure, he eked out a living as an itinerant portraitist and worked briefly as a taxidermist in the Western Museum in Cincinnati, where a few years later a young Vermont Yankee named Hiram Powers was to show his amazing ability to model in wax. Then, inspired by Dr. Daniel Drake, the Museum's founder, Audubon embarked on what was to be the great project of his life, the recording of the birds and animals of North America. All of his amazing energies and abilities, before dissipated in various harebrained business schemes, were mobilized to this end.

The project was an incredibly demanding one, necessitating a tireless search for specimens of wildlife, endless sketching, note taking, record keeping, and the laborious production of drawings, colored and detailed with increasingly critical observation. It was a life which meant years of hardship, not only for himself, but for his wife and their two sons, Victor Gifford and

219

John Woodhouse. Until he became famous in later years, and could afford assistants, he traveled with his gun, his flute, his sketchbooks, and his color box, alone except for the dog which was his constant companion. When in need of money, he drew portraits, gave lessons on the flute or violin, or taught dancing or fencing. During his years of wandering he explored mountains and valleys, swamps and uplands, lakes and rivers, from Canada and the Great Lakes to the Gulf. He went the length of the Ohio and Mississippi rivers, and up the Missouri to the Yellowstone. He traveled the Atlantic coast from southern Labrador to the Dry Tortugas, and the Gulf Coast from Florida to Galveston in the Republic of Texas. And everywhere he went he had fascinating experiences, many of which were recorded in the delightful episodes with which he enlivened his *Ornithological Biography*. In the canebrakes of the Mississippi Delta he found a fugitive slave family. With great courage the father had reunited the family, heartlessly separated by selling parents and children to different plantations, and Audubon arranged to have them taken in by a generous planter who purchased them back from their various owners. In the mosquito-ridden swamps of Florida he saw the battles of bull alligators, and lay at night on the beaches to observe by moonlight the great sea turtles depositing their eggs in the sand.

Starting out at the age of thirty-five on his great undertaking, Audubon faced years of struggle and disappointment as well as adventure. He took his portfolio of drawings of birds to Philadelphia, then the scientific center of the country, to investigate the possible means of publishing his projected *Birds of America*. But he found no support, and New York gave him no more encouragement. Then, following the advice of such interested friends as the painter Thomas Sully and the fellow ornithologist Charles Lucien Bonaparte, a nephew of Napoleon who was then in the United States, he came to an extraordinary decision. Since no American publisher seemed willing to bring out a work to challenge Wilson's, he would try his luck in England and on the Continent. For more than a year not only did the proceeds from Lucy's teaching support the family, but also a portion of the income was regularly set aside for the trip. He gave lessons in French, music, and dancing to add to the travel fund, but his major efforts went into securing specimens, perfecting his technique, and adding to the collection of drawings on which he based his hopes.

In the spring, with savings totaling $1,700, he sailed on the ship *Delos* of Kennebunk from New Orleans for Liverpool, with his precious portfolio and with letters of introduction from such friends as Sully and De Witt Clinton. He found a friendly reception in Liverpool. An exhibition of his drawings at the British Institution there was greeted with enthusiasm, and he went north to Edinburgh, where he met Sir Walter Scott and expressed his admiration for the novelist by noting in his *Journal* that "he looked like Franklin at his best" and reminded him of Benjamin West. The intellectual society of Edinburgh was impressed with his drawings and his fund of knowledge of the natural history of the New World. But best of all, he found in W. H. Lizars a worthy engraver for his plates, and an agreement was worked out whereby Lizars was to engrave and color, at the size of the originals and therefore at life size, a collection of five of his drawings, which Audubon was then to sell to subscribers who, he hoped, would pay for the additional groups of five as they were finished until the whole was complete. He thus undertook to become, on his own, the publisher of a work for which, because of its unusual size and expense, only a limited sale could be expected. It was a risky undertaking and Audubon knew it. And he also knew that he had to commit several years to supervising the quality and accuracy of the plates, all of which had to be colored by hand, and to the selling of sufficient subscriptions at two guineas for each part as it appeared to finance the work as it went along. "With alternate uncertainties of hope and fear," as he wrote in his *Journal,* he determined to go ahead.

In the spring of 1827 the first number of the book was finished, and he set out for London. On the way he stopped in Newcastle, which he thought a mean and grimy place after "fair Edinburgh." There he called on the aged Thomas Bewick, famous for his sensitive wood engravings, and watched him with huge hands expertly cut a block, "with as much ease as I can feather a bird," using delicate tools which he had made himself. Audubon went on to York and then to Leeds and Manchester, showing his work and seeking subscriptions. After a stay in Liverpool he finally arrived in London, where he knew his project faced the critical test of success or failure according to the number of subscribers he could secure. He had just begun to deliver his letters of introduction to those whose support was most necessary when a note from Lizars bluntly informed him that his colorists were on strike, and that Audubon would have to find others in London or the supply of plates would be interrupted. In a flurry of anxiety, Audubon searched the unfamiliar city for colorists. Finally he met a young engraver, Robert Havell, who not only undertook to color the plates but also to make the engravings for subsequent issues as well, and at a lower price than Lizars had charged. Again Audubon could apply all his attention to seeking new subscribers, delivering new issues, exhibiting his work, speaking to various scientific societies and other groups, to the tiresome business of showing his picture to one potential patron after another, and to producing new drawings for the engraver.

He was appreciative of the hospitality with which he was entertained and of the interest shown in his work, but he was disturbed by the signs along the English highways threatening trespassers, and he was disgusted at the idea of shooting half-tame animals and birds in vast quantities as sport. During the long and elaborate dinners to which he was sometimes invited, he would think of the "banks of Thompson's Creek, on the Fourth of July, swallowing the roasted eggs of a large Soft-shelled Turtle," or of Kentucky, "at Henderson, at good Dr. Rankin's, listening to the howling of the wolves, while sitting in security, eating well roasted and jellied venison." When visiting in country houses he would often rise before dawn to sneak outside to enjoy the freshness of the wet grass in bare feet, or strip and dive into a lake or river to escape for a moment the formal patterns of life which he had always done his best to avoid. He had regretfully cut his hair short before going to London because his Scottish friends had told him that the English were very conventional about such matters. But there was no disguising the free stride of the frontiersman and the natural dignity of a man with the assurance which comes, not only from years of self-reliant experience in the wilderness, but also from the sense of purpose, so hard-won in his case, which was the result of his wholehearted dedication to his work.

As in America, Audubon replenished his pocketbook by his art. He sold drawings and made paintings to order after his water colors to support himself and to pay the engravers and colorers. He kept his *Journal* faithfully, starting each day with a greeting to his beloved Lucy and ending with an affectionate good night. Often he wrote of his homesickness for America, for the life of the woods. He was disturbed by "the constant evidence of the contrast between the rich and the poor," he wrote. But he made many friends, and he was especially pleased when Charles Bonaparte looked him up in London and the two sat up late talking of experiences in America. He visited Cambridge and Oxford, where he dined at several of the colleges (Cambridge subscribed to his work, but Oxford did not). It was in the latter place that he was introduced to a judge on his way to court as another possible subscriber, whom he remembered as "a monstrously ugly old man, with a wig that would make a capital bed for an Osage Indian during the whole of a cold winter on the Arkansas River." When he went to France, he noted, to his amusement, that his passport described his complexion as "copper red," since as an American he must be an Indian. In Paris he was hospitably entertained by the famous statesman and naturalist Baron Cuvier. He was greeted by Prince d'Essling as "the gentleman of whom we have heard so much, the man of the woods, who has made so many and such wonderful drawings." He reminisced about America with the Duc d'Orléans, and was greeted by Baron François Gérard, the fashionable portrait painter of the period, as "the king of ornithological painters." He was asked to address the usual meetings of learned societies, something he had learned to do with good grace in Great Britain, but he found the France of the Restoration a far poorer place, having received more subscriptions from Manchester than from Paris, so he returned to England. He finally sailed from Portsmouth for America on April 1, 1829, after a three-year absence, on the packet ship *Columbia,* which he chose, as he noted in his *Journal,* "on account of her name."

It was with a sense of great relief that he returned to the search for new birds and the drawing of those illustrations not yet completed. His sons were now in their teens and proved to be admirable assistants. He followed a schedule of only four hours of sleep a night, devoting the rest of the days to exploring the Great Pine Swamp from his headquarters at Camden, New Jersey. "I wish I had eight pairs of hands," he wrote, "and another body to shoot the specimens." But the work went so well that in 1830 he and his wife embarked for England. He saw many of his old friends and settled in Edinburgh, where he started his *Ornithological Biography.* Finding no publisher for it, he began publishing it himself in 1831, finally completing the project in 1839. After a stay in Paris, they returned to America, and again he was off to the coast of Florida, to Maine, and to New Brunswick. In 1833 he went to Labrador with his son John and a group of Boston friends in the schooner *Ripley.* Victor was in England, supervising the finishing of plates and publication of further parts of the great work. Audubon entrusted Victor with entire authority, writing that if he deemed "it wise to remove the publication of the work to this country, I advise you to settle in Boston; *I have faith in the Bostonians.*"

The *Ripley* sailed from Eastport, Maine. "The hold of the

vessel has been floored," he wrote Victor the last day of May, "and our great table solidly fixed in a tolerably good light under the main hatch." Audubon drew whenever possible, no matter how rough the sea or how stormy the weather. He had breakfast at three-thirty, and noted that "John . . . is overcoming his habit of sleeping late, as I call him every morning at four, and we have famous long days." They explored the rocky, treacherous coast of Nova Scotia, past Cape Breton Island, anchoring in small harbors and dining on lobsters speared in the shallow water, on fresh codfish, on mackerel, and on "hashed Eider Ducks." They approached as close as the heavy seas would allow to the Gannet Rocks, which looked completely snow-covered, so thickly were they populated with the breeding birds.

Audubon averaged seventeen hours of drawing a day whenever he could, and even he felt the pace. "I am much fatigued and wet to the very skin," he wrote in his *Journal*, "but, oh! we found the nest of a Peregrine Falcon on a tremendous cliff, with a young one about a week old, quite white with down; the parents flew fiercely at our eyes." With relief they finally turned back, and when the *Ripley* put in to a small harbor on St. Georges Bay, Newfoundland, they celebrated by attending a ball held in their honor by the inhabitants of the little fishing village. John spelled the local fiddler and others accompanied with flute and flageolet when not dancing with the fishermen's wives and daughters. Many toasts were drunk to England, France, and the United States, and to absent wives and sweethearts. Audubon himself went to bed before midnight, but the rest stayed till nearly dawn, and the sounds of the music across the water proved that the festivities continued until after day had broken. The cabin of the *Ripley* was filled with specimens, bird skins, "large jars . . . with the bodies of rare birds, fishes, quadrupeds, and reptiles, as well as molluscous animals." There were "several pets, too, Gulls, Cormorants, Guillemots, Puffins, Hawks, and a Raven," and many drawings had been completed.

After a winter in Charleston it was necessary to return to England with the new material. John and Victor were able to spend several months studying painting on the Continent while their father saw the continuation of the *Ornithology*; then Victor and his mother stayed on in London while John and his father returned in 1836. Again they spent the winter in Charleston, with Dr. John Bachman, whose two daughters the two Audubon sons eventually married. A cruise exploring the Gulf Coast provided the final material for the *Ornithology*. In 1838 Audubon's great project was done: the double elephant folio depicting at

John James Audubon: *Woodchucks,*
1841,
pencil and water color, 23 x 33¾
(The Pierpont Morgan Library)

224

life size *The Birds of America, from Original Drawings, With 435 Plates Showing 1,065 Figures,* consisting of eighty-seven numbers of five hand-colored copperplate engravings each, published in four volumes (1827-38). The accompanying text, entitled *Ornithological Biography,* was issued in five volumes from 1831 to 1839.

A new project followed, *The Viviparous Quadrupeds of North America,* the first volume of which came out in 1845. The family had moved to Minnie's Land, an estate in what is now a part of New York City, now memorialized by the present Audubon Park, but then still a wilderness on the banks of the Hudson, with a "Painting House" among the trees, and large enclosures with deer, elk, moose, bears, wolves, foxes, and other animals nearby. John and his father worked on the *Quadrupeds,* while Victor was the businessman. It was impossible for Audubon not to return to the wilds again; in 1842 he spent several months in the Canadian woods, and in the following year accompanied an expedition of the American Fur Company up the Missouri for a nine-month journey, following the route of Lewis and Clark, which delighted him, though he admitted to feeling no longer as young as he had been. He stayed with the Bakewells in Louisville, where, he wrote, "I did enjoy myself famously well, with dancing, dinner-parties, etc." From there he proceeded to St. Louis by boat, then up the Missouri, and, finally, to Fort Union, stopping on the way to see the Mandan Indian village described by George Catlin in his famous *Indian Tribes of North America.* He spent some time at Fort Union, collecting specimens for the *Quadrupeds,* exploring the area, and taking a trip up the Yellowstone, before leaving by boat down the river. He stopped at Fort Pierre, Fort Leavenworth, and other places on his return trip to St. Louis. He reached Minnie's Land on November 6. With long hair and full beard, now entirely white, he made such "a

John James Audubon:
Osprey and the Otter and the Salmon,
1844, 38 x 62
(Arizona State University at Tempe,
gift of Oliver B. James)

225

fine and striking appearance" in a green coat with fur collar and cuffs that John painted his portrait in it before letting his father shave.

After that, others did the traveling. John went to the Southwest and sent home drawings and paintings from Texas and California, the latter still a state of Mexico. John's work delighted his father, and when Audubon died in his seventies, on January 27, 1851, John carried on. The plates were published in two volumes (1845-48), and Dr. Bachman completed the text in three (1846-54). Though John's plates for the *Quadrupeds*, about half of the whole, are the work of a first-rate animal painter, and display a real feeling for the drama and beauty of animal life, they cannot equal the fire and spirit of his father's, throughout whose work the passion and the feeling of the immediacy of the experience never flag, as the bold and various compositions express the quickness and the mystery of wildlife.

Birds of America represents an achievement without parallel. In a letter to Bachman in 1831 Audubon had written, "I have labored like a cart horse for the last thirty years on a single work." The result of those labors remains as a permanent monument to one man's determination, ability, vision, and love of nature, the "landmark of my existence" he so hoped to leave behind for his countrymen so that they, too, might share the sense of wonder which gave him lifelong joy.

In 1820, while Audubon was in Cincinnati working at the Western Museum and conducting a drawing school, the expedition of Major Stephen H. Long on the river steamer *Western Engineer* passed through the city on the way to explore the unknown upper reaches of the Mississippi and Minnesota rivers. Many years later Audubon recalled showing his drawings to Major Long and his companions. Among the members of the group was Titian Ramsay Peale (1799–1885), the son of the famous painter Charles Willson Peale and a distinguished artist and naturalist himself. At nineteen he had accompanied a group which explored the south Atlantic coast, and was later to spend some time in Florida collecting specimens and making drawings to illustrate two of the four volumes of the *American Ornithology* of Charles Bonaparte, which appeared from 1825 to 1833. He later went to the South Seas with a government expedition which brought back important information on the culture of Polynesia and observations on Antarctica. Ably instructed by his elder brother Rubens, his work is well up to family standard and reflects that lively curiosity and sharp objectivity characteristic of all the Peales. Titian was for a time director of the Peale Museum, which Audubon considered "so valuable and so finely arranged." The basic concept of the Museum, with its purpose of displaying, in proper Linnaean order, the whole nature of America, combined art and science, much as did the projects of Audubon, Wilson, and others, and it was natural that a similar curiosity about the world and its marvels should run through the work of all the Peales, as it did through that of many other American artists. It appears especially in the delightful still-life paintings of Rubens and Raphaelle Peale, and of James Peale and his daughters Anna,

James Peale: *Still Life, Fruit,*
1820-30, 16 x 22
(Collection of The Newark Museum,
gift of Dr. and Mrs. Earl LeRoy Wood)

Margaretta, and Sarah. Their pictures owe little to the decorative and generally very routine Dutch or Flemish-derived still lifes, examples of which were imported to decorate the walls of eighteenth-century American houses and appear listed in the inventories, especially of families of Netherlandish ancestry in New York and the valley of the Hudson. Instead, these later works are composed with a deliberate simplicity which shows the artists' respect for the subject, not as decorative material to be manipulated arbitrarily into elaborate compositions, but as the fruit of nature, painted appreciatively for its own qualities of beauty and seen freshly and directly, and also with wonder and delight. The subjects are not the opulent masses of flowers, lush fruits, and piles of dead game of the earlier periods, but

227

bunches of grapes, pears, apples, strawberries, and cherries from the vines and trees in the family garden or from the countryside nearby—the bloom still upon them, the foliage fresh and crisp—or a fish caught in a neighboring stream, with a crock, an onion, and a sprig of herbs, or flowers from the border or the roadside.

Similarly, the still lifes of the academically untrained painters—a sliced watermelon, hard-boiled eggs on a plate, or an array of fruits and vegetables on a table with a bunch of field flowers—are expressions of thanksgiving for nature's bounty, the reward for all the labor of felling the trees, of clearing the land, and, finally, of planting and careful cultivation. Like the expertly painted still lifes of the Peales, these, too, reveal the poetry of everyday things, which they celebrate with gratitude and quiet satisfaction.

Anonymous: *Tomatoes, Fruit, and Flowers*, c. 1850, 20 x 31½
(Courtesy, Museum of Fine Arts, Boston, M. and M. Karolik Collection)

THE SEARCH FOR AN AMERICAN ART

In 1825 James Brooks's article "Our Own Country" appeared in the *Knickerbocker Magazine* to tell Americans that God had foretold the country's future greatness through the dramatic landscape of the continent: "It resounds all along the crags of the Alleghenies. It is uttered in the thunder of Niagara. It is heard in the roar of the two oceans, from the great Pacific to the ramparts of the Bay of Fundy. His finger has written it in the broad expanse of our Inland Sea, and traced it out by the mighty Father of Waters." Here was manifest destiny, nature as an expression of divine approval, and high romantic rhetoric to boot. Again and again the critics list the grandeurs of the natural scene, and call for an art "commensurate with our mountains and rivers—commensurate with Niagara, the Alleghenies, and the Great Lakes. . . ." It was in vain that some, James Russell Lowell among them, pointed out, according to Perry Miller in *The Raven and the Whale*, that "There is no system of nature . . . which enables this continent 'to produce great rivers, lakes, and mountains, mammoth pumpkins, Kentuckey giants, two-headed calves,' which by the same token will bring forth great poets and artists."

Two able young Americans, John Vanderlyn and Samuel F. B. Morse, were seeking to make their contribution to American art by painting pictures based on themes of grandeur, inspired by what they saw in the galleries and museums of Europe. The artistic abilities of John Vanderlyn (1775–1852) are demonstrated in his *Ariadne Asleep on the Island of Naxos* (1812), which remained the best nude to be painted by an American artist for many a decade. After living in· the stimulating atmosphere of Paris, where he was honored by Napoleon with a gold medal for his *Marius amid the Ruins of Carthage* (San Francisco), Vanderlyn returned to New York in 1815, to find a country uninterested in the kind of pictures he wanted to paint. He tried his hand at a 165-foot-long panorama of Versailles, to form a continuous circle to be viewed from within, a particularly fascinating example of a notion that many painters had found to be of great public interest and of some profit to themselves from paid admissions. (Robert Fulton [1765–1815], for example, one of the many pupils of Benjamin West, supported

229

John Vanderlyn: *Ariadne Asleep on the Island of Naxos*, 1812, 69 x 88
(The Pennsylvania Academy of the Fine Arts)

himself in Paris, while working on his inventions of the sub-
marine and the steamboat, by painting and exhibiting the first
panorama seen there, a dramatic nocturnal view of *The Burning
of Moscow.*) Vanderlyn obtained a lease from the City of New
York for a corner of the park across from City Hall, constructed
a building he called a rotunda, and showed, not only the *Versailles*, but also his *Ariadne* and other works, including copies
of the old masters. After ten difficult years, the venture failed.
Discouraged and defeated, he eventually retreated to his birthplace, Kingston on the Hudson, driven to portrait painting—
which he hated, as an inferior and mechanical branch of art—for
a meager living.

Samuel F. B. Morse (1791–1872), inspired by West's and
Copley's successes with great historical paintings in London,
early expressed his ambition to "revive the splendor of the
fifteenth century; to rival the genius of a Raphael, a Michelangelo, or a Titian." Like Vanderlyn, he looked down on portrait
painting, though he produced many excellent portraits, among

230

them one of the best of that period, the life-sized, full-length *Lafayette* commissioned by the City of New York, which still hangs in Mangin's and McComb's handsome City Hall. The picture was painted swiftly and brilliantly in the winter of 1825-26, after the old man had revisited the country toward whose independence he had so wholeheartedly contributed his youthful services almost half a century earlier. As the last of the military leaders of the Revolution, Lafayette had become a living symbol of the ideals of that generation, and it is in this way that Morse presents him, a solitary figure against a sunset sky, with the busts of his admired friends Washington and Franklin, both long since passed into history, at his side.

Even such undoubted successes did not reconcile Morse to a career limited to portraiture. He became the head of the National Academy of Design in New York, of which the architect Ithiel Town and the painter Thomas Cole were founding members, and gave the first formal course in art instruction in America. But before long his restless imagination found another outlet in a direction that was to have great appeal to many creative American minds in the years to come. On his voyage back to America in 1832 on the packet *Sully*, with all the pictures he had painted in Europe (including the famous view of the interior of the Salon Carré of the Louvre, in which his friend James Fenimore Cooper may be seen in the background), he got into a conversation about the exciting new experiments of Michael Faraday in "drawing sparks from a magnet." It immediately struck him that such sparks could be used in a code to send messages over a wire. "When you hear of the magnetic telegraph," he told the *Sully*'s captain, "remember it was invented on your ship." And thereafter all of Morse's energies flowed into this new channel of activity.

Emerson's address to the Phi Beta Kappa Society at Harvard in 1837, published among his essays as "The American Scholar," was as hortatory as, if less windy than, the article by James Brooks. "Our day of dependence," Emerson wrote, "our long apprenticeship . . . draws to a close. . . .We have listened too long to the courtly muses of Europe. . . . We will walk on our own feet; we will work with our own hands; we will speak our own minds. . . ." His prophecy was already being fulfilled. While all the talk about Americanism was going on, a genuine flowering of American art was taking place, but it was not appearing where it was supposed to, in those themes of grandeur which Vanderlyn and Morse had wanted so to paint and which had also proved the defeat of Allston. The new nation,

Samuel F. B. Morse: *Lafayette*, 1825-26, 96 x 64 (Art Commission of the City of New York)

in its aspiration and its insecurity, sought its cultural identity in the American scene, in the variety and extent of the gigantic continent, in the overwhelming facts of nature, and in such traditions as had been established during a comparatively short history. Artists and writers were aware of their country's shortcomings in the latter respect. Many deplored the lack of picturesque ruins and of the richness of association such as Europe had (Hawthorne called ours a "landscape without shadows"); while others, perhaps a bit defensively, boasted that the American countryside was unencumbered by relics of past barbarism and cruelty, and lay open to receive the imprint of a new chapter of the world's history, which was to look to the future and not to the past, and to establish the shape of things to come.

Inspired by the writings of Irving and Cooper, Thomas Cole rediscovered the landscape of America as a source, not only for literature, but also for painting, and thus was the initiator of what was in fact the first national school of painting in America, just as the Greek Revival became the first national style in architecture.

"You may fear perhaps," he wrote, "that the wonderful scenery of Switzerland will destroy my relish for my own. . . . Must I tell you that neither the Alps, nor the Apennines, no, nor Etna itself have dimmed in my eyes the beauty of our own Catskills? It seems to me that I look on American scenery, if it were possible, with increased pleasure. It has its own peculiar charm —a something not found elsewhere. I am content with nature, would that I were with art." Cole spent a lifetime trying to capture those qualities he felt so strongly in the natural scene—the wildness, the feeling of limitless extent, of an almost overpowering vastness of a land still so little known that there was an aura of mystery about it, on which man had so far made so small an impression that it seemed to come "fresh from the creation," each valley, each river, each lake, each mountain range a new discovery. Only after the frontier had been pushed westward, and the pioneer's struggle for survival had been succeeded by the ordered life of farm and village, did nature cease to be a hostile force to be feared and battled. Only then were there time and opportunity as well as inclination to contemplate the grandeur of the country with aesthetic appreciation, and to find pleasure in the "wild and romantic qualities" described by Washington Irving, the "rocky precipices mantled with primeval forests; deep gorges walled in by beetling cliffs, with torrents tumbling as it were from the sky; the savage glens rarely trodden except by the hunter."

No American better illustrated this mood of romantic rediscovery than Cole, foremost of the artists misleadingly called the Hudson River School. Actually the scope of their art was far wider than that label suggests, since their work was the expression in landscape of the Romantic movement in America. They were the pictorial counterparts of Irving and Cooper and Bryant. Theirs was a part of that return to nature which was basic to the Romantic attitude, a turning to nature outwardly into the world, exploring all the wonders "of our own bright land," of which Bryant reminded Cole on the eve of his departure for Europe:

> Lone lakes—savannahs where the bison roves—
> Rocks rich with summer garlands—solemn streams—
> Skies where the desert eagle wheels and screams—
> Spring bloom and autumn blaze of boundless groves.

It was also a turning to nature inwardly, an exploration of the self, the feelings, the emotional and imaginative depths of the inner life to discover "the craft with which the world is made," in the words of Emerson, "the power which does not respect quantity, which makes the whole and the particle its equal channel, delegates its smile to the morning, and distills its essence into every drop of rain." Thus the expression of Romanticism in the arts in America represented a reaffirmation of that individualism which had been forged by experience of the impersonal and unfamiliar circumstances of the environment of the New World. But its focus had shifted from the practical to the ideal, a luxury which could be afforded only by a generation which knew and accepted the fact of the conquest, at least along the eastern coast and in the longer-settled areas, of that wild nature which had been to the first comers a fearful and "howling wilderness."

In painting, as in literature, the conscious emphasis was on subject, yet in both the distinction lay deeper, in the attitudes with which the artists approached and interpreted that subject. Cole and his followers pursued different aims from those which animated their European contemporaries, and their ideals prevailed until late in the century. Similarly, following the early and tentative trials of Alvan Fisher, a number of artists rediscovered the poetry of everyday things which increasingly took on, with the rapid growth of industrialism toward mid-century, the nostalgia of a simpler and less urban existence, and became the subject of a flourishing school of genre painting celebrating rural virtues and rustic joys, until it dissolved into the stereotypes of Currier & Ives and the saccharine sentimentalities of the latter part of the century.

233

Thomas Birch: *Skating*, c. 1830, 20 x 30
(Courtesy, Museum of Fine Arts, Boston, M. and M. Karolik Collection)

THOMAS COLE AND THE BEGINNINGS OF THE HUDSON RIVER SCHOOL

Cole had few American predecessors as landscape painters. As early as 1800 Ralph Earl (1751–1801) had recorded the spacious view *Looking East from Leicester Hill* (Worcester) across the green fields of his native Litchfield, Connecticut, but he was primarily a portrait painter whose interest in landscape was literal and incidental. Thomas Birch (1779–1851), of Philadelphia, was trained in the European topographical tradition, and developed, especially in his marines, an airiness and sweep which represent considerable enlargement of that formula but rarely if ever transcend it. Robert Salmon (c. 1780–after 1841), "a small man, most unmistakably Scotch in his appearance and conversation . . . of very quick temper, and one who generally called a spade a spade," turned up in Boston in 1828 after having painted, according to the catalogue he kept all his life, his 627th painting, with a mature style derived from the Baroque seascape, and established himself in a ramshackle studio with living quarters on the marine railway wharf overlooking the harbor. The nautical accuracy of his ships bears out his account of having been in the British navy, though virtually nothing is known of his earlier life.

John Trumbull (1756–1843), the gifted but irascible son of Governor Jonathan Trumbull of Connecticut, onetime aide of Washington and pupil of West, also did occasional landscapes as well as his justly famous historical paintings of the stirring events of the Revolution. Touched by the coming spirit of Romanticism, he produced a series of views of waterfalls, including several of Niagara. Although his approach is rather stiff and unimaginative, as was his personality, a sense of grandeur comes through in his Niagara pictures, though they lack the qualities of those by John Vanderlyn. The latter, Allston's companion in Paris, was unique among Americans in that he had chosen to study there instead of in London. He was the protégé of the notorious Aaron Burr, vice-president under Jefferson and murderer of Alexander Hamilton in the famous duel on the wooded heights of Weehawken, New Jersey. Vanderlyn's earliest views, dating from 1801, are the first paintings of what was considered America's greatest natural wonder since its discovery by Europeans in the seventeenth century, but his best was

Samuel F. B. Morse:
View from Apple Hill,
c. 1829, 22¾ x 29½
(New York State Historical Association,
Cooperstown, N.Y.)

his *Niagara* of 1827, now in the Senate House Museum in his native Kingston, New York. It has the blasted tree of Allston's *Elijah,* but otherwise still remains largely descriptive rather than expressive. The falls appear in the distance, while a man with an ox team and his farm dog suggest the taming of the wilderness of which the falls themselves are the symbol. These and the other landscapes done in the first quarter of the century were occasional work of men who were primarily portraitists or the efforts of those who were trying to establish a reputation as history painters. Into the latter category fall the American scenes by S. F. B. Morse, such as his charming *View from Apple Hill,* which is rather a portrait of a place which also includes smaller portraits of two members of the family that lived there.

Only two artists during these years really devoted themselves to landscapes, Alvan Fisher (1792–1863) of Needham, Massachusetts, and Thomas Doughty (1793–1856) of Philadelphia.

Fisher worked for many years as a clerk in a general store in Dedham, not far from Boston, and his earliest efforts appear as sketches in the margins of the store's account books. He was largely self-taught, though he studied briefly in Boston with John R. Penniman of Roxbury, who did such excellent decorative painting as the still life of sea shells which enriches the top of a luxurious semicircular commode of mahogany and satinwood made by Thomas Seymour of Boston for Elias Hasket Derby of Salem in 1809. According to an inscription in one of his sketchbooks, Fisher took up landscape painting professionally in 1815. He increasingly turned to scenes of rural life in New England, which were unique in their day and establish him as the leader in another aspect of the rediscovery of America—the recognition of the charm and also of the significance and dignity of everyday life—which was to lead to the works of William Sidney Mount, Eastman Johnson, the early Winslow Homer, and others, in a tradition of American genre painting of considerable variety.

Thomas Doughty, however, developed into a more accomplished artist. A native of Philadelphia, he gave up the trade of leather merchant and was listed as a landscape painter in the Philadelphia directory for 1820. He was an inveterate hunter and fisherman, and it was probably his love of sport which first aroused his artistic interest in the natural scene; his many paintings of woodland, lake, and stream are enlivened by tiny figures of solitary fishermen or of hunters with gun under arm and a dog trotting alongside. With the encouragement of Robert Gilmor of Baltimore, one of the leading patrons of the day, Doughty became the first American to specialize in landscape, and he

Thomas Doughty:
View of Baltimore from "Beach Hill,"
1822, 14¼ x 18¼
(Courtesy, Museum of Fine Arts,
Boston, M. and M. Karolik Collection)

made a successful career of it. In 1821 Gilmor praised "his studies from Nature on the spot, which are his best performances," an interesting remark because it implies that Doughty did outdoor painting. This method is supposed not to have been employed before Corot's work in Italy from about 1825, and was later used by the Barbizon School, which led to French Impressionism. A charming and freely handled oil sketch entitled *View of Baltimore from "Beach Hill,"* Gilmor's estate, dated 1822, is probably an example of the kind of work which won him patronage and praise. Sully's influence helped to enrich his palette; he traveled and exhibited at home and abroad, and in Boston he was briefly the art teacher of the attractive invalid Sophia Peabody, who was to become Mrs. Nathaniel Hawthorne. His pictures were widely reproduced in gift books and annuals. His style always remained allied to the topographical tradition, though in later years he developed a silvery tonality and a generality of treatment which added a breath of the romantic.

Thomas Cole (1801-48) was seventeen when he and his family came from England to America. They landed at Philadelphia and then set out by wagon for Ohio. Though a brief experience with engraving had been his only art instruction, he taught drawing and painting to help out his family, then decided to try his luck as an itinerant portrait painter. With a pack on his back, he made his way from one frontier village to another, entertaining himself and others with his flute, and spending the night with hospitable settlers who were glad to talk with a pleasant young stranger of twenty and hear the news he had

237

picked up on his journey. But he found that wherever he went other painters had just preceded him, and when he did get a commission he was paid not in money but in goods, so he returned penniless to Pittsburgh and then to Philadelphia. He drew at the Pennsylvania Academy, and eked out an existence with whatever odd jobs he could find, such as japanning tinware and decorating bellows. Two years later he packed up his painting equipment again and set out for New York.

In 1825 three Catskill landscapes in the window of Coleman's frame shop caught the frosty eye of old Colonel John Trumbull. Deeply impressed, he immediately bought one of them for $25, and carried it over to show his friend William Dunlap, who years before had been a fellow student in London, and who was to be, in his *History of the Rise and Progress of the Arts of Design in the United States*, published in 1834, the first chronicler of the arts in America. Equally enthusiastic, Dunlap bought one for himself, and together they sought out the twenty-four-year-old artist to congratulate him on his work. What a change it must have been for Cole, a shy young man who had spent his recent years without adequate clothing or food in pursuit of an ideal entirely his own. He wanted to produce not the fashionable high-style subject piece so popular in Europe, or the necessary face-painting which seemed all one could sell in the United States, but to portray the American scene in all the grandeur and freshness which so impressed him. The genial Philip Hone, diary-keeping ex-mayor of New York, also acquired his pictures; and in the following year Cole was one of the founding members of the National Academy of Design, in whose initial exhibition he had three paintings. He settled in the town of Catskill, whence he wandered the countryside, exploring far into the mountains, visiting Niagara Falls and the White Mountains (where he climbed Mt. Chocorua), and recording all in his sketchbooks.

Cole had American forebears and so had convinced his family that their future lay in the United States. But the fact that he was brought up in the milder, more pastoral landscape of England may have made him all the more sensitive to the special qualities of the American scene, just as only in Europe did the lore of the Hudson and its Dutch past become clear enough to Irving so that he could set it down on paper in "The Legend of Sleepy Hollow" and the tale of "Rip Van Winkle." (Similarly, Cooper wrote what Balzac considered the "masterpiece of literary landscape painting," *The Prairie*, in Paris.) It was Thomas Cole's function to show his fellow Americans the epic qualities of their native landscape.

238

From the beginning his pictures were completely outside the topographical tradition. They were not attempts to describe a place but to express a spirit and a mood of nature meaningful to man. During lonely boyhood years he had sought the solace of the English countryside to forget for the moment the dreariness of life in a Lancashire factory town. It was then that a book describing the beauties of the Ohio Valley had first fired his imagination with the vision of America. Years of bitter poverty to follow—in Pittsburgh, Philadelphia, and New York—had been made bearable for him through his love of nature. All his life he walked, daily if possible, through forests and fields, alone with sketchbook and flute, but never feeling alone because nature was all around him. Like Cooper's Natty Bumppo, he saw in the wilderness "creation! . . . all creation, lad . . . and none know how often the hand of God is seen in the wilderness, but them that rove it. . . ." "To walk with nature as a poet" he wrote, "is the necessary condition of a perfect artist." Typically for the Romantic period, his notebooks contain almost as many verses as sketches.

His first return trip across the Atlantic in 1829 was made possible by Robert Gilmor of Baltimore. He also had the benefit of the advice, through a mutual friend, of Washington Irving, who felt that half of Cole's time should be spent in England; there Turner was the leader in the landscape field. Then, after a short stay in France and a couple of months or so in Switzerland, all the rest of the time should be devoted to Italy. "You say that your friend is a passionate admirer of nature," Irving wrote. "Let him never lose his love for her. . . . The young artist should study nature and pictures together." He followed Irving's advice to seek out the works of "the best masters"—Claude Lorrain, Titian, Nicolas and Gaspard Poussin, and Salvator Rosa—and he especially admired, as he wrote Gilmor, Claude and the younger Poussin. With London as his headquarters he worked diligently, producing a number of paintings. These were included in the Royal Academy exhibition, but, to his chagrin, they were skied, being hung in the top row close to the ceiling, to give major place to what he felt were minor works by minor artists. So he was happy enough in the spring of 1831 to pack up and cross the Channel.

He did not stay long in Paris, for the current French taste for the sensational struck him as exaggerated and undignified, so he set out for Italy. He went down the Rhone (which reminded him of the Hudson) and, like the young Charles Bulfinch nearly half a century earlier, continued by boat to Leghorn. During nine weeks in Florence he enjoyed the companionship of the American sculptor Horatio Greenough, who had recently settled there. He explored the valley of the Arno and the Tuscan countryside, and was deeply impressed by Volterra, whose medieval walls surmount a yet more ancient Etruscan citadel. In Rome he found a studio which was to be his headquarters for the next seven months. It was said once to have belonged to his hero, Claude Lorrain, and was situated in the Via Babuino, not far from the Piazza di Spagna, in the district which has been a center of artistic life in Rome for centuries.

Cole did not think much more of contemporary Italian painting than he had of the French, but he was overwhelmed by Raphael's great fresco *The School of Athens*, and by other works of the old masters. Though Cole wrote that Europe's natural scenery could not equal America's, he found much food for the imagination in the evidences of time and history—the ruined temples and the hoary relics of the Middle Ages, all abundantly patinated with age. He saw and painted the landscape of Europe just as he had that of America, but now with a freer and surer brush, his mind filled with thoughts of the passage of time, of the transitoriness, not only of individual life, but also of whole ages, epochs, and civilizations.

Cole had also reached the conviction that there is a music of color. "I believe," he wrote, "that colors are capable of affecting the mind, by combination, degree, and arrangement, like sound." Color was the subject of much thought among the painters of the Romantic movement, and though few if any carried the idea of communication through color as far as Allston, there were many experimenting to enrich a palette somewhat dulled and limited by Classicism. Among these artists was a group of Germans whose leaders were Philip Otto Runge and Caspar David Friedrich. Similarities of approach between Cole and these slightly older painters seem too great for coincidence. They looked at nature emotionally and poetically, finding there an experience which was not, as was to be the case with the French Impressionists, a purely visual delight, but, instead, a personal and deeply moving symbolic one. It is very doubtful that Cole ever saw the work of Runge or Friedrich, but it is highly possible that he became acquainted with their theories at second hand through members of the German colony in Rome.

He seems also to have had the idea of a kind of color organ, with translucent sheets in various hues activated by a keyboard so that they would rise before a lamp in whatever combinations, chords, or sequence the operator might desire. Such notions

240

were the natural result of the attitudes of the times. In fact, Runge planned something which later would be called a "happening." His idea was far more grandiose, however, than such usually somewhat shabby shockers. He conceived a combination of pictorial, musical, and architectural elements, including a chorus, a long poem for libretto, and symphonic music supplied by colored instruments, each of which were to project a color as well as a tone, so that the walls and whole interior of the specially constructed building would be suffused in visual and aural harmonies joined with a balletlike choral performance. About the only thing left out was some sort of enlistment of the sense of smell; and there actually was a scent organ invented during the period, though it remained for a later age to conjecture the "feelies." With this sort of thing in the air, it is not remarkable that Cole, too, should have experimented with a systematic use of color as a means of emotional expression.

Thomas Cole:
The Course of Empire—Destruction,
1835-36, 51 x 76
(Courtesy of The New-York Historical
Society, New York City)

While still in Florence, he started what he called a "romantic landscape with appropriate savage figures," which proved to be a trial run for the first of the five canvases of *The Course of Empire.* The very concept of this series emphasizes the artistic weaknesses of the Romantic approach as well as the breadth of thought and depth of imagination which it stimulated. It was to comprise five scenes (which might equally well have been thought of as five books of what Cooper considered an epic, five acts of an opera, or five movements of a symphony, elaborately orchestrated in every detail) to show the development of man from *The Savage State,* through *The Arcadian or Pastoral State* to *The Consummation of Empire,* an architectural fantasy giving

241

Thomas Cole: *The Titan's Goblet,*
1833, 19⅜ x 16⅛
(The Metropolitan Museum of Art,
gift of Samuel Avery, Jr., 1904)

the effect of an opera or motion-picture set, colossal even by Hollywood standards, and realized to a degree of detail to win the admiration of the most spectacle-minded movie mogul. In *Destruction* the imperial city is shown sacked by a barbarian horde, while the final *Desolation* is a Virgilian landscape showing the world of Bryant's *Thanatopsis:*

> . . . the dead are there:
> And millions in those solitudes, since first
> The flight of years began, have laid them down
> In their last sleep—the dead reign there alone.

Cole's Italian experience had also strengthened a vein of fantasy which had already appeared in a small picture of 1833 —*The Titan's Goblet,* an amazing work of surrealist intensity— and was to recur in later years. Two years after the completion of *The Course of Empire,* Cole painted for William van Rensselaer a pair of pictures entitled *Departure* and *Return* (Corcoran), based on memories of medieval monuments seen in Europe, and reflecting the fast-rising taste for the Middle Ages inspired by the poetry and prose of Scott and the ballads of Uhland and Chamisso, widely known through Bryant's translations. With the best of the architecture of Alexander Jackson Davis, Richard Upjohn, and James Renwick, Jr., these paintings represent the height of the Gothic Revival in the United States.

The problems of architecture which Cole had encountered in painting the central episode of *The Course of Empire* turned his serious attention to the subject, and he actually entered a design in competition for the Ohio State Capitol in 1838, and was awarded third prize. Because all of the first three schemes deeply impressed the legislators, A. J. Davis was employed to combine the best features of each, and wrote that "Cole's plan was altered and executed." So, to a degree which shall probably remain forever somewhat uncertain, he had a hand in a building which Talbot Hamlin considered among the few "representing the very best ideals of the Greek Revival movement expressed in public buildings," even though the cylindrical cupola is obviously incomplete. The Capitol's finished appearance may be suggested by a detail of *The Architect's Dream*—which Cole painted in 1840 for Ithiel Town, Davis' partner—in the Classic building to the right with its unbroken façade, colossal order of pilasters, simple architrave, and horizontal mass.

Still preoccupied with ideas of time's passage, he embarked on his second series of pictures, *The Voyage of Life* (now in Utica, New York), commissioned by a prominent New York

Thomas Cole: *The Architect's Dream,*
1840, 54 x 84
(The Toledo Museum of Art,
gift of Florence Scott Libbey)

lawyer, Samuel Ward. Because the paintings were to hang in a drawing room, he planned them in contrasting pairs, *Childhood* and *Youth* lighter and fresher, and *Manhood* and *Old Age* darker and more shadowed. Each is a complete composition, yet each pair also composes, and the pairs echo across in a way to be completely understood only when the pictures are hung in the manner intended by the artist and patron.

A second trip abroad in 1841 led him again to Italy. In Rome he painted his richly romantic *Valley of the Vaucluse* (Metropolitan), from sketches made of Petrarch's castle, crowning a lofty cliff high above the river; it is executed with greater freedom and dash than anything he had done to date. His *The Roman Campagna* and *An Evening in Arcady* (both, Hartford) represent the ripening of his talent. In one, the gigantic fragments of the Claudian aqueduct, marching toward the distant Alban Hills, cast long shadows across the Campagna, empty but for a lonely goatherd, his dog, and his flock—the evocation of the Golden Age—are lighted by a setting sun. Painted in the year of Allston's death, they share with his ideal landscapes a mood of reverie and of waking dream, and are rightly recognized as among the achievements which give him a respectable place in the history of the Romantic movement.

As before, a renewed association with Europe also refreshed Cole's vision of the American scene, and it is, rather, in his American landscapes of this period, in which he brings the same ease and maturity to an interpretation of his native countryside, that he makes his greatest contribution. In such pictures as *The Oxbow* of the Connecticut River near Northampton, Massachusetts, of 1846, the bold panorama—now adroitly but unobtrusively composed—has, like his late Catskill scenes, the scope and drama of nature, which provided for him and for his period such a meaningful revelation. "Scenes of wild grandeur," Bryant called them, "peculiar to our country," which carry the

Thomas Cole: *The Oxbow*
(Connecticut River near Northampton),
1846, 51½ x 76
(The Metropolitan Museum of Art,
gift of Mrs. Russell Sage, 1908)

243

James Smillie: Engraving after Thomas Cole's *The Voyage of Life—Childhood*, 1850, for the American Art-Union (Courtesy of Kennedy Galleries, Inc., New York)

James Smillie: Engraving after Thomas Cole's *The Voyage of Life—Manhood*, 1850, for the American Art-Union (Courtesy of Kennedy Galleries, Inc., New York)

James Smillie: Engraving after Thomas Cole's *The Voyage of Life—Youth,* 1850, for the American Art-Union (Courtesy of Kennedy Galleries, Inc., New York)

James Smillie: Engraving after Thomas Cole's *The Voyage of Life—Old Age,* 1850, for the American Art-Union (Courtesy of Kennedy Galleries, Inc., New York)

eye "over our aerial mountaintops with their mighty growth of forest never touched by the axe, along the banks of streams never deformed by culture, and into the depths of skies bright with the hues of our own climate . . . and through the transparent abysses of which it seemed that you might send an arrow out of sight."

Late in 1845 Cole started a third series of paintings called *The Cross and the World,* for which only a few sketches were completed. In the Brooklyn Museum there is a study for the *Triumph of the Pilgrim of the Cross,* which represents as near a reduction of allegory and symbolism to abstract forms of light and dark as anyone had yet attempted, and shows that tendency of Romanticism to push the expressive powers of art almost beyond its possible limits, an attempt that has been given free rein only in our own times.

On New Year's Day, 1848, Cole wrote in his journal: "I thank God for the blessings of the past year. They have been manifold. Another year, a stranger whose face is yet unknown to us, is announced. Mysterious strangers they are, these years. Pilgrims of time that wander through eternity. . . ." He was not to know much of it. He died suddenly in February of a congestion of the lungs, at the age of forty-seven. The day of his funeral was a solemn holiday; in Catskill all business ceased. His friend Bryant gave an eloquent funeral oration, which, when published by popular demand, became a best seller, so highly were both men regarded.

Though the very notion of life as a voyage, much less so portraying it, seems to us incredibly banal, for countless people *The Voyage of Life* provided a kind of a text for living, the naïve allegory lending dignity and meaning to day-to-day existence. These pictures were, during the greater part of the century, as famous and as widely known as any works of art in history. Sixteen thousand engravings of them were sent out in one year alone by the American Art-Union, and they continued to sell for decades to come, finding their way from New England farmhouses and Southern plantations to frontier cabins and goldminers' shacks, from European cottages and castles to the outback in Australia. Jacksonian America greeted *The Course of Empire* with almost equal enthusiasm, finding in it a more optimistic thesis than the intended vanity of human greatness, for Americans interpreted it as portraying the inevitable downfall of the kingdoms of the Old World, deprived as they were of the benefits of the American democratic system! Such was the confidence of the age.

Thomas Cole:
The Dead Rising from Their Tombs,
c. 1847, 7½ x 10¾
(The Art Museum, Princeton University)

246

THE FOLLOWERS OF THOMAS COLE

Frederic E. Church and the Painters of Epic Landscape

Factuality dominated the work of the panoramic landscapists as strictly as any contemporary critic's passion for *vraisemblance* (the then fashionable term) might demand. It was a quality derived both from temperament and from experience, and it was strengthened by the fact that from early days a great many American painters had had their first training as engravers. And those that did not, inevitably studied engravings as a necessary means of learning about pictures in a country that did not yet have many to exhibit, those few to be seen only in the larger cities. Engravings, on the other hand, especially after the popularity of gift books and illustrated annuals, and with their distribution by the American Art-Union, could be found almost everywhere. It is understandable, therefore, that a dominant feature of American landscape painting should have been tonal, in terms of what might be called, in an expression borrowed from television, the gray scale, but that it should also tend to sharp delineation and to structure of composition by linear rather than pictorial means. An example of this is the art of Asher B. Durand (1796–1886), who was acknowledged as the country's leading engraver after his plates of John Trumbull's *The Declaration of Independence* and Vanderlyn's *Ariadne* appeared. Both attest his unusual skill and craftsmanship, and explain the demand for his services, which kept him constantly occupied and won him general acclaim.

Though Durand was almost five years older than Thomas Cole, he did not take up painting until about 1834, and his style was much influenced by his younger contemporary. Luman Reed, the New York merchant who was a Maecenas to so many American artists, encouraged him to turn to painting and commissioned several works, and Jonathan Sturgis, Reed's son-in-law, made it possible for him to tour Europe. In 1840 Durand sailed on the *British Queen* with three of his pupils. These were Thomas P. Rossiter, who later traveled through Switzerland with Cole and then settled for several years in Rome before returning to make a name for himself as a history painter; John W. Casilear, who had been a fellow apprentice of the engraver Peter Maverick; and John F. Kensett, who studied and worked in Europe for seven years before returning to become one of the

Asher B. Durand: *Valley Landscape,* 1859, pencil, 7¹³⁄₁₆ x 5⁷⁄₁₆
(The Walters Art Gallery)

most admired artists of his period. Though Durand did many portraits, it is as a landscapist that he is best known, and perhaps his most charming picture is that in which he appropriately combined the two genres by painting Cole and Bryant in a Catskill glen—the famous *Kindred Spirits* in the New York Public Library, a memorial to Cole on his death in 1848. Two years earlier Durand had succeeded Morse as president of the National Academy, an office he retained until he resigned in 1861, so deeply was he respected by his fellow artists. The unprecedented choice of a landscape painter for a leading position in the country's cultural life did much to add prestige to this branch of art, and undoubtedly had a great deal to do with the tremendous emphasis on landscape painting in America for the rest of the nineteenth century and on into the twentieth.

Because of his training as an engraver, it is natural that Durand should have based his painting on a fine and controlled line and taken full advantage of his highly developed sense of tonality, so essential to that medium. Yet he had a natural feeling for color and for light, and was one of the first Americans consistently to paint out of doors, observing the natural scene. Thus he was able to combine solidity of composition with an increasingly sensitive expression of atmosphere.

A boyish interest in studying foliage, which Tuckerman later recorded, gave a sense of structure and coherence to his woodland scenes, such as the early *In the Woods* (Amherst), which was painted a year before *Kindred Spirits*. Here the moss-clad trunks have firmness and a rugged texture contrasted with the delicacy of leaves and branches. The whole is broadly composed with rich shadows and sensitive gradations of light, yet displays the grasp of substance, which has been a fundamental purpose of so much of American art, and which represents the approach that Durand urged younger painters to assume.

In his "Letters on Landscape Painting," which appeared in *The Crayon* (an important magazine devoted to art, founded by W. J. Stillman, a former pupil of Church, which gave great currency in America to the writings and ideas of John Ruskin), Durand wrote: "Go not abroad in search of material for the exercise of your pencil while the virgin charms of our native land have claims on your deepest affections." He advised them to search out "the lone and tranquil lakes embosomed in ancient forests, that abound in our wild districts, the unshorn mountains surrounding them with their richly-textured covering, the ocean prairies of the West, and many other forms of Nature yet spared from the pollutions of civilization. . . ." Here in 1855, when so much of the continent was still unspoiled, is an expression of that attitude toward wild nature, which, fed by the spirit of romanticism, became a dominant trait of mind of a great number of Americans, a point of view today on the defensive against the also typically American confusion of change with progress, but which nonetheless maintains the fight for conservation against the blind exploitation of the national heritage.

"Go first to Nature to learn to paint landscape," Durand urged, "and when you shall have learned to imitate her, you may then study the pictures of great artists with benefit. . . ." Though such advice runs counter to the standard practice of European painting, and has been criticized as a result, it follows the same idealistic purpose of Cole and of virtually all the best American landscape painters thereafter. Their essential aim was not to demonstrate theories or produce graceful compositions, but somehow to express the "lessons of high and holy meaning" which they found in the natural scene in America and wished to share with all their countrymen. They felt themselves to be instruments through which this spirit could flow, and they sought to perfect their art so that no intrusive personal idiosyncrasies should muddy those clear natural waters which they believed rose fresher from the New World's springs than from anywhere else on the globe.

Durand's best pictures effectively illustrate this philosophy, perhaps none better than those smaller studies from nature, carried out entirely on the spot, such as *Lake George, New York* (Karolik Coll., Boston). It was probably painted in his old age because, though his pictures were in great demand, it was found in his studio at his death and appeared in the executor's sale held in New York in 1887. Its loving rendering of detail, the luminous quiet, and the untroubled serenity of vision are true expressions of his own spirit. In his long and admirable life Durand did much to keep this attitude alive, and he was a constant supporter of younger artists, generous with advice and encouragement.

It was the ambition of almost all the artists of the following generation to study in Europe. Many went to Germany, where the sculptures of Thomas Crawford were so deeply admired, and where Emanuel Leutze (1816-68) was for years a leader of the school of Düsseldorf. Later Leutze painted *Westward the Course of Empire* for the Rotunda of the Capitol in Washington, and his immense *Washington Crossing the Delaware* (Metropolitan), in a pose as much at variance with the great man's natural prudence as with the seamanship of the sailors from

Jasper Cropsey:
Eagle Cliff, New Hampshire,
1851, 37 x 53
(Courtesy, Museum of Fine Arts, Boston,
M. and M. Karolik Collection)

Marblehead who were in charge of that significant operation. Some of the artists, however, sought to realize in Europe "The dream of Arcadia," a title given by Thomas Cole to one of his most evocative and Septembral landscapes. John Gadsby Chapman (1808-89), foremost of American etchers and book illustrators of the time, and painter of *The Baptism of Pocahantas* for the national Capitol, walked the rugged hills of Calabria, clad "in the goatskin and untanned shoes of a peasant," Tuckerman tells us, while he drew and painted mountaintop towns, medieval towers, and the empty, rocky southern coast. Jasper Francis Cropsey (1823–1900), architect of the fanciful stations of the Sixth Avenue Elevated Railway in New York City, was another passionate admirer of the Italian scene, and walked and painted his way through the hills and across the Campagna, though his favorite subject was the fall coloring in America, in the treatment of which he won the praise of the critic of *The Times* of London because he resisted the temptation to be "a Turner of the forest." Though "his autumn is still brilliant," the critic wrote, it is "not quite lost to sobriety, as we have sometimes, we think, seen it in that Western World." Even Emerson's friend Christopher Pearse Cranch (1813-92), Unitarian minister turned painter and poet, and translator of the *Iliad,* whom William James called "a mild and melancholy humorist," was inspired by the Italian atmosphere to join the rest. He scaled the steep slopes of Sorrento and Amalfi, painted Paestum's ancient temples by moonlight, and met with Bierstadt, Gifford, Durand, Kensett, and other artists of all nations at the Caffé Greco in Rome, the haunt of Canova, Irving, Byron, Goethe, and a host of other luminaries of the world of the arts from the days of Benjamin West down almost to our own.

Thomas Cole had many followers but only one pupil, Frederic E. Church (1826–1900), of Hartford, Connecticut. Church early determined on an artistic career, and went to Catskill, New York, to study with Cole in 1844. Although his master died four years later, Church became infected with Cole's love of nature; but his own inclinations inspired him to seek wider and different horizons. Just as Cole had wandered the Catskills and Italy, Church explored North and South America, Labrador, and the Near East.

The world of the artists of this generation was a constantly enlarging one. It was an age of exploration, led by such adventurous individuals as Alexander von Humboldt, the great German naturalist, whose work, published in translation as *Personal Narrative of Travels to the Equinoctial Regions of America* in 1852, inspired the young American to penetrate the innermost valleys of the Andes and to put down on epic canvases their snow-capped peaks and vast distances. Church visited Ecuador and Colombia in 1853 and again in 1857; he stayed in the same house in Quito which von Humboldt had occupied half a century earlier, and he made many sketches of the ranges and jungles of New Granada. These were usually done in oil on paper and retain all their freshness and convey the keenness with which he felt what von Humboldt had called the "peculiar attraction" of the place, a "feeling common to all men who have been brought up in the habits of civilization. You find yourself in a new world, in the midst of untamed and savage nature." But in the naturalist's earlier book lies Church's immediate source of inspiration. Much read in its own day but completely neglected since, no doubt because its scientific basis so rapidly became antiquated, *Kosmos* represents the attempt of a scholar and scientist of adventurous and inquiring mind to sum up man's idea of the universe in the light of the latest discoveries and speculations of his day. As was almost inevitable for a cultured man of his generation, von Humboldt was much preoccupied with the changing relation of man to the natural world, and devoted an entire chapter in *Kosmos* to the subject of landscape painting as a means of understanding nature. He could not help but wonder that if painters had been able to create important works of art based upon the more austere landscape of Europe, how much wider would be the horizons of art, and how much richer its content, when all the luxuriance and color of the tropical scene were available both as subject and as inspiration. He felt that it was the task of the landscape painter to resolve the apparent differences between man and his environment by revealing "the great enchantment of nature," glorying in all its diversity but suggesting its underlying unity. It was in this spirit that Church painted, whether his subject was Andean peaks or, excited by the accounts of the famous Arctic explorer Elisha Kent Kane, icebergs off the coast of Labrador in 1859, or the lush foliage of Jamaica in 1865, or, later, the holy landscape around Jerusalem and views of the Pyramids, the Alps, and the Parthenon.

Church sought to know nature with the completeness of a scientist. In him the pious pantheism of Cole has been transmuted by a scientific age, but the underlying spirit, the sense of wonder, is still there. Tuckerman wrote that "Church exhibits the New England mind pictorially developed. . . . He goes to nature with the patient intrepidity of a student; he is keenly

Frederic E. Church: *Floating Icebergs*, 1859, pencil and oil on cardboard, 6 x 10 (Courtesy of the Cooper Union Museum)

251

on the watch for facts. . . ." As his sketches demonstrate, he endeavored to learn nature like a Chinese painter of the classic period—to observe the patterns of growth of trees and plants, the structure of rocks, the convolutions of leaf and tendril, the light of dawn in an Arctic sky, the reflection of sunset in an Adirondack lake, the rippling of foliage in the wind. He tried to synthesize all the wonders of the mountain chains and tropical forests of South America in his *The Heart of the Andes* (Metropolitan), which was exhibited to admiring crowds both in the United States and in Europe. Though the picture is colossal in scale, the consistency of detail is remarkable, as is the spaciousness of the distances, achieved with the subtlest possible command of aerial perspective—the minute gradations of color intensity and clarity being sifted out of our vision by the atmosphere as our eyes look at ever-increasing distances. As in Chinese landscape scrolls, in all of Church's larger pictures we can move around within the painting, exploring the tremendous depths he has created, complete to the utmost detail but all so subordinated to the demands of truth that we find no discontinuities to trouble our experience of the remarkable unity of the whole.

Church's best works represent an amazingly sustained and realized performance. The completeness of detail is not the result of the compulsive finicking which the century was to see so much of. Instead, it was the result of a glorious enthusiasm for nature's visual and formal richness which it is the artist's constant joy to celebrate, and is an expression also of the essential factuality so strongly ingrained in the American mind. At his best—as in the sparkling cliffs and pinnacles and the glacial chill of his icebergs, or in his view of the Ecuadorean volcano *Cotopaxi* (versions in the Smithsonian and Reading, Pennsylvania), with a lurid cloud of smoke rising against a sunset sky throwing the foreground, with its immense waterfall, into a strange unearthly light—Church achieves the expression of the force and impersonality of nature's power, to which he dedicated his amazing energies and skill.

He had just hit his stride in his art when, at the age of fifty-one, an attack of rheumatism permanently crippled his right hand. Undaunted, he taught himself to paint with his left, but then that, too, was attacked, and his career as an artist was over. He devoted himself to collecting and was among the first to value for aesthetic qualities, rather than merely as curiosities or as artifacts of anthropological or archaeological interest, the pottery of Peru, pre-Columbian sculpture, and Near Eastern weaving and ceramics. Church housed his collection, which also included paintings by European artists and by his own master, Thomas Cole, in one of the period's most interesting and romantic structures, the Villa Olana, a mountaintop palace of Moorish style, commanding a superb view of the Hudson and the Catskills. Designed by the painter himself with the help of his friend the architect Calvert Vaux, it has been preserved by the State of New York as a landmark of Romantic architecture. Though crippled and in pain, Church continued to travel, exploring early ruins in Mexico and Central America with the same spirit which animated his artistic aim to paint the world for his fellow Americans, and through his painting to reveal its truth and unity.

Albert Bierstadt (1830–1902) was another artist-explorer. A contemporary of Church's, he was born abroad but brought to New Bedford, Massachusetts, as an infant, so his education, upbringing, and experience were entirely of the New World. He returned to his native Germany to study art, however, and the large pictures which brought him fame in his day are visual demonstrations of that prevailing influence. His Rockies look rather like the Alps, and the operatic cloud effects which he so

Frederic E. Church: *Cotopaxi*, 1855, 28⅛ x 42⅛
(Courtesy of the Smithsonian Institution National Collection of Fine Arts, gift of Mrs. Frank R. McCoy)

often contrived make his large paintings seem to us more Wagnerian than American. In his sketches, however, he forgot his stylistic self-consciousness and recorded immediately observed impressions of freshness and vigor. In 1858 he joined Frederick W. Lander's expedition to map an overland wagon route to the Pacific. The group went west from St. Louis, crossed the desert, followed the Platte River, went through the Laramie Mountains by way of Fort Kearny, South Fork, and Honey Lake Road. Bierstadt spent the summer sketching in the Wind River and Shoshone country and then left the expedition to return east by easy stages, sight-seeing as he came. He brought back innumerable sketches of the Far West—scenes of mountains, rivers, plains, and Indians—and from these he composed large panoramas which won him instant fame. Thereafter, though he often traveled to Europe and elsewhere, the Rocky Mountains were his particular artistic province.

Bierstadt's popularity was immense. His paintings were highly praised in both Europe and America, and he built a thirty-five-room marble studio-palace overlooking the Hudson at Irvington, where he and his wife entertained such illustrious guests as the Grand Duke Alexis of Russia, for whose amusement he made arrangements through the War Department to stage a buffalo hunt. In answer to the artist's request, General Sheridan wrote that "if his Royal Highness desires the Buffalo hunt I will place myself at his service & can take him to Largeheads south of McPherson on the Union Pacific Road say from fifty to sixty to seventy miles. Spotted Tail's branch of Sioux Indians & Whistlers band are in the neighborhood and I can give to them such inducements as will cause them to join us at least I think so. It will be cold but not half so cold as Russia. . . . He can kill Buffalo to his heart's content, but must be willing to rough it a little."

Deeply interested in wildlife, Bierstadt made a special study of the wild horned animals of North America, and filled his studio with trophies of the West, until it looked like a natural history museum. He was a charter member of the Boone and Crockett Club, founded by Theodore Roosevelt, and was well known for his lively reminiscences of adventures with animals and Indians, and of the fabulous landscape of the Far West in which America, in this period of expansionism, was becoming increasingly interested. When his immense painting of *The Rocky Mountains* (Metropolitan) was first exhibited in New York in 1863, banners strung across Broadway dramatically announced the event. He had an attractive personality and a natural flair for publicity. From the early 1860's, for twenty years he was, according to a contemporary observer, "probably the most talked of artist in New York." And his prices, ranging from $5,000 to $35,000, were the highest on record for his day.

In his later works the less fortunate aspects of the Düsseldorf manner seem increasingly to dominate; his color becomes hot and his surfaces harder, while detail, never so well drawn or so skillfully subordinated as by Church, becomes insistent. He was less perceptive than Church and lacked Church's constantly rechargeable enthusiasm. He probably never again equaled a sketch which embodies the excitement of the first impact upon him of the West, a record of what he obviously was deeply aware was an historic and symbolic confrontation. Entitled *Indians near Fort Laramie*, it was almost surely painted in 1858, while he was with the Lander expedition. Even the snapshotlike composition helps to convey the immediacy of the scene. Bierstadt forgot his usual technique and used sharp nervous strokes which detail the figures sufficiently so that they can be recognized as members of the Teton Dakota or Western Sioux and show the combination of trade goods and native manufactures that was typical of the Indians of the Oglala or the Brule tribes at that time. Fort Laramie was a fur-trading post

Albert Bierstadt: *Indians near Fort Laramie*, c. 1858, oil on paper, 13½ x 19½ (Courtesy, Museum of Fine Arts, Boston, M. and M. Karolik Collection)

established in 1834 by one of William H. Ashley's original mountain men, William Sublette, at Laramie Fork in the North Platte River, "square on the crossroads," Bernard De Voto tells us in *Across the Wide Missouri*, of "the north and south Indian trail that was older than any record, and the Oregon Trail. . . . Here with a desert to the east and a worse one to the west, and grueling travel in both directions, here and there was rich grass, cottonwood groves, clear water, and Laramie Peak in the sunset to suggest the mountains that lay ahead. Emigrant trains invariably halted here as if coming to an oasis. . . . It would draw all wandering trappers, all Indians who came to the Laramie plain to hunt or en route anywhere east of the mountains, the Oglala Sioux, and finally the United States Army who would take over the post and try to keep a third of the West peaceful from this site." It was here that Indians still came to trade, as perhaps was the case with those whom Bierstadt painted, watchful and motionless in the light-drenched, empty landscape stretching uninterrupted to the distant hills; one can feel the tension and the silence, as modern man—heir to centuries of civilization stemming from the shores of the Mediterranean, Europe, and the Holy Land—and Stone Age man meet face to face.

John Frederick Kensett and the Painters of Light

Church was the first of the far-wandering artists, but there were others as well. His friend Martin J. Heade (1819–1904), who had been born in a little town in the Pennsylvania hills, but who had traveled the length and breadth of North America and much of Europe while still a young man, painted orchids and hummingbirds in the high Andes and haycocks on the marshes of Newport, Rhode Island, with a more personal sensitivity to light and atmosphere. A feeling of mystery pervades his pictures and sometimes rises to a dramatic crescendo, as in his *Approaching Storm, Beach near Newport* (c. 1860), a painting of frightening power as an expression of the sinister force in nature. Ominous black clouds fill the sky, and the strange light which falls across the familiar shore makes it look as alien as a landscape on the moon, while the sails of boats fleeing to harbor gleam white against the dark sky.

During the middle decades of the nineteenth century there was a growing fascination with light, both scientifically and aesthetically. The results may be seen in Europe equally in the invention of photography and in the painting of Corot. It

Martin J. Heade: *Approaching Storm, Beach near Newport,* c. 1860, 28 x 58½
(Courtesy, Museum of Fine Arts, Boston, M. and M. Karolik Collection)

also appears in the work of a group of artists who gathered in
Barbizon in the 1840's, whose approach to painting, influenced
by the Englishmen Constable and Turner, was to establish them
as precursors of Impressionism. At the same time that the Barbizon group, whose works were so admired by George Inness
and William Morris Hunt, were rediscovering the natural landscape of France, a number of other Americans, including Heade,
were carrying forward the development of American landscape,
after the rediscovery of its possibilities for painting by Thomas
Cole, with an equal interest in the effects of light. These artists
have been called Luminists by Edgar P. Richardson, because
of their search for a means of expressing their feelings about
the American countryside in atmospheric terms. Their style was
based in the firm naturalism of Durand—the belief in the faithful study of nature—but for them the beauty of light was but
a further expression of the wonder of the natural world with
which they felt so at one. Much of what they did was instinctive,
for American art was untroubled by the theoretical considerations which pitted Romantic colorists against Neoclassicists in
France, and was comparatively untrammeled by an overload
of literary paraphernalia, as in the German schools; there was
even less of the sentimentality of the English, such as appears in
Leslie and Wilkie, though there was to be an overdose of it
later in the century. Instead, the Luminists had a feeling of identification with the American scene, an emotional sense of its

257

qualities, seen and felt with unselfconscious appreciation, and painted with delight so that others might share their joy and satisfaction.

John Frederick Kensett (1816-72) was a leader of this group. Twenty years younger than the long-lived Durand, he also started as an engraver, and the basic firmness of drawing that results from that discipline underlies all his work. But unlike the older artist, he was interested in light and air, in the enveloping atmosphere that gives each moment a special character, and he developed his own serene style. He sketched in England and on the Continent, sharing a Paris studio with Benjamin Champney (1817–1907) from Boston and one in Rome with Thomas Hicks (1823-90) from Pennsylvania, between trips through Germany, Switzerland, France, and Italy. In America he explored the area west of the Rockies with Sanford R. Gifford (1823-80) and Worthington Whittredge (1820–1910). But he was most at home with the mountains and lakes of New England and New York, and with the coast of Long Island Sound and around Newport, which he painted with the silent visual poetry that pervades all his pictures. He was one of the most popular painters of his period in America, and his work was also known and respected abroad.

John F. Kensett: *Thunderstorm, Lake George,* 1870, 13$\frac{13}{16}$ x 24$\frac{1}{8}$
(The Brooklyn Museum, gift of Mrs. W. W. Phelps)

Worthington Whittredge:
Old Homestead by the Sea,
1883, 22 x 32
(Courtesy, Museum of Fine Arts, Boston,
M. and M. Karolik Collection)

Where the mood of Kensett's paintings is almost always one
of hushed quiet, occasionally tending toward a vague sadness,
that of Gifford's is warmer and brighter. Gifford delighted in
the effects of distance seen through an atmosphere suffused with
sunlight, and he developed an aerial perspective based on a
system of greater contrast than appears in Kensett's canvases.
In *Lake Como* (Utica) the mountains of the far shore are seen
across the water from the deep shadows of the tunneled road-
way cut in the cliff above the lake; in *Kauterskill Falls* (Metropolitan), the wooded heights beyond a Catskill lake are barely
visible through a golden mist. His pictures were painted, as an
artist friend noted, with "a brush dipped in sunlight." Gifford
traveled widely in Europe with Worthington Whittredge; there
is much in common in their work, though their backgrounds
could not have been more different. Gifford was the son of a
Hudson River Valley ironworks owner and never had to worry
about money, while Whittredge came of a frontier family settled
in Ohio.

Whittredge somehow knew as a boy that he was destined to
be an artist, before he even saw a work of art. He left home for
Cincinnati with two dollars and a half in his pocket, studied
drawing books, and supported himself as a sign painter. At
twenty he was taking daguerreotypes in Indianapolis, where he
became ill and was given a home by Henry Ward Beecher,
whose family's portraits he painted in gratitude. In Cincinnati
he had been delighted with Hiram Powers' by then famous
animated three-dimensional scenes illustrating some of the more
lurid descriptions in Dante's *Inferno*, and by the paintings in
the collection of Nicholas Longworth who, with other patrons,

259

aided him in his plan to go abroad to study. He spent several years in Düsseldorf, where, like so many other Americans, he posed for Emanuel Leutze's famous *Washington Crossing the Delaware* (Metropolitan), and where he also welcomed young Albert Bierstadt, fresh from New Bedford, into his studio. He traveled widely, visiting museums and sketching, from Holland to Italy, supporting himself by the sale of the paintings he sent back to Ohio.

On Whittredge's return to the United States in 1859 he settled in rooms in the Studio Building at 15 Tenth Street in New York City, which he retained for the rest of his life. Here he enjoyed the companionship of Church, Bierstadt, Gifford, and, later, of John La Farge and Winslow Homer, among many others. The Studio Building was designed in Romantic style in 1857 by Richard Morris Hunt, who was to be one of the leading architects of the country after the Civil War. It was a center of artist life, with handsome exhibition galleries that were always crowded and "Artists' Receptions" that attracted all interested in art, literature, music, and the theater. Bachelors lived there, and the artists who were married kept studios, all taken care of by a housekeeper who, according to a friend of the Giffords, "was certainly an institution. . . . It is probable that no living woman, beautiful or plain, ever sat for her portrait oftener than she. . . . It would be impossible for any one building, at the present day [1900], to equal the interest possessed by the Tenth Street Studio . . . it was pervaded by a mental atmosphere quite removed from that of the prosaic, work-a-day world. Camaraderie and good fellowship prevailed, and there was little of the striving, envy, and personal ambition which seem at present inseparable from the pursuit of art."

Before Whittredge settled down to work, he hid for months, as he wrote, "in the recesses of the Catskills. But how different

Worthington Whittredge:
Outskirts of the Forest,
c. 1880, 25½ x 35½
(Courtesy, Museum of Fine Arts,
Boston, M. and M. Karolik Collection)

260

was the scene before me from anything I had been looking at for many years! The forest was a mass of decaying logs and tangled brushwood, no peasants to pick up every vestige of fallen sticks to burn in their miserable huts, no well-ordered forests, nothing but the primitive woods in their solemn silence reigning everywhere." The scale, the light, the weather were all utterly different, and he turned to "Durand's truly American landscape," finding it "such a faithful if in some parts sombre delineation of our own hills and valleys, I confess the tears came to my eyes." The tightness of the Düsseldorf style that Bierstadt almost never overcame gave way to Whittredge's broad, atmospheric approach, and the multitude of details fell into place as he recaptured the sensitivity to nature of his early years. Aware of the subtle elements that differentiate each time and place, he interpreted the character of the scene, the time of day, the season of the year, with self-effacing admiration expressed in a luminous and atmospheric unity.

George Loring Brown (1814-89) seems to have had no such trouble adjusting to the home scene after his twenty years of study and work abroad. Like so many of his countrymen, he found a spiritual home in Italy, where he became the most celebrated American landscapist in Europe. His friend Nathaniel Hawthorne was amused by his twangy New England speech and greatly admired his serene pictures, and when he remarked in wonder at the long hours and painstaking attention that produced them, the artist exclaimed, "It isn't patience; it's love." And the results, whether scenes on the coast of the Amalfi Peninsula or the homely *Medford Marshes* (Boston) near where Brown found a home after his return from Europe, reveal him as one of the Luminists.

One of the most interesting marine painters America has produced was then working quietly on the New England coast north of Boston. Like Heade, Fitz Hugh Lane (1804-65) has been called a Luminist, because of his sensitive perception of light. On November 5, 1851, the Gloucester, Massachusetts, *Telegraph* proudly reprinted an opinion of his work by the anonymous critic of the Boston *Transcript,* who stated that "since Salmon's death, we have no one who can paint a ship and ocean prospect like him. His 'squalls at sea' are the best thing of the kind that we remember to have seen." Lane was then forty-six, and had been drawing and painting since boyhood. And for a man who had been stricken so severely with polio at the age of two that he lived largely in a wheel chair and could not move without crutches, he had an amazingly successful career.

At twenty-eight he became an apprentice in one of the most productive lithography shops in the country, that of William Pendleton of Boston, for whom Alexander Jackson Davis and William Rimmer, artist and anatomist, also worked. Benjamin Champney, a fellow apprentice, reported that "Lane, afterward well-known as a marine painter, did most of the views, hotels, etc. He was very accurate in his drawing, understood perspective and naval architecture perfectly as well as the handling of vessels, and was a good all-round draughtsman. . . ."

In 1849 Lane returned to Gloucester and, with the help of his brother-in-law, Ignatius Winters, built a curious and picturesque stone house on Duncan Point. Constructed of massive blocks of the local granite, it had steep gables, Gothic windows, and groined vaults. On the top floor was his studio, with a glass roof for the best possible light, and with wide windows giving a panorama of Gloucester harbor. Around the house he laid out a series of terraces descending to the shore. Here he worked in his garden, famous for its flowers and fruits, of which he was very proud. He advertised in the local paper that "Mr. Lane's rooms are open at all hours of the day"; and, its editor urged, "all our readers who have any love of art are advised to call there and look at his paintings." Despite the effort that it must have cost him, he sailed along the Maine coast to Penobscot Bay and Mt. Desert, stopping off at Blue Hill, Castine, Owl's Head, and other picturesque places; he also visited New York, Baltimore, and probably got as far as the West Indies, and perhaps even farther. He was a familiar figure around Gloucester, where he was often seen driving his carriage on sketching expeditions. Many oils and drawings are preserved in the collections of the Cape Ann Scientific, Literary, and Historical Association in Gloucester, and through scholarly detective work many more have been rediscovered and disentangled from those of a few followers, including Mary B. Mellen, a pupil who managed on several occasions to emulate his distinctive style with unexpected success. The resulting body of work established as Lane's proves him to have been a marine painter of unusual quality.

Lane's method was first to make simple topographical sketches, many of which are preserved in the Cape Ann Historical Association collection. They are disarmingly brief and usually entirely linear, though occasionally he did water colors also. Studying the sky, the harbor, the sea, and the headlands at all times of day and night and in all sorts of weather, year round, from the studio atop his house like the bridge of a ship, he experimented with effects of light and atmosphere. Sometimes he used a limited palette, as in the *Maine Inlet* (Karolik Collection, Boston), where all is pervaded with the soft, pale tones of falling twilight. Sometimes he would depict a rising fog bank at sea, the moon shining across still water, or the morning sun gleaming through mist over the harbor. He knew the moods of the ocean, whether rolling in lazy swells or with a stiff breeze kicking up a chop and blowing spray from the whitecaps, and every detail of his sailing vessels is of such impeccable accuracy that it seems to prove his actual experience on the water. He could have had no severer critics than the many seafaring people among his patrons and also his fellow townsmen, who were scarcely to be considered landlubbers themselves, and who were his enthusiastic admirers.

New Englanders had a special interest in ships' portraits. But there are few within hailing distance of that which Lane did of the famous clipper brig *Antelope*, "the only square-rigged vessel which could beat through the Formosa Channel against the northeast monsoon." She was built by Robert Bennet Forbes of Boston, and when under his command or that of the hard-driving Captain Dumaresq, she gained a tremendous reputation for speed. In his *Brig Antelope in Boston Harbor* (1863, Karolik Collection, Boston), Lane shows her as she

Fitz Hugh Lane: *Owl's Head, Penobscot Bay, Maine,* 1862, 16 x 26
(Courtesy, Museum of Fine Arts, Boston, M. and M. Karolik Collection)

proudly sailed down the harbor, bound for China, in 1843, never to return to Boston. She was caught in a typhoon in 1848 in the China Sea and dismasted; rerigged as a bark, she lost her speed and was wrecked four years later near Woosung.

Lane is at his most memorable in those quiet canvases that are cool with the clear northern light in which even distant outlines are firm and definite against the transparent depth of sky. Such a one is his *Owl's Head, Penobscot Bay, Maine* (1862). The water is calm, barely rippling on the pebbly, shelving beach; there is a sense of profound stillness. The standing figure gazing out away from us across the bay toward the ghosting brig is isolated and alone. Here Lane has struck a note heard again and again in American art and literature, concerning the place of man in nature—man as solitary as only those who have known the limitless wilderness of the New World or the vastness of the endless sea from prolonged experience know him to be.

VI

Democracy
and
the
Arts

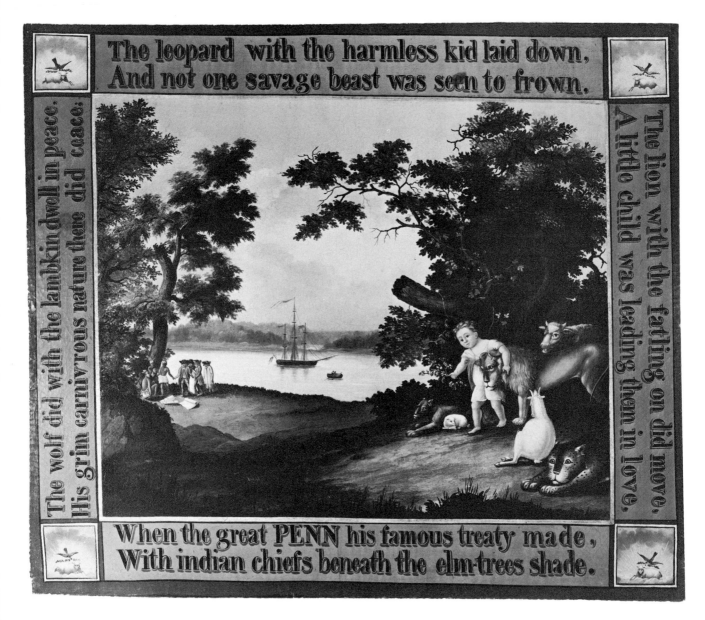

Edward Hicks: *The Peaceable Kingdom*, 1830-35, 30¼ x 36¼
(New York State Historical Association, Cooperstown, N.Y.)

EVERY MAN HIS OWN ARTIST

The do-it-yourself idea started early in America. Captain John Smith had complained bitterly at being given a group useless as colonists because they knew no trade. He asked for fewer gentlemen and more practical men who knew a craft and could work to establish a settlement, "artificers, labourers, and husbandmen." There never were enough "honest and good artificers," so from the beginning it was every man for himself, in the arts as in everything else. Though a few minor painters reached these shores, there was little to attract trained artists to the New World, especially during the earlier years of settlement. Yet people wanted something in the way of art, and from sign painting men turned to portraiture, mural decoration, mourning pictures, and whatever else might be desired. Thus the profession of the academically untrained artist began with local and itinerant limners, working in a tradition having roots in earlier centuries, influenced by the academic only at some remove—through engravings, perhaps, or seeing European pictures or wallpapers imported by a wealthy house owner. From the craft of the sign painter there evolved a native school of painting that spread across the country as settlement grew, and from the craft of the tombstone maker and the ship carver a native tradition in sculpture developed.

The Self-Trained Artisan

In the German settlements expert blacksmiths not only produced the superbly useful American ax and the long rifle, but also made fanciful weathervanes, firebacks, wafer molds, latches, locks, hinges, and occasional "fancy pieces." Other artisans carried on the medieval craft of illumination of documents and manuscripts, from deeds to school certificates, known as fracturs. The colonists of German ancestry who have come to be called the Pennsylvania Dutch also made the colorful slip-ware pottery and the charmingly painted furniture that is so distinctive of that group.

Shaker interior
(Hancock Shaker Village, Hancock, Mass.)

The Shakers, more formally known as the United Society of Believers in Christ's Second Appearing, in their celibate communities of hard-working farmers and craftsmen in New York, New England, and the Middle West produced everything for self-sufficiency, including the simple, clean-lined chairs, tables, benches, and cupboards that provided the model for the Scan-

267

Rev. George Geistweite:
Illuminated fractur, religious
text dated Aug. 19, 1801, 12½ x 15
(Philadelphia Museum of Art,
Titus C. Geesey Collection;
photograph by A. J. Wyatt,
Staff Photographer)

dinavian furniture of a later day which has been called Danish
Modern. Their belief in "true Gospel simplicity," and that any
object that "has in itself the highest use possesses the greatest
beauty," kept the artistic level of their monastically simple and
perfectly ordered architecture—limited almost entirely to meetinghouses, schools, dwelling houses, and barns—at a height that
puts to shame most of the building of their own day as well as
of ours, just as it dominated their admirable craftwork. The
beauty of a dedicated life shines through in the harmony of line
and form in everything the Shakers made, and also in the in-
spirational drawings and paintings of visions received during
quiet hours of labor and meditation, such as that "seen and
received by Hannah Cohoon in the City of Peace [Hancock,
Massachusetts] Sabbath Oct. 9th 10th hour A.M. 1845, drawn
and painted by the same hand." Below her water color of *The
Tree of Light or Blazing Tree* she described precisely what she
drew and colored with such sensitivity:

The bright silver color'd blaze streaming from the edges of each green
leaf, resembled so many bright torches. N.B. I saw the whole Tree as
the Angel held it before me as distinctly as I ever saw a natural tree.
I felt very cautious when I took hold of it lest the blaze should touch
my hand.

Though the development of machine-made articles gradually
eliminated the traditional handcrafts throughout most of the
country during the second half of the nineteenth century (except for such isolated areas as the settlements of the Pennsyl-

Round barn, 1826
(Hancock Shaker Village, Hancock, Mass.)

vania Dutch and the Shakers, and other utopian communities),
for many years quilting bees provided an opportunity for imaginative variations of traditional themes. Coverlets were woven
of linen and wool in patterns known as "Washington's Victory,"
"Missouri Trouble," "Rose in the Valley," and "New Jersey
Dream." Samplers, embroidered pictures, toleware, pierced tin,
quillwork, scrimshaw, calligraphy, and the products of all sorts
of minor crafts showed the ingenuity of innumerable anonymous Americans.

When Mrs. Anna Jameson, the author of still useful handbooks on "sacred and legendary art," came to America in 1837,
she "was struck by the manner in which the imaginative talent
of the people had thrown itself forth into painting; the country
seemed to swarm with painters." They were everywhere, in the
cities, towns, and villages, and they even turned up in remote
frontier settlements. Many of them are totally unknown today,
like the obviously untrained but gifted individual who painted
in about mid-century an enigmatic *Meditation by the Sea*,
which becomes, as we look at the little figure standing on a
beach and contemplating an endless, restless ocean, a disturbingly apt symbol, charged with emotional overtones, of the
solitariness of man in the vastness of the New World. The
austere figure of Henry Ward Beecher, carved in chestnut and
pine in about 1840 by an unknown Indiana artist whose name
may have been Corbin, perfectly expresses in the upward gaze
and the large Bible held in tiny hands the moving fervor of
the famous divine.

Though most of the foreign-born artists who came to America had received some academic instruction, the Englishman
Thomas Chambers, active in New York, Albany, and Boston
from about 1832 to 1866, belongs rather to the craft tradition

Hannah Cohoon: *The Tree of Life*,
1854, ink and water color, 18½ x 22
(Hancock Shaker Village, Hancock, Mass.,
gift of Dr. and Mrs. Edward D. Andrews)

Anonymous: *Meditation by the Sea*,
c. 1850-60, 13½ x 19½
(Courtesy, Museum of Fine Arts,
Boston, M. and M. Karolik Collection)

269

of painting. His lively and fresh landscapes were freely borrowed from many sources—prints, wallpaper, and other paintings—but all were transformed with a joyous and lyric fancy in a style that has led some to conjecture that he may have originally been a painter of canal boats or Gypsy caravans.

Most such artists were native-born, however. Edward Hicks (1780–1849) of Bucks County, Pennsylvania, who was trained as a coach and sign painter, was also a Quaker preacher who became famous for his eloquence. He traveled around the country at his own expense, speaking of brotherly love to groups everywhere as a dedicated missionary of the Friends. Distrusting sometimes the facility of his gifts as an orator, and disturbed over divisions within the sect, he turned for solace to the same theme in his paintings, a vision of the "peaceable kingdom," sometimes envisioned on this earth (as in the views of the farm of David Twining, where he grew up), and sometimes seen as a symbolic presentation of the prophecy in the eleventh chapter of Isaiah, which the artist paraphrased in his own homely verses:

> The wolf did with the lambkin dwell in peace,
> His grim carnivorous nature there did ceace,
> The leopard with the harmless kid laid down,
> And not one savage beast was seen to frown,
> The lion with the fatling on did move,
> A little child was leading them in love,
> When the great PENN his famous treaty made,
> With indian chiefs beneath the elm-trees shade.

He often painted a frame on the edge of the picture, complete with appropriate inscription, carefully lettered in gold in the style he used for signs and wagons. He painted more than a hundred versions of *The Peaceable Kingdom*, each a different combination of the familiar animals, the gentle-eyed ox with monumental bulk and spreading horns, the outstretched leopard, the awkward bear, cows, sheep, and goats that might have belonged to David Twining, the docile wolf, and the worried, human-faced lion with which he seems to have identified himself. Often the treaty of William Penn with the Indians, the beginning of "Penn's holy experiment," appears in the background; and sometimes the Natural Bridge in Virginia or the Delaware Water Gap is depicted as a sign of nature's wonders, God's gift to mankind. None of these paintings was ever sold. All were given to friends as a reminder of the opportunities of the New World as a place where the age-old dreams of man for a heavenly kingdom might be realized even on earth, in anticipation of that to come.

Henry Ward Beecher,
attributed to Corbin,
c. 1840, chestnut and pine, h. 21½
(Abby Aldrich Rockefeller Folk Art
Collection, Williamsburg, Va.)

In the town of Leverett, Massachusetts, in the Connecticut River Valley, Erastus Salisbury Field (1805–1900) was also painting Biblical scenes, dramatic episodes from the Old Testament of miracles and disasters, set in an exotic landscape that could exist only in the artist's fertile imagination. Field did flat, decisive portraits of his relatives and neighbors throughout a career as long as Titian's, but his most attractive works are the treatments of *The Garden of Eden,* which somehow reflect his own origins on a New England farm, despite the presence of feather-duster palm trees to suggest the tropical lushness of the garden which "God planted . . . eastward in Eden." The animals are all there, neatly paired, while Adam, like a good farmer, watches them, his nudity discreetly screened by a clump of iris such as no doubt grew in Field's own garden, and Eve, shielded by a clump of peonies, reaches up to pick a summer sweeting, sheepnose, or other familiar variety of apple that seems more likely to be put into a pie than used to tempt her husband from the path of innocence, though there is a spotted serpent lurking in the shadows nearby.

Field's most ambitious work was inspired by his intense love of country and his faith in its future. To celebrate the hundredth anniversary of independence, he painted, at the age of seventy, a nine-by-thirteen-foot *Historical Monument of the American Republic.* In an architectural fantasy of remarkable multiplicity of detail, ten towers rise—covered with inscriptions and decorated with simulated reliefs of episodes from American history, and adorned with innumerable busts and statues of all the nation's heroes and leaders—from a colossal base whose style suggests the origins of our culture and history from the ultimate Classical, Egyptian, and Biblical past. The seven tallest towers are connected at their topmost stage by weblike suspension bridges, across which steam locomotives pull their trains, all converging on the most massive tower, while the tower above the central portal is dedicated to Abraham Lincoln and the Constitution. Far below, splendidly uniformed troops march in precise ranks along an avenue, bordered with plants and trees and enlivened with playing fountains, in a Fourth of July parade for admiring fellow citizens who have turned out in holiday dress for the occasion.

Unique in American art, Field's allegory pursues the symbolizing tendency seen in such other works as Thomas Cole's *Course of Empire* to an ultimate degree of organization and detail, in a quaint but somehow compelling vision. Both Hicks and Field belong to the group of painters of the imagination, who

Erastus Salisbury Field:
The Garden of Eden, 1860's, 34¾ x 46
(Courtesy, Museum of Fine Arts,
Boston, M. and M. Karolik Collection)

271

spin the web of their art out of their inner selves, as did Rimmer and Inness, Ryder and Blakelock, and others—artists whose painting reflects the strain of fantasy and mysticism which continues into our own day.

There were also those who pursued a completely opposite aim, that of a searching realism, in which they employed the same painstaking emphasis of detail that Field displayed in his *Historical Monument,* and which seems a common characteristic in the work of many of the academically untrained artists. Outstanding among these are three sculptors—John Frazee, Hezekiah Augur, and John Henri Isaac Browere—all contemporaries of Samuel F. B. Morse. Two of these artists, Frazee and Augur, were friends of Morse's who were inspired by his widely admired sculpture *The Dying Hercules,* which had won its twenty-two-year-old creator the praise of Benjamin West and the gold medal of the Adelphi Society of the Arts in London in 1813.

Erastus Salisbury Field: *Historical Monument of the American Republic* (detail), 1870, 111 x 157 (From the Morgan Wesson memorial collection, Museum of Fine Arts, Springfield, Mass.)

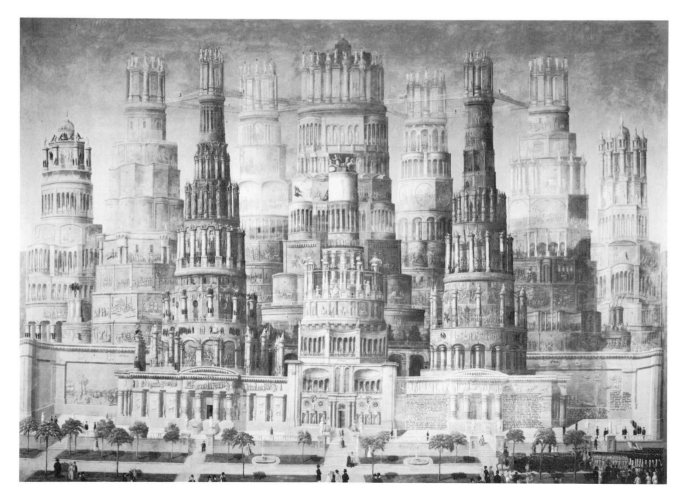

Samuel F. B. Morse:
The Dying Hercules, 1812, plaster, h. 20
(Yale University Art Gallery)

John Frazee (1790–1852) was one of the founders, with Morse, Ithiel Town and others, of the National Academy of Design. He supplied stone lions, eagles, urns, and other architectural details for many of the buildings designed by Town and his younger partner, Alexander Jackson Davis. Born in Rahway, New Jersey, Frazee was the tenth child of a Scottish carpenter and grew up on a farm, a neglected and lonely boy whose only amusement was whittling. After working as a bricklayer and a waiter in a tavern, at eighteen he undertook to carve a stone inscription for a bridge. He did it so well that he was offered a job, and began his career, as he later told William Dunlap, "among the tombstones," working after hours with an older cutter to learn technique. He opened his own yard on Broadway in New York City in 1818.

Dissatisfied with the current style of ornament, derived entirely from old manuals and design books, Frazee turned to the native vines and the flowers of the countryside in which he had grown up, learning to carve with crispness and authority. His business flourished as he produced tombstones, mausoleums, memorial tablets, elaborate marble mantelpieces, ornamental door frames and all sorts of wood carvings, from lion feet for cabinetmakers to capitals for architects and builders, North and South. His initial effort at sculpture in the round was a posthumous portrait in marble of John Wells, to be placed in Ren-

273

wick's handsome Grace Church in New York. Dating from 1825, it was the first bust in stone ever made by a native-born American, according to Dunlap. The success of this sculpture led to a commission by the Boston Athenaeum to produce seven others of New England worthies of his day, all of which show the relentless realism of his approach.

Frazee's career had an almost exact parallel in that of a New Haven carpenter, Hezekiah Augur (1791–1858), whose name sounds as though he should have been a character in one of Cooper's novels. After an early struggle, he, too, achieved a successful business with a wood-carving shop. At the suggestion of Samuel F. B. Morse, he also experimented in marble, cutting a head of Apollo directly in the stone, and then sculptured a pair of small figures, *Jephtha Meeting His Daughter*, carried out in the same unsparing detail, with every tiny fold of drapery and hair defined with minute attention.

Both Augur and Frazee scorned the necessity of Italian study for a sculptor's career. Though they were both successful men in their chosen field, they never abandoned the essentially descriptive approach of the folk artist. Their portraits have none of the bland generalization characteristic of the universally admired works of their more famous compatriots Hiram Powers, Horatio Greenough, Thomas Crawford, and the others who labored under the overwhelming influence of the Neoclassicism learned in Rome and Florence. They are rivaled only by the busts of a curious and dedicated contemporary, John Henri Isaac Browere (1790–1834), who learned the technique of making life masks in Paris, perhaps from Houdon himself, and determined, like Henry Dexter later, to start a national portrait gallery by thus recording the real appearance of the great Americans of that time. The aged Jefferson nearly had his ears torn off when the plaster dried too fast, and the equally ancient John Adams has a set to his mouth which may record the pains of the sculptural operation as much as those of the ills of old age.

Browere laboriously assembled a large series of busts in plaster made from the masks, only to have President Madison refuse government support for the project, since they were, he decided, made by a mechanical process, and were therefore not genuine works of art. Long after Browere's death, they were discovered, stored on a remote upstate New York farm. Finally cast in bronze, they are now exhibited at the New York State Historical Association at Cooperstown, New York. Amer-

Hezekiah Augur:
Jephtha Meeting His Daughter,
marble, h. about 16
(Yale University Art Gallery,
gift of the Citizens of New Haven)

274

icans can be grateful today for Browere's efforts, as they look
at the familiar features of the famous heads (which are incongruously set off, as are Frazee's busts, by togalike drapery).
They look like Roman senators who could more than adequately
have held their own in that more ancient forum just as they did
so effectively in ours of more recent time. Despite the awkward-
ness of presentation, or perhaps because of it, the busts are impressive, firsthand records of character, and they represent the
furthest extent of America's search for total realism.

The two extremes, represented by the artists who recorded
visions and those who sought the maximum of objective truth,
define the broad area within which American art developed,
though it tended toward the former pole more strongly in the
folk tradition and toward the latter in the academic. Realism,
however, was the general and unquestioned aim of even the
most freely imaginative portraitists and landscapists, and often
shines through the mannerisms of their style with power and
conviction. Instinctively, they selected those qualities and elements that revealed the character of a sitter or a place and organized them in a strong pattern to enhance the effectiveness
of the whole. The contrast between a bust by Powers (who was
so famed for the telling accuracy of his likenesses that he was
credited with reproducing "the porosity of the skin") and one
by Frazee makes manifest the essential difference. The polished
generalities of the former appear empty and meaningless beside the detailed realism of the latter, which seems almost
grotesque in its lack of compromise, but always has the genuine
ring of truth.

While the storytelling and mythmaking that allowed Americans to believe that the *Greek Slave* was not nude but clothed
in her own virtue, and led them to see imaginary qualities in
the other works by the most admired Neoclassic sculptors, in
general, they shared a belief in objective realism as the only
true measure of artistic quality. The remarkable diversity of
result from a consistent unity of purpose is the measure of the
strength of the individualism of both the artists and their
patrons in their freedom of interpretation of a common aim, and
nowhere does it appear more strongly than in the variety of the
folk and popular arts of nineteenth-century America.

John Henri Isaac Browere: *John Adams,*
life mask, bronze cast from the original plaster
(New York State Historical
Association, Cooperstown, N.Y.)

275

Itinerants

and

Amateurs

When visiting America in 1837-38, Mrs. Jameson found everyone on the move—families going west, the rough and potholed roads thronged with wagons and caravans, river and coastwide vessels crowded. Spring brought the itinerant painter with the returning robins, and no matter how inept he was, there always seemed to be someone who was willing to trade something—perhaps only lodging and meals for a day or so—for a likeness by him of one of the family, for a new signboard, for an overmantel panel, or for a parlor wall decorated with stencil or landscape. With a pack on his back, or pushing a handcart, or riding horseback, or with a horse and wagon (like the Yankee peddler, who also took to the roads with the coming of spring), the itinerant artist wandered across America, from the Atlantic coast to the frontier, carrying his prepared canvases or panels and his color box, palette, brushes, and precious pigments contained in squirrel and mouse bladders. He took a room in a country inn or at the house of a prospective patron, and passed out handbills or ran a notice in a local newspaper announcing himself ready to "take likenesses," and also to undertake a variety of other tasks, from "Varnishing, Gilding, etc. Coaches, Chaises, Signs, Fire-buckets, fancy Chairs, Standards, &c. painted in the neatest manner," to painting and "gilding on glass . . . paper, Vellum, Silks &c."—all performed in a fashion "to merit the approbation of those who may please to employ" him. The quality of the work varied from rank crudity to an extraordinary skill and power within the traditional limits of the style.

Many an artist started in this way and then moved up, to become proficient according to academic standards. Chester Harding, who momentarily outshone the great Gilbert Stuart himself, Thomas Cole, George Caleb Bingham, who so effectively recorded the life of the middle frontier—all were at one time itinerant painters. Morse turned of necessity to the same practice to feed his family; he painted portraits at fifteen dollars apiece when he found that Americans were not interested in the grandiose allegories he, like John Vanderlyn, so wanted to paint. Audubon did the same to support himself while on his endless journeys in search of the birds and animals of America. Rufus Porter (1792–1884), who painted portraits with the aid of a camera obscura of his own invention mounted on a handcart, went on foot from his home in Boxford, Massachusetts, and painted his way to the remote Appalachian valleys of western Virginia in 1819. His little book entitled *A Select Collection of Valuable and Curious Arts,* published in Concord,

John Brewster, Jr.:
Francis O. Watts with Bird,
1805, 35¼ x 26¼
(New York State Historical
Association, Cooperstown, N.Y.)

New Hampshire, in 1826, became a useful compendium of the crafts of the itinerant, not only for fellow wanderers, but also for the householder who wished to embellish his front room with a fireboard decorated with fruit or flowers, or to try his hand at stenciling the floors in the brightly colored substitutes for the carpets which were far too expensive for most to afford.

The ranks of academically untrained professionals were swelled by many who took to painting out of necessity as a means of livelihood. Joseph Whiting Stock (1815-55), whom an early accident confined to a wheel chair, painted hundreds of pictures—including portraits (some "from corpse"), miniatures, landscapes, anatomical drawings, and transparent window shades—during his short career. John Brewster, Jr. (1766–after 1846), son and brother of physicians of Hampton, Connecticut, who was born a deaf-mute, wandered throughout New England and beyond, producing some of the most delightful portraits of children in American art, painted with a sensitivity perhaps enhanced by the empathy he felt for them from the isolated, silent world in which he lived.

Far less is known about most of the artists of this group. Joseph H. Davis, for example, more than a hundred of whose colorful miniature portraits have survived, painted in northern

Joseph H. Davis: *Caverly Family of Stafford, N.H.*, c. 1836, water color, 15¾ x 11½ (New York State Historical Association, Cooperstown, N.Y.)

New England in the 1830's but is otherwise unrecorded. The elegant nonchalance of his male sitters—who are shown reading newspapers, signing documents, or merely balancing a shiny top hat on one knee—and the fashionable ease of his ladies—depicted sewing or embroidering while they watch the children, also dressed in their best—must have pleased his clients as much as the decorative details of the rooms with garlanded walls in which he represented them, seated facing each other across a table with a basket of fruit or a vase of flowers, the family Bible, and perhaps another volume or two, while the family cat gambols on a carpet of unbelievable color and design. James Sanford Ellsworth (1802-74) of Windsor, Connecticut, was another miniaturist with a native gift about whom little is known. Self-taught and reportedly "very eccentric," he "kept himself away from society, and read Shakespeare incessantly." He described himself as "a weather-beaten wanderer" with "an old dog as his only friend," but he made beautiful and distinctive portraits from New England to Ohio. His work is immediately identifiable by the characteristic stylized cloudlike forms that provide a kind of ambiance for the heads in profile and terminate the half-lengths he seems almost invariably to have preferred.

Learning, perhaps, from Rufus Porter's handbook or else in one of the innumerable female academies that sprang up during the early years of the nineteenth century, many young ladies (and often those not so young) indulged their "natural taste for drawing" as "an accomplishment very well adapted both to the taste and delicacy of [the] sex." They learned how to make "theorems"—paintings on velvet made with the aid of stencils carefully cut from stiff paper to make an endless variety of still-life compositions; and to make Grecian or sand-paper paintings with charcoal heightened with chalk on a ground of marble dust, which produced a romantic *sfumato* effect, often of moonlight; as well as to draw with crayons, as pastels were then called.

Ruth Henshaw Bascom (1772–1848) was one of the most accomplished in the last technique, in addition to being known for her skill in weaving, spinning, and embroidery. Her second husband was a minister who had parishes in Massachusetts and New Hampshire, but who was called as far afield as Charleston, Savannah, and other cities of the South. Her diaries record a happy and useful life, including many a sociable evening during which she took profiles of her friends and their children. Her method was to place her sitter with a light to

James Sanford Ellsworth:
Lady of the Folts Family of Albany,
c. 1845-50, water color, 4¾ x 3½
(New York State Historical
Association, Cooperstown, N.Y.)

Anonymous: *Flowers and Grapes,*
c. 1820, theorem painting, 11¾ x 16½
(New York State Historical
Association, Cooperstown, N.Y.)

Ruth Henshaw Bascom: *Mary Chamberlain,*
of Brattleboro, Vt., 1837, pastel, 19 x 14
(New York State Historical Association,
Cooperstown, N.Y.)

Ruth Henshaw Bascom: *Eliezur Chamberlain,*
of Brattleboro, Vt., 1837, pastel, 19 x 14
(New York State Historical Association,
Cooperstown, N.Y.)

cast on a sheet of paper the shadow of the profile which she
traced at life size, coloring the drawing the next day; sometimes
she would place it against a blue background, though occasionally she cut it out and mounted it against a piece of wallpaper
or a sheet of another shade or design. According to Nina
Fletcher Little, a leading authority on American folk artists,
she "supplied the glass and framed her own pictures," and
"during her infrequent trips to Boston, she purchased crayons
and drawing paper for twenty-five cents at Burdit's, 'on the way
to Hanover St.' "

One of the most prolific of the professional unacademic
artists was William Matthew Prior (1806-73), who was born in
Bath, Maine, the son of a shipmaster who died early, leaving
the boy on his own when still in his teens. At twenty-one he
advertised in the Maine *Inquirer* as an ornamental painter who
would also produce "drawings of machineries of every description executed in good order and on shortest possible notice,"
likenesses at a reasonable price, and "side views and profiles

William Matthew Prior: *Mrs. Lawson*, 1843, 30 x 25
(Courtesy Shelburne Museum, Shelburne, Vt.)

William Matthew Prior: *Rev. W. Lawson*, 1843, 30 x 25
(Courtesy Shelburne Museum, Shelburne, Vt.)

of children at reduced prices." He varied his style to suit the pocketbooks of his sitters, announcing that he would produce head-and-shoulder portraits on academy board in one-hour sittings "without shade or shadow," framed and glazed, for two dollars and ninety-two cents. His larger and more complete portraits, those of children and usually including a dog or cat, often ran to twenty-five dollars or more. He also did landscapes, such as views of Washington's tomb at Mount Vernon and "Moonshines," romantic moonlit scenes derived from prints but never slavishly copied.

After his marriage in 1828 to Rosamond Clark Hamblen, he lived for a while in Portland and then moved to East Boston and bought a house at 36 Trenton Street, where, in what he called his "painting garret," he and his brother-in-law Sturtevant Hamblen, and other members of the painting Prior and Hamblen households turned out innumerable pictures in a style so consistent that, unless there is a signature, it is impossible to tell the work of one from another. Prior himself took frequent trips, traveling with horse and wagon, by coastal steamer, and up and down the Eastern seaboard by railroad, painting portraits on the spot and taking orders for other works, such as landscapes or copies of Stuart's Athenaeum *Washington*. Many of these were done on glass and neatly mounted in a frame of gold, veneered mahogany, or plain pine painted to resemble that more elegant wood. The standard of quality maintained by Prior and his assistants is remarkably high. His sitters are thoroughly convincing, and even their frequently included pets have a vitality which lends his compositions great charm. He managed at once to satisfy that basic American desire for realism, since he was a keen-eyed and sympathetic observer, and also to create colorful compositions of great decorative value. A passionate abolitionist, he remains among the few artists of the period who often painted Negro subjects, who are depicted with the dignity and deep respect he accorded all his sitters. His *Three Sisters of the Coplan Family* (Karolik Collection, Boston), one of his most delightful group portraits, and the pair of likenesses of the Reverend Mr. Lawson and his wife, each composed with a vista of landscape seen through the window, remain outstanding examples of his work.

The crafts of the sign and wagon painter provided a livelihood for many. The eccentric John Quidor (1801-81), who so vividly transformed scenes from Irving into eerie visions, made the greater part of his living as a painter of fire engines. His robust Indian maidens, painted in brilliant colors against the bright red of the polished hand tubs, aroused great admiration among the firemen and the small boys who frequented the firehouse. Sign painting kept Edward Hicks and his family sheltered and fed, and gave Chester Harding his start, as it had so many other less famous men. There were also other special fields in which a few artists found careers. James Bard (1815-97) and his twin brother, John (d. 1856), who were born in a house overlooking the Hudson and spent their entire lives in New York City, became famous for their portraits of the steamships that plied the river and docked at the piers along the lower shores of Manhattan. At the age of twelve James did a picture of the *Bellona,* the first steam vessel owned by Commodore Vanderbilt, and thus discovered his lifework. He haunted the shipyards, sketching and measuring, checking every detail and color, until shipbuilders admiringly testified that they could lay down the lines of a vessel from the paintings that resulted. So accurate and decorative were the Bards' pictures that they often had to produce several of the same vessel, for captain, owner, or satisfied passenger, though no two were ever alike.

Far better known, however, are the painters who portrayed the sailing vessels of the nineteenth century which reached their peak of perfection and beauty in the brief but glorious reign of the clipper ship starting at mid-century. James E. Buttersworth (1817-94) and Clement Drew, who worked in Boston from 1841 to 1860, are but two of the clipper-ship painters whose names have been recorded. The works of such artists were submitted to the most exacting criticism of expert sea-

Ship Carvers and Other Craftsmen

James Bard:
Hudson River Steamboat: "Rip van Winkle,"
1854, 31¼ x 53
(Courtesy, Museum of Fine Arts,
Boston, M. and M. Karolik Collection)

283

men, who expected every detail of rigging and hull to be precise. The results are always decorative and picturesque, but they rarely rise to the artistic heights of those of William Bradford (1823-92), from the old whaling port of Fairhaven, Massachusetts, who made several trips far into Arctic seas, painting the effects of light on the ice floes and the bleak coasts of the Far North. His *Dashing Wave* of 1855 (Peabody Museum) is an excellent example of his ship portraiture, with its feeling of the sea in motion and of canvas taut with the fresh sweep of a spanking breeze.

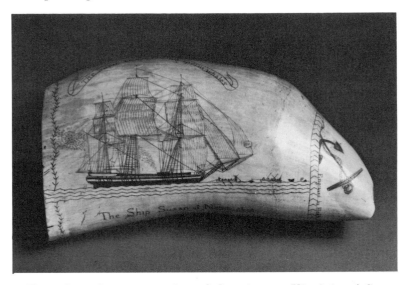

Anonymous:
The Ship "Susan" of Nantucket,
19th cent., scrimshaw
(Courtesy of the Peabody Museum
of Salem, Mass.)

Ever since the construction of the pinnace *Virginia of Sagadahock*, at the mouth of the Kennebec in 1607, the shipbuilding industry kept generations of craftsmen busy before the decline of the wooden ship and the austerity of the later steamships no longer demanded the services of the ship carver for figureheads, billetheads, trail boards, and stern designs. The ancient craft seems to have produced dynasties—such as the famous Christmas workshop in England, which was responsible for so much of the spectacular and ornate grandeur of the British ships of the line and royal barges for over a century or more, from the Restoration on. There were firms of brothers, like the Littlefields of Portland, and father-and-son firms, like the Gleasons of Boston. The major American dynasty of ship carvers was that of the Skillins, started by Simeon Skillin (1716-78), of Boston, whose three sons, John, Simeon, Jr., and Samuel, continued the tradition. Samuel moved to Philadelphia, where he carried out carved work for a number of Pennsylvania State naval vessels and privateers before returning to Boston, where he remained active until his death in 1830. Samuel's son, Simeon III, worked in New York from 1792 until his death in the same year as his father's, while his uncles, John and Simeon, Jr., monopolized the craft in Boston, making figureheads and other work for virtually every ship of importance—merchantman, privateer, or naval vessel. They did most of the carving for the large fleet of Elias Hasket Derby of Salem, the largest shipowner and richest man in the country at the time, and also executed the charming sculptures for his garden pavilion and the Hercules figurehead for the famous frigate U.S.S. *Constitution*, which was designed by William Rush of Philadelphia.

Samuel McIntire, architect and cabinetmaker of Salem, also is known to have been a ship carver, but only one work can with any certainty be attributed to him, a figurehead of a woman holding an oval medallion-portrait of a man. It is an attractive but stiff figure, and, like the work of the Skillins, is entirely in the style of the British ship carvings of the same period. Solomon Willard, best known as architect of the Bunker Hill Monument, also did marine work. The bust of *Washington* for the seventy-four-gun ship of that name built at Portsmouth, New Hampshire, in 1816, shows the qualities of directness and strength one would expect from such a forthright individual.

It remained for William Rush (1756–1833) to usher in "what was certainly," according to Commander M. V. Brewington in his definitive *Shipcarvers of North America*, "the grand period of American marine decoration." The son of a shipwright, Rush grew up in the shipyards of Philadelphia, was apprenticed at fifteen to an English-trained carver, Edward Cutbush, and while still in his teens was acknowledged the leader in the field in the city. During the Revolutionary period he had seen two French frigates undergoing repairs at the yard of Joshua Humphreys, the designer and builder of the *Constitution*. From the time of Colbert, the French navy had conducted schools of ship carving under distinguished artists, and what Rush saw gave him an entirely new idea, not only of what a figurehead could be, but of what all sculpture might be. His work thereafter showed the influence of the style, however remote, of Pierre Puget, the greatest of French Baroque sculptors, of whom Rush had in all probability never heard. Puget's designs, made during the second half of the seventeenth century when he worked in the navy yard at Toulon, served as models for generations of ship carvers of France. Instead of the stiff, wooden

Figurehead, attributed to Samuel McIntire, late 18th cent., painted wood, h. about 42 (Courtesy of the Peabody Museum of Salem, Mass.)

images that had adorned the bows of American ships up to that time, Rush designed and carved figures full of motion. The awkward, thrusting pose of the earlier heads was replaced by a free-flowing, dynamic composition, the male figures striding or gesturing with energy, the female figures moving with floating grace.

Rush's figureheads caused a sensation wherever the vessels carrying them put into port. When the ship *William Penn* docked in London, "carvers there would come in boats and lay near the ship and sketch the designs from it," her captain reported. "They even came to take casts of plaster of Paris from the head." And when the ship *Ganges* reached Calcutta, "the Hindus came off in numerous boats to pay their admiration and perhaps reverence" to her river-god figurehead. Orders for what came to be known as Philadelphia-style figureheads poured in from London, from shipbuilders up and down the Atlantic seaboard, and even from the dey of Algiers, for whom Rush carved "2 Lyons, very airy &c different attitudes, one tearing a Fox to pieces, the other destroying a Tiger or Lioness, Painted," according to a contemporary description, "to the Life." So great was Rush's fame that in 1794 he was commissioned to design all the heads for the six frigates of the original United States Navy. The most elaborate of these was one described by Rush himself in the *American Daily Advertiser* as "the genius of the UNITED STATES: she is crest with a Constellation, her hair and drapery flowing . . . and reclining on her bosom is the portrait of her favorite son, George Washington President of United States; her waist bound with a Civic Band. In her right hand which is advanced she holds a spear suspended to which is a belt of wampum containing the Emblems of Peace and War. On her left . . . is a tablet which supports three large columns which relate to three Branches of Government. . . . The Left Hand suspends the Constitution over the book, &c. on the Tablet; the Eagle with his wings half extended, with the . . . Arms of the United States on the Right . . . the attributes, Commerce and Agriculture, and a modest position of the Arts and Sciences."

Unfortunately, this carving, like almost all of Rush's other figureheads, did not survive the buffets of the seas and the toll of the years. He brought a freedom of movement into all his work, as may be seen in the lively and amusing figures of *Tragedy* and *Comedy* sculptured for a pair of niches on the façade of the Chestnut Street Theatre, and in his *Water Nymph and Bittern* (all in the Philadelphia Museum), executed for

Center Square in front of the Pump House, Philadelphia, which was designed by his friend and admirer Benjamin Latrobe. But there is more to his style than the results of his study of the Neoclassicism of the age, enlivened by the movement derived from the Baroque of a previous epoch. He also looked at nature directly and objectively, and strove to realize what he saw and felt as the result of that analytical scrutiny. Though the finished figure was to be draped, tradition has it that, uniquely, he worked from the nude for his statue of the *Water Nymph*. The daughter of a friend is said to have posed for it, properly chaperoned by her mother, and this in a city that was to ostracize Thomas Eakins for the same offense half a century or more later. This vigorous and searching realism pervades all his work, from the portrait busts, such as those of *Lafayette* (Pennsylvania Academy) and *Franklin* (the latter perhaps the most perceptive of all the innumerable portraits of the great American philosopher) to the masterfully carved models of organs of the human body, which are still used in the study of anatomy. His life-sized *Washington* in Independence Hall, clearly inspired by that of Houdon in Richmond, translates the suave forms into the more vigorous expressionism of his wood-carving technique, giving the figure the force that made his figureheads, as a contemporary observed, "seem rather to draw the ship after them than to be impelled by the vessel."

There were few to approach the quality of Rush as a ship carver in later years. John W. Mason, who worked in Boston during the middle decades of the nineteenth century, must have been one of the more accomplished carvers, because his drawings, all preserved at the Peabody Museum in Salem, provide an interesting record, though none of his actual carvings remain. But with the passing of the clipper-ship era, the craft declined. There are countless examples of the work of later men, done most often for the schooners that continued to be built throughout the century for coastwise trade. Few have any distinction, though several carvers achieved at least a local fame. Harvey Counce of Thomaston, Maine, lent his skills to the adornment of houses in the village, with cleanly cut trim for porches, and bargeboards carried out with greater sculptural feeling than usual. Edbury Hatch, also of Maine, created handsome side panels in designs of grapevines and acanthuslike crestings for the front doors of a number of houses in Damariscotta and Newcastle, where he lived, and elsewhere in the region. One of the best known in the craft was John Bellamy (1836–1914) of Kittery Point, Maine, who spent a lifetime as a ship carver in the

William Rush: *Benjamin Franklin*, c. 1785, wood, h. 21 (Yale University Art Gallery)

287

neighboring Portsmouth Navy Yard, and became famous for his abstract and stylish American eagles, such as that with a wingspread of eleven feet executed for the U.S.S. *Lancaster*. Bellamy was honored with exhibitions in Boston and elsewhere, and lived on as a leading citizen of Portsmouth, the last of a proud profession, until almost the eve of the First World War.

During the same period a similarly fanciful art was adorning, with a profusion of nymphs, animals, warriors, and chimeras, in a style that might be called Barnum Baroque, circus wagons and floats for all of Barnum's would-be rivals and many successors, most of whom were eventually absorbed into "The Greatest Show on Earth" of the Ringling Brothers. Brightly decorated, and gleaming with scarlet and gold, they were produced by craftsmen largely of German and Swiss descent. They share, as do the horses and other beasts of the merry-go-round, much of the vigor of the ship carvings, though they far outdid the figureheads in a brash gaudiness matched only by the brassy blasts of the calliope, that most unmusical instrument whose stirring sound so appropriately conveys the carnival spirit.

More sedate, though stylistically related, were the three-dimensional shop signs, such as the neatly carved sheep to denote the wool merchant, the famous little navigator in New Bedford, perpetually shooting the sun with his sextant, to show where nautical instruments were sold, and the fierce Indian brave or buxom Indian maiden to mark the tobacconist's shop. All the better works of these many carvers—whether intended for a ship, a circus wagon, a carrousel, or as a shop sign—have an explicitness of significant detail and a completeness of formal realization which were intended to enable them to be effective at a distance and thus fulfill their essential function, and which today convey the power and vitality of the men and the period from which they came. None of them, however, achieves the monumentality of a sculpture by the self-taught artist David Gilmour Blythe (1815-65).

Though he was born in Ohio and lived most of his life in Pittsburgh and western Pennsylvania, Blythe occasionally traveled as an itinerant jack-of-all-trades through the middle frontier. In 1847 he carved a nine-foot figure of *Lafayette*, from a block made of poplar planks spiked together, for the top of the dome of the Fayette County Court House in Uniontown, in southwestern Pennsylvania. The sculpture is said to have been based on the artist's youthful recollections of the return in 1824 of the aged veteran to America. Lafayette had traveled throughout the

Circus wagon, c. 1900
(Circus World Museum, Baraboo, Wis.)

288

United States, his visit a triumphal tour, since, as a companion-in-arms of Washington, he was, in American eyes, a living symbol of the nation's beginnings. It is thus that Blythe portrays him, with a presence closely reminiscent of Morse's famous portrait, in a boldly simplified style which is not only appropriate for the statue's original lofty situation, where detail could not be seen, but which also gives it the seriousness and dignity befitting an historic personage who had become an almost legendary folk hero.

During the nineteenth century the popular arts of America produced a variety of results, ranging from the naïve charm of a homemade weathervane or child's toy to the monumentality of Blythe's *Lafayette,* and from the flights of idealizing fancy of Hicks and Field to the detailed descriptive realism of Augur and Frazee. At best, all the examples convey in some measure the impact of personality, which is an expression of individualism. It appears in the carved birds and animals of Wilhelm Schimmel (1817-90), the lumbering and morose Pennsylvanian who, as an itinerant sculptor, wandered the fertile countryside of the Cumberland Valley, selling for a few cents the birds and animals he had whittled out of pine and colored with what paint he could find, or else trading one for a drink of whiskey, a meal, or a night's lodging. His roosters and squirrels, lions and eagles are infinitely varied, all instinct with a vitality derived both from acuteness of observation and from the consistent ruggedness of his direct technique. When he died in the almshouse in Carlisle at the age of seventy-three, there was hardly a house, restaurant, or barroom throughout the area that did not boast a defiant spread eagle or some other product of his jackknife, bristling with the cantankerous independence that the old man himself had had in such full measure.

The same acuteness is evident in the decoys—ducks and geese, curlews, plovers, herons, and swans—made by countless enthusiastic gunners during the cold winter evenings in anticipation of the season to come. Far from being a slavish copier of nature, the maker of good decoys reduced the form and attitude of the bird to its essentials in a process of simplification possible only with a complete and instinctive knowledge based on years of observation and experience, the result of the individual's intimate relation to nature, fostered by the environment of the New World. The same approach that had made it possible for Audubon to produce his expressive panorama of the birds and quadrupeds of America, had also allowed one Andrew L. von Wittkamp, M.D., unknown except for his signa-

David G. Blythe: *Lafayette,*
1847, painted wood, h. 108
(Courtesy of Board of County Commissioners,
Fayette County, Uniontown, Pa.)

289

ture on a single picture, to turn that canvas into an unforgettable image of his black cat, sprawled across a yellowish chair, portrayed with an almost surrealist intensity.

American folk art reached its height during the period before the Civil War, and after it went into a decline and virtually disappeared, except for vestiges here and there, by the end of the century. When in 1839 Samuel F. B. Morse transported M. Daguerre's ingenious invention of two years before across the Atlantic, it meant the end of the charming art of the miniaturist, and those portraits that continued to be painted became increasingly luxurious products for the comparative few who were rich enough to afford them and wanted something more prestigious than a mere photograph. From the beginning, people had relied on the artist to record the appearance of members of their families, likenesses all the more treasured because of the toll of hardship, accident, and disease during the difficult early years of the country's history. Portraits were carried when the family moved, providing a link with the past. The artist's skill preserved for bereaved parents the appearance of the child that did not live to grow up, and thus helped to keep the family circle complete.

With no more demand for portraits, the opportunity which had supplied so many men and women with a respectable and respected livelihood and a useful place in the community, and which had discovered and nourished so many varying talents, vanished, and the nation was incalculably the poorer for it. Some artists took up photography. Those who continued to paint for a diminishing clientele, even the successful leaders in the field, with few exceptions tended to adopt the hard outlines, textureless surfaces, and murky tones of the photograph. Just as advancing technology and the development of the machine brought an end to most of the traditional handcrafts, the camera provided competition that the portrait painter, whether professional or amateur, could not survive.

The portrait had been the basis of the painter's art in America, and without it the position of the artist in society underwent an abrupt and alarming change. Thereafter, if a person aspired to a career in art, he could no longer learn the rudiments of the craft from some local practitioner, because unless he lived in a fair-sized community there was no longer a local artist. If he persevered, he had to teach or carry on some other sort of activity to support himself, unless he were one of the gifted and fortunate few, and the dilemma of the artist of our

Andrew L. von Wittkamp:
Black Cat on a Chair,
c. 1850-60, 36 x 29¼
(Courtesy, Museum of Fine Arts,
Boston, M. and M. Karolik Collection)

own day, with the insecurity of a position dependent upon fashion rather than function for the sales to produce the income essential to life, was the result. The artist ceased to have an accepted and understood position in the community, and art was never again to occupy the same unselfconscious and intimate place in the everyday life of Americans, for whom it had provided generous enrichment during so many earlier generations throughout the land.

Dr. William Hallowell: *The Peaceable Kingdom*, 1865, pen drawing, 15¾ x 19¾
(New York State Historical Association, Cooperstown, N.Y.)

Currier & Ives: *The Great East River Suspension Bridge* (Brooklyn Bridge), 1877
(Courtesy Kenneth M. Newman, The Old Print Shop, Inc.)

ART FOR EVERYONE

Though Americans have always tended to express an admiration for art as an unexceptionable good, like Virtue and Motherhood, they have also seemed to enjoy it most if mixed with something a bit tastier. *The Greek Slave* presented a nice combination of art with the female nude, a very rare commodity in the age that held that even tables had limbs rather than legs. And P. T. Barnum offered "THE ALBINO LADY and 500,000 curiosities" as an added inducement to art lovers to come to see "the great picture of CHRIST HEALING THE SICK IN THE TEMPLE, by Benjamin West, Esq." in his famous museum.

The American Art-Union and the Growth of the Popular Arts

James Herring, a little-known artist turned dealer, hit on an unbeatable scheme, significantly borrowed from a highly successful Scottish precedent, when he spiced an enjoyment of the arts with the added ingredient of gambling in his creation of the Apollo Association by offering a free painting to lucky ticketholders who had subscribed to his Association. The appeal of culture plus something for nothing was too great to resist. By the middle of the century, little more than a decade since its inception, the American Art-Union, as it came to be called, had almost 20,000 members paying five dollars a year, spread across the country from coast to coast as well as in Canada, Great Britain, on the Continent, and as far distant as Brazil and New Zealand. Each of the members annually received "a large and costly Original Engraving from an American painting" and a numbered ticket which might prove to be one of the lucky ones, entitling its holder to an original painting, at the annual drawing held in the Broadway Tabernacle, the largest available public hall in New York. For months in the meantime the Art-Union gallery's exhibition of works of American art, bought with the proceeds from the subscriptions, had delighted crowds of visitors, half a million in 1849, and the dramatic climax in the Tabernacle was played to capacity crowds. Presided over by William Cullen Bryant, who could always be counted on to do everything possible to advance the cause of the arts, the gathering heard various addresses, including a report on the year's purchases (selected by a jury of prominent artists), membership, and receipts collected by a dedicated group of volunteers. Finally, the numbers were drawn by two little girls dressed in their best. During the eleven years of its existence the Union distributed nearly twenty-five hundred paintings and sculptures, not including the annual premium engravings, to its members. Hardly a town of any size in America lacked its winner, and, for many, the illustrated *Bulletin* sent out by the Union was the first publication devoted to the arts that they had ever seen, and their first introduction to the artistic achievements of their countrymen.

It was too good to last. Art seems inevitably to arouse controversy in America, and a few artists, disgruntled because the Union had not bought enough of their works, and a crusading press, more interested in increasing circulation than in fostering the arts, combined to force an issue with the courts, which resulted in outlawing the scheme as a lottery and therefore illegal in the sovereign State of New York. Its pattern, however, was successfully followed by other cities from Boston and Philadelphia to Cincinnati and Sandusky. Though the life of the American Art-Union was short, during its brief existence the idea that the arts were for everyone was firmly implanted in the public mind.

Among those people who awoke to the fact was Andrew Jackson Downing's friend and admirer Nathaniel Parker Willis, who had developed a fine taste for the world of fashion when still at Yale. Upon graduation, he hastened to New York, where he managed to get himself appointed a foreign correspondent for the New York *Mirror* so that he could observe and enjoy yet more exalted society than he had found at home. His facile style, superficial but lively observation of people and manners, and good humor lent just the right tone to the reports he sent home from the capitals and watering places of Europe, and exactly suited a generation of feminine readers who were beginning to become somewhat painfully aware of American social deficiencies, after having had them all too clearly pointed out by such critics as Mrs. Trollope and Harriet Martineau. People were suddenly conscious of taste, and insecurities unknown to such confident souls as Cooper and Irving, who were at perfect ease everywhere, beset the wives of those whose fortunes were or hoped to be rising in the rapidly shifting society of the post-Jacksonian era. Byron now shared the stage with the more elegant and equally aristocratic Bulwer-Lytton, and by some mysterious process taste was rapidly becoming the exclusive property of women who were then in the early throes of the feminist movement. To show their independence of mind some of them were even to take to wearing the curious garment intro-

T. H. Matteson: *Distribution of the American Art-Union Prizes,* lithograph by Sarony & Major, 1848 (Courtesy, Museum of Fine Arts, Boston, M. and M. Karolik Collection)

duced by Mrs. Amelia Bloomer of Seneca Falls, New York, in her attempt quite literally to have the ladies wear the pants in the family. Determined to achieve culture, they avidly subscribed to the various periodicals prepared to improve their taste without unduly taxing their intellects, chief among these was *Godey's Lady's Book,* expertly and relentlessly edited by the redoubtable Mrs. Sarah Josepha Hale with an unbeatable combination of soggy sentiment, spiritual uplift, moral verses, snippets from "the great authors," messages from Harriet Beecher Stowe, sound advice from the editor, and the latest news in fashions.

Willis' style and approach were exactly gauged to just this audience, and his novels, poems, sketches, stories, and reports, expertly and frothily written, were far and away the best of their kind. As editor as well as author he was equally successful, and his contribution to the growth of the gift-book industry (for such it rapidly became after its start in 1825 with *The Atlantic Souvenir,* an immediately popular volume issued by Carey and Lea of Philadelphia in imitation of the British *Forget-me-not* of two years earlier) was significant. *The Atlantic Souvenir* proliferated into countless volumes directed toward various interests of the feminine audience. *The Lover's Gift* and *The Marriage-Ring* were for brides; *The Wreath,* "a selection of elegant poems from the best authors," was for those addicted to sentimental numbers; and *The Cypress Wreath* or *The Mourner's Chaplet* for those who had suffered recent bereavement. Some were published year after year (like *The Pearl, or Affection's Gift, The Rose of Sharon, The Token,* and *The Hyacinth*), while others were issued singly, all appearing, however, during November or December, in time for the Christmas market. Many titles were taken from the jeweler's shop, there being a whole run of *Opals, Rubies, Pearls,* and other *Gems,* while floral titles sprouted in large numbers (*The Lily of the Valley, The Violet, The Passion Flower, or A Gift of the Heart, The Mignonette, or The Graces of the Mind, The Iris,* and *The Rose*).

For those so piously inclined that the regular stiff doses of religious sentiments administered in the average gift book were inadequate, there was *The Christian Parlor Book Devoted to Science, Literature, and Religion,* or *The Religious Souvenir,* which Mrs. Sigourney herself certified pure. "Not a line in this book will cause a Christian to hesitate," she stated. These seem to have been supplied with most of their material by clergymen, who no doubt hoped to get a little more mileage and some needed extra money from printing their sermons. They were also

295

filled with such informative and practical information, to cite the partial contents of one such volume, as the manner of addressing petitions to the Sublime Porte; an illustration and accompanying list of the 46 "loftiest buildings in the world," from the steeple of the Park Street Church in Boston to the Temple of Shomadu in Pegu; lines by Mrs. Felicia Hemans, England's opposite number to Mrs. Sigourney, set to music in "fresh and inspiriting songs for the music-loving public"; and reams of verse on such edifying subjects as "The Dying Child" and "On Suddenly Seeing a Maniac Smile." But there were also views and plans of model cottages designed by Downing, the plans and elevations of "O. S. Fowler's Gravelwall and Octagon House," with a strong recommendation of it as "a practical, common-sense production, and well worthy the study of all house-builders," and a view and description of the circular house, "recently erected by Enoch Robinson, Esq., at Spring Hill, Somerville, Mass."

Their publishers endeavored to make the gift books as attractive as possible by the use of colored frontispieces and dedicatory pages where, in a heart-shaped cartouche of lilies of the valley or moss roses, one could write the name of the lady who was to receive the gift. Large numbers of steel engravings were included, and sometimes wood engravings also, in lower-priced gift books. Many gift books had elaborate bindings in bright colors, stamped in gold with appropriate designs, and some had a series of color plates of flowers that might be removed for framing. Though the general tone of all the books was condescending, moralizing, and cloggingly sentimental, they contained works of leading contemporary writers, among them Bryant, Longfellow, Emerson, Holmes, Whittier, and Poe, several of whose stories, including "The Pit and the Pendulum" and "The Purloined Letter," first appeared in *The Gift*. The engravings were often made after genuine old masters, such as Raphael and Claude, and after the works of recent and contemporary British artists—such as Constable, Turner, Wilkie, and Landseer—as well as those of such Americans as Cole, Durand, Doughty, Bingham, Church, and many less well known. There were also views of the great cathedrals, Egyptian temples, the Parthenon, the Roman Forum, and other architectural monuments, accompanied by explanatory text. The gift books were, in short, the nineteenth-century equivalent of the hard-covered periodicals on the cocktail table in today's conversation pit. With the immensely popular magazines, such as *Gleason's, Peterson's, Appleton's Journal, Harper's,* and the *Atlantic,* they introduced innumerable Americans to the art and literature of their own country and beyond, and were a force of incalculable influence in the spread of ideas of culture and the course of American taste.

Many an American artist got his start as an engraver. Durand, for example, produced some of the finest works in the medium done in America, such as his large plates after Trumbull's *Declaration of Independence*, the major picture in many an American household, and Vanderlyn's *Ariadne*, which was only for those advanced enough in their tastes so that they could allow a nude in the house. Durand's portfolio of 1830, *The American Landscape*, which consisted of expert engravings after the major painters of the Hudson River School and a text by Bryant, contained prints of the highest quality. John Sartain introduced the mezzotint technique from England in the same year, with immediately popular results in many of the annuals. William (1795–1879) and John (1798–1866) Pendleton opened the first lithographic shop in the United States in Boston in 1829. A number of expert draftsmen and painters, among them Fitz Hugh Lane and Alexander Jackson Davis, supplied their designs, and their excellent views of cities and towns, famous buildings, and important landmarks were in great demand. In 1838 and 1839 an Englishman, William Henry Bartlett, came to America to make sketches for his engraved plates for N. P. Willis' *American Scenery* of 1840, and the views that he produced rivaled those of the Pendletons in popularity.

The Pendletons soon took on an apprentice named Nathaniel Currier (1813-88), who learned the trade well, because when he set up for himself in New York in 1835, along with J. H. Bufford, who later started his own business, he made an immediate success. In 1857 he took a minor painter named James Merritt Ives (1824-95) into partnership, and the most famous firm in American popular printmaking was established. It turned out dozens of prints of topical subjects, famous men, views familiar through paintings of Cole and his followers (like that of the Hudson at West Point), scenes of skating in Central Park, suburban villas in Italianate style which would have had Downing's approval, life on the farm and in the West, children and animals, burning buildings, patriotic subjects, railroads, steamboats, and clipper ships. The prints cost little enough at the time—from twenty-five cents to three dollars—so that almost anyone could afford them.

First printed in black and white, the lithographs were colored by hand by a group of young women, each of whom was in charge of a single tint, though later they were entirely printed in a color process. Artistically unimportant, they are nevertheless interesting as giving an insight into the taste of the times, because they were bought in unbelievable quantities both in America and abroad. As Harry T. Peters' *Currier & Ives, Printmakers to the American People* demonstrates, the prints are always idealized, with everybody happy and well fed except when they are sorrowing over the loss of some loved one. Dogs are noble and cats playful, and Indians die with stoic dignity as the white man wins the West. In the most popular pictorial art that America has ever had before the development of the cinema, the prints of Currier & Ives embodied the images and the attitudes of the generality of Americans for half a century.

Meanwhile another ingenious Yankee had hit the jackpot of popular taste, but with works of a far higher standard of quality. Originally from Salem, Massachusetts, John Rogers (1829–1904) tried his hand at a number of things, including becoming an expert mechanical draftsman. Then his little sculptured group called *The Checker Players*, full of storytelling detail, became the hit of a charity fair at the Cosmopolitan Bazaar in Chicago in 1859 and was auctioned off for $75, an event which, as he remarked, "set him to thinking." He had spent a brief time studying art in Rome, but he did not care for the Neoclassic frigidities being produced there. He was really more interested in people than in art, and he liked to finish his small clay figures with the utmost detail so that they told a story with clarity and often with humor. He learned from an Italian craftsman in Chicago how to make molds and casts, then modeled with great care a group he entitled *The Slave Auction*. It included a Negro family of four, sympathetically portrayed, and a sinister Simon Legree as the auctioneer. With *The Slave Auction* Rogers launched his career in New York. When a leading abolitionist, who saw the propaganda value of the piece (for Rogers himself felt very strongly on the subject of slavery) commended it enthusiastically, success was assured.

Rogers gradually assembled a group of expert workmen who made the many casts of the master models he himself worked up with such care. His subjects were episodes from stories by Irving and Cooper and from American history, and included family groups and portrayals of the famous actor Joseph Jefferson as Rip van Winkle and in other popular roles. Those groups inspired by the Civil War are among his most eloquent. His *Fugitive's Story* and other antislavery subjects were almost as

John Rogers: *The Council of War*, 1868, plaster, h. 24
(Owned by the Henry Ford Museum & Greenfield Village)

helpful to the cause of abolition as *Uncle Tom's Cabin*. He mailed his circulars all over the country and abroad, listing the pieces, in plaster, at from $6 to $25 because, as he said, "I want them to be within the means of everyone to buy." Between 1860 and 1890, Russell Lynes tells us, "about 100,000 Rogers groups were sold." He was an artist about whom everyone was in accord, from the members of the National Academy, which early elected him to their group, to inhabitants of farm and frontier.

His early notion that "high art" was neither for him nor for the American people led to his becoming one of the most popular artists in history, whose works are avidly collected by some even today, despite the intervening convulsions of style and taste. Furthermore, he had attacked head on the problem of making art objects available to the many, one that has bothered many a socially conscious artist and critic. He simply used good production methods. From John Rogers' point of view and that of his countless customers, he had resolved the dilemma to complete satisfaction. No less a critic than James Jackson Jarves, whose collection of medieval and early Renaissance painting is today the great glory of the Yale University Art Gallery, could join Henry Ward Beecher, John Greenleaf Whittier, Abraham Lincoln, and the man in the street in admiration of his work. People liked his observant realism, just as they did the works of William Sidney Mount and the other contemporary genre painters, and as today they acclaim the illustrations of Norman Rockwell, the pleasures of recognition being still more satisfying to many than those of discovery. Today's critics, however, unlike those of the last century, are more sensitive to the dangers of an attempt at total realization, and to the banal triviality that inevitably results from the disproportion between an indiscriminate elaboration of means and the end sought. In his most effective works, Rogers successfully avoided this pitfall, though they are never without the narrative element, so satisfying to popular taste but anathema to the purists of today.

At this time methods were being perfected to allow production of the color prints known as chromolithographs, some of which, such as those made by Louis Prang in Boston, are of excellent technical quality. Though subjects were usually taken from sentimental genre painting of the day, his reproductions of the paintings of Western scenery by Thomas Moran, a later artist of the Hudson River School, remain handsome examples of their kind. Imported murky-toned "art prints" after Renaissance and later masters began to appear on the dormitory and study walls of art-loving undergraduates and Concord transcendentalists alike, to be followed, later in the century, by the once familiar photographs of European monuments and views.

There were also those who took a leaf from the book of Currier & Ives, and employed groups of young women to produce "genuine oil paintings" for a less sophisticated market, with the use of sponges and brushes in a curiously careless, impersonal, and abstract style in half a dozen or so standard compositions copied with great generality from typical scenes by the artists of the Hudson River School. On muslin rather than canvas, and packaged in the cheapest of false-gilt simulations of the heavy and ornate frames then in vogue, they are the nineteenth-century equivalents of the plastic-framed, mass-produced reproductions, complete with "brushwork," of "masterpieces by the world's great artists" of more recent date, except that they had the slight advantage of being, after a fashion, actually painted instead of turned out by machine. Produced in great numbers, they were once sold in furniture and other stores, as were the vastly superior Rogers groups, and were also hawked by peddlers along with books and household wares, during the second half of the century.

In the larger cities the activities of the American Art-Union and its successors, stimulated an interest that led to frequent exhibition of the works of European and American contemporary artists, and in some cities to the starting of commercial galleries, such as that of J. J. Gillespie, which opened in Pittsburgh in 1832, and was said to be "the oldest Art Establishment in America." Probably the first to show both domestic and foreign works in formal exhibitions west of the Alleghenies, Gillespie's gallery became a meeting place for artists of the region and beyond; it served as headquarters for Sully, Harding, and others when they visited Pittsburgh to carry out portrait commissions, and it was there that David Gilmour Blythe saw his first paintings and showed his own curious and forceful works.

In 1846 young Michel Knoedler arrived in New York to open a branch gallery of the famed Paris firm of printsellers and engravers Goupil & Cie, which became, eleven years later, M. Knoedler & Company, today one of the world's greatest art dealers. In 1849 the Prussian consul in New York, John G. Baker, started the once popular Düsseldorf Gallery. And in the following year an active and ambitious young man named Seth Vose established the Westminster Art Gallery in Providence, Rhode Island, and shortly afterward started another in Boston, where he sold to adventurous New Englanders, inspired by the enthusiasm of William Morris Hunt, works of the forward-looking European artists of the day—Millet, Courbet, Delacroix, and other leaders in the movements that were to contain the future of French painting, artists unknown to the German-oriented taste of New York. For more than half a century Seth Vose and his son were to be almost the sole source for collectors who lived at a distance from the Eastern seaboard, for the firm, which today specializes in American old masters, once sent annual exhibitions of important European paintings around the country. Eagerly anticipated, these attracted the most rapt attention wherever they were shown.

In 1855 *The Crayon* was established in New York by John Durand, son of the painter Asher B. Durand, and by William J. Stillman, friend of Ruskin and Dante Gabriel Rossetti and others of the Pre-Raphaelite group. It was the first American magazine devoted to the arts and successfully challenged the British *Art Journal* for readership. In an early issue Stillman was one of the first to acclaim "the wonderful vigour of thought and intensity of purpose" of the irregular verses written by a young Brooklyn editor named Walt Whitman in his *Leaves of Grass. The Crayon* lasted only six years, however, publication ceasing when Stillman left to become United States consul in Rome. The *American Art Journal* was not to appear till after the Civil War.

Speedier and more efficient presses made the production of generously illustrated magazines possible, and opened the way for a new school of popular illustrators. Important among them are F. O. C. Darley (1822-88), whose prolific production has tended to obscure his considerable gifts as an interpreter of character and incident, Alonzo Chappel (1828-87), once famous for historical illustrations, and Theodore Russell Davis (1840-94) and Alfred R. Waud (1828-91), swashbuckling combat correspondents who, with the taciturn Winslow Homer, have left us the most vivid pictorial record of the Civil War.

Davis and Waud actually saw more of the crucial fighting than almost any individual soldier, since both had the co-operation of the armed forces, a grasp of the over-all patterns of the conflict, and a highly developed instinct for guessing the time and place of climactic engagements. Both wore buckskins and went armed to the teeth. Davis was twice wounded, and, according to *Harper's Weekly*, in which his drawings were published, "witnessed the capture of Port Royal; the battle between the *Monitor* and the *Merrimac*; the conflict at Shiloh; the capture of Corinth; the first bombardment of Vicksburg by Porter; the battle of Antietam; the surrender of Vicksburg . . . ; the battle of Chickamauga; the siege and battle of Chattanooga; the

Alfred R. Waud: *Union Troops Crossing the Pontoon Bridge at Berlin, Md.*, probably 1862, pencil and chalk, 8 x 12½ (Courtesy, Museum of Fine Arts, Boston, M. and M. Karolik Collection)

301

Thomas Nast:
"Let us cease these contests for spoils,"
1880's, pen and wash, 27½ x 19
(Courtesy, Museum of Fine Arts,
Boston, M. and M. Karolik Collection)

Atlanta campaign and the Grand March to the sea. . . ." Waud came through unscathed, despite being "in every advance, in every retreat, in every battle, and almost in every reconnaissance" of the army of the Potomac, and was credited with knowing "more about the several campaigns, the rights and wrongs of the several fights, the merits and demerits of the commanders, than two out of three wearers of generals' shoulder-straps." Homer was attached to no particular unit and saw less action, but he recorded the life in camp and in the field in incidents showing that the boys then recruited from farm and city had much in common with the GIs of Bill Mauldin.

Thomas Nast (1840–1902), the greatest political cartoonist of the period, was also a combat artist, though he started with the army of Garibaldi in Sicily at the age of twenty, having been on his own from fifteen. His sketches and reports of the triumphant march of the red-shirted hero and his legions appeared in both the London and the New York *Illustrated News*, and found an especially enthusiastic reception among Americans, who watched the tide of the *Risorgimento* with the same sympathy they had earlier shown for the liberation of Greece. Nast's wartime drawings for *Harper's Weekly* set forth in dramatic symbols the issues at stake. A dedicated and tireless champion of right, he played a leading part in the crusade for reform in postwar years, and his devastating cartoons exposing Boss Tweed and his ring remain outstanding among their kind.

*The
Painters
of
Panoramas*

Americans of the nineteenth century were notoriously restless, and it sometimes seemed that motion was the object rather than destination, as in the case of the New Hampshire farmer whom Alexander Mackay, a visiting London barrister, met in a crowded country hotel in Connecticut on a stormy winter evening in 1846. Forced by the bad weather to miss the next day's sailing from New York to Oregon, the Yankee confided, between expectorations of "filthy distillations" of tobacco into a distant spittoon "with unerring certainty," that he might as well "go west . . . to Illinois State" instead, it being all the same to him. Habits of travel and the quest for culture led to an increased curiosity about the world, which was reflected in the flood of travel articles in magazines. There one could examine illustrations of the temple at Karnak and the newly rediscovered shrines and cities of Central and South America; read about adventures in Abyssinia and Kordofan; see engravings of the great ecclesiastical buildings of the world, from the fantastic turnip-domed Church of the Assumption in Moscow to the Gothic Seaman's Mission then floating around the harbor of Philadelphia; admire ghost-haunted castles perched on Rhenish crags, the Bazaar at Cairo, the bridge across the Ebro at Saragossa, the picturesque ruins of Tintern Abbey, the temple of Pachacamac, and the palace of the Incas; and thrill to the romantic scenery of the Vale of Kashmir, the Bay of Funchal, and the Delaware Water Gap, all in a single subscription.

Another way of satisfying the travel urge was that adopted by Mr. Booley, an elderly Londoner—apparently the creation of Charles Dickens—who "closed the door of his house behind him at one o'clock in the afternoon of a certain day, and immediately proceeded to New Orleans," then to New Zealand, Australia, Egypt, India, and the Arctic, all in the same afternoon, by visiting various of the panoramas that were then popular in England, as well as on the Continent and in the United States. They were of every conceivable kind, all designed to convey "the results of actual experience," as Mr. Booley explained in "Some Account of an Extraordinary Traveller," "to those who are unable to obtain such experiences for themselves; and to bring them within the reach of the people—emphatically of the people. . . ."

In the panorama, Barnum's formula of combining culture, edification, and entertainment proved as effective as ever. By its magic one could travel around the world, as, for instance, in the "Grand Cozmorama" that was exhibited in St. Louis in 1840. Or one could see London, Paris, Jerusalem, and the Bay of Naples, complete with Vesuvius erupting, belching forth actual smoke accompanied with appropriate subterranean rumblings. Or one could cheer the victory of the American navy over the Barbary pirates, shown with all the strife of battle, according to the prospectus, which describes how "the fleets will meet, and begin the fight; the Tripolitan vessels are burned, their forts blown up, and the depot of the enemy, increases the glory of the American family, and gives immortality to the glorious heroes, Decatur, Preble, and to the host of other brave men who seconded their efforts in the memorable campaign of 1803-4." No red-blooded American could resist the appeal of such vigorous flag-waving. Besides, it was history and therefore educational, and just the thing for the children as well.

The nation's maritime traditions were represented not only by vivid re-creations of the victory of the American fleet at Tripoli, but also by the extraordinary panorama of a whaling

303

Caleb Purrington and Benjamin Russell:
Whaleships at Lahaina, Hawaii,
detail of panorama, 1849, 108 x 168
(Whaling Museum, New Bedford, Mass.)

voyage around the world exhibited in 1849 by two New Englanders, Caleb Purrington and Benjamin Russell, who exuberantly advertised their creation as being three miles in length. Though it is no longer complete, enough is left to form a rare record of great charm. In a palette predominantly light in tone, the partners painted from their own experience of a voyage in 1843 the cruise of a fleet of New Bedford vessels from its home port across the Atlantic to a landfall in the Azores at the Island of Pico. Its cloud-capped peak towers high above the small port, which was a favorite rendezvous for New England whalers. They followed the vessels' course southward around the Cape of Good Hope and into the Pacific to Lahaina, on the Hawaiian Island of Maui, where canoes full of friendly natives are shown visiting from ship to ship. The artists also depict the hunt and the long pursuit, the harpooning, the "Nantucket sleigh rides," the kill, and the messy process of trying out, and, finally, the voyage around the Horn into the Atlantic again and, with a stop at Rio de Janeiro, arrival home.

The two Yankees approached their job with a seamanlike directness. They recorded every aspect of the long voyage, from details of rigging and of the pursuit and capture to a mariner's-eye view of their infrequent ports of call, with the accuracy and immediacy which are the result of experience. Because of this their work suggests something of the rigor, the danger, and the loneliness of a way of life to which Herman Melville was inspired to give such epic expression three years later in *Moby-Dick.*

The Burning of Moscow by Napoleon was a great favorite, and its presentation was made all the more dramatic by the sounds of flames, cannon and rifle fire, booming explosions with showers of sparks, hoarse shouts of command, and the blare of bugles. For those of more sober tastes, there was *Pilgrim's Progress,* painted by one Thomas Coke Ruckle (1811-91), which

304

played to capacity crowds in the Temperance Temple in Baltimore. In Indianapolis James F. Harris' *Mirror of Intemperance* was so well received that he rather single-mindedly followed it with *The Evils of Intemperance,* for good measure. In 1849 John Insco Williams (1813-73) showed *The History of the World from the Creation to the Fall of Babylon,* which was accompanied by such pyrotechnics that it was twice destroyed by fire, twice replaced by the indefatigable artist, whose third version sold for enough to keep him in comfort for the rest of his life.

The panorama was said to have been the invention of Robert Barker, an otherwise unknown portrait painter, who had the idea when in an Edinburgh jail for debt, and patented it in 1787. In 1792 he displayed, in a building especially constructed in Leicester Square for the purpose, a panorama of *The English Fleet at Anchor Between Portsmouth and the Isle of Wight,* which was followed by others of naval engagements, *The Environs of Windsor,* and *The Baths of Margate.* Robert Fulton, the American pupil of West and inventor of the steamboat, picked up the idea at once and financed his scientific researches in Paris with a *Burning of Moscow.* Within three years of Barker's London showing, William Winstanley, a somewhat less than mediocre English landscapist, showed in New York *A View of London,* which was, according to Dunlap, the first panorama to appear in America. The American Edward Savage (1761–1817) opened his version of the same subject in Philadelphia in the same year. John Vanderlyn's *Versailles* (Metropolitan) came to New York City in 1817, and others followed.

It was the effect of being in the actual presence of the scene that the painters of the panoramas endeavored to create. One entered the rotunda through a dimly lit corridor, to find oneself in the center of the building, surrounded by the circle of the painting; it was invisibly lighted from above and, with nothing to distract the observer's attention, the effect was dramatically convincing. A platform with a railing around it in the center of the room kept the spectator at a uniform distance from the pic-

Charles S. Raleigh:
Detail of panorama,
1879, 60 x 132
(Whaling Museum,
New Bedford, Mass.)

305

ture, while a dropped ceiling kept him from seeing the source of the lighting, which came from clerestory windows in the day-time and from gas lamps in the evening. Some rotundas were as large as 150 feet in diameter and could take care of more than a hundred spectators at a time. All sorts of refinements were added to complete the illusion of reality: One might view a sea battle from the deck of a ship, complete with guns and rigging, or see *The Burning of Moscow* with real cannon and other three-dimensional objects nearby, cleverly scaled down to increase the feeling of space and depth. Effects of changing light were achieved by painting on layers of scrim rather than on solid canvas, so that by varying intensities and locations of gas lamps the artist could show the interior of an empty cathedral with day-light streaming through its windows, then the gradual approach of twilight, and, finally, the lighting of hundreds of candles for a Mass with crowds of people. Or he could simulate the effects of a sunset on a romantic landscape, with the fall of night, and then the rising of the moon, whose light was partially diffused, as if seen through a diaphanous mist.

At first, panoramas were stationary, with the spectators doing the moving, but by about 1830 someone had the idea of intro-ducing motion by a presentation like that of the motion picture, moving the continuous strip of painted canvas by rolling it on one cylinder as it was unrolled from another. In this way what John Francis McDermott calls, in his amusing *Lost Panoramas of the Mississippi*, the "newsreel, old style," was born. It was portable and had movement, and it opened the way for a group of Americans to enter into a contest to see who could create "the largest painting in the world." Appropriately, they chose as their subject the country's largest river.

Of the five great panoramas of the Mississippi, two were pro-duced by theatrical scene painters, one by a painter-decorator, one by a carpenter, and one by a youth who had had no artistic training whatsoever. Not a trace of any of them remains today, though the aggregate acreage of canvas must have been colossal, since at most reasonable estimate the panoramas added up to something over a mile in length. A triumph of craftsmanship, showmanship, and determination rather than of artistry, they attracted tremendous attention in their day, and represent an amazing amount of energy and effort poured into a genuinely popular art form more closely allied to the stage than to paint-ing.

Because of the intense rivalry among their creators, it is im-possible to be certain which of the five panoramas was really the first. It is most probable that at least two of the artists were working on their great projects simultaneously. John Banvard (1815-91), the youngest of the group and also the best publicity man (though there was not a slouch among them from this point of view), seems to have been first in the limelight. Born in New York, he headed west at the age of fifteen, and got a job as a clerk in Louisville, Kentucky, but was fired for drawing caricatures of his employer. Jobless, he set up as a painter. Since he had no training and little practice, the venture was understandably unsuccessful, so with some equally youthful friends—he was then sixteen—he designed and painted some dioramic paintings, loaded them in an old flatboat, and set off from New Harmony, Indiana, down the Wabash toward the Ohio. No one knew the river, and they grounded within sight of the wharves at Shawneetown, Illinois, where crowds had gathered, thanks to the advance publicity Banvard had sent ahead. During the night the wake of a passing steamer washed them loose, and they woke up on a sandbar miles downstream.

By the time they reached New Orleans they were rich only in experience and a sack or two of potatoes. Banvard had had it and sold out. Though he had never been nearer Italy than New York Harbor, he painted a panorama of Venice and toured with it successfully until the steamer he was traveling on hit a snag and sank, taking the picture with it. He painted portraits, peddled produce and various miscellaneous items up and down the river, saved his money, and at twenty-five started on his lifelong ambition, which was, in the words of his third-person autobiography, "to paint a picture of the beautiful scenery of the Mississippi, which should be as superior to all others, in point of *size*, as that prodigious river is superior to the streamlets of Europe—a gigantic idea!—which seems truly kindred to the illimitable forests and vast extents of his native land." For more than a year he went sketching up and down the river, from the mouth of the Missouri to the Delta. Then he took a studio in Louisville and started to paint, doing odd jobs of decorating to support himself and to buy canvas. He ground his own pigments, mixed his own paint, cut the wood for his fire, cooked his own meals, and painted tirelessly for six months, until the work was finished in the autumn of 1846.

Exultantly he announced the exhibition of "Banvard's Panorama of the Mississippi River, Painted on Three Miles [*sic*] of Canvas, exhibiting a View of Country 1200 Miles in Length . . . being by far the largest Picture ever executed by Man." He printed a program spiced with highly colored descriptions of

Charles S. Raleigh: Detail of panorama, 1879, 60 x 132
(Whaling Museum, New Bedford, Mass.)

307

the work and of his adventures in achieving it. In renting a hall, he had to pay a special city tax and an enormous deposit for the large number of gas fixtures necessary to light it. The exhibit opened on a stormy night with no customers, so he gave away free tickets to all the rivermen he could find. They were delighted with what they saw, recognizing with shouts all the familiar landmarks along the river's course. The next day all Louisville flocked to look. All agreed with those infallible critics of art, the river boatmen, that it was not only the biggest but also the greatest work of art in the world. At last America had found what it had been so frantically looking for: Nathaniel Parker Willis announced that "Mr. Banvard has refuted the assertions of foreigners, that America had produced no artist commensurate with the grandeur of its scenery." The proud creator of "the largest Picture ever executed by Man" was determined that no one in Europe or America should be denied the privilege and edification of seeing it, and he started on his triumphal tour.

He reached Boston late in 1846, in time to allow Longfellow to study the scenery of the lower reaches of the river so that he could describe it properly in his *Evangeline*. Everyone was delighted with what the papers called "a marvelous monument of the patience, daring ambition, and genius of American character." Congress passed special resolutions in both House and Senate commending Banvard for "boldness, originality, and indefatigable perseverance," and on one of the few occasions in history that that august body has shown any interest, much less enthusiasm, for art in any form, judged it "a truly wonderful and magnificent production."

London was even more enthusiastic than America. A command performance in St. George's Hall, Windsor, followed, and "at the close of the Exhibition," as Banvard modestly announced on subsequent posters, "HER MAJESTY was pleased to bestow upon Mr. Banvard a distinguished mark of her Royal Approbation." A critic of the *Illustrated London News* analyzed the reasons for its popularity. It was presented with dramatic lighting in a darkened hall, while "upon a platform is seated Mr. Banvard, who explains the localities as the picture moves, and relieves his narrative with Jonathanisms and jokes, poetry and patter, which delight his audience mightily; and a pianoforte is incidentally invoked, to relieve the narrative monotony." And never one to waste an opportunity, Banvard had the music printed for sale, with his own lyrics, which contained scarcely subtle references to the "Great Panorama of the Mississippi."

Banvard's monopoly did not last long, however, for John

Rowson Smith (1810-64), an experienced theatrical scene painter, presented in 1848 a "Leviathan Panorama of the Mississippi River," advertised as four miles in length, "depicting nearly four thousand miles of American scenery." Smith's public announcements were condescending toward "the crude effort of the uncultivated artist," a nasty blow clearly directed at Banvard. Smith's panorama was presented at fashionable Saratoga, and the reviewer for the *Daily Whig*, as quoted by McDermott in his *Lost Panoramas*, gives a clue to the reasons for its earning $20,000 during a six-week run: "never has an exhibition given greater satisfaction than this. . . . The immense size of the pictures—the thrilling interest kept up throughout the whole—the burning steamboat, the pilot burnt at the wheel, the captain tearing the planks off the upper deck, the yawl upsetting, and females perishing in a sublime and terrible scene." Smith also included "a longitudinal section of a steamboat of the first class [50 feet long in the panorama], a correct representation of the pilot house, ladies' cabin, social hall, and the main saloon. The lady passengers are seen sitting at the table, while gentlemen who have no ladies under their care remain standing until the steward rings the bell, thus always securing seats for the ladies, no matter how great the crowd. Below the cabins are seen the boilers, and the whole arrangement of a high-pressure engine with the accommodations for the deck passengers; the whole being a correct view of the steamer *Magnolia*."

Samuel B. Stockwell (1813-54), a Boston scene painter, got into the act next, later in the same year. A popular person with a delightful humor, he recounted his experiences in making the sketches for his great work, such as his meeting with a squatter whose cabin he drew, who directed him to make clear "when you show me to them Inglish fellers, jest tell 'em I'm a Mississippi screamer—I kin hoe more corn in a day than any Yankee machine ever invented, and when I hit anythin', from a bullock down to humin Natur', they ginerally think lightnin' is comin'." Stockwell toured successfully in the United States for several months before a disastrous venture in the West Indies put him out of business.

Henry Lewis (1819–1904), an ambitious carpenter turned scene-painter, was next with a version produced by a team of painters. The group made the sketches for it in far greater comfort than any of the others, Lewis having built a floating studio on a catamaran of his own construction, with two 50-foot hulls, which appeared from time to time in the finished work. From its first showing in 1849 in Cincinnati until it was sold four years

309

later in Germany to a Java plantation owner who took it to the East Indies, the panorama earned its creator enough so that he settled down to study painting in Düsseldorf, where he stayed contentedly for the last fifty years of his life.

Also in 1849 Leon Pomarede (c. 1807-92), "determined to produce a painting that would outlive the Mammoth, Gigantic, and Monster daubs, which are scattered at home and abroad," launched his panorama, enlivened by a section on the recent burning of the city of St. Louis, and with the added charm of models of steamers, with smoke pouring from their tall stacks, which passed back and forth to heighten the illusion. After a little over a year of successful exhibition, Pomarede's panorama was destroyed by fire in Newark, New Jersey, and he, like Smith and Stockwell, returned to his original pursuits, spending the rest of his life painting religious and genre pictures for churches and theaters. Banvard returned to America to live for years in the splendor of a castellated mansion overlooking Long Island Sound at Cold Spring Harbor before retiring late in life to an unlikely retreat in South Dakota.

All that remain of any of the colossal portraits of the Mississippi are ancient press notices and a book written by Henry Lewis, illustrated with seventy-eight colored lithographs after his drawings and paintings, entitled *Das illustrierte Mississippithal*. Published in Düsseldorf in parts from 1854 to 1858, it is one of the most attractive and interesting pictorial records of America of the period, and suggests something of "the diversity of the human race . . . the variableness of the scenery . . . and the habitations," to quote from the pamphlet accompanying John Rowson Smith's panorama, that so fascinated countless viewers. "The wild and the city—the mountains and the plain—the swamp, forest, prairie, cataract, and tributary stream . . . in an almost endless changeableness," as seen from the deck of a river steamboat, a "moving palace" with "complicated machinery . . . the fierce fires burning beneath, the long perspective of the superb saloons, the crowd of people, the beauty of the landscape on each shore, and then, when the boat meets the powerful current against her in full force and she staggers a moment, then rushes on impetuous and irresistible," the excitement of the voyage when "you cannot but feel that steam is indeed a mighty power in the hands of American ingenuity and go-ahead-itiveness." It was the same spirit that launched the contest for the largest painting ever made in the dramatic form that was the climax of popular art in nineteenth-century America.

310

THE PAINTERS OF EVERYDAY LIFE

Part of the rediscovery of America, a movement led by Irving and Cooper in literature and by Cole in landscape painting, was a growing consciousness of the charm of everyday life, both in the country and in the city. As the nation became more industrialized and urbanized, rural life became increasingly flavored with nostalgia. The quickening tempo of living and the mounting tensions between North and South made memories of country and village childhood seem more remote and more attractive. The sentimentalizing tendencies of the age are evident in the prints of Currier & Ives and in the ballads of Stephen Foster. The prints, however, are poor things compared with the genuine lyric quality of Foster's disarmingly simple songs, which find their artistic counterpart in the works of a group of genre painters who followed the lead of Alvan Fisher and devoted their attention to recording the simple subjects sung by Foster and by the poets of that time.

The winter scenes of George Henry Durrie (1820-63), several of which were reproduced by Currier & Ives, might have been illustrations for John Greenleaf Whittier's *Snow-bound*. The New England landscape is transformed by the heavy snowfall, the bare trees, with branches, edged in white, against a gray sky, the breath of man and animal vaporous in the cold, and the smoke rising from the farmhouse chimney, suggesting the warmth and hospitality within.

George Henry Durrie:
Winter Landscape: Gathering Wood,
1859, 28 x 34¼
(Courtesy, Museum of Fine Arts,
Boston, M. and M. Karolik Collection)

311

The pictures by William Sidney Mount (1807-68) of Stony Brook, Long Island, were engraved by Goupil & Cie, and were widely known. Mount was twice offered the chance to go abroad, all expenses paid, by Luman Reed and his son-in-law Jonathan Sturgis, both generous patrons of American art, and Goupil offered to stake him for a year, but he refused, preferring a life devoted to painting, frequently fiddling for country dances. He built a horse-drawn studio on wheels, complete with plate-glass windows, ventilation, and a stove for winter. He did almost all his paintings on the spot, often preceded by swift oil sketches, the fluidity and breadth of which never appear in his finished oils. The latter show an unexpected transparency of shadow and an interest in textured surfaces, which, however, never influence the smooth evenness of his neatly applied paint. His pictures have almost a miniaturist's attention to detail, but are controlled by the essential simplicity of his subject matter,

William Sidney Mount: *The Power of Music*, 1847, 17 x 21 (The Century Association)

William Sidney Mount:
Eel Spearing at Setauket,
1845, 29 x 36
(New York State Historical
Association, Cooperstown, N.Y.)

with an episodic rather than narrative interpretation, and are ordered by an instinct for formal composition so well assimilated to his purpose that it has generally gone completely unnoticed. He strove for "the happy but unstudied circumstance . . . the moment should offer," and achieved, without the exaggeration so common to the painters of genre, a quiet unity that conceals both the awareness of his observation and the skill with which the concept has been realized.

A strain of music runs through Mount's paintings, as it did throughout American life of the period. *The Power of Music* shows four figures lost in the melody one is playing on a violin; *The Banjo Player* (Detroit) is absorbed in his instrument; and *The Bones Player* (Karolik Collection, Boston), lacking any suggestion of the grimacing humor usually found in anything concerning the minstrel show, is, instead, a sympathetic portrait, animated by a spirit of gaiety and rhythm. His *Long Island Farm House* (Metropolitan), without figures, has the savor of pale sunlight and the spidery shadows of leafless trees on weathered shingles. His *Eel Spearing at Setauket*, with its abstractly structured geometry of diagonals, shows two figures, concentrated and motionless, in the warm stillness of water, quiet landscape, and lucid sky.

As early as 1815, Henry Sargent (1770–1845) of Boston painted a pair of pictures (Boston), one of a stag *Dinner Party*. The other, of a *Tea Party*, has a Federal elegance; the ladies are dressed in high-waisted gowns and the gentlemen in tight trousers and long-tailed coats, conversing in a spacious

Henry Sargent: *The Tea Party*,
1815-20, 59½ x 48
(Courtesy, Museum of Fine Arts, Boston,
gift of Mrs. Horatio A. Lamb in
memory of Mr. and Mrs. Winthrop Sargent)

James Goodwyn Clonney: *What a Catch!*, 1855, 24 x 34
(Courtesy, Museum of Fine Arts, Boston, M. and M. Karolik Collection)

drawing room lit by candles and warmed by a fire in the fire-place, and furnished with chairs and tables in a French-inspired style very like those of Duncan Phyfe.

James Goodwyn Clonney (1812-67) recorded in *"What a Catch!"* (Karolik Collection, Boston) the pleasures of fishing in Lake Otsego, near Cooperstown, New York, for the famous bass found there. The occupants of two skiffs compare the results of their sport in a good-humored and unpretentious scene mirrored in the clear water. Other artists painted turkey shoots, corn-husking and flax-scutching bees, country dances, country fairs, horse trading, interiors of village stores, and scenes of gathering the harvest, winnowing grain, haymaking, winter sleigh rides, summer outings, and children going to school; and of blacksmiths at work as if in illustration of Longfellow's famous poem. In 1848 Richard Caton Woodville (1825-56) recorded the excitement with which news of the Mexican War was received, with reports of the latest exploits of General Zachary Taylor ("Old Rough and Ready") and General Winfield Scott ("Old Fuss and Feathers") and of two young officers, Captain Lee and Lieutenant Grant, who were to share the limelight in a later and more desperate conflict. In the 1850's Jerome B. Thompson (1814-86) painted *A "Pic Nick" in the Woods of New England* that is full of lively observation and incident.

Jerome B. Thompson: *A "Pic Nick" in the Woods of New England,* c. 1850, 41 x 62 (Courtesy, Museum of Fine Arts, Boston, M. and M. Karolik Collection)

In 1851, he painted *The Peep Show*, with a group of fascinated children on a New York street. In the 1850's and 1860's John McLenan (1827-66) was sketching the humor of the urban scene for *Yankee Notions: or, Whittlings from Jonathan's Jackknife.*

George C. Lambdin (1830-96), famous in his day for portraits and still lifes, could occasionally catch the essence of early spring, with its tentative sunlight breaking through a cloudy sky, as in *Pruning* (Karolik Collection, Boston). In 1853 John Whetten Ehninger (1827-89) pictured the arrival of *The Yankee Peddler* (Newark), his canvas-covered wagon chock-full of fascinating wares. While he shows yard goods and a coffee mill to interested customers, his horses drink at the trough.

Other artists recorded the busy shipyards, the waterfront, and the cityscape, with new buildings crowding the old and the streets full of activity. John F. Weir (1841–1926), who had gone to Rome with Horatio Greenough and returned to teach drawing at West Point, painted *The Gun Foundry* (Putnam County Historical Society) with its cavernous interior dramatically lighted by the fiery brightness of the white-hot metal being

Jerome B. Thompson: *The Peep Show,* 1851, 25 x 30 (Courtesy, Museum of Fine Arts, Boston, M. and M. Karolik Collection)

poured, the glare emphasizing the concentration and the strain of the workmen and engineers.

Almost every aspect of city life was visually chronicled— slave auctions and street brawls, fires and firemen, ships entering busy harbors, trains puffing in and out of stations, troops on parade during Fourth of July celebrations, men eating and talking politics in an oyster house, people in shops and post offices, a sailor's wedding, funeral processions, church services, theatrical performances, newsboys and street hawkers, carriages with mettlesome horses, and political rallies. Most of the works themselves are of no great importance artistically, though they often have an added charm of recording fashions and events of bygone days. But the best of the genre painters, among whom Mount is a leader, did work that was far from negligible and often rises to a quiet and evocative poetry whose undemanding tone is welcome in a strident age.

George Caleb Bingham (1811-79) was the outstanding artist of the group of genre painters who chronicled the life of the advancing frontier. Though he was born in Virginia, he was taken at the age of eight to a small settlement named Franklin Habitation in Missouri, and there grew up with a catch-as-catch-can sort of education. He read some theology, learned to roll cigars, became a cabinetmaker's apprentice, probably not a very skilled profession at that time in Missouri, read some law, and amused himself copying engravings and coloring the drawings with homemade paints. Then the frontiersman-turned-artist Chester Harding (1792–1866), himself still only a self-taught primitive at the time, came through the little settlement on his way to look for Daniel Boone, whose portrait he wished to paint. The boy was deeply impressed—as were all who met Harding—and determined to become a portrait painter also. In his wanderings he managed a few months of study during 1837 and 1838 at the Pennsylvania Academy in Philadelphia, where he saw the works of Allston, West, Sully, and others, and settled in Washington for a while, painting vigorous portraits whose archaisms were no doubt not apparent to the not very discriminating clientele he found there during the post-Jacksonian years.

In about 1844 Bingham went back to Missouri, determined to paint a visual record of life there. He had discovered that, to the inhabitants of the Eastern seaboard, episodes from the frontier life in which he had grown up were interesting and picturesque, rather than routine, as they seemed to him. As he began to look at the life around him, he became conscious that these episodes were indeed important, that history was being made. He shows us scenes of the rambunctious political life he loved. He had campaigned hard to elect William Henry Harrison and was locally famous for his political banners. His *County Election, Stump Speaking,* and *The Verdict of the People* (Boatmen's National Bank of St. Louis) are full of the livelist observation and, undoubtedly, of portraits of his friends, neighbors, and political opponents. All the rough-and-tumble of hardcider persuasion, whiskey vote-getting, and ranting frontier eloquence is present at meetings attended by local worthies deeply conscious of their dignity, and also by drunken raftsmen, small boys, and dogs. The pictures are carefully composed, after the manner of the paintings he had seen at the Pennsylvania Academy, but with a subtlety of organization few of his models approached, and all are unified with a tonality that is uniquely his own. His local tones are clear and appear in defined areas—shades of browns and earth colors, enlivened with reds, blues, and greens that are almost high-keyed. Patterns of light and shade are arbitrary and appear knowingly conceived, though they are probably intuitive, as may be, also, the hazy, luminous atmosphere which gives an unexpected visual beauty to the whole, and which somehow does not seem out of keeping with the boisterous subject matter. Individual figures are carefully studied—there are sheaves of drawings to prove the point —and are often strongly expressive and filled with humorous observation.

The scenes of river life—as familiar to Bingham from boyhood as they were to the young Samuel Langhorne Clemens, born twenty-four years after Bingham—supplied both with similar subject matter, since Arrow Rock on the Missouri and Hannibal on the Mississippi had much in common. The river and the life of the river pulse through the adventures of Tom Sawyer and Huckleberry Finn, just as they do through Bingham's pictures of raftsmen and wood-boatmen, which proved so popular when engraved and circulated through the American Art-Union. The most famous is probably the *Jolly Flatboatmen,* the original version of which, engraved for the Union and pirated by Currier & Ives, has been lost. His most effective painting, however, is his *Fur Traders Descending the Missouri.* Drifting out of the river's mist in a dugout canoe, the two motionless figures look out at us, silent and enigmatic, while shapes of trees loom palely through the vaporous air to suggest the setting, as insubstantial as the reflection in the smooth, slow-moving water. The sharp silhouette of the little black animal tied to the prow seems a very symbol of the wildness of the environment in which these men led their hazardous and solitary lives. One can hear the stillness and feel the brooding solitude.

George Caleb Bingham: *Fur Traders Descending the Missouri*, 1845, 29 x 36½
(The Metropolitan Museum of Art, Morris K. Jesup Fund, 1933)

It is both an amazing document and, more important, a piece of
visual poetry in which all Bingham's limited but not inconsequential talents combine to evoke the heroic spirit of life beyond the frontier. Strong design and curiously personal color
relations give a sense of timelessness to his pictures of the life
of the river, and his work as a whole remains the most vigorous visual record we have of the frontier folkways of Jacksonian
democracy.

In 1856 Bingham went to Düsseldorf to study, and it was the
ruination of his art. He returned to a nation torn with factions.
A passionate believer in the Union, he was nonetheless appalled
at the portents of the coming disaster of which he seems to have

been more sensitively aware than many of his countrymen. He ran for public office and no doubt found as much if not more satisfaction in actually taking part in the politics that he had recorded so colorfully in his art. Successively state treasurer of Missouri and adjutant general, he enlisted when the conflict came, and painting took a back seat to war and politics. But the pictorial record remains. He alone of the painters of the frontier was himself a frontiersman born, and he lived what he painted.

Eastman Johnson (1824–1906) also studied in Düsseldorf, and then at The Hague around mid-century but, as in the case of Thomas Cole earlier, his European experience seems merely to have sharpened his perceptions of the American scene. Born and brought up in Maine, where his father was for thirty years Secretary of State, he determined at eighteen to become a portrait painter, and embarked on what was at once a successful career, since during the ensuing sixty-four years he was in constant demand. His *Two Men* (Metropolitan) shows Robert W. Rutherford and a painter friend of Johnson's, Samuel W. Rowse; it is rich in dark tonalities, and uses shadow and highlight for expressive purpose with a result approaching Thomas Eakins in powerful insight and unity of feeling. His *Family Group* (Metropolitan) remains a fascinating statement of the formidable dignity and restraint of a privileged New York family of the Victorian era.

The paintings for which Johnson is most respected today are his scenes of country life—of cranberrying on Nantucket and of blueberrying at Kennebunkport. In these pictures there is no longer any episode, merely figures in an open landscape drenched with clear sunlight. In his scenes of a maple sugar camp in Fryeburg, Maine—such as *Measurement and Contemplation*—light and shadow on tree trunk and foliage, and on weathered wood and snow, mingle with the smoke of the fires and the steam from the great kettles, to create an environment of which the figures are an integral part. Swiftly and loosely but surely painted, these pictures reveal no trace of the Düsseldorf tightness that was the ruination of Bingham and sometimes hardened and deadened passages in Johnson's portraits. Devoid of both storytelling and sentiment, these paintings are subtly observed and felt. Richly luminous, they reveal his figures as one with their natural world, unified by light and mood.

Only Winslow Homer (1836–1910) was to surpass Eastman Johnson as a genre painter. Homer's early work for such magazines as *Ballou's Pictorial* and *Harper's Weekly* led him naturally to subjects of episodic interest—playing croquet, walk-

Eastman Johnson:
Measurement and Contemplation,
1860's, 20 x 24
(Courtesy, Museum of Fine Arts,
Boston, M. and M. Karolik Collection)

319

ing on Boston Common, skating in Central Park, boys clambering up a steep dune to rob the nests of cliff swallows, and children on a beach. But Homer's art was to pass far beyond these early illustrative works, and was to develop the same theme that Johnson had treated with such sensitive observation, the relation of man to nature, into an heroic expression that is one of the highest achievements of American art.

Winslow Homer: *Croquet Scene*, 1866, 15⅞ x 26 1/16
(The Art Institute of Chicago, Friends of American Art Collection)

VII

A World Changed: Painting after the Civil War

THE LURE OF EUROPE:
THE
EXPATRIATES

As 1876 approached, the city of Philadelphia—where the Declaration had been signed and the two Continental Congresses had been held—prepared to celebrate the hundredth birthday of American independence with a great international fair. Exhibits were invited from all over the globe, and the world flocked to see the five great halls with their 70 acres of floor space. Memorial Hall, later to be turned into the Pennsylvania Museum, was crowded with works by the famous and the near-famous painters and sculptors of the day. Duly admired by the multitude, these provided the first experience for most American artists to see what was being done by their contemporaries in England, France, and Germany, and inspired many to go abroad to study. But the real center of the exhibition was the immense cast-iron and glass building containing 12 acres of mechanical display. There were great guns from the Krupp works, to impress the world with Germany's military might; a British steam hammer that could deliver a blow of hundreds of tons or be lowered so delicately that it would not crack the crystal of a watch; the newly invented telephone shown by Alexander Graham Bell, which shocked Dom Pedro, the Emperor of Brazil, by talking to him; George Westinghouse's new safety air brake for railroads; George Pullman's newest sleeping and dining cars; turret lathes and milling, grinding, and other machines, including the "Mohawk Dutchman," a band saw to turn out at a great rate the intricate patterns increasingly popular in the architecture and the furniture of the day; and the Hoe press, which could print the unprecedented number of 25,000 sheets an hour.

When the Centennial Exposition was opened by President Grant's setting the great Corliss engine in motion, it was clear that the engine was the heart of the show. The largest steam engine yet constructed in the world, it weighed 1,700,000 pounds, and its uncompromising bulk loomed 40 feet above its base. It delivered enough power to drive the whole machinery exhibit, yet it was tooled with such precision that it ran effortlessly and without vibration. Some complained that its design was unaesthetically bare, because it lacked the debased Gothic moldings and cusps, the mechanical Renaissance scrollwork, or

President Grant and the Emperor of Brazil starting the great Corliss engine, Centennial Exposition, Philadelphia, 1876 (From *Record of the Centennial Exposition*, by Frank Leslie)

323

Mary Cassatt: *The Bath*, c. 1892, 39½ x 26
(Courtesy of The Art Institute of Chicago, Robert A. Waller Collection)

the wiry Corinthian colonnettes usually applied—so incongruously, to a modern eye—to everything, from sewing machines to locomotives. But others agreed with the French sculptor Bartholdi (the gigantic hand of whose *Statue of Liberty* was completed in time for the exhibition), who saw in the engine "the beauty and almost the grace of the human form." The visitors who returned again and again to watch the rhythmic alternation of its colossal pistons as it generated an unprecedented 1,600 horsepower were catching an exhilarating and startling glimpse into the future. In 1860 the United States had been primarily an agricultural country, but under the pressures of the Civil War, she had become, almost before the world was aware of the extent of the change, a predominantly industrial one. The great Corliss engine was the frightening symbol of the age to come.

Donald McKay's beautiful clipper ship had been replaced by the swift transatlantic steamer. Railroads spanned the continent; and the petroleum industry, launched only seventeen years earlier in Pennsylvania, had already devastated whaling. Tycoons of business and industry were relentlessly demonstrating the social application of Darwin's theories of the survival of the fittest in the jungle of the world of free enterprise. Commodore Vanderbilt and the unscrupulous partners Jim Fisk, Jay Gould, and Daniel Drew were feuding for the control of a railroad empire; Swift and Armour were cornering the meat market; Boss Tweed was the ruthless dictator of New York; and Rockefeller, Morgan, Huntington, and other empire builders were making huge fortunes and creating the vast corporations that were to outlast and, finally, to dwarf even them.

Materialism was rampant, and the era of the entrepreneur was under way, a period which Mark Twain and Charles Dudley Warner called the Gilded Age. And gilded it was—certainly not golden. In a lavish display of conspicuous consumption, immense quantities of the new money were spent for culture and respectability, both of which were largely thought to come in such gaudy packages as pseudo-French châteaux on Fifth Avenue, in Newport, and in other places chosen as socially correct. Art also became a means of achieving an elevated position in a socially competitive era. In general, the taste displayed in its avid pursuit was that of the unsure and uninformed middle class, from which the new rich had so suddenly sprung.

The genuine movement toward the democratization of culture of the middle of the century, with the flourishing of the American Art-Union, had been forgotten. Europe was all the rage.

324

The rich bought European art on the familiar theory that the imported is always better than the native product. At a time when Manet, Courbet, and other leading French artists were demonstrating at the Salon des Refusés the low state of affairs in the official Salon, American millionaires were vying with one another to purchase the latest official medal winners, the empty machines by Meissonier and Bouguereau and others of their kind. American artists flocked to Europe—to Munich, Rome, Antwerp, and, especially, the crowded ateliers of the Paris masters—to study the fashionable styles. Like the novelist Henry James, many permanently fled the noisy vulgarities of the new America for the more refined and sophisticated environment of Europe. Some, like Ryder, Inness, and Blakelock, turned to a cultivation of the inner life of the imagination; and others, like Homer and Eakins, remained stubbornly independent of the hurly-burly of life around them and concentrated on the more fundamental aspects of man and nature.

James Abbott McNeill Whistler (1834–1903) was one of the first of the expatriates of that era. His father was an engineer of international reputation who in 1842 laid out the railway from St. Petersburg to Moscow. The younger Whistler was born in the mill town of Lowell, Massachusetts, a fact he preferred not to think about. But he grew up largely in Europe and studied art in St. Petersburg. Later he entered West Point, and a less likely candidate for the military can scarcely be imagined. An aggressive aesthete, he flunked out in 1854, ostensibly because of failure to pass in chemistry, but it was a clear case of incompatibility. He spent a year with the Coast and Geodetic Survey as a draftsman, painted a few portraits, and in 1855 took off for Paris. There he settled down to student life on the Left Bank, studying in the famous atelier of Charles Gleyre, making friends with Fantin-Latour, Alphonse Legros, and the great pioneer realist Gustav Courbet, and finding a young milliner, whose nickname was *La Tigresse*, to pose for him and live with him. When an early canvas was turned down by the French Salon but accepted by the Royal Academy in London in 1860, he went to England, and the picturesque Chelsea district of London became his home from then on. He rapidly made a name for himself as a wit and a dandy, using his capacity for verbal pyrotechnics—as shown by his book *The Gentle Art of Making Enemies*—to cultivate a reputation as a controversial and colorful character, while as an artist he remained extremely serious and dedicated.

Though he was of the same generation as Cézanne, Manet, Monet, Pissarro, and others who were to emerge as the artistic leaders of the period, and although he remained acutely aware of the dramatic developments in France, Whistler developed his own style quite independently. His work shows the influence of the Pre-Raphaelites, but his approach to the world was too direct to follow their path of romantic withdrawal. He remained deeply involved with objective reality. Like his contemporary Degas, he was among the first to discover and to study the art of the Far East through the Japanese print. He evolved a subtle skill in composition, at first glance snapshotlike, but actually carefully calculated in structure.

During the 1870's his vision sharpened and his work matured. He painted many portraits, some of them among the outstanding examples of their kind of the period, the most famous being the *Arrangement in Gray and Black No. 1: The Artist's Mother*, the similarly composed *Thomas Carlyle* (Glasgow Art Gallery), and the delightful Miss Cecily Alexander, with butterflies hovering around her head, which he entitled *Harmony in Gray and Green* (National Gallery, London). But most remarkable are the Nocturnes, so titled with musical connotation because they "so poetically say all I want to say and *no more* than I wish." Among these are the magical studies of Old Battersea Bridge and the *Nocturne in Black and Gold—The Falling Rocket* (Detroit), an almost nonobjective example of the purely visual poetry that he sought. "As music is the poetry of sound," he wrote, "so painting is the poetry of sight, and the subject matter has nothing to do with the harmony of sound or of color." Like Baudelaire, and like Blakelock, Poe, and Melville, he had a special feeling for nightfall, "when the evening mist clothes the riverside with poetry, as with a veil, and the poor buildings lose themselves in the dim sky, and the tall chimneys become campanili, and the warehouses are palaces in the night, and the whole city hangs in the heavens." The River Thames appears again and again in his canvases, an ever-changing but constant motive. And like his contemporary Winslow Homer, Whistler was preoccupied with the sea. For him the technique was the picture, the means by which he conveyed his personal vision of the real world seen through an almost abstract atmospheric space. In his grasp of factuality as the basis of his art, Whistler was true to the American tradition; and in his stubborn refusal to try, through multiplication of detail or by overly defining a subject, to govern the spectator's response, he anticipated an important aspect of the art of today. Like Allston, he

James A. McNeill Whistler:
Arrangement in Gray and Black No. 1:
The Artist's Mother,
1872, 56 x 64
(Louvre, Paris)

326

James A. McNeill Whistler: *Battersea Reach*, c. 1865, 20 x 30
(In the collection of The Corcoran Gallery of Art, bequest of James Parmelee)

created paintings of mood, but rather than definite statements
or records, they are, like many of the best paintings of our own
day, points of departure for a voyage of personal discovery.

After a good deal of European travel, Mary Cassatt (1845–
1926), born of a wealthy Philadelphia family, went to Paris
in 1868, and became a respected member of the artistic society there. A friend and admirer of Degas, she joined the
group of the Impressionists, and spent a long career painting
sensitively observed figure pieces, especially on the constantly
recurring theme of the mother and child. Pictures of great
charm, they are devoid of sentimentality, and are based upon
an objective realism of form and a quiet awareness of individual personality.

Theodore Robinson (1852-96) sought out Monet at Giverny
in 1888, and, with John H. Twachtman (1853–1902) and
Childe Hassam (1859–1935), formed a group of what have
been called American Impressionists. These artists did not,
however, seek to emulate the purely optical approach which

327

Childe Hassam: *New England Headlands*,
1899, 27 x 26¾
(Courtesy of The Art Institute of
Chicago, Walter H. Schulze Memorial
Collection)

is the basis of Impressionism, the objective recording of the purely visual effects of light and atmosphere rather than the objects themselves. They strove, instead, to enrich and enliven their vision and expression through the brilliant, broken handling developed by Monet and the others. Just as in the works of Mary Cassatt, the substance is always there because it is the substance rather than merely the way of looking that was of primary importance to them. At their best, they combine a light palette, liveliness of touch, and freshness of observation that relate their work to their Luminist predecessors and give them a legitimate place in American art.

Although John Singer Sargent (1856–1925) was born abroad, he was actually an American, the son of a Philadelphia physician who was living in Florence at the time. His extraordinary natural facility in the handling of the brush, and an innate capacity as a draftsman, led to precocious development during a brief time in Paris in the studio of Carolus-Duran, one of the highly trained and competent second-rate French artists of the day. The amazing completeness and objectivity of Sargent's vision combined with his virtuosity and his sense of the elegant to make him a leading fashionable portrait painter of the period, both in America and in Europe. But in his works in other categories—such as the brief and dashing oil sketches, like *Luxembourg Gardens at Twilight* (Minneapolis), saturated with the soft light of the dying day and the rising moon, and his shadowy interiors of Venetian palaces—the theme is a pervading mood effortlessly expressed. And his personal, bravura handling of water color resulted in a brilliance that was surpassed only by Winslow Homer in American art, and did much to establish the medium as a serious artistic vehicle.

Sargent was a true cosmopolitan, as at home in Europe as in America. He lived and worked in Paris for a time before turning to London in 1885 as his transatlantic headquarters,

John Singer Sargent:
Venice—Under the Rialto,
probably 1911, water color, 10¾ x 19
(Courtesy, Museum of Fine Arts,
Boston, Charles Henry Hayden Fund)

and when in the United States, he stayed mostly in Boston. There, in the newly completed Public Library designed by Mc-Kim, Mead, and White, he painted a large mural decoration, commissioned in 1890, one of the more successful essays in the Renaissance manner so popular at the time.

Most of the notable figures of the day were recorded by Sargent's facile brush—college presidents, captains of industry, and leaders in society and the arts. A portrait of the fascinating Mrs. Jack Gardner, shown in a black dress and wearing her famous pearls, is enshrined in the Venetian palace she built on the Fenway in Boston to house her remarkable collection of art. There, too, is Sargent's early *El Jaleo,* with the life-sized whirling dancer and the intent musicians caught in a fiery

John Singer Sargent: *The Daughters of Edward D. Boit,* 1882, 87⅝ x 87⅝
(Courtesy, Museum of Fine Arts, Boston, gift of the daughters of Edward Darley Boit, in memory of their father)

rhythm and unified with a swirling, dramatic pattern of light and shade. The picture is Sargent's homage to Spanish art and to Spain, from which he had just returned in 1880, and whose tradition was as important to his artistic development as it was to Manet and Eakins. All three artists had been deeply impressed by Velázquez's totality of vision and by the drama in the crowding shadows that fill Spanish painting and become a frightening dark world in Goya's later work.

Perhaps the finest of all of Sargent's many portraits was that done in 1882, shortly after his Spanish visit, and entitled *The Daughters of Edward D. Boit*, now in the Boston Museum of Fine Arts, just across the Fenway from Mrs. Gardner's palace. The smallest child sits on an oriental rug, while the next stands apart to the left, and the other two merge into the shadows to the rear. A pair of immense oriental vases in blue and white establish the scale, and the combination of transparent shadow and flooding light suggests the extension of the interior beyond the confines of the picture. The poses are caught with the momentary swiftness of vision for which the artist was famous. The whole conception looks unstudied and informal, a happy accident, until one starts to analyze the subtlety of the composition in terms of light and dark—a gamut from white to black—and of the atmospheric re-creation of a moment which unifies the vivid individuality of the four portraits within a world of their own.

In Munich young Frank Duveneck (1848–1919), of Ohio, and William Merritt Chase (1849–1916), of Indiana, learned the dark, warm tonalities and fluent brushwork which they in turn passed on to their pupils. Duveneck taught in Florence until his wife's death in 1888 sent him, sorrowing, back to Cincinnati, where for a quarter of a century he was the head of the Art Academy. In 1878 Chase became an instructor at the newly founded Art Students League in New York City, where he continued to teach for more than thirty years, regarded as the very personification of the cosmopolitan artist. Dapper in dress and dashing in manner, his mustache and neat beard bristling with enthusiasm, he urged his students to cultivate the visual grasp of Sargent's approach, and his own swift attack.

The ambitious young Americans who had flocked to Munich to study at the Royal Academy or with Duveneck, or to Paris to the ateliers of Gérôme, Gleyre, Carolus-Duran, and Julian, where so many of them worked, or to the many other studios, returned to their native land with a sound technical basis, but found there neither the ready patronage that a previous generation had enjoyed nor the same picturesqueness that had delighted them in Europe. The light in America seemed harsh and hard. There were no colorful peasants with donkeys and oxen, but only ordinary Americans like themselves, working the land with the newest in mechanized agricultural equipment. They found sprawling, ugly cities with teeming, dirty slums, smoking factories, sweatshops, and crooked politics. Some went back to find a minor place in the European art world. Others taught in the art schools that were springing up in the United States, and dreamed of their carefree student days, because they could not compete with the imported Paris novelties of such now fortunately forgotten "geniuses" as Koek-Koek, Achenbach, Rosa Bonheur, and Meyer von Bremen, whose works were avidly being sought by the rich American collectors.

Art galleries had proliferated to meet the insatiable demand. Although most collections were all too alike in the dull monotony of then famous names, there were a few collectors—like Mrs. Gardner and Henry Adams Shaw in Boston, Henry Walters in Baltimore, Henry G. Marquand, Benjamin Altman, and J. P. Morgan in New York, and John G. Johnson in Philadelphia—who assembled collections of real quality and importance. Good art also began to be available to the public through the museums founded in the same period. Unfortunately, however, very few collectors and curators paid any attention to contemporary work, and the lot of the artist became precarious, as it has largely remained to our own time.

As 1900 approached, the European-trained painters and sculptors became increasingly remote from booming, crude, progressive America, for theirs was an art of nostalgia and introspection. As Horatio Greenough had prophesied a half-century earlier, the creative genius of the nation was flowing in other channels. It appeared among the engineers who designed the great bridges, like the far-sighted John A. Roebling (1806-69) and his heroic son, Washington (1837–1926), whose Brooklyn Bridge, begun in 1867 and completed in 1884, remains as a monument to their determination and vision, a triumph of human ingenuity, which, even more than the mighty Corliss engine, became a symbol of the future.

In architecture it was expressed, not by the fashionable firms expertly designing derivative palaces made up of a collection of literal details taken from French or Italian Renaissance monuments, but by the imaginative creators of the early skyscrapers, which, significantly, first appeared in Chicago, "the hog butcher of the world," rather than in Boston, New York, or Philadelphia, which were the traditional centers of American culture.

Winslow Homer: *The Country School*, 1871, 21⅜ x 38⅜
(City Art Museum of St. Louis)

WINSLOW HOMER AND THE EPIC OF MAN

"He is almost barbarously simple," wrote the young Henry James of three paintings by Winslow Homer (1836–1910) in the National Academy of Design's annual exhibition in 1876, "and, to our eye, he is horribly ugly; but there is nevertheless something one likes about him. What is it? For ourselves, it is not his subjects. We frankly confess that we detest his subjects—his barren plank fences, bald, blue skies, his big, dreary, vacant lots of meadows, his freckled, straight-haired Yankee urchins, his flat-breasted maidens, suggestive of a dish of rural doughnuts and pie. . . . He has chosen the least pictorial range of scenery and civilization; he has resolutely treated them as if they *were* pictorial, as if they were every inch as good as Capri or Tangier; and to reward his audacity, he has incontestably succeeded." James's grudging appreciation of Homer's genre scenes are as significant a commentary on the critic as on the artist. Already a much-traveled cosmopolitan, the novelist had formed his opinions from a study of the older and more elegant contemporary painting of Europe, and his judgment was undoubtedly shared by many Americans. The general public, however, took to Homer's work from the beginning, recognizing its freshness of observation, and accepting its lack of spurious romanticism because of its firm basis in essential fact.

Homer came of a long line of New England Yankees, and grew up self-reliant and independent. A boyhood spent out of doors gave him a love of the country, but he was ambitious to get ahead. At nineteen he was apprenticed to the well-known Boston lithographer John H. Bufford, thus receiving the same technical training as so many American artists. He despised the work, but kept at it until he was twenty-one, when he set himself up as a free-lance illustrator. He worked for *Ballou's Pictorial* in Boston for several years before going to New York, encouraged by commissions from *Harper's Weekly*, the leading periodical of its kind. He rendered his subjects in clean line and broad masses so that they might lend themselves to the process of translation by the wood engraver who made the blocks from which they were printed, and during the '60's and '70's his illustrations stand out among all the rest for effectiveness of design. He went briefly to a drawing school in Brook-

AND NATURE

lyn, took an evening course at the National Academy, and had a few lessons with a minor French painter, Frédéric Rondel, but otherwise was self-taught.

At the outbreak of the Civil War he went south with the Union forces and sent back many illustrations to *Harper's*, and in 1862 he did his first paintings in oil, and showed two of them, both wartime subjects. Ever since the drudgery of work at Buford's, he had refused any regular job. "From the time I took my nose off that lithographic stone, I have had no master," he remarked, "and never shall I have any." Nevertheless he swore that if the two pictures did not sell, he would take the regular job that *Harper's* offered him. His older brother Charles bought them secretly, and when Winslow found out about it years later, he was so angry that he would not speak to Charles for weeks, but by then he had made a success and was well launched on his career. The first oil to attract attention was another subject from the Civil War, *Prisoners from the Front*. Without bloodshed or violence, it combined the defiant Confederate in ragged uniform with the neatly dressed, serious young Union officer in a revealing study of temperaments. First shown at the National Academy in 1866, the painting created a sensation. The following year it was exhibited at the Paris Exposition, where its effective directness impressed European observers. Thereafter Homer might be hard up or his work adversely criticized, but he could not be overlooked.

During 1866-67 he spent a few months in Paris. He investigated the Louvre, wandered about the city, visited a dance hall, and went home. Although he must have seen the work of at least some of the contemporary Frenchmen who were the avant-garde of the day, his painting shows no sign of their influence since, characteristically, he pursued his own thoughtful and independent way. The early discipline of black and white led him to compose in broad masses of light and dark, with firm and simple forms, and when he turned to water color in 1873 he found

Winslow Homer:
Prisoners from the Front,
1866, 24 x 38
(The Metropolitan Museum of Art,
gift of Mrs. Frank B. Porter, 1922)

334

Winslow Homer: *The Berry Pickers*,
1873, water color, 9¼ x 13⅛
(The Harold T. Pulsifer Memorial
Collection at Colby College)

a medium that naturally suited his inclinations. Even the earliest are big and broad in concept though small in scale, and
all have a great freshness because of his direct approach—
painting out of doors, face to face with his subject. He painted
children picking blueberries in the rough meadows near the
ocean, lying on the rocks in the sun, wading in the shallow
water, sitting in a beached dory, or lugging a basket of clams;
or girls on the shore, leaning against a fence or sitting on a
stone wall. His pictures are drenched in sun and fresh with
the wind blowing off the sea, and are painted without a trace
of sentimentality.

By nature a wanderer, Homer saw much of rural New England, climbed the White Mountains, explored the New Jersey
shore, and in 1876-77 visited Virginia, where he painted Negroes—at work in the cotton fields, sitting on a rickety porch,
or dressing up for a carnival—with an old-fashioned respect
for the dignity of physical labor and for those who live by it.
In his pictorial records of childhood and country life—like the
Country School of 1871, *Snap the Whip* (Youngstown) of 1872,
Weaning the Calf (North Carolina Museum) of 1875, and *A
Fair Wind, or Breezing Up* (National Gallery) of the following year, in which one can feel "the force of the wind and the
pull on the sheet"—an idyllic strain underlies the disarming
ease of his unsentimental observation, linking him, as Lloyd
Goodrich has pointed out, with "such fellow New Englanders
as Thoreau and Whittier." Homer's children have the total lack
of nostalgia of Mark Twain's famous urchins, one of whom,
Tom Sawyer, appeared in print also in 1876.

In 1870 Homer made his first visit to the Adirondacks, where he and his brother Charles returned afterward season after season. In that year he began a long series of water colors in which he moved toward the theme that became central to his mature work. He painted fishermen on the lake, guides bearing packs, woodsmen, loggers, trout leaping above the water strewn with the leaves of water lilies, and deer drinking. He gained increasing breadth and control and greater richness of tone. From the beginning his water colors sold so well that he gave up illustration entirely, and in 1881 he went to England, where he spent two summers at the North Sea port of Tynemouth. These years were a turning point in his art. He painted the sea and the shore, the fishermen and their boats, their wives and daughters. Perhaps influenced by English water colors, or perhaps by the English climate, his pictures became more atmospheric. He made figure studies, and his forms became fuller and more monumental.

After his return he left New York for good, to settle on a storm-battered point at Prout's Neck on the Maine coast. There, close to the high, rocky shore, he built the studio that was to be his home for the rest of his life, where the constant sound of the surf became thunderous when savage northeasters struck the coast, and where there were always the cries of the gulls and the mingled smells of the pines on the shore and the salt of the sea. Prout's Neck is now a summer resort, but then, as the artist wrote, "My nearest neighbor is half a mile away—I am four miles from telegram & P. O. & under a snow bank most of the time." But he was no recluse, as has been said. He had been a bit of a dandy in his younger years and had had, as a friend recalled, "the usual number of love affairs"; and he has left us some of the most delightfully appreciative pictures of attractive girls in American art. Homer's move to Maine was not a retreat from life. He had never liked the city. He had found his vocation, and with typical determination he set out to follow it. He traveled every year, often visiting his brothers in Boston and going to the Bahamas, Nassau, Cuba, or Florida during the winter, and to the Adirondacks, the Catskills, or Quebec in the summer or autumn. His brothers had summer houses not far away in Maine, and he was a friend of the fishermen who lived nearby. In 1884 he voyaged with the fishing fleet to the Grand Banks off Newfoundland, and on his return began the series of heroic paintings on the theme that preoccupied him for the rest of his life.

It was a theme introduced into American art, as Edgar P.

Winslow Homer:
After the Hurricane, Bahamas,
1899, $14\frac{15}{16}$ x $21\frac{3}{8}$
(Courtesy of The Art Institute of Chicago,
Mr. and Mrs. Martin A. Ryerson
Collection)

Richardson has pointed out, by Copley with his *Watson and the Shark*. It recurs in Cooper's *Leatherstocking Tales*, in Melville's *Moby Dick*, in Allston's *Rising of a Thunderstorm at Sea*, in Dana's *Two Years Before the Mast*, and in the paintings of Thomas Cole, Fitz Hugh Lane, Martin J. Heade, and others. It is the theme of man and nature, of man as a part of nature yet apart from it, of individual man as solitary as he can be only when faced with the immensity of the wilderness of the New World or with the even greater immensity of the endless sea. It appears throughout Homer's later works, developed with perspicacity and skill. *The Life Line* (1884, Philadelphia) shows a breeches buoy swinging perilously on its heaving cable in the foaming trough of a sea. *The Fog Warning* (1885) depicts a solitary fisherman rowing his dory against choppy waves toward a distant schooner, while an ominous fog bank rises against a cloudy sky. Heroic sou'wester-clad figures are seen against storm-blown clouds and a frothy ocean in *Eight Bells* (1886, Andover). In *"All's Well"* (1896, Boston) there is a compellingly fragmentary glimpse of the lookout and the fog bell against a moonlit sky, while the slant of taut sheets and the tilt of the rail suggest the heaving of the deck.

The same theme of man and nature is to be found again in Homer's Adirondack water colors—in the lonely figure of *The Woodcutter* (private collection) standing on a height looking out across the wild, forested landscape to a far horizon; and in the

Winslow Homer: *The Fog Warning*, 1885, 30 x 48
(Courtesy, Museum of Fine Arts, Boston, Otis Norcross Fund)

stolid *Huntsman and Dogs* (1891, Philadelphia) alone on an autumn hillside. It recurs in *The Gulf Stream* (1899, Metropolitan), which shows an exhausted Negro fisherman lying on the deck of his dismasted boat with hungry sharks following, and a waterspout on the horizon.

In the later paintings, the figures tend to become smaller, as in the view from his studio window, *Winter Coast* (1890), in which the hunter is almost lost in the rough brush and rocks of the stormy shore, dwarfed by the immensity of the thundering surf. In the tremendous seapieces that are the climax of Homer's art, figures often disappear from the picture entirely. Yet man is somehow always a part of the scene, whether he is represented by tiny silhouettes atop a cliff, as in *High Cliff, Coast of Maine* (1894, National Collection), or is shown in a small boat driven by a howling wind, as in *Summer Squall* (1904, Clark Art Institute), or is there only by implication, as in *West Point, Prout's Neck* (1900, Clark Art Institute) and *Early Morning after a Storm at Sea* (1902, Cleveland)—one of the last of the series—in which man is represented by the unseen presence of the painter himself and by whoever looks at the picture and thus becomes a part of it, for the essential subject of man's relation to nature remains the constant theme, a theme basic to Homer's life and to life in the New World.

Like those of the fisherman and the woodsman, and like those of our pioneer ancestors, his senses were constantly alert. He was acutely conscious of the direction of the wind and of the set of the tide, with an awareness unknown to city dwellers. Like the Bartrams and Audubon, like Cole and Heade, and like Morris Graves and Andrew Wyeth today, he identified himself more and more with the natural scene. Like Ryder, he needed solitude to mature his art. As he became more famous, there was an increasing stream of visitors to waste his time. He was often brusque, and is said once to have put a sign on his door saying, "Go away. I am out," and he had a rubber stamp made to answer autograph collectors. But he was at heart no misanthrope, as his fisherman neighbors and close friends could have told.

"This is the only life in which I am permitted to mind my own business," he once wrote. "I suppose I am today the only man in New England who can do it. I am perfectly happy and contented." On the eve of his fifty-ninth birthday he wrote his brother Charles, "The life that I have chosen gives me full hours of enjoyment for the balance of my life. The Sun will not rise, or set, without my notice, and thanks."

Winslow Homer: *Winter Coast,* 1890, 36 x 31½ (John G. Johnson Collection, Philadelphia)

338

THOMAS EAKINS AND THE BIG TOOLS OF ART

During the months when Winslow Homer was making his sole visit to Paris, the twenty-two-year-old Thomas Eakins (1844–1916) was studying at the Ecole des Beaux-Arts. He attended classes under Léon Bonnat, who was admired as one of the leading portraitists of the day, worked more briefly with a sculptor named Augustin Alexandre Dumont, and most intensively with Jean Léon Gérôme, then generally considered the greatest living French painter. Gérôme had developed a style of photographic naturalism so minutely detailed that in his ingeniously contrived compositions of historical anecdote or imagined dramatic episode from Arab life its effect was almost surrealistic. His pictures were greatly admired and brought huge prices from American as well as from European collectors. Most of his pupils imitated his elaborately devised illustrative subjects, though none carried them off with the conviction of their master. Eakins, however, could not have been less interested in subject. What fascinated him was Gérôme's controlled academic drawing and modeling, his realization of every detail. Eakins worked so hard that he became ill and went to Spain for six months, where he fell under the spell of the great Baroque masters Ribera and Velázquez—"the good Spanish work," he called their paintings, "so strong, so reasonable, so free from every affectation." Where Gérôme used his technique to achieve a minute and rather trivial illusionism, Eakins used the academic drawing learned from him in an inexorable search for truth.

"I have seen big paintings here," he wrote home from Madrid. "The big artist does not sit down monkey-like and copy a coal scuttle or an ugly old woman like some Dutch painters . . . but he keeps a sharp eye on Nature and steals her tools. He learns what she does with light, the big tool, and then color, then form. . . . The big artists . . . had the greatest confidence in nature, and when they made an unnatural thing they made it as nature would have made it, and thus they are really closer to nature than the coal-scuttle painters ever suspect. In a big picture you can see what o'clock it is, whether morning or afternoon, if it is hot or cold, winter or summer and what kind of people are there and what they are doing and why.

Thomas Eakins:
Starting Out after Rail,
1874, 25 x 20
(Roland P. Murdock Collection,
Wichita Art Museum)

. . . The sentiments run beyond words." Eakins was to produce as many "big pictures" as anyone in American art.

Like Homer, whom he regarded as the best contemporary painter in America, he was a pronounced individualist from youth, and know that he wanted to be an artist when he was graduated from high school. In Philadelphia, where he was born and lived all his life (except for the few years he spent abroad and some very occasional later trips he made in the United States), he took drawing at the Pennsylvania Academy of the Fine Arts and at the same time studied anatomy at the Jefferson Medical College. He disliked dissection but considered it essential "to increase . . . knowledge of how beautiful objects are put together to . . . be able to imitate them. . . ." However, he later warned his students, "This whole matter of dissection is not art any more than grammar is poetry." But he learned that grammar so well that he became the only American artist to equal William Rimmer as an anatomist. To understand anatomical function he developed, under the auspices of the University of Pennsylvania, a method of photographing athletes and animals in motion which was an advance on the famous experiments of Eadweard Muybridge and proved important to the development of the motion picture camera. His strong scientific turn of mind fostered a love of mathematics, which he felt closely related to painting and sculpture. He had a blackboard in his dining room so that anyone could illustrate with sketches or equations whatever points might arise in discussions during meals. He was a natural linguist who spoke perfect French, and his favorite authors were Dante, Rabelais, and Whitman, whose *Leaves of Grass* he read again and again.

Like Homer also, Eakins loved the out-of-doors, and painted many such subjects as sculling on the Schuylkill, sailing on the Delaware, shooting rail, and swimming in the river, with a luminous, controlled completeness of vision that reflects the severe self-discipline of his approach to art. In every one "you can see what o'clock it is." Every detail is pondered, understood, and subordinated to a whole which has the totality of vision he sought. Though the pictures look uncomposed, as if things just happened that way, they are in fact most carefully structured, and then studied until they are made to appear unstudied, thus embodying the objective truth, not merely of a single momentary episode brilliantly recorded, but of a time, a place, and an attitude toward life.

The same totality of purpose runs throughout all Eakins' work, whether a small sketch of a dead bird, a drawing of a stand with decanters and wine glasses, or a large, complex canvas with groups of people. And in all of them "light, the big tool," fuses the composition into visual completeness at the same time that it expresses the severe and often almost somber turn of the artist's mind. The atmosphere of all his interior scenes, whether portraits or groups, is shadowy, and the light falls in a way that is utterly natural but also calculated to express with greatest significance the special qualities of the subject. There were few sitters in Philadelphia who dared to face the scrutiny of his penetrating eye and the revelation of the inner as well as the outer truth of the resulting canvases. "Distortion," he wrote, "is ugliness"; for Eakins, truth and beauty were synonymous. His idea of beauty was based on function and an understanding of function, hence his preoccupation with anatomical research. The resulting understanding was the basis not only of his paintings but also of the several sculptures that he executed.

Potential patrons, however, wanted to be flattered in their portraits, not exposed to the world in their essential humanity, with its weaknesses as well as its strengths. When he returned from his European study, Eakins therefore turned for subjects to outdoor scenes and to his own family. He painted Katherine playing with the family cat in her lap, the light falling across the canvas from the left to model face, hands, and details of her creamy white dress and red fan. In *Home Scene* (Brooklyn), another sister is seated at the piano watching a child playing on the carpet with a slate. In *Elizabeth at the Piano* (Andover) his subject's face is shadowed except for high lights that suggest her profile and model one expressive hand at the keyboard. *The Chess Players* (Metropolitan) shows a sober Victorian interior with two elderly men at the chessboard while the artist's father stands looking on.

In 1875 he undertook one of the two most ambitious projects of his career, *The Gross Clinic* (Jefferson Medical College, Philadelphia). Like *The Agnew Clinic* of 1898, it embodies his ideals in art as well as his intense interest in science in the same inseparable fashion in which they were combined in his own approach to life. Both pictures are so large that the major figures are life-sized. In the well of the operating theater, Dr. Gross pauses momentarily, scalpel in hand, to explain a point of procedure to the attentive audience of doctors and medical students. The plunging light falls across his face, revealing its thoughtfulness and concentration, and on the operating table where his assistants proceed with the incision in the patient's

leg. The atmosphere of scientific seriousness is sharply emphasized by the contrast of the emotional reaction of the patient's
mother, who is seated at the left, for the law then required the
presence of a member of the family in charity cases. Her arm
is thrown up to hide the scene from her eyes, her hands tensed
in a gesture of horror and fear. Because of the lack of knowledge about antisepsis at that time, there are none of the white
gowns that appear in the later *Agnew Clinic;* in the somber
interior, the carefully controlled highlighting expresses the subject with an intense drama that gives the composition an heroic
and almost religious exaltation.

The painting was finished in time for the Centennial Exposition of 1876, but though several of Eakins' other pictures were
included, *The Gross Clinic* was denied admission to the art
section because its subject matter was considered unfit for public exhibition. Because he showed blood on the doctor's hand
and exuding from the incision, the artist was called a butcher.
One Philadelphia critic wrote that "the more one praises it
the more one must condemn its admission to a gallery where
men and women of weak nerves must be compelled to look at
it, for not to look at it is impossible." The picture was finally
shown as a part of the medical exhibit of the fair, and thus
was not seen in its true significance as a masterpiece of monumental figure painting which can hold its own in its category
beside almost any other example. At thirty-two Eakins had
reached the high point of his career, and in the same year he
took over the anatomy classes at the Pennsylvania Academy
of the Fine Arts, where he taught for ten years without salary,
since, owing to his father's generosity, he was, fortunately, fi-
nancially able to do so.

As a teacher, Eakins was revolutionary and compelling. Unlike Gérôme, he taught his students to draw with paint, beginning with the main masses of the body, and building up the
figure from the inside, rather than outlining and defining and
then filling in. The constant emphasis was on the human figure—first, by making casts, then, by using nude models, and,
finally, through dissection. He was always serious and always
kind, rarely praised, but was never sharp or negative in his
criticism, and his pupils adored him. "If he liked a student's
work," a biographer has written of him, "his face lit up." His
students never forgot him or their experience in his classes, and
his uncompromising integrity, tireless pursuit of excellence,
generosity of spirit, and joy in their achievements became legendary. They absorbed his belief that "if America is to pro-

342

duce great painters and if young art students wish to assume a place in the history of the art of their country, their first desire should be to remain in America, to peer deeper into the heart of American life." When, however, he insisted on the use of a naked male model in the classes for women students, he was too far in advance of his times. There were protests. He refused to compromise his scientific and professional principles, and in 1886 was forced to leave. Almost all his students signed a petition asking his reinstatement, but the governing board refused to reconsider its decision. The Academy lost the most gifted and powerful teacher it has ever had, and Eakins was more than ever cut off from the community in which he lived.

Many of the students were so loyal that they left the Academy with him and founded the Philadelphia Art Students League, where he continued to teach for some years. In 1888 he began a six-year stint of teaching at the National Academy of Design in New York. It was at this time that he undertook the only other project to rival *The Gross Clinic*. *The Agnew Clinic* was completed in 1898 at the same scale, but the contrast between the two reflects a change not only in the artist's approach, but

Thomas Eakins: *The Agnew Clinic*, 1898, 74½ x 130½
(University of Pennsylvania)

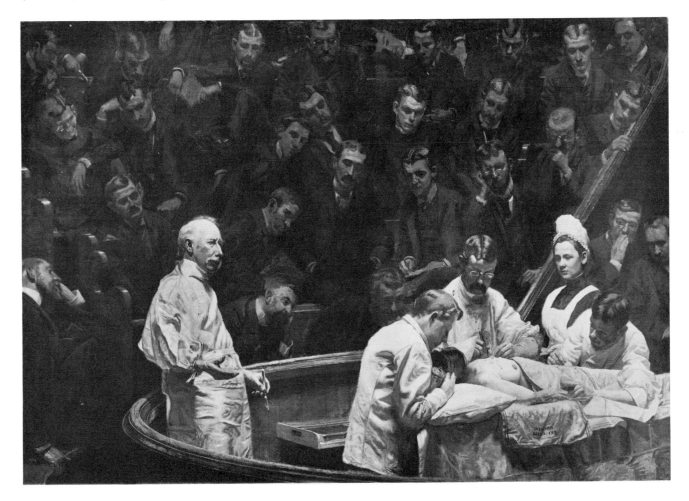

also in the progress of medicine during the intervening years. There is none of the dramatic heroism of the earlier picture, reflecting Eakins' feeling for the miracle of developing science. Instead, the mood is quieter, though equal in intensity. The introduction of the white, sterile robes for the surgeon and his assistants, unknown when the earlier picture was painted twenty-three years before, creates a lighter atmosphere. The light is more diffused, and the composition more open, with the single, eloquent figure of Dr. Agnew on the left balanced by the group to the right surrounding the patient on the table. The play of light on the gowns is beautifully studied, and the still concentration of each individual, whether spectator or participant, is a tribute to the dedication of the medical profession.

Though Eakins regarded the study of the nude as essential to art, it appears in his work only in his pictures of athletic events—such as *Taking the Count* (Yale) and *Salutat* (Andover), boxing subjects painted in 1898, and *Wrestlers* (Philadelphia) of the following year—and in the extraordinary *Crucifixion* (1880, Philadelphia), in *The Swimming Hole* of 1883 (in spirit so like Whitman's "twenty-eight young men [who] bathe by the shore"), and—the only female nude—in the versions of his imaginary re-creation of *William Rush Carving the Allegorical Figure of the Schuylkill River*, the most successful of which is that painted in 1877 (now in the Philadelphia Museum). As in so many of his other pictures, the slanting light models the back of the standing figure, picks up the details of the clothing on the chair in the foreground, and emphasizes the repose of the girl's mother, who sits to the right, quietly knitting. To the far left, Rush works directly on the life-sized wooden sculpture with mallet and chisel. The figures are en-

Thomas Eakins: *The Swimming Hole*,
1883, 27 x 36
(Collection Fort Worth Art Association,
Fort Worth Art Center Museum)

344

veloped in the warm, shadowy atmosphere of the workshop, in which there are various pieces of ship carving, sculptures, tools, and materials. The whole composition has a quiet lyricism which far transcends the expert factual statement and strikes a rare note in Eakins' work.

In 1887 he asked Walt Whitman to pose for him, and a warm friendship resulted. "The Eakins portrait . . . sets me down in correct style without feathers," the poet decided. "Tom's portraits, which the formalists, the academic people won't have at any price . . . are not a remaking of life but life, its manifest, just as it is, as they are."

There were few sitters after that, except for the professional colleagues and friends who were sympathetic to the artist's approach. The result is a memorable series of eloquently expressive likenesses, penetrating in their psychological understanding, devoid of a trace of the idealism he hated as distortion, but based in a profound human sympathy. Among the most impressive of the later works are *Mrs. M. S. Stokes* (1903), in the Art Gallery at Canajoharie, New York, and the extraordinary *Self-Portrait* (1902), in the National Academy of Design, to which he was unanimously elected in the same year. Few artists, no matter how objective in approach they may intend to be, have both the courage and the character to face themselves with such unflinching truth as Eakins displays in his *Self-Portrait*. It reveals both the underlying intensity and the controlled sensibility that made possible the fruitful pursuit of his uncompromising artistic life in the troubled period of dislocation after the horror of the Civil War. It shows, also, his tragic awareness of the times, when people, insecure and saddened by the conflict, sought escape, and he alone faced the facts of things as they were, and found the resources within himself to transform his experience and insight into one of the most remarkable records of creative accomplishment in the history of our art. No artist has ever peered deeper "into the heart of American life" than he.

Thomas Eakins:
Mrs. M. S. Stokes,
1903, 24 x 20
(Canajoharie Library and Art Gallery,
Canajoharie, N.Y.;
photograph, Lebel Studio)

Thomas Eakins: *Self-Portrait,*
1902, 30 x 25
(National Academy of Design;
photograph, Frick Art Reference Library)

WILLIAM M. HARNETT AND THE PURSUIT OF

Homer's painting gained public acceptance, and he earned his living from his art, first as an illustrator, and later with his oils and water colors, although his pictures never came anywhere near the price range of the imported trivialities from the Paris Salon. (His water colors commanded $175 apiece for most of his career, and even his large oils fetched only a few hundred dollars apiece.) Eakins sold comparatively few pictures during his entire lifetime. But the nation's appetite for descriptive realism, which, however, Americans were not willing to face in a portrait, was completely satisfied by a group of painters who specialized in trompe l'oeil still lifes, led by an Irishman named William M. Harnett (1848-92).

Brought to Philadelphia when he was one year old, Harnett started out, like so many others in this country, as an apprentice to an engraver, and made a living engraving silver until he was twenty-seven, first in Philadelphia and then in New York. He attended classes in drawing at the Pennsylvania Academy and at the National Academy of Design and Cooper Union in New York. He began painting oils in 1875, and the following year he returned to Philadelphia to concentrate on still-life painting. From then to 1880 he turned out many carefully painted studies, small in scale and based on the work of James and Raphaelle Peale of half a century earlier. Certain motives recur again and again in his work—a pipe, a beer mug, a quill pen, old books, newspapers, and Confederate currency. These he arranged and rearranged, and in four years he sold enough canvases so that by 1880 he had enough money to go to Europe —at a time when Eakins could sell almost nothing.

Harnett remained abroad for six years, staying mostly in Munich, making a living as a painter. During this period his pictures became increasingly full of such German *kitsch* as porcelain pipes, elaborate tankards, and ornate metalwork, but he greatly improved his technique. He seems to have studied some of the tighter academic work of contemporary continental artists, but, more important, discovered Dutch still lifes of the seventeenth century, from which he learned a more lustrous and richer manner, and a broader range of light and dark. In 1886 he returned to New York to paint his most notable pictures in which, often at considerable scale, he maintained a

Raphaelle Peale: *A Deception*,
1802, pencil and India ink, 16 x 10¾
(Courtesy of Kennedy Galleries, Inc.,
New York)

347

William M. Harnett: *Old Models*, 1892, 54 x 28
(Courtesy, Museum of Fine Arts, Boston, Charles Henry Hayden Fund)

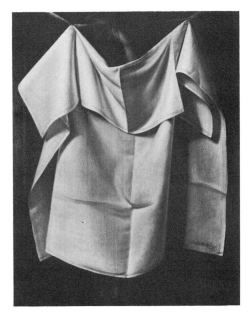

Raphaelle Peale: *After the Bath*,
1823, 29 x 24
(Nelson Gallery-Atkins Museum,
Kansas City, Mo., Nelson Fund)

richly textured illusionism in his veristic treatment of a complex of objects in a studied arrangement. Sometimes these are compositions in depth, like *The Magic Flute* (1887), but more often the objects appear as if hung against, or fastened to, a weatherbeaten door, as in *The Old Violin* (1886), with its careful spotting of the curling sheet music, newspaper clipping, and wrinkled envelope. In *The Faithful Colt* (1890, Hartford), the revolver hangs against a battered door in a striking diagonal balanced by a tiny scrap of newspaper. His *After the Hunt* (1885, California Palace), shown in the Paris Salon of 1885, where it received some critical praise, was sold, on his return in 1886, to a famous New York saloon, where less sophisticated throngs than those which attended the Academy and other more formal galleries were wildly enthusiastic about it, filled with admiration for the verisimilitude of the textures of the dead rabbit and the game birds and the other related objects shown hanging against a door with elaborate decorative hinges.

Old Models (1892) is one of his most attractive works. A dented bugle hangs at the upper left against sheet music, while a violin and bow rest on a shelf against the battered green cupboard door that is the background of the picture. At the lower left, a tall blue-and-white Dutch jug stands on two ancient volumes, while another volume, bound in vellum, leans at an angle, and another sheet of music protrudes below. Every tear, spot, and mark of use and of wear is lovingly delineated. The painting is executed with a sustained and communicable enthusiasm for the objects, their distinctive colors and textures; their existence in the shallow space is realized almost atmospherically as the light, falling from the left, models their forms and casts soft shadows on the worn and sympathetic surface of the cupboard door. The handling is painterly, the colors glow, and the effect is magically luminous.

Soon there were others to challenge Harnett's achievements. John F. Peto (1854–1907) used similar subjects but usually at much smaller scale and with no such extreme attempt at the same degree of illusionism, so that an almost romantic softness pervades his best pictures. *Poor Man's Store* (1885), which shows a partly opened window with small toys, candy, cookies, and fruit for sale, is sensitive in color and strangely effective. In the Harnett boom that occurred in the 1940's, a great many paintings by Peto, who had been totally forgotten in the quarter of a century after his death, were sold with forged Harnett signatures, though the mood, handling, color, composition, and scale of Peto's paintings are utterly different. In a brilliant piece of artistic detective work, Alfred Frankenstein rediscovered Peto and disentangled the various elements of the whole trompe l'oeil movement, which lasted throughout the last two decades of the nineteenth century and the first two of the twentieth; he published the story of his discoveries in an entertaining and scholarly book appropriately called *After the Hunt,* the title of one of Harnett's best-known works.

There were several other painters in the group. Jefferson David Chalfant (1856–1931), a Wilmington, Delaware, cabinetmaker, applied his craftsmanship to painting a newspaper clipping on a small plaque of enameled copper and sticking a two-cent postage stamp on it next to one that he had painted, titling the result *Which is Which?* (private collection). John Haberle (1856–1933) painted paper money so accurately that he was threatened with indictment for forgery by the United States Secret Service. His most remarkable and amusing success was *Torn in Transit* (private collection), which shows a painting wrapped for shipment, its covering apparently torn to reveal portions of a canvas painted in the Hudson River landscape style then current, a trick that effectively dramatized the relentless completeness with which the illusionism was pursued.

This whole movement involves an element of spoofing. It is based on fooling the eye. It achieves a disturbingly complete degree of realism and thus appeals to the American search for the tangible and the real at the same time that it reflects the strong materialistic bent of American society. Yet, by its studied arrangement and very completeness of illusion, it denies that very reality it pretends to represent. The perfection of its surfaces invites touch, but there is nothing there. In attaining that particular kind of perfection, it heightens the intensity of the apprehension of the objects, so ordinary in themselves, but lent thereby a kind of magic. At their best, such pictures suggest to perceptive observers the nostalgia of outworn things and the mystery that lies behind the commonplace. In this way this movement anticipates the modern cult of the found object and is not unrelated in some of its implications to Pop Art. Its great appeal is a significant indication of American taste and instinctive preference. When Homer's greatest oils were selling for a hundred dollars, and Eakins' finest achievements were selling not at all, Harnett, with such paintings as *Emblems of Peace* (1890, Springfield), was enjoying a vogue that recalls the earlier triumphs of Albert Bierstadt and Frederic E. Church with their heroic-sized and minutely detailed landscapes. Art attempted to be reality rather than merely to reflect it or represent aspects of it, but the resulting counterfeit turned out to have a curious validity of its own.

John Peto: *Poor Man's Store,*
1885, 35½ x 25½
(Courtesy, Museum of Fine Arts,
Boston, M. and M. Karolik Collection)

349

Albert Pinkham Ryder: *Toilers of the Sea*, 1884, oil on wood, 11½ x 12
(The Metropolitan Museum of Art, George A. Hearn Fund, 1915)

ALBERT PINKHAM RYDER AND THE PAINTERS OF THE VISION BEYOND

"Have you ever seen an inch worm crawl up a leaf or a twig, and then, clinging to the very end, revolve in the air, feeling for something to reach something? That's like me. I am trying to find something out there beyond the place on which I have a footing." In this way Albert Pinkham Ryder explained to a friend the way he created his strange and compelling visionary paintings, which bring to a climax the inward-looking tendencies so strong in American art. There had been many who had sought "to find something out there," many who had recorded their dreams, like the yearning for *The Peaceable Kingdom* that filled the soul of Edward Hicks, the hoped-for return to innocence of Erastus Salisbury Field's *Garden of Eden,* and the prophecy of future greatness of his *Monument to the Republic.* The inward search is expressed in the quiet reverie of Allston's and Cole's Arcadian landscapes, the gigantic symbolism of the latter's *Titan's Goblet,* the demoniac fancies into which John Quidor translated episodes from Washington Irving's innocent tales, the frightening enigma of William Rimmer's *Flight and Pursuit,* the tragic vision of his *Night, or Fall of Day,* and the impending gloom of Heade's ominous *Approaching Storm.*

It was George Inness (1825-94) who transformed the romantic realism of the Hudson River School into subjective and dreamlike expression. Largely self-taught, he gradually developed a broadly naturalistic approach, dissolving the linear-

John Quidor: *The Money Diggers*,
1832, 16¾ x 21½
(The Brooklyn Museum)

351

ism of Durand and other earlier artists into a pervading atmosphere expressed with freer, looser handling. Two large landscapes of 1865, *The Delaware Valley* and *Peace and Plenty* (Metropolitan), represent the culmination of the first stage in his career. They are grand in conception and have something of the autumnal mood of Allston and Cole, though they are more broadly brushed and freely massed, and they glow with afternoon light. In them can be felt the artist's growing conviction that "A work of art does not appeal to the intellect. It does not appeal to the moral sense. Its aim is not to instruct, not to edify, but to awaken an emotion."

Experience gained on Inness' frequent trips to Europe gradually turned his efforts into a different direction, for he visited Barbizon and fell under the spell of Millet and the others who were painting out of doors in the picturesque Forest of Fontainebleau. In 1870 he spent four years abroad, mostly in Italy, where he wandered the Campagna and painted the Alban Hills south of Rome—with their blue lakes and misty distances, and the deep shadows beneath the thick groves of ancient trees—the olive-clad slopes of the valley of the Tiber, and the steep countryside near Perugia, with its winding roads and medieval farms. This series of Italian paintings is not only among the most delightful of the period, but also includes the most impres-

George Inness: *The Monk*, 1873, 39½ x 64
(Addison Gallery of American Art, Phillips Academy, Andover, Mass.,
gift of Stephen Clark)

sive of his works—the large, twilight landscape entitled *The Monk* of 1873. Beneath colossal stone pines, their wide-spreading branches meeting high overhead, almost black against the evening sky, stands a hooded monk, rapt in meditation, a tiny figure alone with gnarled olive trees and a crumbling wall, in a scene of brooding silence unified by the soft, crepuscular light. It remains one of the best of American Romantic paintings, and marks the height of Inness' art. Thereafter, under the influence of his increasing Swedenborgian mysticism, his painting becomes more subjective, until the forms almost disappear, shimmering vaguely through a misty atmosphere as if through water. His colors grow more muted, his tone darker, and the pictures, drenched in a soft glowing light, become almost subjectless except for the mood alone. During the last quarter of the century Inness' work was enthusiastically admired, and he was among the few American artists of the time to vie with the European in popularity among critics and collectors.

There were others during the period who showed a similar growth from the older type of landscape painting into a newer, more personal and expressive style. Among them were Alexander H. Wyant (1836-92), a country boy from Ohio. While apprenticed to a harness maker, he painted signs and drew from nature during his time off. He went to Cincinnati, where the sight of some of Inness' work encouraged him to a painting career that followed a similar direction. Homer Dodge Martin (1836-97) was another. Inspired to go to Europe by seeing some of the first paintings by Corot imported to America, Martin was influenced, like many other Americans, by the Impressionists in handling, but he did not adopt their point of view, because his art was essentially contemplative, and he did not borrow their light-toned palette. After living for several years in France he returned to America, and, painting from recollection, with his eyesight almost gone, he synthesized a lifetime's experience in his large and spacious *Harp of the Winds* (1895) by combining, as James Flexner has pointed out, the panoramic view of nature of the Hudson River School with the subjective expressiveness of a controlled personal style. Its consistency of tone and sustained mood caused it, not without reason, to become one of the most famous paintings of its day.

More important, however, were William Morris Hunt (1824-79) of Boston and his friend and pupil John La Farge (1835–1910) of New York. William Morris Hunt was the elder brother of Richard Morris Hunt, the leading architect of the Gilded Age. The Hunt brothers were the sons of a congressman from

Homer Dodge Martin: *Harp of the Winds: A View on the Seine,* 1895, 28¾ x 40¾
(The Metropolitan Museum of Art, gift of several gentlemen, 1897)

353

Vermont and hailed from Brattleboro, though they were brought up largely in Europe. Richard studied architecture at the Ecole des Beaux-Arts, and in 1847 William studied painting in the studio of Thomas Couture, later to be Manet's teacher, before discovering Millet and the Barbizon School three years later. Couture and Millet represented the experimental group of modernists of the day. In 1856 William Morris Hunt returned to America, not only to spread the new gospel, but to paint in the broad, atmospheric fashion, with a rich impasto, the portraits, small landscapes, and poetic figure studies that were to have a considerable influence on his younger contemporaries. Hunt was also important as a teacher, numbering among his early pupils the future novelist Henry James, his brother, the philosopher William James, and John La Farge. Because of his enthusiasm, such painters as Corot, Millet, Daubigny, and Rousseau gained a following in Boston before they were accepted in their native France, and through his influence, Paris began to replace the German centers and Italy as the place for young Americans to go to study art.

About 1860 Hunt painted the life-sized portrait of *Chief Justice Lemuel Shaw* (County Court House, Salem) of the Massachusetts Supreme Court, standing with documents in one hand and the other firmly resting on a leather-bound legal volume on the table, covered in dark green, at his side. In this painting, one of the few portraits that can compare with the work of Eakins of the following decades, Hunt has less portrayed an individual than created a symbol. The ponderous figure, rising in a dark silhouette to the massive, craggy head, simply and broadly modeled, looming against a yellowish-brown wall, is the personification of the New England conscience and of the dignity of the law, bearing the sober weight of the Puritan tradition.

Hunt's most ambitious work was one of the few important mural commissions up to that time, and the most successful mural by any American artist of his generation. In 1875 he accepted the task of painting two large sections of the Assembly Chamber of the State Capitol in Albany, New York, but the areas were not finished when promised, and three years later Hunt was faced with having to plan and complete the painting of two colossal lunettes, each measuring 16 by 45 feet, within six months. He went to work furiously and in four months worked up the sketches and completed the cartoons of *The Discoverer*, suggesting both the finding of the New World and man's perpetual and hopeful search for a better life, and,

William Morris Hunt:
The Flight of Night,
study for New York State Capitol mural,
c. 1878
(The Pennsylvania Academy of the
Fine Arts)

far more successful artistically, *The Flight of Night,* based on
a Persian poem about Anahita, goddess of the heavens, used
by the painter as an allegory of the light of culture and learning banishing the darkness of savagery.

In the two remaining months, working tirelessly on the high
scaffold, Hunt completed the murals, painting in oil directly on
the light-colored stone because of the shortness of time. Though
far from great, they were among the very few respectable works
of their scale in the country and were greeted with enthusiasm.
Their appearance is known today only through the preparatory
studies, because within a matter of weeks the leaking of the
faultily constructed vault started the swift course of their inevitable ruin. Judging from the sketches and photographs taken
in process, *The Flight of Night* was by far the more successful
of the two. The wild action of the three great horses plunging out of the clouds is balanced by the slumberous curve within
which lie a sleeping mother and child; above, the goddess sits
enthroned on a cloud before a crescent moon, seen against the
lightening sky of dawn. Exhausted by his efforts, Hunt was
prostrated by the prospect of the destruction of his work, and
late that summer his body was found floating in a tide pool on
the Isles of Shoals.

John La Farge realized the achievement of monumental decoration that had been denied Hunt. With a rich imagination and
an acute and inquiring mind, he had similar advantages of education and travel, also studied briefly with Couture, and at
Hunt's urging took up painting professionally. He did landscapes, nature and figure studies, and detailed still lifes of an
almost trompe l'oeil character with great delicacy and feeling.
An example of the latter type is the painting of a wreath of

flowers hanging against a scarred, rough-plaster wall entitled *The Greek Love Token* (1866). Among his close friends were the outstanding architect H. H. Richardson, the sculptor Augustus Saint-Gaudens, the statesman John Hay, and the philosopher Henry Adams. Like Adams, La Farge also spoke and wrote with distinction.

When Richardson won the commission for Trinity Church in Boston in 1872, he persuaded La Farge to take over the decoration of the vast and solemn interior, the most important commission of its period. Undaunted by lack of experience with anything approaching such a scale, La Farge assembled a group of young artist assistants, including his friend Saint-Gaudens, and, with little time for proper preparation, in four months completed perhaps the most successful monumental interior carried out by an American painter. Drawing on his recollections of decorative schemes seen in Europe, La Farge organized a design in glowing color—gold, blue-green, and orange—of choirs of angels floating beneath the massive, dark beams of the roof. The light is filtered through stained-glass windows which La Farge also designed, in the opaline tones later to appear in the glass of Louis Tiffany. With the paintings, the windows complement the great scale and virile grandeur of Richardson's conception. Such a success was bound to lead to other commissions, and La Farge, who trained a generation of muralists (none of whom, unfortunately, rose above pallid mediocrity), left such major works as *The Ascension*, in the Church of the Ascension in New York City, and a composition of painting, stained glass, and sculpture—the last by Saint-Gaudens—in the chancel of St. Thomas', also in New York.

La Farge's work was very uneven, reflecting the conflict of the times between an overinsistent realism, expressing itself in a clutter of detail and triviality of interpretation, and large design broadly stated in color and form. But nowhere does he show greater charm and sensitivity of observation and feeling than in his drawings and smaller paintings in oil and water color. In 1886 he, Richardson, Saint-Gaudens, Hay, and Adams went on a trip to the Far East and the South Seas. La Farge's oils and water colors are a delightful record of the experience. They show his fascination with oriental art and interpret both the scenery and the mythology of Japan with a sense of its mysterious poetry. Those done in the Pacific islands reflect his sympathy for the natives' carefree life and a delight in the sun-warmed sands and the palms blowing in the trade winds; they suggest Melville's idyll on Fayaway's island in *Typee*.

John La Farge: *The Greek Love Token*, 1866, 23½ x 12¾
(Courtesy of the Smithsonian Institution National Collection of Fine Arts, Gallatly Collection)

356

Both the strain of mysticism in La Farge's art and the powerful masses and rough textures of Richardson's architecture show their relationship to the romantic tendency toward emotional expressionism that runs through so much of American art. It appears in the mood of Hawthorne and Melville, in the strange imagery and macabre flavor of Poe, and in the rhapsodic outpourings of Whitman. In architecture it continues in the work of Louis Sullivan and flowers again in the long career of Frank Lloyd Wright. It also appears in the work of his contemporary Bernard Maybeck (1862–1957), whose Palace of Fine Arts in San Francisco (1915), has, as Wayne Andrews has pointed out, the sense of time and of history seen in Thomas Cole's *Course of Empire*. Its "keynote," the architect noted, is "that of sadness . . . of melancholy . . . seen in the engravings of Piranesi . . . whose remarkable work conveys the sad minor notes of old Roman ruins covered with bushes and trees."

In painting, this tendency reached a peak late in the nineteenth century in the work of Albert P. Ryder, his exact contemporary Ralph Albert Blakelock, and Elihu Vedder (1836–1923), an upstate New Yorker who studied briefly in New York and in Paris and evolved a curious style entirely his own. After five years abroad Vedder returned to New York in 1861, and supported himself during the war years by doing sketches for *Vanity Fair*, various kinds of hack illustrations (including diagrams of exercises with dumbbells for an athletic instructor), and comic valentines, proving that the old versatility of American artists had not entirely disappeared. Yet it was during those same years that, as he worked alone in a room on Beekman Street, fantastic and haunting visions came to him as they were to come to Ryder in his solitary room a decade and more later. Vedder gave form to these fancies in such paintings as *The Questioner of the Sphinx* (1863, Boston), in which, as Tuckerman described it, "the cold daybreak reveals a lonely Arab in the desert, with his lips at the mouth of the vast mystical image, asking for the great secret." *The Lost Mind* (1864, Metropolitan) shows a mysterious figure wandering through a wasteland. *The Lair of the Sea Serpent* (1864) is a panoramic landscape, atmospherically painted, of dunes with a scrubby growth of parched grasses and bushes and the calm sea beyond. Coiled across the sunlit sand lies the immense steel-gray monster, showing that it is alive only by the baleful glitter of a dark reptilian eye. The model for the serpent was actually a large eel that had been washed up on the shore, but Vedder transformed it, as Samuel Isham pointed out in his pioneering work of 1905, *History of American Painting*, "into a type of the

Louis Comfort Tiffany:
Peacock decanter,
c. 1896–1900, h. 14¼
(From the collection of Hugh F. McKean,
President, Rollins College,
Winter Park, Fla.)

357

Elihu Vedder:
The Lair of the Sea Serpent,
1864, 21⅛ x 35½
(Courtesy Museum of Fine Arts,
Boston, bequest of Thomas Gold Appleton)

terror and mystery of the sea." Though there is a narrative element in these pictures which makes them partake of illustration and hence has caused them to fall from fashion, they actually display an extraordinary capacity for the creation of symbols that have a suggestion of surrealism and a curious emotional power.

Vedder moved to Rome in 1866 and remained there for the rest of his life, exploring the Campagna that Allston and Cole had loved and the remote hill towns of central Italy, about which William Dean Howells wrote so appreciatively in *Tuscan Cities.* He was especially attracted to Perugia and painted the mountains of Gubbio from his villa there at the same time that Inness was trudging the roads winding through the same countryside and recording similar views in his atmospheric landscapes. Vedder did many small oils, warm and golden in tone, with touches of bright color, that are full of the flavor of Italian life and sun, and recall the timeless Italy that through the centuries attracted artists and writers from every country like a magnet, and was an Arcadia for Americans from the days of Benjamin West and John Singleton Copley.

Vedder did a number of mural paintings, one for the Walker Art Gallery of Bowdoin College, where La Farge is also represented, and others for the Library of Congress in Washington, D.C. At his villa in Perugia a friend first showed him Fitz-Gerald's translation of Omar Khayyám, whose hedonism and exoticism so attracted him that the result was the extraordinary series of illustrations in black and white, drawn during months of work in his studio outside the Porta del Popolo in Rome, which appeared in the 1884 edition of the *Rubáiyát.* Vedder's imaginative images and symbols are revealed in a sinuous and elastic line that seems to echo the grace and vague melancholy of the verses. The book became one of the most famous of its day and the illustrations are the work for which the artist is best known.

Ralph Albert Blakelock (1847–1919) was a self-taught artist who, at twenty-two, went on a western tour through the desert, the Rocky Mountains, and the West Coast, recording his experiences with swift sketches showing a distinctive jagged line. While on this trip he saw a sight that haunted the remainder of his days—an Indian encampment among trees at dusk with the dull glow of campfires and the soft light of the rising moon. Though not all his pictures were night scenes, he returned again and again to moonlight themes, often with the Indian tepees in the shadows. Working from memory, he gradually built up his paintings, sometimes grinding the surface of the thick impasto down with pumice stone before washing the final delicate glazes across the canvas to pull the composition together. He worked instinctively, using knowledge and judgment but allowing the picture to grow organically until it reached its own natural completion. He constantly studied the effects of nature, the textures of bark and stone and of weathered surfaces, and patterns of clouds and water. Even the effect of paint peeling from a zinc bathtub gave him the idea for *Brook by Moonlight* (1885-90), with its delicate lacework of branches against a moonlit sky.

At twenty-nine he married, and he was soon plagued by ill-health and the growing needs of his family. The dealers and collectors who bought his pictures took such vicious advantage of his necessities that he sold the paintings for little. So consistently was he victimized that in 1899 he became insane and had to be committed to an asylum. Ironically, at about the same time popular taste caught up with his work, and a growing appreciation of the original and valid poetry of his vision led to his being elected at first an associate and finally a member of the National Academy, long after he could have had any knowledge of the event. His paintings sold for larger and larger sums, without benefit to him or to his destitute wife and nine children.

A gifted daughter started to paint to help support the family, and when she realized that an unscrupulous dealer was forging her father's signature to her paintings and selling them as his, she, too, had a breakdown from which she never recovered. The story is horrifying beyond anything in the history of American art, but no breath of sadness or suffering entered Blakelock's paintings. Each is a variation on a theme, carrying the landscape of mood, introduced into American art by Allston, into a realm of personal expression in chords of color

Ralph Blakelock: *Brook by Moonlight*, 1885-90, 72 x 48 (The Toledo Museum of Art, gift of Edward Drummond Libbey)

359

and tone whose quiet resonance re-echoes his lifelong love of music. His habit of musical improvisation helped him to achieve the momentary freedom from the growing pressures of life which enabled him to paint his visions of a more beautiful world than fate allowed him to know.

Albert Pinkham Ryder (1847–1917) also evolved his fantasies from deep within the recesses of his instinctive being. The youngest of four brothers, he was born of an old seafaring family in New Bedford, then the greatest whaling port in the world. He grew up in a house across the street from that occupied by Albert Bierstadt. When he was twenty-one the family moved to New York. The sea was in his inheritance, he lived near it throughout his life, and it constantly recurs in his painting. Two of his brothers went "on the water," and a vivid memory from his boyhood was of one who was so happy to be back from a long and arduous voyage that he even kissed the pig.

From his childhood Ryder drew and colored and as he grew older he started to paint by himself. Later in life he described a turning point: "When I grew weary with the futile struggle to imitate the canvases of the past, I went out into the fields. . . . In my desire to be accurate I became lost in a maze of detail. Try as I would my colors were not those of nature. My leaves were infinitely below the standard of a leaf, my finest strokes were coarse and crude. The old scene presented itself one day before my eyes framed in an opening between two trees. It stood out like a painted canvas—the deep blue of a midday sky—a solitary tree brilliant with the green of early summer, a foundation of brown earth and gnarled roots. There was no detail to vex the eye. Three solid masses of form and color—sky, foliage, and earth—the whole bathed in an atmosphere of golden luminosity. I threw my brushes aside; they were too small for the work in hand. I squeezed out big chunks of pure, moist color and taking my palette knife, I laid on blue, green, white, and brown in great sweeping strokes. As I worked I saw that it was good and clean and strong. I saw nature springing into life upon my dead canvas. It was better than nature, for it was vibrating with the thrill of a new creation. Exultantly I painted till the sun sank below the horizon, then I raced around the fields like a colt let loose, and literally bellowed for joy."

In New York, where his brother became a successful restaurant and hotel owner, Ryder continued to paint small idyllic recollections of the country and village life of his boyhood,

360

with cows grazing, sheep in a fold in the moonlight—familiar forms transmuted into elements of dream, seen in a softly glowing light. Small in size and intensely personal, Ryder's pictures, as his biographer Lloyd Goodrich has observed, are the "product of a mind that lived in a world of its own—a mind as self-sufficient as that other New Englander, Emily Dickinson," whose poems are similarly concerned with homely images, enlarged by a vivid imagination and private vision to another dimension. His ideas often came from things he read—from the Bible, Shakespeare, Chaucer, Byron, Tennyson, Coleridge, Browning, Poe, Scott, and the traditional border ballads—from opera, and from recollections and memories. But unlike so many artists of his period, Ryder was not a literary or illustrative painter. The subject, whatever its genesis might be, became a compelling image with a life and curious overtones of its own and the illogical coherence of a dream.

At twenty-seven he exhibited at the National Academy, which was then made up of the older generation of artists to whom all that the younger men were doing either in Europe or America was dangerously revolutionary. So, like a number of others, Ryder was accepted by the Academy only once in the next seven years. In the meantime the American branch of Cottier & Company, a British firm of art dealers, invited a group of these artists, Ryder among them, to show in opposition to the Academy, an event which led to the formation in 1877 of an independent group, the Society of American Artists, of which Ryder was a founder. "Modern art must strike out from the old," he said, "and assert its individual right to live. . . ." He showed regularly at the Society's exhibitions, and through Daniel Cottier he attracted the attention of a small and discriminating group of collectors, especially Thomas B. Clarke, the generous patron of Inness, who was deeply interested in the American art of his day. In 1885, when Clarke had purchased two of his pictures, *Christ Appearing to Mary* (National Collection) and *The Temple of the Mind* (Buffalo), inspired by Poe's poem, "The Haunted Palace," from his "The Fall of the House of Usher," Ryder wrote, "I find myself . . . so upset with a little appreciation that I can hardly be quiet to acknowledge the source. . . . For a long time I have observed a marked change in the attitude not only of the press but also of collectors toward the possibilities of something being done here amongst us: to you much of the credit belongs: and I am so happy to be identified with your mission. . . . I can not but feel some way that in both the Temple and the religious picture I have gone a lit-

361

tle higher up on the mountain and can see other peaks showing along the horizon."

His small *Self-Portrait* (private collection), only six inches high, shows how he looked at about thirty, with an intense but dreamy gaze and a reddish beard, neat collar, and black bow tie. He was more than middling tall, had a husky frame and a very gentle and courteous manner. He has been called a recluse, but the record scarcely substantiates the description, since all his life he had a devoted group of friends and was remembered as a delightful dinner companion with a good sense of humor who could tell a good story. He went abroad several times, spending a month in London in 1877 and five years later returning to the British Isles with Daniel Cottier and, joined by the sculptor Olin Warner, going on to Holland, France, Italy, Spain, and North Africa. Twice later he sailed with his friend Captain John Robinson on vessels of the Atlantic Transport Line, and spent most of his time, day and night, on deck watching the sea. On these occasions he stayed in London merely long enough to wait for the return trip.

All his life he lived alone. Like a good New Englander, he never threw anything away, and since in New York he had neither attic nor woodshed, as he had had during his early years in New Bedford, his two rooms were increasingly filled with an accumulation of junk to which he was completely oblivious. "I have two windows in my workshop," he wrote, "that look out upon an old garden whose great trees thrust their green-laden branches over the casement sills, filtering a network of light and shadow on the bare boards of my floor. Beyond the low roof tops of neighboring houses sweeps the eternal firmament with its ever-changing panorama of mystery and beauty.

Albert Pinkham Ryder: *The Race Track*
or *Death on a Pale Horse*, 1910, 28¼ x 35¼
(The Cleveland Museum of Art,
purchase from the J. H. Wade Fund)

362

I would not exchange these two windows for a palace with less a vision than this old garden with its whispering leafage."

Here, with the sound of the "whispering leafage," he painted his visions, of *Siegfried and the Rhine Maidens* (National Gallery), inspired by hearing Wagner's *Götterdämmerung*, in which the twisting of the branches of the trees become as expressive as the gestures of the maidens; of Celia and Rosalind wandering through the enchanted landscape of *The Forest of Arden*, from *As You Like It*; and of *Macbeth and the Witches* (Phillips Collection) meeting on the blasted heath, which takes on a sinister presence in the ominous moonlit sky. Sometimes he stayed close to nature, as in the elegiac and strangely moving little study of *The Dead Bird* (Phillips Collection), so reminiscent of Whitman's fated "feather'd guest from Alabama" in "Out of the Cradle Endlessly Rocking." At other times the visions came unbidden out of his mind, as of Death on a white horse endlessly galloping around *The Race Track* (Cleveland), an idea that came to him when he learned that one of the waiters in his brother's hotel, a man he knew, had lost all his savings on a bet and had committed suicide. But perhaps the most unforgettable are the marines, such as the famous *Toilers of the Sea*—a solitary boat by moonlight—and *Homeward Bound* (Phillips Collection) with its luminous sky and endless horizon.

For Ryder, as for Melville and Whitman, the sea becomes a symbol of eternity, infinitely vast and timeless, yet subject to moods equally of terror and of peace. He often shares with Cole and with Emerson the idea of life as a voyage "across the wild ocean, now bright on the wave, now darkling in the trough of the sea; but from what port did we sail? Who knows? Or to what port are we bound? . . . There is no one to tell us but such poor weather-tossed mariners as ourselves, whom we speak as we pass. . . . But what know they more than we? They also found themselves on this wondrous sea. . . . Over all their speaking-trumpets, the gray sea and the loud winds answer, Not in us; not in Time. . . ." But in his painting of *Jonah* (National Collection), Ryder suggests the source of his own inner peace and serenity of spirit, for though the boat's hull is wracked by the fierceness of the stormy seas and the great monster bears relentlessly down on the hapless sacrifice, from the storm clouds God emerges in a golden light above the tumult.

"I've carried the idea for some of my pictures around in my head for five years before I began to put them on canvas," Ryder told a friend. "The artist must buckle himself with infinite patience. . . . His eyes must see naught but the vision beyond. He must await the season of fruitage without haste, without worldly ambition, without vexation of spirit. An inspiration is no more than a seed that must be planted and nourished. It gives growth as it grows to the artist, only as he watches and waits with his highest effort." The vision continued to grow as he worked out the forms with an increasingly thick impasto, developing organically, slowly, as a plant grows until finally it is complete; the material of the paint was so mixed with the immaterial of the creative imagination that the whole has a heightened intensity.

As Ryder grew older his creative powers slowed, and he reworked some of his paintings again and again, much to the detriment of their lasting qualities, since he was notoriously careless about method and materials. Night after night he walked the streets and parks and the waterfront of New York. In the old coat and stocking cap he wore (unless he were going out to dinner or the opera, when he dressed in a top hat and tail coat), he became a familiar figure in the neighborhood of West Fifteenth Street, where he lived, and was a friend of all the children. He loved to stop in of an evening with Charles Fitzpatrick, who had been to sea in his youth, and his wife, who was an amateur painter. They would sing sea chanteys together, and Ryder would get better food than he was accustomed to cook for himself on the grill in his fireplace. Or when Captain Robinson's ship was in port he would spend the night on her deck watching the lights in the harbor and the vessels passing.

It was thus that the younger artists—among them Marsden Hartley and Walter Pach—knew him; Hartley painted his portrait in the knitted sailor's cap. His reputation as an artist grew, and he was dismayed to learn that forgeries of his work had begun to appear on the market. After his death they came in such a spate that it was estimated recently that there were five times as many forgeries as originals. As time passes, Ryder's own conviction that his pictures "spoke for themselves" is being increasingly substantiated. Without the long process of creation, the forgeries are unlike the genuine works in physical structure and aspect. But more important, the free plastic expression of feeling and idea are absent in the imitations; there is no haunting image, none of the revelation of the truth of vision and of dream that was his unique contribution to American art.

VIII

Architecture
and
Sculpture
after
the
Civil War

Richard Morris Hunt: Biltmore, near Asheville, N.C., 1895
(Biltmore Estate, Asheville, N.C.)

HENRY HOBSON RICHARDSON CHANGES THE COURSE OF ARCHITECTURE

Richard Morris Hunt (1828-95), the younger brother of the painter William Morris Hunt, was the first American to study architecture at the Ecole des Beaux-Arts. He designed the famous Caen-stone château for William Kissing Vanderbilt on Fifth Avenue in 1881, the first of the spectacular palaces he produced for the leading tycoons of the day. Ochre Court, a late-Gothic château for Ogden Goelet, followed in 1888, then Belcourt for the Belmonts in the style of Henri IV. He built Marble House, in a late eighteenth-century French design, for the W. K. Vanderbilts, and the famous Breakers, an adaptation of a sixteenth-century Genoese marble palace, for Cornelius Vanderbilt II. For George W. Vanderbilt he designed the most spectacular example of architectural magnificence of its kind ever achieved in America, Biltmore, whose foundations cover five acres. Superbly situated on an enormous estate in the Great Smokies near Asheville, North Carolina, it is now open to the public. After five years the house, a picturesque exercise in the style of the Loire Valley, was completed in 1895, with acres of landscaping and handsome gardens planned by Olmsted, all looking as if they had been there for years. But the genial designer of the house had died a few months before, leaving the field of millionaire architecture for its few remaining years to men of a younger generation, outstanding among them being the famous firm of McKim, Mead, and White.

Though the châteaux have disappeared from Fifth Avenue to be replaced by anonymous apartment houses and office buildings, fortunately several outstanding examples of such architectural expressions of conspicuous consumption, in Veblen's phrase, are preserved at Newport, Rhode Island, and are open to the public, to suggest something of the determined splendors of life among those who were or aspired to be members of the plutocracy designated by its social arbiter, Ward McAllister, as the Four Hundred. Significantly, the styles of their dwellings, as well as the fashions of their clothes and the patterns of the marriages of many of their daughters, were as determinedly European as possible. Andrew Jackson Downing had earlier remarked on the foolishness of an attempt to establish

Richard Morris Hunt: The Breakers, Newport, R.I., 1893
(Photograph courtesy The Preservation Society of Newport County)

great estates in a democratic and swift-changing country. The vast palaces of the Gilded Age, with their implications of the artificiality of the patterns of life of their inmates, seem as remote from today as the temples of the Aztecs, even though many of them date from "only yesterday."

While Richard Morris Hunt was busy satisfying the megalomania of the robber barons—who were as competitive in architecture as in business—and producing some highly impressive examples of picturesque eclecticism in the process, Henry Hobson Richardson (1838-86) was pursuing a different course. Born on a plantation in St. James Parish, Louisiana, he went to Harvard, where he met Henry Adams (who became a lifelong friend) and developed a fondness for Boston which was perhaps not unrelated to the fact that he became engaged to a charming Boston girl. After graduation he went abroad, traveling through the British Isles and on the Continent. He ended up studying, not engineering, as he had at first intended, but architecture, at the Ecole des Beaux-Arts in Paris. The outbreak of the Civil War cut off his income from home and prevented his returning, so he gave up his studies and got a job with a good French architectural firm, though after hours he often rejoined his friends in the atelier at the Ecole. Despite all difficulties, he determined to master his profession.

At the end of the war Richardson returned, married, and built a house on Staten Island. He found the going difficult. Architecture, especially in New York, was a disorganized and misunderstood business, scarcely yet accepted as a profession. People thought they could get along without an architect for most projects, builders often supplied designs for houses, and fees were not standardized. Richardson barely got along during these early years, though no one would ever have known it, since, as Wayne Andrews notes in his amusing and perceptive *Architecture, Ambition and Americans*, "He wore his clothes with an indescribable air of ease." In 1872 he won the commission for Trinity Church in Boston that marked the turning point in his career. Something of his remarkable abilities was already known there, since he had done one previous building in Boston, the new Brattle Square Church on the corner of Commonwealth Avenue and Clarendon Street (often irreverently called the "Church of the Holy Bean Blowers" from the handsome trumpeting angels in Bartholdi's frieze around the top of the tower). But successful as the Brattle Square Church undoubtedly was, Trinity outshone it by far. In five years the triangular lot on the eastern end of what later became Copley

Henry Hobson Richardson: Trinity Church,
Boston, 1872-77
(Photograph, Wayne Andrews)

Square—"a desert of dirt, dust, mud, and wind," Bishop Lawrence called it—was transformed by the masterpiece of Richardson's all too short career.

The architect himself called Trinity "a free rendering of the
French Romanesque," and the tremendous success of the design
brought about a Romanesque Revival similar to the earlier
Gothic Revival. But it was more than that. Certain aspects and
details were obviously derived from the architect's studies of
medieval monuments in Europe, for Trinity combines elements
of the churches of Auvergne, the Torre del Gallo in Salamanca,
and the portal of St-Gilles in Arles. But Richardson was no
archaeologist. He interpreted these elements freely, and the
bold massing, the powerful use of rough-textured Milford granite, and the contrasting color of the Longmeadow freestone trim
are a direct expression of the exuberance of his creative personality. Its interior displays his feeling for the dramatic qualities

369

of space, which are further enhanced by La Farge's decorations and windows, which effectively filter and diffuse the light. Because the building is located on a lot surrounded by streets, Richardson used a Greek-cross plan with the parish house attached to the church by arcades so that the composition composes from every angle. The church is especially impressive from Copley Square, which it dominates, its virile bulk and rough masonry making the Public Library built by McKim, Mead, and White in 1887, ten years after Trinity was finished, look dry and academic by comparison.

Richardson was a man of heroic proportion physically as well as emotionally. When, with two American companions of equal stature, he once walked through the streets of a French provincial town, small boys asked when the circus was coming since the giants had already arrived. He was energetic, outgoing, and gregarious, yet capable of intense concentration in his work. He loved good food and good wine, of which he was a connoisseur, often wore yellow waistcoats with his impeccably tailored suits, and, despite a slight stammer which had kept him out of West Point, was a witty and humorous conversationalist. His generous vitality appears in his architecture, in the organic and fluid handling of the interiors of his houses, in his preference for native New England fieldstone and weathered shingles, with which he created the rambling, broad-windowed cottages that hugged the ground with a new feeling for their environment, and which were prototypes of the "shingle style."

In an age that was undergoing breathless change, he built massively, optimistically affirming a future that many feared. Increasingly, he stripped his buildings of ornament, allowing the uncompromising qualities of the rough masonry he loved to speak for themselves. As Lewis Mumford has observed, he used the autumnal colors of New England, "of the sumach and the red oak, the sweet fern and the lichened rock, the pine tree and the butternut." Constantly aware of construction in a period that had come to dress its buildings' skeletons in such borrowed and vulgarized fancies as were momentarily in vogue, he exploited the new freedom of balloon framing in his houses, and in his last design, the Pray Building in Boston, he anticipated the coming domination of steel construction by using almost continuous strips of window to minimize the solidity of the wall and emphasize openness in a fashion that was in advance of the first skyscraper builders in Chicago.

His railroad stations, instead of being, like so many previously designed, flights of fancy that might have been conceived by a reminiscent Yankee returned from King Arthur's court, were direct statements of function, carried out with great style in stone with tile roofs, and with a sweeping protective overhang for both departing and arriving passengers. The Boston & Albany Station (1881-84) at Chestnut Hill, Massachusetts, is outstanding among them. His bridges were severe and satisfying; that on the Fenway in Boston shows his sculptural handling of rough masonry in simple yet dynamic forms. Sever Hall, completed in 1880 in the Harvard Yard, shows his equal mastery of brick.

The City Hall (1880-82) in Albany, New York, puts the larger State Capitol across the park to shame by the power of the great granite tower anchored by the heavily rusticated façade, and the composition of the Allegheny County Court House and Jail in Pittsburgh (1884-87) is superbly varied and organically adapted to its site. The stone work, with a carefully calculated gradation from the colossal blocks in the lower ranges and the eight-foot voussoirs surrounding the arched openings to the comparatively smaller stones in the upper ranges, is cyclopean in its massiveness.

Richardson once remarked that most of all he wanted to design a grain elevator and the interior of a river steamboat. Unfortunately, he lived to do neither, but the remark shows that his approach to architecture was in the tradition of Bulfinch, for he gave equal care and individual attention to each problem at hand, applying the same standards to the public library he did so successfully in Quincy, Massachusetts, in 1883 as to Trinity Church and to the tremendous Wholesale Store he built in Chicago for Marshall Field (1885-87). The latter, a gigantic business block which was razed in 1930, was seven stories high, expressing its commercial purpose with clifflike walls, and with no decoration whatsoever except a ruggedly detailed cornice. "A monument to trade," Louis Sullivan called it, "to the organized commercial spirit, to the power and progress of the age, to the strength and resource of individuality of character; spiritually it stands as the index of a mind, large enough, courageous enough, to cope with these things, master them, absorb them, and give them forth again, impressed with the stamp of a large and forceful personality."

The work poured out of Richardson's office as he tried to cram as much as possible into a life that he came to know was to be short. He maintained the same intense activity up to the day he died, shortly before his forty-eighth birthday in 1886. From the mid-seventies on, his dynamic personality dominated

Henry Hobson Richardson:
Allegheny Court House, Pittsburgh,
1884-87
(Photograph, Wayne Andrews)

Henry Hobson Richardson: Marshall Field Wholesale Store,
Chicago, 1885-87
(Chicago Architectural Photographing Company)

the scene. Though born in the South, he inherited the New England tradition and gave it national application, uniting the romantic and the utilitarian currents, which had become increasingly separated. In his bursting vitality Richardson expressed the spirit of the times and changed the course of American architecture.

As Montgomery Schuyler observed, "The great and merited success of Richardson was as personal and incommunicable as any artistic success can be." Although there were many who attempted to follow the course he had set, most ended up with heavy proportions, round arches, and little substance, the misunderstood externals of a personal style.

The waves of revivalism were not entirely spent, however, and some of the best of the eclectic architecture of the period that was abruptly to end with the outbreak of war was in the Renaissance style. Among the leaders of this phase were the members of the firm of McKim, Mead, and White, the leading inheritors of the practice of Richard Morris Hunt. Charles Follen McKim (1849–1909) completed his excellent training at Harvard and the Ecole des Beaux-Arts in Richardson's office, where he met the versatile and dynamic Stanford White (1853–1906). In 1879 they went into partnership with William Rutherford Mead (1846–1928), the brother-in-law of the novelist William Dean Howells. Their company went on to become the most successful and the best-known architectural firm in America, maintaining its leadership until shortly before the First World War. The firm produced a number of the outstanding examples at Newport and elsewhere of the vaguely romantic "shingle style," important for the future of domestic architecture, and, after Hunt's death, such handsome Renaissance palaces as the Villard Houses (1885) on Madison Avenue opposite St. Patrick's Cathedral, the University Club (1899) on Fifth Avenue, and the Boston Public Library (1887).

By the beginning of the second decade of the twentieth century, their world had already begun to become obsolete. Signs of change were in the air, and in 1913 Congress ratified the Income Tax Amendment to the Constitution. The older generation of industrial tycoons, the "gigantic lizards and armored reptiles" of the age of "carboniferous capitalism," as Lewis Mumford has called them, were dying out, and the lead in architecture passed from the East to Chicago, the birthplace of the skyscraper, and returned to a course in which Richardson had so imaginatively pioneered.

LOUIS SULLIVAN AND THE MAGIC CITY

The skyscraper was made possible by two practical elements, the passenger elevator and steel construction. The first efficient passenger elevator was installed in 1857 in the cast-iron-fronted Haughwout Building in New York City, and in 1883, the same year in which the Roeblings' magnificent engineering achievement, the Brooklyn Bridge, was opened, William Le Baron Jenney (1832–1907) designed the ten-story Home Insurance Building on the southwest corner of La Salle and Adams streets in Chicago, which was completed in 1885. Jenney, a native of the whaling port of Fairhaven, Massachusetts, had studied engineering in Paris and served with distinction on the staffs of Generals Grant and Sherman in the Civil War. His strength may not have been as a designer, but he was an ingenious engineer. The structural framework of the building was a wrought-iron skeleton, but after construction reached the sixth floor, Bessemer steel could be supplied and was used from there up. Whatever its architectural merits, the Home Insurance Building proved that with elevators and a steel frame there was almost no limit to the heights to which a building might soar.

The year after the Home Insurance Building was completed, William Holabird and Martin Roche, both of whom had worked in Jenney's office, designed the fourteen-story Tacoma Building, completed in 1888 (unfortunately demolished in 1929) for the northwest corner of La Salle and Madison streets in Chicago. It was the first building to use a riveted steel structure. The thin terra cotta walls, whose function was enclosure, not structure, dramatically demonstrated the essential characteristics of the skyscraper. In 1889 John Wellborn Root (1850-91), who had received his training under James Renwick, Jr. (architect of Grace Church and St. Patrick's Cathedral in New York), and who later formed a famous partnership with Daniel H. Burnham (1846–1912), designed the Monadnock Building on the southwest corner of Chicago's Jackson and Dearborn streets. It rose sixteen stories without a suggestion of ornament, "an amazing cliff of brickwork, rising sheer and stark," according to Louis Sullivan, "with a subtlety of line and surface, a direct singleness of purpose, that gave one the thrill of Romance." The lesson of Richardson's Marshall Field Wholesale Store had been well learned.

Daniel H. Burnham and
John Wellborn Root: Monadnock Building,
Chicago, 1891
(Photograph, Hedrich-Blessing)

373

Dankmar Adler and Louis Sullivan:
Auditorium Building,
Chicago, 1889
(Photograph, Hedrich-Blessing)

In the meantime another and far more creative talent had appeared on the Chicago scene. Young Louis Sullivan (1856–1924) was the son of an Irish violinist and a Swiss pianist. Born in Boston, he studied architecture under that austere classicist William R. Ware at the Massachusetts Institute of Technology. He worked briefly in Philadelphia—a "large quiet village," he called it—and with Jenney in Chicago, before going to the Ecole des Beaux-Arts in Paris in 1874. Though he felt that the Ecole "lacked the profound animus of a primal inspiration," and that "beneath the law of the school lay a law which it ignored unsuspecting," he got a great deal out of his experience in Paris, and after he returned he enunciated the law beneath in the succinct and famous statement that "form follows function," a credo of modern architecture. In Dankmar Adler (1844–1900), an experienced engineer, Sullivan found the perfect partner. In 1886 the firm began work on the Auditorium Building on Michigan Avenue, between Congress Street and Wabash Avenue, in Chicago. The building again shows Sullivan's deep respect for Richardson's Wholesale Store, then nearing completion nearby in the Loop. Of solid masonry construction, the Auditorium Building established its architect as a designer of the first order. Its opening in 1889 was a triumph for the firm and for the leadership of the Chicago School. The auditorium itself was a masterpiece of Adler's subtle knowledge of acoustics and of Sullivan's rich and individual sense of ornamental enhancement of design. The predominating gold of the decorative scheme was relieved with accents of rich color.

With this success under his belt, Sullivan was then free to turn his talents to the skyscraper, to make it "every inch a proud and soaring thing." And this is what he did, beginning with the Wainright Building in St. Louis, completed in 1891, in which, as he pointed out, "the steel frame . . . was first given authentic recognition and expression." His finest skyscraper was the Guaranty Building (1895) in Buffalo, in which the verticality is still more emphatic. The red terra-cotta panels, decorated with delicate, dynamic, scroll-like patterns based on natural forms, were inset above and below the windows to form stripes rising to a row of oculus windows beneath a similarly ornamented cornice. The ornament on the Auditorium Building and in Sullivan's later work is closely related to the current movement in Europe of Art Nouveau, yet Sullivan seems to have evolved his decorative vocabulary from Gray's *Botany*, combined with recollections of Gothic Revival ornament and that of Richardson, to produce an extraordinarily personal and effective expression.

374

Sullivan's most outstanding work was perhaps the building he designed in 1899 for the dry goods firm of Schlesinger & Mayer on the northeast corner of State and Madison streets in Chicago, now occupied by Carson, Pirie, Scott & Company. Completed in 1904, the strict geometry of the "Chicago windows," with a single large sheet of glass between much smaller movable sashes, is an amazing anticipation of the architecture of a later generation. The cast-iron panels of lush decoration in swirling organic patterns of the two lower stories emphasize the essential austerity of the building all the more, and exemplify his theory that "ornament is a mental luxury, not a necessary," which must be properly subordinated to the concept of the building as an entity.

Despite the example of Richardson and Sullivan, when the World's Columbian Exposition of 1893 came along, it was to Richard Morris Hunt and McKim, Mead and White that Burnham and Root, who had been entrusted with its architectural supervision, turned for leadership. Hunt was, at sixty-five, the grand old man of American architecture, and was unanimously elected leader of the large group of designers who worked on the project. Frederick Law Olmsted and his gifted assistant Henry Sargent Codman planned the layout, which turned empty acres along the lake shore into a masterly combination of squares, avenues, and lagoons, on which floated the Venetian gondolas sketched by Winslow Homer. The scale was immense, and the perspectives were grand. Within a matter of months acres of buildings began to rise in Jackson Park, endless lath and plaster colonnades appeared, and the White City began to take shape. Edwin H. Blashfield, arriving in Chicago to paint

Dankmar Adler and Louis Sullivan:
Carson, Pirie, Scott & Company
(originally, Schlesinger & Mayer)
Building, Chicago, 1904
(Photograph, Hedrich-Blessing)

Lagoon,
World's Columbian Exposition,
Chicago, 1893,
photograph by Robert Logan
(From *W. H. Jackson's Famous Pictures
of the World's Fair* [Chicago: The White
City Art Co., 1895])

375

murals for the Fair, looked on in wonder. "Here on every side," he reported, "were groups of a half dozen men debonairely picking up a colossal fluted thing that looked like a monolith, standing it on end and with light tackle fitting a Corinthian cap to it; white walls were rising as you watched and domes seemed big iridescent bubbles in the vapor of the lagoons. My chin dropped."

The list of artists participating reads like a Who's Who in the arts of the day. John La Farge, Elihu Vedder, Mary Cassatt, Kenyon Cox, and Edwin Blashfield were among the vast number of painters, directed by Frank D. Millet, who were working away at cartoons for murals, lunettes, domes, and vaulted ceilings throughout the many buildings. Saint-Gaudens captained the team of sculptors, which included Daniel Chester French, whose sixty-five-foot statue of the Republic, "a golden colossus" on an immense base, rising from the waters of the long reflecting pool in the Court of Honor, looked westward to the high-domed Administration Building by Hunt and the grandiose fountain by Frederick MacMonnies. The fountain showed Columbia riding proudly in her barge, rowed by graceful maidens, with a winged Fame piloting at the prow and Father Time at the tiller, while playful sea horses sported among high-spraying jets. The interminable classic façades formed by McKim, Mead, and White's Agricultural Building on one side—with Saint-Gaudens' *Diana*, borrowed from the Madison Square Garden in New York, crowning its central, Pantheon-like dome—and the Manufacturers and Liberal Arts Building, designed by George Brown Post, on the other, reminiscent of Thomas Cole's painting of *The Architect's Dream*, were enlivened by sculptures, banners, and flags. William Dean Howells saw it through the eyes of his Altrurian Traveller: "I feel as if I had caught a glimpse of the glorious capitals which will whiten the hills and shores of the east and the borderless plains of the west, when the New York and the Newer York of today shall seem to all the future Americans as impossible as they would seem to any Altrurian now." For the public, it was the Magic City, especially so at night, its white buildings and statues lit by "the hundred moony arc-lamps of the esplanades," and the "clustered electric jets."

In sculpture, as in architecture, the Fair was a triumph for eclecticism. Though a small army of sculptors was involved, Augustus Saint-Gaudens (1848–1907) and Daniel Chester French (1850–1931) dominated the field. Saint-Gaudens had studied at Cooper Union and the National Academy of Design before going on to the Ecole des Beaux-Arts, to Rome, and to

Frederick W. MacMonnies: Grand Fountain, World's Columbian Exposition, Chicago, 1893 (Photograph, Courtesy of The Art Institute of Chicago)

376

Florence. As a young man he had worked under La Farge on the decorations for Richardson's Trinity Church in Boston before showing his American heritage in the taut naturalism of the sinewy and masculine *Farragut Monument* in Madison Square, New York, in 1881, a commission he received through the recommendation of the older sculptor J. Q. A. Ward. The power and sobriety of the lanky standing *Lincoln* he sculptured for Chicago six years later reflected the hero worship arising out of his childhood memory of the President. His 20-foot nude *Diana*, as graceful and as unprovocative as a Gibson girl, had been raised to its position atop the tower of McKim, Mead, and White's Madison Square Garden three years before it was borrowed for the Exposition. And the *Sherman Monument*, commissioned in 1892, was not to be installed at the corner of Fifty-ninth Street and Fifth Avenue until a decade of hard work had been expended to make it his single most famous work. With something of Rodin's richness of surface, the contrast of the vitality and solidity of horse and rider with the winged grace of the figure of Victory belies the Southerner's wry comment that "it's just like a damnyankee to make a lady walk."

French was self-taught except for a few lessons from Dr. William Rimmer in Boston and J. Q. A. Ward in New York. He had been only twenty-five in 1875 when he sculptured the figure of *The Minute Man* at Concord, whose idealized youthfulness seems soft compared to the gritty realism of Ward and the naturalism of Saint-Gaudens. French's career was to be even longer than Saint-Gaudens', reaching a climax in the colossal *Lincoln* seated within Henry Bacon's classic temple on the Mall in Washington. Commissioned in 1915, the sculpture was not completed until years later, in which time the sculptor had evolved the concept of the brooding figure, the Piccirilli brothers had enlarged and carved it in Georgia marble, and the endless experiments with lighting had taken place, finally transforming it into a monument of tremendous size (30 feet, including the pedestal) and with the formal dignity which has been so much admired. Though he achieved suavity and control, French never equaled Saint-Gaudens in either strength or sensitivity. Neither of these two sculptors had the hard realism of the older Ward. But their work and those of the others represented at the Exposition set a standard of classicizing idealism which characterized most of the monuments and public commissions from then on, and which still retains a grip like *rigor mortis* on the vast majority of the works that receive the patronage of government.

Louis Sullivan:
Transportation Building,
World's Columbian Exposition,
Chicago, 1893
(Photograph, Courtesy of
The Art Institute of Chicago)

The Columbian Exposition, as the contemporary architectural critic Montgomery Schuyler observed, was "a triumph of ensemble" and "very eminently a success of illusion," its architecture "holiday building . . . festal and temporary." But Louis Sullivan saw it as "an imposition of the spurious . . . a naked exhibitionism of charlatanry in the higher feudal and domineering culture, enjoined with expert salesmanship of the materials of decay. . . ." He foresaw that there would be "a violent outbreak of the Classic and the Renaissance . . . contaminating all it touched," and in a way he was right, for the nation's official architecture, like its sculpture, has remained white and pallidly derivative in its Classicism, as may be seen even in current building in Washington, D.C. But without Olmsted's and Codman's planning, Burnham would never have conceived his famous Chicago Plan, nor would he and McKim have been able to revive L'Enfant's plan for Washington. It took a long time for the white Classic tradition to peter out, but there were two buildings in the Fair which did not follow the Classic style and presaged eventual change. The Richardsonian Fisheries Building, designed by the Chicago architect Henry Ives Cobb, and Sullivan's own Transportation Building, with a façade enriched with gold, orange, red, and yellow in a vigorous expression of individualism, stood out like sore thumbs among the rest. And there was a young man from Wisconsin working in Sullivan's office who was to play a great part in dissipating that tradition—Frank Lloyd Wright.

Sullivan's later life was troubled. The depression of 1893 led Adler to retire, terminating the partnership, and Sullivan never forgave him. The Schlesinger & Mayer Building was Sullivan's last great commission. After that there were banks in small towns in Indiana, Ohio, Wisconsin, and Minnesota, all imaginative designs that show none of the despair that he felt. Brought up on the idealism of Emerson and Whitman, he, too, had envisioned an architecture "Mightier than Egypt's tombs, Fairer than Grecia's, Roma's temples. . . ." He had sought "the genius of the modern . . . to build a grander future," and somehow the dream had gone awry.

Louis Sullivan: Drawing of architectural ornament, 1903
(Courtesy of The Art Institute of Chicago, Burnham Library Collection)

Frank Lloyd Wright: Broadacre City
(Reproduced from *The Drawings of Frank Lloyd Wright*, by permission of
The Frank Lloyd Wright Foundation and the publisher, Horizon Press, New York)

FRANK LLOYD WRIGHT'S ARCHITECTURE

FOR A DEMOCRACY

"Early in life," Frank Lloyd Wright (1869–1959) once remarked, "I had to choose between honest arrogance and hypocritical humility. I chose honest arrogance, and have seen no reason to change." During a long and varied career, Wright's consistency in this regard never faltered, and the period during which he lived was such as to try even his brand of determination. Of Welsh descent and with a couple of generations of dissenting preachers behind him, Wright was brought up with a Jeffersonian passion for individualism and a distrust of the city that never left him. He had inherited Emerson's trust in self-reliance and Whitman's faith in democracy and the common man. From Sullivan, in whose office he worked until even that fairly loose rein felt too tight, he absorbed many of the ideas on which he based his theories of "organic architecture" as the only possible architecture for a democracy, "the modern ideal . . . so much needed if we are to see the whole of life . . . to serve the whole of life, holding no 'traditions' essential to the great TRADITION. Nor cherishing any preconceived form fixing upon us either past, present or future, but—instead—exalting the simple laws of common sense . . . determining form by way of nature of materials, the nature of purpose so well understood that a bank will not look like a cathedral, nor a fire-engine house resemble a French château, or what have you? Form follows Function? Yes, but more important now *Form and Function are One.*" For Wright, as for the ancient Chinese philosopher whom he liked to quote, Lao-tzu, "the reality of a building consisted not in the four walls and the roof but inhered in the space within, the space to be lived in."

Inspired by a burning sense of purpose, armed with a quick intelligence and rare creative imagination, and bucklered by stout prejudices against the effete East and any art but architecture, Wright propagated his gospel, a happy warrior stimulated by opposition. The fact that he was a past master in the art of publicity aided his cause and at the same time riled his enemies, thereby giving him double satisfaction. With a tossing mane of hair and a flowing tie, he delighted in shredding pretension and other people's prejudices from the lecture platform with a charm and wit that were as great as his self-assurance. After examining the hundreds of tedious trivialities in the vast art exhibit at the Columbian Exposition, he decided that "the arts are today cursed by literature. Artists attempt to make literature of music, usually of painting and sculpture, and . . . of architecture also." His understandable distaste for contemporary mediocrity hardened into a permanent contempt. But the Japanese exhibit at the Fair utterly charmed him, and he was, like Whistler and Degas, captivated by the Japanese print. Here was a tradition with a consistent aesthetic which could be applied to all the arts. Its power of simplification and abstraction, its sensuous awareness of the textures and qualities of natural materials, and its relation of art to nature, strongly appealed to him. And its very remoteness from the West gave him a vantage point from which to see clearly the overwhelming and massive inheritance of outworn forms which so confused all the current aesthetic issues for American artists, and for Western artists generally. The objectivity gained from this fresh point of view enabled him to clarify basic principles of all art and gave him added strength in his own work.

Wright's initial training had been as an engineer at the University of Wisconsin, which he left at the age of eighteen to talk Louis Sullivan into giving him a job. At nineteen, he tells us, he was "the best paid draftsman in the city of Chicago." He deeply admired Sullivan and soon proved how sensitively he could interpret the older man's concepts in the drawings he turned out. At twenty-two he was entrusted by the firm with designing the James Charnley House on Astor Street in Chicago in 1891, in the planning of which he "first sensed the decorative value of the plain surface." In 1893, he recalled in his autobiography, Daniel Burnham, the chief executive officer of the Fair, was deeply impressed by the brash young man, and offered to pay his way through four years of the Ecole des Beaux-Arts and add two for study in Rome if, when he returned, he would take a job in Burnham's office. "The Fair, Frank," the older architect told him, "is going to have a great influence in our country. . . . I can see all America constructed along the lines of the Fair, in noble, 'dignified' classic style. The great men of the day all feel that way about it." But the twenty-four-year-old Wright did not agree. He knew that Louis Sullivan also did not, and was sure that neither Root nor Richardson would have if they had been alive. For him that was "the uncreative way," so he opened up his own office to practice what he was so consistently to preach.

Wright's early houses show him groping toward the freedom he sought. His own house (1889) in Oak Park, Illinois, was a

382

shingled Richardsonian design, and he went on to experiment
with modified Colonial in the Blossom House in Chicago (1892),
with the Tudor style, after Sullivan, and even in the so-called
Queen Anne style which was then proliferating throughout
American suburbia with the ghastly results still to be seen. After
1900 his interest in the Japanese had become sufficiently digested
so that it could be brought to bear in his work, and the totally
different series of designs that resulted was heralded by the
Winslow House of 1893 in River Forest, and included the
Willitts House of 1902 in Highland Park. In the latter, the clean-
cut geometry of its plain light walls articulated with the dark
trim echoed the Japanese Palace he had seen almost ten years
before at the Fair. The generous roof overhangs, the sprawling
but highly organized plan, and the balance approaching symmetry became typical of a number of the houses of this period. The

Frank Lloyd Wright: Willitts House, Highland Park, Ill., 1902 (Reproduced from *The Drawings of Frank Lloyd Wright*,
by permission of The Frank Lloyd Wright Foundation and the publisher, Horizon Press, New York)

Martin House in Buffalo followed the next year, and the famous
Prairie style, which was to revolutionize the concept of the house
in America, had been launched.

Declaring that democracy deserved something better than the
box to live in, Wright conceived plans with a flowing and continuous interior space, arranging successions of rooms growing
from a central core, often interpenetrating, and following the
logic of use adapted to the particular site. In the flat or gently
rolling landscape of the Middle West that Wright loved, these
houses hug the ground and seem to grow from it in an expression
of that organic ideal that permeated his architectural thinking.
The sweeping roof overhangs were at once practical—in that
they sheltered windows from the glare of the summer sun, yet
welcomed the more slanting rays of the sun in winter—and
stylistically effective—in that they emphasized the low breadth

of the complex masses and echoed the contours of the land. The interiors were as carefully calculated as the exteriors, with colors, textures, furniture, and decorations—such as the architect allowed (and he became increasingly severe in such matters)—all designed by Wright himself. He pioneered in built-in furniture, as in the revolutionary low-cost housing unit he designed for Francisco Terrace and the apartments on West Walnut Street in Chicago, for his ideal was to build for a democracy, not just for the happy few whose patronage supported the practice of most architects. Wright was thus an outsider, and he gloried in it, spreading his gospel in lectures, articles, and by example.

One of Wright's finest houses is appropriately in Riverside, Illinois, the suburb of Chicago that had been so picturesquely laid out by Olmsted years before. Both the architect and the landscape designer shared a similar sense of place, a sensitive awareness of the specific characteristics of terrain and environment. Olmsted's plan was conceived to take advantage of the natural features of the landscape, with its groves of oaks along the banks of the Des Plaines River; and Wright's house, designed for Avery Coonley in 1908, was marvelously adapted to its generously spacious site. It is a design made up of a complex of low-lying units of pavilionlike buildings and gardens with terraces and pools organically interrelated in the continuously flowing fashion that represents Wright's dynamic concept of space. This kind of freedom from "the box," against whose confinement he was constantly to inveigh, was only possible through the development of central heating, and Wright's quickness to take advantage of the potential it offered is typical of his objective attitude toward all such technological advances, and his total lack of preconceived notions of form.

In his freedom of space-planning Wright brought to a climax the inheritance that had begun with Charles Bulfinch, who started to experiment with a freer arrangement and shape of rooms, and was carried on by Alexander Jackson Davis with his ingenious suites and sequences; it was taken on again by Richardson in his awareness of the dramatic qualities of space, and carried yet further by Wright's *"lieber Meister"* Sullivan. Wright realized the ideal of Andrew Jackson Downing in designing each building in relation to the site, as the houses he designed in the Prairie style show, and was to reach the greatest degree of perfection in his own houses—Taliesin East at Spring Green, Wisconsin, and Taliesin West near Phoenix, Arizona— and, at Bear Run, Pennsylvania, in the most superb house of its kind in America, Falling Water, built in 1936 for Edgar J. Kaufmann of Pittsburgh.

Taliesin East was twice burned, and the present version dates from 1925. But dates are misleading, because it was constantly being added to and changed. Built of the very stuff of the hill on which it stands, it exemplifies Wright's dictum that "no house should ever be *on* a hill or *on* anything. It should be *of* the hill, belonging to it, so hill and house should live together each the happier for the other."

Taliesin West was first laid out in 1938, sprawling across the desert, around and including great boulders, its red local stone melding with the site, and the diagonals of its roof line and dense shadows of its overhangs broken by the grotesque forms of the strange cacti that crowd in upon it as if it were, like themselves, a natural outgrowth of the desert sands.

Falling Water is the most complete interblending of house and site that it seems possible to achieve. The architect took advantage of newly available techniques of concrete construc-

Frank Lloyd Wright: Falling Water, Bear Run, Pa., 1936
(Photograph, Hedrich-Blessing)

tion; the hovering cantilevers bridge the rushing stream and grow out of the colossal boulders of the valley in which it is built. The changes of level and flowing interior space express not only the function of the various areas but also the unevenness of the site, until the man-made and the natural become one, like an oriental fantasy such as might be seen in a Chinese scroll painting of a mythical Han palace.

In the Administration Building executed for the Larkin Company in Buffalo in 1904, the architect showed his grasp of the principles of business structures. He organized the floors of offices around a central well in a fashion similar to the yet more masterly Administration Building he designed for the Johnson Wax Company in Racine, Wisconsin. Begun in 1936 (the year that saw the completion of Falling Water) and finished in 1939, the Johnson Wax Building is an abstract composition of plain brick with windowless walls, curved in simple forms; its tall interior rises to a ceiling of Pyrex glass tubing, naturally lighted, supported on columns which taper downward from lilypadlike disks of concrete to the pavement. The Research Center, added in 1951, is a tower with rounded corners, rising in alternating bands of brick and Pyrex tubing to complete a composition unparalleled in industrial construction for subtlety and simplicity.

In his Unitarian Meeting House in Madison, Wisconsin, the eaves sweep the hillside, and the roof, like a folded leaf, rises to a tall gable in front, through which the light floods an interior with walls built of the stone of the hill itself. In 1940 he laid out the campus of Florida Southern College in Lakeland, with the various units scattered about a landscape of lush foliage and blue water, their shapes ingenious variations on a geometric theme interpreted in the gleaming white of concrete blocks, and connected by covered walks that wind from one to another to form an additional compositional as well as practical whole. The result is a blending of nature and art such as Davis had also achieved at Llewellyn Park, New Jersey, though Wright's design is in an idiom entirely of the mid-twentieth century.

In 1901 Wright addressed the Society of Arts and Crafts at Hull House in Chicago, one of the many such societies that had sprung up under the influence of William Morris and others who saw the threat of the machine to all that was individual and of human value in the arts and crafts. "In the machine," Wright announced, "lies the only future of art and craft—as I believe, a glorious future." Since ours is an industrial age, the machine is a fact of life, he declared, not to be deplored but to be em-

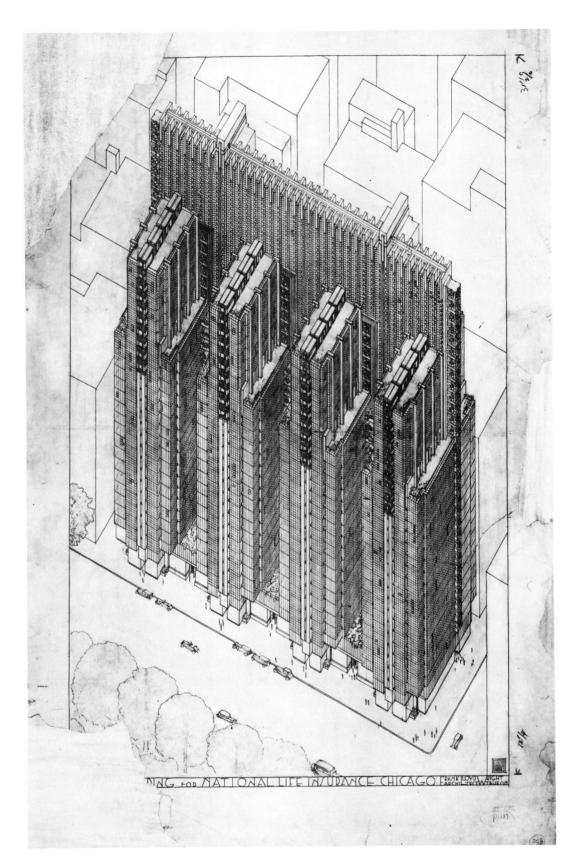

Frank Lloyd Wright: National Life Insurance Company Project, Chicago
(Reproduced from *The Drawings of Frank Lloyd Wright,* by permission of
The Frank Lloyd Wright Foundation
and the publisher, Horizon Press, New York)

387

ployed, not to be used to imitate the old-fashioned handwork, but to reveal the beauty of the natural materials—of wood, steel, cement, and terra cotta. Greece used "the chattel slave as the essential tool of its art and civilization"; we have the machine to save "the most precious thing in the world—human effort."

From the beginning of the century on, Wright's theories and his buildings received a good deal of attention, at home and abroad. His so-called "style" was being copied by followers with about as much understanding as that shown by the followers of Richardson a few years earlier.

In 1908 the forgotten Sullivan wrote his long-unpublished *Democracy: A Man-Search,* in which his idealism came strongly through his growing despair to assert the greatness of the challenge of democracy, for "democracy is ever a revolution . . . an aspiration . . . seeking form for its superb and calm spirit." And in the same year Wright published in the *Architectural Record* his "In the Cause of Architecture," illustrating with eighty-seven examples of his work the principles of organic architecture that were based on Sullivan's convictions, founded on nature, an expression of function—free, individualistic, practical—lovingly exploiting the natural qualities of materials, and relying on them alone for decoration. Wright was sought out by visitors from at home and abroad; his works were published and discussed in Germany, France, Holland, Austria, and Scandinavia, where they were of profound influence on the emerging new architecture in Europe.

Yet it was a time when traditional stylists were receiving the great commissions in America, from the Woolworth Building in New York, designed by Cass Gilbert as a Gothic tower in 1909, to the adaptation by Raymond Hood and John M. Howells of the famous late-Gothic Butter Tower at Rouen, blown up to colossal size, for the Chicago Tribune Building in 1924 to satisfy Colonel McCormick's sense of romance. As McKim wrote Stanford White's son in Europe, "the scale is Roman." His firm turned the Baths of Caracalla into the Pennsylvania Station in 1903, while half a dozen years later Trowbridge and Livingston topped the Bankers Trust Company Building on Wall Street with a replica of the tomb of Mausolus at Halicarnassus.

A major postwar change was the shift from town house to suburb, and apartment houses in the prevailing orthodox style started their swift rise along Park Avenue, which had suddenly become fashionable. During the First World War Wright was designing the Imperial Hotel in Tokyo with a fine feeling of oriental fantasy and a new structural approach that allowed it

388

Philip Johnson: Glass House,
New Canaan, Conn., 1949
(Photograph, Alexandre Georges)

to weather the earthquake of 1923—balanced, as he explained,
like a tray on a waiter's fingers—undamaged when all about it
was destroyed. In the same year that the Pennsylvania Station
was begun, Ralph Adams Cram was reviving the Middle Ages
by adding a Chapel and Post Headquarters at West Point,
buttressed and massive enough to withstand the assaults of Richard the Lion Heart, and redesigning in Gothic the Cathedral of
St. John the Divine in 1911, thus seeking to recapture the faith
and purpose that had been translated into the medieval cathedral
by returning to medieval forms. Meanwhile, Wright was
announcing that twelfth-century structures could not express
twentieth-century ideas, and was designing a skyscraper for San
Francisco that recalled Sullivan but went far beyond him in
grandeur—a great upthrusting concrete slab, topped with extended cornices, that was so far in advance of the times that no
one had the courage to build it.

During the 1920's the modern style was burgeoning in Europe
—with Walter Gropius (1883–) and the Bauhaus (founded
in 1919 in Weimar, Germany), with J. J. P. Oud (1890–)
in Holland, whose rectilinear simplicities suggested those of his
countryman, the painter Mondrian, and with Le Corbusier
(1887–1965) in France, whose definition of a house as a
"machine for living" rivaled the motto of Miës van der Rohe
(1886–) that "less is more," which he illustrated with a cold
and impeccable purism. The European developments were
deeply indebted to the works and theories of Wright, but the
latter found himself in the odd position of being a godfather of

389

an architecture he did not approve because of its dehumanization and anonymous approach. Some seemed to look upon him as a kind of Rip van Winkle who had slept through the period of the First World War and the 1920's, only to wake up in a changed world after the United States had suddenly discovered the International style through an important exhibition handsomely staged in 1932 at the Museum of Modern Art by Philip Johnson (1906–   ). Johnson himself was to become a leading American architect, first as an ardent follower of Miës van der Rohe and then as master of his own style.

Wright's Jeffersonian ideals, his Whitmanesque language, and his dedication to individualism may have seemed anachronistic in the cool climate of the post-Depression years, but Falling Water, Florida Southern College, the Johnson Wax buildings, the Guggenheim Museum, and much else was yet to come. Gradually, many of the puritanical austerities of European theory became modified by transplantation to the New World, much as had been the case centuries earlier, when the first settlers had tried to re-create their remembered homeland in the wilderness along the Atlantic shores but found that they were gradually creating something else instead. Today there are few who do not recognize Wright as the embodiment of those forces that made the vital difference.

IX

A
World
Divided:
The
Arts
in the
Twentieth
Century

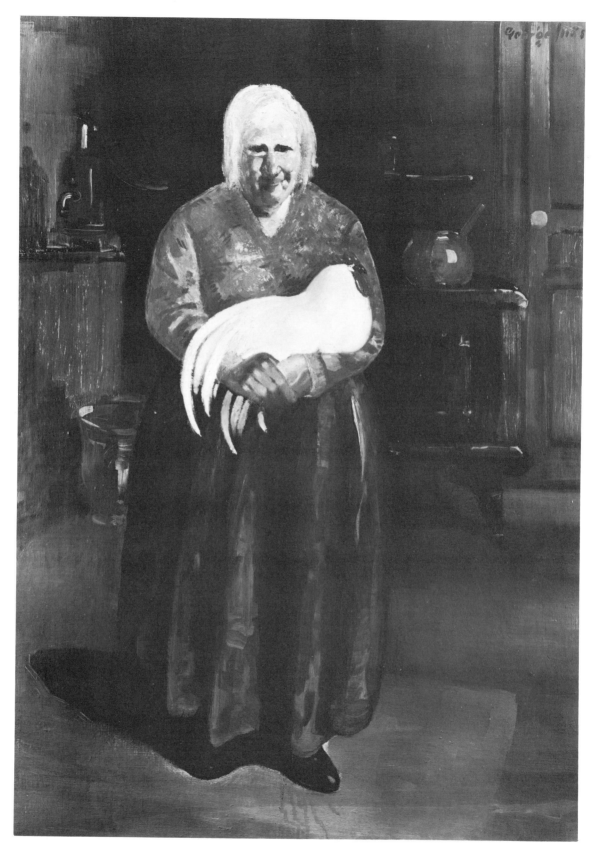

George Luks: *Mrs. Gamley*, 1930, 66 x 48
(Collection Whitney Museum of American Art, New York)

THE EIGHT AND THE ARMORY SHOW

The year 1908 was a significant one for the arts in America. It saw the adoption of Daniel Burnham's updating of the L'Enfant plan for Washington. Louis Sullivan finished writing his *Democracy: A Man-Search*, and designed the National Farmers' Bank in Owatonna, Minnesota, while his pupil Frank Lloyd Wright built Unity Temple in Oak Park, Illinois, and the Coonley House in Riverside. A whole new group of young Americans was studying and working abroad, mostly in Paris, and in New York the sculptress Gertrude Vanderbilt Whitney started a small gallery to give encouragement and a chance to unknown painters and sculptors to show their work. The gallery became the Whitney Studio Club, whose vigorous director, Mrs. Juliana Force, later became the head of the Whitney Museum of American Art, a final evolution from the little gallery of 1908.

Three years earlier the famous photographer Alfred Stieglitz had opened three small rooms in a brownstone on Fifth Avenue, to become famous as "291." There, the most important series of exhibitions showing the work of advance-guard European and American artists before the First World War was presented. Stieglitz's support of the work of experimental artists during these years was invaluable, but his greatest significance was his influence on the developments which are a part of the story of the course of American art after the war. The leaders during the 1920's and later were largely recruited from among the artists associated either with Stieglitz's gallery or with the Studio Club.

It was in such places as these that the artists, newly returned from abroad, found a place to talk, to show their works, and to see those of others. In Paris they had seen the paintings of Matisse and the other Fauves (the "Wild Beasts," as they were called when their colorful canvases were first shown in the Salon d'Automne in 1905); of the German Expressionists, whose movement was launched by the exhibition of Van Gogh in Berlin in 1901; and of the Italian Futurists, who proclaimed the high-powered automobile more beautiful than the *Victory* of Samothrace. The earlier stages of the artistic revolution led by Cézanne, Gauguin, Van Gogh, and others had been supplanted by a newer and yet more adventurous generation. Braque and

Picasso were developing Cubism, which found its interpreter in Guillaume Apollinaire, whose *The Cubist Painters: Aesthetic Meditations* was published in 1913 to proclaim a purer and profounder approach to art than that of external realism.

When the Americans came home, they found a nation ignorant of everything that had gone on in art since Monet. The accepted painting was a pallid Impressionism, and the reaction that was bound to result from such a confrontation took two directions. The first, which flourished during the first two decades of the century, was toward a healthy and earthy realism of subject— such as often appeared in Stieglitz's sensitive photographs—in the tradition of Emerson, Whitman, and Homer, interpreted in fuller color with direct and zesty brushwork. The second was toward an increasing subjectivity and intuitive exploration in the trend established by Ryder, Blakelock, and others, in the tradition of Hawthorne, Melville, and Poe. This second direction became much the stronger during the period after the First World War, since it was in direct reaction to the scientific naturalism and rampant materialism of the times. It was fed and influenced by the rediscovery, as art rather than as artifact, of the arts of primitive peoples, and by the rediscovery of the unconscious and the inner life in the movement in which Freud was a pioneer. The first was a revolt in attitude expressed in choice of subject. The second was a revolt in the whole approach to art—indeed, in the idea of what art is and might be. It, therefore, became protean in the variety of its directions and experiment, proliferating into the many diverse forms we see today. Since it emerged strongly only during a later period, the account of its development belongs to a subsequent chapter.

The great American public was totally unaware of all this, and with but a few exceptions the established world of art was equally uninformed. The shows put on at "291" and occasionally in a few other galleries scarcely attracted attention except as the trivial irrationalities, important only as minor symptoms of an unrest, of a small lunatic fringe, who were classified along with anarchists, nihilists, and other foreigners that unaccountably disturbed this best of all worlds. The courtly and genteel members of the National Academy and the Century Club lived serenely in their comfortable past. They were profoundly shocked when, in 1907, the jury's refusal to accept the work of George Luks, John Sloan, and William Glackens for the annual National Academy exhibition produced a reaction that was to shake the American art world to its very foundations.

The first of these tremors was an exhibition at the Macbeth

Alfred Stieglitz: *The Steerage*, 1907, photograph
(Collection, The Museum of Modern Art, New York)

Gallery the following year entitled simply "Eight American Painters." When his friends' paintings were turned down by the Academy, Robert Henri (1865–1929), whose pupils they had been in Philadelphia, refused to allow his own pictures to be shown, though they had been accepted. And when William Macbeth, sure that there were better works by younger Americans than those appearing in the annual exhibition at the Academy, asked Arthur B. Davies, a prominent artist who often showed at his gallery, to assist in assembling a group, Davies joined forces with Henri, Glackens, Luks, Sloan, and another pupil of Henri's, Everett Shinn, along with Ernest Lawson, a pupil of Twachtman, and Maurice Prendergast, an older independent from Boston who had traveled and painted abroad more than the rest. Some of Davies' own pictures were included as well.

Henri was the dominant member of the group. He was born in Cincinnati, but had studied under Thomas Anshutz, Eakins' assistant and successor at the Pennsylvania Academy, and at the Académie Julian and Ecole des Beaux-Arts in Paris. As a teacher in Philadelphia, he had a buoyant approach to life as well as to art, which brought him many pupils and friends, among them Glackens, Luks, Sloan, and Shinn—young newspaper artists working for the Philadelphia *Press*—who turned from illustration to painting under his inspiration. They approached art with the same interest in everyday life that they had had in their reportorial work and that was to be found in the short stories of O. Henry and in the novels of Theodore Dreiser and Frank Norris. When they moved to New York, they continued to make a living as illustrators while they kept on with their painting. Henri had settled in New York in 1900 where his influence was more valuable for the future as a teacher than as a painter, because he was really more interested in people than in pictures. He managed to impart to his pupils and followers his own gusty, Whitmanesque love and joyous acceptance of life, so well reflected in the collection of his opinions published in 1923 as *The Art Spirit*.

Glackens (1870–1938) had also studied at the Pennsylvania Academy. In 1895 he had gone abroad, where he saw the work of Manet, Renoir, and others, haunted Paris cafés with Henri and other artist friends, and bicycled about Europe before returning to settle in New York. He did comic drawings and other illustrations for the New York *Herald* before departing for Cuba as a combat artist for *McClure's* to cover the exploits of the Rough Riders and other American forces in Teddy Roosevelt's "splendid little war." Later, he contributed skillful and humorous drawings to various newspapers, did covers for *Collier's,* and made a name as an illustrator while his reputation as a painter steadily grew.

George Luks (1867–1933), with whom Glackens briefly shared a studio, was another successful newspaper artist. A good-humored, tireless extrovert, he told tall tales about his imaginary early life as a pugilist named "Chicago Whitey, the terror of the Windy City." After initial training at the Pennsylvania Academy, he, too, had gone abroad before returning to draw a comic strip for the New York *World* and to gain fame, not only as a painter, but also as a teacher at the Art Students League, where he enjoyed a devoted following. Attired with a bespatted stylishness to rival the very proper William Merritt Chase, Luks occasionally delighted his students by entering the studio, cane in hand, and breaking into an expert buck and wing accompanied by ingenious and often bawdy improvisations on some popular song of the day.

John Sloan (1871–1951), early showed himself to be an accomplished illustrator in black and white who had a sharp reportorial eye which he turned toward the everyday world about him. He settled in New York in 1904 and thereafter devoted himself primarily to painting the activities of people in the streets and parks, in bars and restaurants, on the elevated, in the moving picture palaces, in the back yards of tenements, and along the waterfront. His lively observations are among the outstanding examples of genre painting in more recent American art. They are at their best in such examples as *McSorley's Bar,* where his interpretation of the smoky scene is expressed largely in warm neutral tones with touches of quiet color to give the very feel and smell of the place; or his group of girls drying their hair in the sun on a rooftop; or a city back yard with ash cans and a lean black cat slinking over the snow.

As Ira Glackens recalls in his delightful *William Glackens and the Ash Can Group,* Everett Shinn (1876–1953), the youngest of The Eight (as the group came to be called), was so stage-struck that he wrote and produced such deathless dramas as *Ethel Clayton, or Wronged from the Start* and *Hazel Weston, or More Sinned Against than Usual,* in which the genial Glackens played the villain with Mephistophelean intensity, perhaps to be outdone only by Shinn's own frightening portrayal of Glucose Smith in *Lucy Moore, or the Prune Hater's Daughter.* Amazingly, these preposterous farces, written for fun, were taken over by vaudeville, then translated into several languages and

John Sloan: *McSorley's Bar*, 1912, 26 x 32
(Courtesy of The Detroit Institute of Arts)

performed for many years in Europe. Shinn found some of his
favorite themes for his art in the streets of Paris but he took far
more from the theater, with the pretty girls and the flashy gents
of vaudeville and revue caught in the glare of the lights to express all the tinselly color and tinkling charm of the world of
popular entertainment that he loved.

Lawson, Prendergast, and Davies really fall outside this
group in style and approach, though all were good friends, admired one another's work, and were involved in the same crucial
artistic developments. Although Ernest Lawson (1873–1939)
was of British parentage, he became such an enthusiastic American that he even played professional baseball for a while before

settling down to the painting career to which his early experiences in Paris had committed him, and from which his personal interpretation of the Impressionists' vision was derived. Prendergast was by several years the eldest of The Eight. Shy and solitary, he pursued his own very individual way, and became, all unknowing, a pioneer of the art that was to come in the following period.

Arthur B. Davies (1862–1928), who proved to be the arch-revolutionary of the time, was as unlikely a person to be cast in such a role as could well be imagined. Suave, reserved, and distinguished in manner, he painted landscapes rendered in soft

Arthur B. Davies: *Unicorns*, 1906, 18¼ x 40¼ (The Metropolitan Museum of Art, bequest of Lizzie P. Bliss, 1931)

and muted tones, "in which attenuated nudes walked in rhythmic strides borrowed," as Guy Pène du Bois remarked, "from the languors of lovers," in a sophisticated continuation of the romantic tradition. With European experience, he was a perceptive and intelligent connoisseur of current trends totally unknown to most of his American contemporaries, including Henri and his followers. They continued the darker naturalism of Daumier and Manet, and for them subject was more important than manner because they carried over into their painting the social commentary that had sharpened and given direction to their work in black and white.

The impact of The Eight seems today out of all proportion to the character of the works shown in the exhibition of 1908. The paintings of the participants were already known from inclusion in numerous other exhibitions, and the subjects seem far from shocking. Henri's *Dutch Soldier* gazes, rather truculently to be sure, out of a canvas painted in that artist's bravura manner. Glackens' *Chez Mouquin* includes a mustachioed man suggesting John L. Sullivan in husky masculinity, but who was actually James B. Moore, the wealthy lawyer who ran the Café Francis as a favorite meeting place for his artist friends. Neither he nor

Robert Henri: *Dutch Soldier*, 1907, 32⅝ x 26⅛ (Munson-Williams-Proctor Institute, Utica, N.Y.)

the chic young lady seated beside him could exactly be regarded as low life. Ernest Lawson's pleasantly impressionistic landscapes, Prendergast's mosaics of broken color, freshly lyric in mood, and Davies' palely poetic figures seem unexceptionable. And Shinn's small theatrical vignettes, Luks's freely brushed portraits, and Sloan's humorous observations of life in the streets of New York strike a somewhat nostalgic note today. Yet the critics reacted with horror at "the despicable vulgarity" of what they termed the "Ash Can School" and the "Revolutionary Black Gang." Ernest Lawson was even accused of deliberately choosing the ugliest aspects of nature to paint. The exhibit was regarded by many as a deliberate conspiracy to blacken the eye of America by besmirching her classic beauty with such impolite elements of life, which should obviously remain outside the proper domain of art.

Not everyone disapproved, however. Seven paintings were sold—four to that generous patron Gertrude Vanderbilt Whitney—and the Pennsylvania Academy borrowed the exhibition complete and circulated it among eight other museums for more than a year. But its critics hadn't seen anything yet. The banner of revolution had been raised, and the battle was about to begin.

Two years later several artists of the group held a big, unjuried exhibition in a rented building on West Thirty-fifth Street, which turned out to be a mixture of something of everything and included a number of the modernists. Stieglitz put on the first American all-modern show at "291" in the same year, and in 1911 there was an exhibition at the Madison Gallery, which was largely supported by Mrs. Whitney, of the work of Walt Kuhn (1880–1949), Jerome Myers (1867–1940), Elmer L. MacRae (1875–1955), and Henry Fitch Taylor (1853–1925). Kuhn had started as a cartoonist from Brooklyn; Myers, a former scene painter, who had studied at Cooper Union and in Paris, painted small darkish canvases of the Lower East Side with a touch of fantasy; MacRae painted in oil and pastel in an impressionistic style; while Taylor was a painter who arranged the shows for the Madison Gallery.

The exhibiting artists and their friends dropped in to the gallery to talk, and from their conversations grew the Association of American Painters and Sculptors. All of The Eight were included in this group except Shinn, who was asked but who seems to have been too busy at the moment with a mural in Trenton, New Jersey, to join. Among the younger artists were George Bellows (1882–1925), who loved to paint prize fights and street scenes; Guy Pène du Bois (1884–1958), a witty painter-illustrator; the pugnacious sculptor Gutzon Borglum (1867–1941), a

William Glackens: *Chez Mouquin,* 1905, 48³⁄₁₆ x 36¼ (Courtesy of The Art Institute of Chicago, Friends of American Art Collection)

399

pupil of Rodin's who was to make a name for himself by carving, with pneumatic drills and dynamite, the colossal heads of four great presidents on the lofty sides of Mount Rushmore in South Dakota; and Jo Davidson (1883–1952), later famous for his life-sized sculptured heads of notables. All were independent spirits. None of the Stieglitz group was included, apparently because none of them was known to the founders.

Inevitably, Davies emerged as a leader and was elected president. As Milton W. Brown remarks in his excellent account in *The Story of the Armory Show*, "his was truly a hand of steel in a suède glove"; "a dragon evolved from that very gentle cocoon," du Bois recalled. With the assistance of such interested friends as the collector and attorney John Quinn, the group set about finding space for the exhibition which was their reason for being, and eventually secured the Sixty-ninth Regiment Armory on Lexington Avenue between Twenty-fifth and Twenty-sixth streets.

Late in the summer of 1912 Davies received a copy of the catalogue of the comprehensive Sonderbund Exhibition of recent and contemporary works in Cologne, Germany. He sent it off to Kuhn, who was painting in Nova Scotia, along with a short note saying, "I wish we could have a show like this." Kuhn wired back to get him reservations on the next boat, met Davies on the dock, and sailed for Europe, reaching Cologne the day of the closing of the exhibition. He was overwhelmed by what he saw—125 works of Van Gogh, 26 by Cézanne, 25 by Gauguin, 18 by Signac, 16 by the explosively new Picasso, 32 by the Norwegian Expressionist Edvard Munch, and others by the German Expressionists and the leading Fauves. He looked up Wilhelm Lehmbruck and asked for several pieces of his sculpture, including the famous *Kneeling Woman* now in the Museum of Modern Art. In Paris, Alfred Maurer (1868–1932), whose father had been an artist for Currier & Ives, and who had been abroad since 1897, knew the art world well and made many suggestions. The younger Walter Pach (1883–1958), who had been carried away with the excitement in the artistic atmosphere there and who already knew his way around, took Kuhn to studio after studio and introduced him to galleries, critics, and collectors. Davies came over to join them briefly, and they sought out the brothers Duchamp-Villon and secured a number of oils by Marcel Duchamp and Jacques Villon as well as sculptures by their brother, Raymond Duchamp-Villon.

They chose sculptures in the more Classic style of Rodin, Bourdelle, and Maillol, and more experimental pieces from

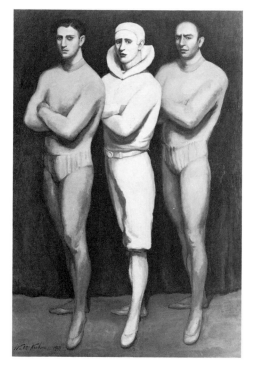

Walt Kuhn: *Trio,*
1937, 82½ x 60
(Collection: Colorado Springs
Fine Arts Center,
gift of the El Pomar Foundation)

Archipenko and Brancusi. Among the paintings were some by Cubists, including Léger and Delaunay, by Gleizes and Picabia, both of whom later came to America, and by the Fauves Matisse, Dufy, and Derain. The famous dealer Ambroise Vollard offered several paintings by Cézanne and Gauguin as well as many lithographs by them and others. Durand-Ruel lent a number of Impressionist pictures by Monet, Renoir, Sisley, and Pissarro, while Emile Druet supplied Pointillist work by Seurat and Signac, paintings by the great Post-Impressionists Cézanne, Van Gogh, Gauguin, and Toulouse-Lautrec, and more of the Fauves. Daniel-Henry Kahnweiler promised Derains, Vlamincks, Picassos, and Braques. There were many other paintings also, including a large group by Odilon Redon, whose magical color and dreamlike images fascinated Kuhn. Within a few weeks the three had collected a remarkable assemblage of important works that would ordinarily have taken months of search and negotiation to secure. Kuhn and Davies hurried home, and Pach took care of the packing and shipping from Europe.

In his recollections in *A Queer Thing, Painting*, Pach tells how he piloted the indefatigable pair around Paris, and introduced them to Gertrude Stein's famous Saturday evenings, where Alfred Maurer was always sure to turn up, and where Davies was deeply impressed with the avant-garde collection he saw there. Pach's account tells much about the sureness of Davies' taste, and his keenness when faced with the brand-new and the strange.

Davies and Kuhn stopped off in London on their way home to see the Second Post-Impressionist Exhibition at the Grafton Galleries, organized by the forward-looking critic Roger Fry, and they were so impressed with the Matisse sculptures and paintings that they wrote Pach urging him to enlist the aid of the Steins and to visit Matisse himself in order to borrow more. The buoyant energy of the three is amazing. When Kuhn got back he wrote Pach that "It will be like a bomb shell. . . . Everybody is electrified . . . I feel as though I had crowded an entire art education into these few weeks. . . . We have a great opportunity in this show, and must try to make it truly wonderful. . . . We want this old show of ours to mark the starting point of the new spirit in art, at least as far as America is concerned. I feel that it will show its effect even further and make the big wheel turn over both hemispheres. . . . Had supper in Child's tonight. Oh you Laperouse!"

With that kind of energy and Davies' extraordinary organizational ability, committees were formed, the publicity was planned, and the arrangement of the galleries, made with burlap partitions to form a series of octagonal rooms, was laid out. Bills kept coming, and though there was no money in the treasury, Davies somehow kept paying them. News releases poured out, articles appeared in the press, and du Bois ghostwrote an entire issue of *Arts and Decoration* on the coming show. Some even looked into the possibility of hiring an electric sign in Times Square. Mrs. Clara Davidge, in whose Madison Gallery the Association of American Painters and Sculptors had come into being, raised money to support the cause as effectively as Davies himself. Gutzon Borglum resigned in a huff from the chairmanship of the sculpture committee because the rest did not want to fill the available space with white marble monuments. Opinions were aired in the press, charges were made and refuted, and out of the ferment came an exhibition that lived up to Kuhn's predictions.

In the five days before the opening, the partitions were built, the temporary arc lighting was installed, the festoons of yellow streamers were hung from the center of the ceiling, the sculptures were mounted on their pedestals, 2,400 running feet of wall were hung with pictures, flags were raised, the interior was strung with green garlands, and pine trees—a symbol borrowed from Revolutionary days—were spotted about. Posters had been distributed across the country and lapel buttons made, all carrying the pine tree emblem, and a catalogue was ready at the opening. True, it was not complete, since entries continued to be received up to the last minute, and a supplement had to be issued, but that it was there at all was a miracle.

The evening of February 17, 1913, saw 4,000 guests milling about the octagonal galleries, listening to the lively music of the Sixty-ninth Regiment Band playing from the balcony, and inspecting each other in the immemorial fashion of openings, as well as looking at the spectacular selection of works of art. The small group that made up the Association of American Painters and Sculptors had done the impossible. They had staged the largest and most important art exhibition ever held in America, something the Academy had stated could not be done. As John Quinn said in his opening address, "The members of this association have shown you that American artists—young American artists, that is—do not dread, and have no need to dread, the ideas or the culture of Europe. They believe that in the domain of art only the best should rule. This exhibition will be epoch-making. . . ."

From the beginning, Davies seems to have had a didactic purpose in mind: to trace with actual works the derivation of mod-

Armory Show, interior
(Photograph, The Museum of Modern Art, New York)

ern art from Goya, Daumier, Corot, and Delacroix to the Impressionists, Post-Impressionists, Fauves, Cubists, Pointillists, and artists of all the other movements down to the actual opening date of the exhibition. And if The Eight had been a tremor, the Armory Show was a major quake.

About 70,000 people paid admission to see what Pach estimated to be the 1,600 works, including groups of drawings and prints. Among the visitors were several outstanding collectors, such as Lillie Bliss, who, astutely advised by Davies and, later, by Kuhn, started the magnificent collection of modern masterpieces that eventually became the backbone of the collection of the Museum of Modern Art. John Quinn also bought, as did Arthur Jerome Eddy of Chicago, another attorney and a brilliant collector. Walter Arensberg, whose collection is now in the Philadelphia Museum, also made purchases, as did the terrible-tempered Dr. Albert C. Barnes of Argyrol fame. The latter, with the astute advice of his old schoolmate William Glackens, was laying the foundations of his Barnes Collection; not yet up to Matisse, he satisfied himself with a tamer Vlaminck instead. Stephen C. Clark bought a Lehmbruck sculpture. Marcel Duchamp's *Nude Descending a Staircase* was purchased by a West Coast firm of dealer-decorators for $324—certainly one of the outstanding bargains of the show—while Cézanne's *Poorhouse on the Hill* fetched $6,700 from the Metropolitan Museum of Art, the highest price paid and the first painting by the artist to enter the collections of an American museum.

Other visitors included Albert Ryder, a stocky, bearded patriarch, forgotten by the public, who had taken his stand for modern art more than thirty-five years before, and whose works in the show were a fascinating discovery for many younger artists. Edward Lamson Henry, a minor painter of genre then in his seventies, was taken through by Jerome Myers. He looked at everything and then turned to his guide and said, "Mr. Myers, they told me there was a lot of crazy wild art here, but I really found it wonderfully interesting and I am very glad to have seen it." The two elderly artists were far more open-minded than many visitors, including ex-president Theodore Roosevelt, who was reported to have been "most gracious, but noncommittal" by some, and by others to have been observed shaking his head and crying, "But is it art? But is it art?" Some observer recalled seeing a woman so overcome by laughter that she rolled on the floor. Whatever the reaction, it was not neutral.

The public response to the exhibition was understandably mixed, though most thought it a great lark and enjoyed its carnival atmosphere. The press was enthusiastic over the works of Odilon Redon, with their delicious color and poetic symbolism, for which Whistler's and Davies' tonalities and subjects had apparently prepared the way. From the point of view of sales, the Duchamp-Villon brothers were way ahead, with Marcel Duchamp selling all four of his paintings, Jacques Villon all nine of his, and Raymond Duchamp-Villon three of his four sculptures.

But the single work that was the most talked about was the *Nude Descending a Staircase* by Marcel Duchamp, and though the gallery of the Cubists became popularly known as "the chamber of horrors," the *Nude* was the center and the symbol of the show. The American *Art News* offered ten dollars to anyone who could find the nude in the painting, and it was often surrounded by hordes of earnest school children, pencil in hand, trying to win the prize. It was ridiculed, lampooned, vilified, called an example of degeneracy, and dismissed as a joke, but it was never overlooked, and it became, overnight, one of the most famous pictures in the world. One of the better spoofs it inspired was J. F. Griswold's cartoon in the *Evening Sun* of rush hour in the subway, captioned "The Rude Descending a Staircase." Milton Brown lists several of the descriptions and titles of the painting offered by its scarcely admiring critics; these include "an elevated railroad stairway in ruins after an earthquake," a "dynamited suit of Japanese armor," and, most popular of all, "an explosion in a shingle factory."

As the exhibition moved on to Chicago, it provided material for more would-be wits and, also, for the always numerous self-appointed protectors of the nation's morals. The exhibit was called degenerate, insane, diseased, lurid, vicious, anarchistic, and a leering effrontery, and all the arguments against modern art that have been repeated *ad nauseam* ever since were directed upon it. But from reading the serious critics, one must sympathize with the shock felt by men who, without preparation, were suddenly brought face to face with the facts of the art of their own day; with but very few exceptions, the critics knew as little as the people in general of what had been going on, not only in Europe, but also in the studios of many of their own countrymen.

After the fumes of prejudice had cleared and the shrill screams of the outraged moralists had died down, the general feeling seemed pretty much that enunciated by Theodore Roosevelt, whose article "A Layman's Views of an Art Exhibition" appeared in *The Outlook*. He complimented the exhibitors and agreed that they were "quite right as to the need of showing to our people in this manner the art forces . . . in Europe, forces which cannot be ignored." He felt that "a glance" at the American work "must convince anyone of the real good that is coming out of the new movements. . . ." He affirmed the spirit of change, was pleased to find no "note of the commonplace . . . not a touch of simpering, self-satisfied conventionality . . . no requirement that a man whose gift lay in new directions should measure up or down to stereotyped and fossilized standards." But he ridiculed the "Cubists and the Futurists, or Near-Impressionists" and lumped all of the more experimental artists with "the lunatic fringe," apparently seeing no difference between Lehmbruck's *Kneeling Woman*, a Cubist painting by Braque, and a sculpture by Brancusi, and showing no interest in trying to find out. For the moment art was headline news, but it was not the significant aspect of life

405

for any appreciable number of people that it had started to become before the Civil War and is today beginning to be again.

When William M. Chase, as dapper as if he had just stepped from a portrait by his greater rival John Singer Sargent, joined the dense crowd of visitors to the Armory Show on the eve of its closing on March 15, he was looking, whether he knew it or not, into the future. Despite the gaps recognizable today in the survey of contemporary art that the organizers had intended to present, the spectrum was there, from the descriptive realism of the conservative inheritors of the Hudson River School tradition, through the various degrees of abstraction represented by Impressionism, Cubism, Expressionism, and other movements, to the nonobjective style of such artists as Kandinsky. The newer developments were to come mainly from the latter extreme, but in subsequent American art all shades were to be represented, from one end of the spectrum to the other, and the variety that was so shocking at the Armory was to continue.

There were many of Chase's generation who must have become suddenly aware that a world that they had known and felt themselves a part of had ended. Realists like Henri, who had been leaders in American art, overnight found themselves among the conservatives. There were, no doubt, many who agreed with Jerome Myers that "Davies had unlocked the door to foreign art and thrown the key away. Our land of opportunity was thrown wide open to foreign art, unrestricted and triumphant; more than ever before, our great country had become an art colony; more than ever before we had become provincials." But such fears proved unfounded. A new group of Americans, whose talents had been encouraged by Stieglitz and the Studio Club, was ready to step upon the stage. And, like their predecessors, they were influenced but not dominated by the foreign styles that seemed so disturbing to men of Henri's and Myers' generation.

After the doors of the Armory had closed on the last evening, the members of the Association, their friends, the guards, the ticket sellers, the guides, and members of the Sixty-ninth Regiment held their own festivities, snake-dancing through the galleries, and drinking toasts in the champagne that John Quinn had supplied. The celebration was at once a wake and a jubilee, because for the world of art the Armory Show was a divide. It marked the end of one era and the beginning of a new one. Whether one liked it or not, and there were plenty who did not, its result was, as the *Globe* told its readers, that "American art will never be the same again."

406

EUROPEAN INFLUENCES AND AMERICAN REACTIONS

The First World War came hard on the heels of the Armory Show, and matters of art took a back seat to the problem first of staying out of the conflict and then to the far greater problems of taking part in it. After it was over, the nation reacted by suspiciously withdrawing into itself and seeking "normalcy" in a period of internal disruption and corruption in government. The years after the Civil War had not given Thomas Nast any richer material than that which inspired the brilliant cartooning in the same fearless tradition by Boardman Robinson (1876–1952), Art Young (1895–1944), and William Gropper (1897–   ). It was a period that produced the scandal of Teapot Dome, with the pillaging of oil reserves by public officials. It was an era in which the nation voted for prohibition and spent its energies flouting the law. It was a time when Al Capone terrorized Chicago and the rackets flourished in Jimmy Walker's gaudy New York, and when hooded Klansmen practiced violent bigotry in the South, where the Scopes trial proved it was still impossible to teach the theory of evolution. It was a period of Babbitts and isolationists, of speakeasies and the Charleston, and of the flapper and her coon-coated collegian, so aptly illustrated by John Held (1889–1958). Its heroes included Jack Dempsey and Rudolph Valentino, Charles Lindbergh and Babe Ruth, Gloria Swanson and Mary Pickford. Charlie Chaplin filmed *The Gold Rush* and George Gershwin composed *Rhapsody in Blue*. It saw the transformation of the patterns of American life by the automobile and the motion picture, the explosive development of radio from a cat whisker and a crystal to a means of world-wide communication, and the growth of that characteristically American popular art form, the musical comedy, from vaudeville, variety, and jazz.

As was the case after the Civil War, so unsympathetic to the arts did America seem in the years following the Armistice of 1918 that an increasing number of writers, painters, and sculptors, in growing disillusionment, left home for Europe. Though the poet T. S. Eliot, like Henry James in an earlier generation, found a refuge in England and Anglicanism from a world he saw as a wasteland inhabited by hollow men, Paris was the center to which most artists gravitated. A number of them al-

BETWEEN
TWO
WORLD
WARS

Stanton MacDonald-Wright:
Embarkation, 1962, 48¼ x 36⅛
(Collection, The Museum of Modern
Art, New York, gift of Mr. and Mrs.
Walter Nelson Pharr)

ways turned up at Gertrude and Leo Stein's Saturday evenings to rub shoulders with the latest of the avant-garde. There was much restless wandering, and many of the more famous expatriates, among them Ezra Pound, the young Ernest Hemingway, and F. Scott Fitzgerald, lingered at café tables to "sit in a corner and drink thinks and think drinks," in the verses of E. E. Cummings, "in memory of the Grand and Old days:/ of Amy Sandburg/of Algernon Carl Swinburned." When in 1925 the French government invited the United States to participate in the international *Exposition des arts décoratifs*, President Calvin Coolidge replied that the United States had no arts to send. And most Americans, unaware of what was going on in the art world both in Europe and at home, would quite cheerfully have agreed with their chief executive.

Americans have generally tended away from theory and toward direct experiment and statement. The only consciously created American movement in art was that of Stanton Macdonald-Wright (1890–) and Morgan Russell (1886–1953), in Paris in 1913. They called it Synchromism and endowed it with manifestoes and expressions of purpose that they themselves immediately began to transcend. They explored the use of color in a manner related to Kandinsky's music-inspired compositions and to the Orphism of Delaunay and Kupka, who arranged disks and segments of brilliantly orchestrated tones.

The First World War brought to the United States Francis Picabia and Marcel Duchamp (1887–) who, with the American painter and photographer Man Ray, in reaction to the unthinkable destruction that had been unleashed, experimented in directions parallel to those of a group of artists in neutral Zurich who allied themselves in the protest movement in the arts which in 1916 was named Dada. After the war the movement was largely centered in Paris, where in turn it gave birth to Surrealism, the exploration of the unconscious disclosed by the development of psychoanalysis and the psychological studies of Freud and Jung.

In this same period the first European experiments were made with totally abstract or nonrepresentational art. The Russian Casimir Malevich launched what he termed Suprematism in 1913; the Dutchman Piet Mondrian in about 1917 introduced the rectilinear geometry which came to be called Neoplasticism or *De Stijl*; and the Russian sculptors the brothers Naum Gabo and Antoine Pevsner declared themselves champions of an abstract Constructivism in 1920. The tendency was in the air, because the first wave of American abstraction dated from the decade of the Armory Show, from about 1910 to 1920.

The works of two Americans who were perhaps more closely identified than most with contemporary European movements, Alfred Maurer (1868–1932) and Max Weber (1881–1961), reveal a succession of Expressionist, Fauvist, and Cubist phases. None of these remained exclusively dominant, a fact which shows the changeability characteristic, especially in the 1920's, of much of the art, which was in the process of searching for a means to embody a statement appropriate to a complex and revolutionary period. It was a time full of conflict and violence, not least of which, for the artists, was the opposition of European ideas and American attitudes.

From early in the century, Alfred Stieglitz played a unique role in the development of American art. Argumentative and doctrinaire, he was dedicated to the cause of modern art with an almost religious fervor. He showed in his galleries the work of most of those whom time has revealed as the classic American artists of the period. There the few who sought them out

Max Weber: *Chinese Restaurant*, 1915, 40 x 48
(Collection Whitney Museum of American Art, New York)

could see the experiments of Maurer and Weber, the organic abstractions of Arthur Dove, Marsden Hartley's stark expressionism, the clean, symbolic forms of Georgia O'Keeffe, the joyous hieroglyphs of John Marin, Charles Demuth's sophisticated visual commentary, and the suave marbles and witty bronzes and woods of Elie Nadelman.

Stieglitz showed experimenters in all mediums, including the photographs of Clarence White, Gertrude Kasabier, Paul Strand, Edward Steichen, and others as well as his own superb prints; the swiftly washed drawings of Rodin; the paintings and sculptures of Matisse; Cézanne's water colors; Brancusi's sculptures; and the work of Picasso in its many forms. He also exhibited African primitives and the work of children, to show the depth of the roots of modern art in the instinctive life of man.

"If ever institution in America came to bring the challenge of the truth of life to the land of the free, and to show the face of expressivity to a trading society living by middle-class conventions, it was the little gallery '291,'" wrote Paul Rosenfeld in *Port of New York* in 1924. He described "291" as "an art gallery that was itself a work of art. Exhibitions of baffling work were hung there with a white austerity . . . like scientific presentations of fact. And though each exhibition demonstrated the quintessential spirit of an artist . . . the many separate shows contributed to a single demonstration that grew like a tree—the demonstration of the world hour. It was a place where the work of the heart was let be, set clear of commercial entanglements . . . where the spirit of life came alive . . . where people got very hot and explanatory and argumentative about rectangles of color and lumps of bronze and revealed themselves . . . where quiet unobtrusive people suddenly said luminous things in personal language . . . and revealed life. . . . It stood, perpetual affirmation of a faith that there existed, somewhere, here in very New York, spiritual America."

In 1925 Stieglitz moved from the Photo-Secession Gallery (better known as "291") uptown to open the Intimate Gallery, which was followed four years later by An American Place. Other gallery owners followed the lead of Macbeth, Stieglitz, and Mrs. Whitney in presenting the works of contemporary painters and sculptors to a public which was gradually increasing in size and interest. Like the Macbeth Gallery and An American Place, the Daniel Gallery, where Demuth first exhibited, no longer exists. But the Rehn Gallery (where Charles

Burchfield showed) and the Kraushaar Galleries remain active, and, with a group of others, including Edith Halpert's Downtown Gallery, have carried on the same tradition of commitment and leadership.

Various periodicals also furthered the cause of the arts. The *Art News* was founded in 1902, and in 1908—the year of the showing of The Eight—*The American Magazine of Art* was established by the American Federation of Arts, an institution whose benevolent encouragement of the arts has outlived the *Magazine*, good though it was. In 1916 *The Dial*, which was responsible both for perceptive criticism and for producing the best reproductions of paintings then available, moved its headquarters from Chicago to New York. Like *Seven Arts*, also established in this period, it concerned itself with the more experimental group of artists. In 1920 Hamilton Easter Field established *The Arts* with the backing of Mrs. Whitney, and when Forbes Watson assumed its editorship three years later it became the best art periodical of the times and a thoughtful and forthright supporter, without chauvinism, of the best in American art. In 1925 the urban and urbane voice of Harold Ross's *New Yorker* first was heard speaking of metropolitan affairs to a metropolitan audience rather than to "the little old lady from Dubuque," and providing sophisticated commentary on the artistic scene. The drawings of James Thurber and Peter Arno which enlivened its pages, as well as those of Gluyas Williams and others which appeared in Frank Crowninshield's *Vanity Fair*, rivaled in satire and expressive draftsmanship the work of the political cartoonists, which appeared in *Punch, Life*, and *Judge* as well as in newspapers. These drawings give evidence why the period has been called "a golden age of illustration."

The 1920's also saw the beginning of the rediscovery of the American past, which sparked a sudden interest in folk art. It was activated by an exhibition arranged by the painter Henry Schnakenberg at the Whitney Studio Club in 1924, and fostered by the formation, during subsequent years, of several collections, among them that of Abby Aldrich Rockefeller (now at Williamsburg) and of Mrs. J. Watson Webb at Shelburne, Vermont, and the three collections given by Maxim and Martha Karolik to the Museum of Fine Arts in Boston. The Depression project of the Index of American Design, under the auspices of the Works Progress Administration, recorded the unexpected richness of the anonymous creations of Americans of all regions in earlier years; water colors and drawings were made

James Thurber: Drawing from
The Beast in Me and Other Animals
Copyright © 1948 James Thurber
(New York: Harcourt, Brace & World, 1948;
originally printed in *The New Yorker*)

411

of the folk art and crafts of the nation, ranging from figure-heads, weathervanes, and shop signs to furniture, ceramics, and needlework. Further aspects of the country's heritage were also explored. Fiske Kimball published his scholarly classic on *The Domestic Architecture of the American Colonies and of the Early Republic* in 1922, Vernon Parrington's examination of *Main Currents in American Thought* was almost completed at his death in 1929, and in the 1930's Van Wyck Brooks began his *Makers and Finders* series, a study of American literature from *The World of Washington Irving* to *The Confident Years: 1885–1915.*

In the early 1930's the raw power of contemporary Mexican art suddenly made its impact on the United States. For more than a decade Diego Rivera, David Siqueiros, and José Orozco, the greatest of the three, had been monumentalizing the new spirit of man in a revolutionary era of their country. In 1932 Rivera embodied the monstrous force of industry in his murals in the Detroit Institute of Arts, and in his fresco for Dartmouth College Orozco revealed with frightening stridency the barbarity of the modern world. Patriotic citizens of Detroit and loyal alumni of Dartmouth rose in righteous wrath at allowing such dangerous "Bolshevists" and "nihilists" to display their subversive ideas in happy, healthy America. When a head of Lenin was discovered among the crowds of people Rivera painted on the walls of Rockefeller Center, the murals were hastily covered and then destroyed. But the damage had been done. The new force had entered the stream of American art to give added strength and bite to the painting of social protest which appeared during the Depression years, when the government became a patron of the arts because of the sharpness of human necessity in a period of unemployment and economic disruption. Through the Federal Arts Project of the Works Progress Administration, the process of democratization of the arts, forgotten since before the Civil War, was taken up again, as actors, writers, sculptors, musicians, painters, and photographers were able to bring their talents to a public that was hungry for the arts it had been deprived of. A nationwide crafts movement was implemented, and a feeling of responsibility for the spiritual as well as the material well-being of citizens prevailed during these crisis years.

The atmosphere of social consciousness of the 1930's encouraged artists to take a more active part in both national and world affairs. In 1936 the First Artists' Congress was held in New York to assert its members' awareness of their responsibilities as citizens in the face of the rapidly worsening world situation, and it went on record as being against the spreading infections of Fascist and Nazi dictatorship. For the greater number of American artists, there was a cause to be joined, and they identified themselves with the liberalism burgeoning in America during these years which were haunted by the brutality of Mussolini's rape of Ethiopia, Japan's ruthless adventuring in China, and the horrors of civil conflict in Spain, and which were to end with greater violence in 1939, when Hitler's blitzkrieg on Poland precipitated a second and even more terrible world war.

In that same year the United States Congress, despite impassioned pleas from leading artists, actors, and critics, tabled and thus killed the Fine Arts Bill, which would have provided a continuing role for government in the nation's artistic development. The Federal Arts Projects limped on for a few months with diminishing resources until the outbreak of war brought to an end the unique experiment which had employed the diverse talents of more than 5,000 artists in almost every state in the union, and which had adorned a multitude of public buildings with more than a million works of art. A majority of these works is mediocre in quality, and the murals, an art for which that generation of Americans had had no training whatsoever, are especially weak. Yet Jacob Lawrence's visual symbolism of his people's tragic history in his *Migration of the Negro* series, Henry Varnum Poor's *The Story of the Land Grant College* for the Pennsylvania State University at University Park, and Ben Shahn's monumental illustration of Whitman's thesis that "Democracy rests finally upon us" in the Bronx Post Office remain as landmarks of a significant era in American art and history.

There had been overtones of social comment in the work of the Ash Can School; and, in a sense, most of The Eight had been regionalists, in that they discovered the main material of their art in the urban life of America, especially in New York. Theirs was a rediscovery for art of an aspect of the American scene that had been deliberately overlooked and avoided as unworthy of attention by anyone except policemen and social workers, certainly not by artists. Most of The Eight continued to paint during the 1920's and 1930's, and Sloan and Glackens did some of their best work during these years.

Another group of artists developed a new and more specifically geographical regionalism in the 1930's, however, in reaction to the First World War and the expatriation in the earlier part of the century. The movement showed itself at its strongest in the paintings of Grant Wood, John Steuart Curry, and Thomas Hart Benton.

Wood (1892–1941) interpreted American history as a 'folk tale in his *Paul Revere's Ride* (Metropolitan), a bird's-eye view of a toylike town on that fatal midnight. In his *Parson Weems' Fable*, he shows the Parson himself drawing aside a curtain to reveal George Washington as a boy, but looking like the Stuart portrait, standing, hatchet in hand, by a felled cherry tree to illustrate Weems' apocryphal tale. But Wood could show sharpness of observation in his tightly composed *American Gothic* (Chicago) and biting satire in the group portrait of smug narrow-mindedness he entitled *Daughters of Revolution*.

Grant Wood: *Daughters of Revolution,*
1932, 20 x 40
(Cincinnati Art Museum,
The Edwin and Virginia Irwin Memorial)

Curry (1897–1946) is at his best in the large, airy landscapes of the Midwest, with fields flowing horizonward under cloud shadows. In his dramatic *John Brown* (Metropolitan) he gives the Harpers Ferry raider the elemental force of a folk hero.

Benton (1889–), the grandnephew of the famous senator from Missouri, spent early years in Paris during which, in his own words, he "wallowed in every cockeyed ism that came along" until the Depression brought him home and he turned to a self-conscious mannerism based upon Baroque precedent. He used it most effectively in such commissions as the mural, now in Indiana University, for the Indiana State Building at the Chicago Century of Progress Exposition of 1933.

During the 1930's Benton's denunciations of everything foreign and his lauding of everything native American—meaning from the Midwest—were matched in spread-eagling only by the chauvinistic trumpetings of the critic Thomas Craven in an exaggeration of the anti-intellectualism inherited from the days of the frontier. The paintings themselves, however, were even more

414

powerful representatives of the regionalism of the Midwest, just as were the poems of Carl Sandburg, Vachel Lindsay, and Edgar Lee Masters, and the novels of Sherwood Anderson and Sinclair Lewis for the same region, and the writings of Steinbeck and Saroyan for the West Coast, Faulkner for the South, and Frost for the Northeast. Yet many young provincials felt, like Thomas Wolfe, the yearning for "the enfabled rock" of Manhattan, the New York of *The Great Gatsby*, whose excitement and glamour had been celebrated, already nostalgically, by F. Scott Fitzgerald. For during both periods, the Jazz Age of the 1920's and the years of depression and recovery under the New Deal, New York remained the artistic capital of America.

The broadest European influence on American art during these decades was that of Expressionism. It was a generalized influence, however, because it touched upon the native inclination in this direction, which may be traced variously through such artists as Allston, Cole, Quidor, Blythe, Rimmer, Blakelock, and Inness. It reappeared in the work of several painters and sculptors who emerged in the period immediately following the Armory Show, and its direction varied strongly with each individual. Some carried their Expressionist tendencies over into total abstraction, while the greater number used them in the achievement of a personal style that stopped short of the nonobjective.

The painters and sculptors who became the real leaders during the 1920's and 1930's avoided either extreme of provincialism or expatriatism, and, though they came to feel a new sense of belonging and of purpose, they followed their own independent paths. European influence or experience liberated and matured their talents and confirmed their chosen directions rather than controlled their expression. As far as most Americans were concerned, however, these artists formed almost an underground movement during the 1920's, when the nation was so busy enjoying the excesses and inconsistencies of the Jazz Age, and during the post-Depression 1930's, while the country was sobering up.

For the greater number of the small minority of those interested in art, only the works of the Ash Can School enlivened the artistic scene, to be joined in the 1930's by the art of the regionalists. Yet it was during these twenty-odd years between two world wars that the small but diverse group of artists, whose work was to lead on to dramatic postwar developments, hit their stride and accomplished some of their most significant achievements.

There were no true Cubists, Fauves, or Futurists among them, just as there had been no true Impressionists in the earlier generation. There was a stubborn conservatism in the way they clung to their own way of seeing, based essentially on a traditional realism. Yet such European movements as German Expressionism and Fauvism strengthened similar inclinations in American art, though these were interpreted individually by each artist. Cubism gave greater structure to composition, and increased the tendency toward sharp definition, which had originated in the tradition of engraving and draftsmanship, as a common basis of the American artist's training. Futurism—which, among the European movements of the time, was backward-looking in its emphasis on subject and strongly romantic in its emotional identification with the machine—may have encouraged, along with Cubism, the recognition of the aesthetic qualities of the urban scene and in the mechanical details and surfaces of the industrial landscape.

The various European movements of the period served to encourage in the Americans a spirit of experimentation, which increased its pace as time went on and eventually produced the artists who became world leaders of the avant-garde of the mid-century and of today. The experiment assumed such individual forms that the subsequent course of American art took on an increasing complexity, within which the traditional realistic approach was reinvigorated, to flourish alongside the most extravagant manifestations of novelty-seeking as equally expressive of the American tradition.

When the Museum of Modern Art appeared upon the scene in the Depression year of 1929, a new force was loosed which soon assumed the leadership of the cause of modern art. From its earlier years in an old brownstone through its various stages of growth, it presented significant exhibitions which exerted the greatest influence on the course of the arts and on public opinion of them. Starting with *Living American Painters* in its first year, the Museum mounted an impressive series of shows of the works of the major European modernists, of Cézanne and the Impressionists, of the Fauves, of German Expressionists, of Dadaists, of Surrealists, and of other groups and movements. Alfred H. Barr, Jr., for some years the Museum's director and always a leading spirit, was the first to apply the scholarly approach of art history to the works of contemporaries in catalogues, books, and articles of the highest standard. The exhibition of works of naïve and untrained artists signalized a shift in vision in the earlier 1930's which was strengthened by the exhibits of the primitive arts of Africa and the Americas, installed by René d'Harnoncourt in a style that provided a model for museum display.

When Stieglitz died at eighty-two in 1946, the Museum of Modern Art had become an institution of world-wide renown and influence. For Barr and his associates the arts were a serious matter. Following the lead of Stieglitz, they regarded photography and cinema as artistically important, and they included in the Museum's scope such other fields as architecture and stage design, as well as methods of art education. They presented a varied program of lectures, musical performances, poetry readings, and other activities within the broad area of the Museum's concern. In this manner, the Museum of Modern Art showed the same urge toward the democratization of the arts that had characterized the period before the Civil War. In a similar spirit both exhibits and publications had a didactic purpose, which recalls the aim of Davies in assembling the Armory Show. This was perhaps especially apparent in the Museum's display of utilitarian objects, chosen for good design, in recognition of the fact of the machine and machine production, not as representing a debasement of quality, but as a vital change of means opening the new opportunities that had been heralded by Frank Lloyd Wright.

In its policy and its philosophy, the Museum continued the Puritan inheritance of essential seriousness of purpose and an association of utility with aesthetic quality, which are important American attitudes. Modern communications and techniques vastly increased the scope of its operations and influence, and the new gospel was spread far and wide as its exhibitions were circulated and its publications sent across the country and around the world. Its program emphasized the growing internationalization of the arts, which resulted from the increase of world contacts, from the migration of artists to New York because of disturbances abroad, and from the emergence of New York as a major center of the avant-garde. The cause of experimental art in America was no longer supported merely by the imaginative dedication of a few individuals working virtually alone. Except that the artists working in the realist tradition were not often represented in its galleries, the Museum's exhibitions during the late 1930's served to show the state of the arts in America before the Second World War, much as the Armory Show had both summarized and looked ahead before the advent of the First. By the time of the outbreak of the Second World War, the Museum of Modern Art had become as much of a tastemaker as Andrew Jackson Downing had been a century earlier.

Maurice Prendergast: *Piazza di San Marco*, c. 1889, water color, 16⅛ x 15
(The Metropolitan Museum of Art, gift of the Estate of
Mrs. Edward Robinson, 1952)

THE STIEGLITZ GROUP AND SOME OTHERS

Maurice Prendergast (1859–1924), who had exhibited with The Eight and at the Armory Show, provided a link between the older generation of painters and the new. He kept pace with European developments without being unduly influenced by them, and his very individual achievement made him a pioneer. His paintings remain fresh and lyric and have a quality of timelessness that sets him apart from his contemporaries, whose work may be vigorous but seems strongly dated by contrast. Prendergast—like Ryder, who was only twelve years his senior—belongs to the group of solitary, creative individuals who followed their own vision. He was a reserved and retiring man, whose correctly formal manners and dress seemed to belong to an earlier age and masked a gentle disposition and quiet humor. He had grown up in Boston, where he lettered signs for a living and then ran a frame shop with his brother Charles, who was a gifted cabinetmaker, before they moved to New York in 1914. Both brothers had a strong sense of craftsmanship and both experimented with art, Maurice with water color and, later, in oils, and Charles by making richly decorated chests and carved panels, painted and gilded with a delightful fantasy.

Maurice studied in Europe as early as 1886. He knew the works of the Impressionists, who were preoccupied with visual effects of light rather than objects, and of the Pointillists, whose theory was to paint with tiny dots of clear color to build up areas to be mixed in the eye of the beholder to create tones of greater vibrancy. Georges Seurat, Prendergast's exact contemporary, exhibited his first great Pointillist work, *Sunday in Summer on the Island of Grande Jatte* (Chicago), at the last Impressionist exhibition in the same year the young American reached Paris. By the early 1890's Prendergast had developed a personal water-color style which owed something to Impressionism and Pointillism, as well as to a number of other experiments in painting technique going on in Europe at the time, yet which followed none of these styles and was distinctively his own.

Maurice Prendergast was very deaf, an affliction which he said he considered a great advantage because, as he explained, if something worthwhile was said he was sure someone would pass it along to him, and in the meantime neither the ceaseless sounds of the city nor foolish talk distracted him from his beloved painting. His deafness probably increased his natural shyness and, perhaps by compensation, the acuteness of his observation. His eye for color was preternaturally keen and his vision extraordinarily objective, so that the tiny scraps of Renaissance fabrics which he found in Italy and kept in a pair of antique Persian pottery jars, and the little box full of brilliantly colored tesserae from ancient mosaics, which he stored under a bench in his studio, were a constant source of revelation and inspiration to him. Painting was his life, and though he was by nature solitary, he loved the pageantry of crowds ·in the streets, in parks, and at the shore. He painted horseback riders, carriages, promenaders, families on a Sunday in spring or summer, nursemaids with perambulators, and children with dogs, in scenes sparkling with sunlight and dappled with shade. All these subjects—often the same ones that interested his friends Sloan, Glackens, Shinn, and others of the Ash Can School—Prendergast turned into pictures of poetic elegance in which all elements are woven together by his firm and delicate brush into a vivacious and personal vision, at once serene and gay.

Later, he translated into oil his mosaiclike treatment of color and design, but with a body appropriate to that medium and with an equally painterly feel for it. In his freedom from domination by the various movements of the time while making use of their discoveries in the evolution of his own style, Prendergast continued a pattern of independence that has characterized the best of American creative life, an example followed by the leaders in American art during the post-Armory years.

Arthur Dove (1880–1946) was the first and the wittiest of the native abstractionists. In Europe in 1907 he had undergone a personal revolution in his art, brought about by the work he saw there, and before 1910 he was painting in a manner close to Kandinsky, though there is no reason to suppose any connection between the two. He alternated his successful career as an illustrator with farming and experimental art, including both painting and collage. He often displayed a light touch in his collage portraits, such as that of *Ralph Dusenberry* (Metropolitan) of 1924, which is made up of fragments of shingles suggesting a fish and a kingfisher because his subject "could dive like a Kingfish and swim like a fish"; the yacht's ensign is present because "the Dusenberrys lived on a boat near us in Lloyd's Harbor"; a torn piece of music records that the subject "when tight . . . always sang 'Shall we gather at the river'";

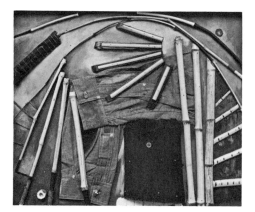

Arthur Dove: *Goin' Fishin'*,
1925, assemblage, 19½ x 24
(The Phillips Collection, Washington, D.C.)

420

and the whole is framed in a carpenter's rule because Dusenberry was an architect and builder. Another delightful collage, entitled *Goin' Fishin'*, is made up of sections of a bamboo rod, various items of fishing tackle, and a blue denim shirt, to suggest the passionate interest of the subject. Whether one knows the private language of such symbolism or not, the impact of both wit and humor is genial and definite.

Dove's painting style is organically abstract, a rhythmic interplay of forms originating in nature—a cow, a goat, plants, trees, and rocks—transformed from momentary perceptions into separate creations which embody the essence of whatever they were based upon. He sought visual equivalents of sounds as well, transmuting the blasts of a foghorn into looming shapes. He felt as close to nature as had Audubon, and there found the limitless material for his personal variations on the theme of the unity of the natural world.

John Marin (1872–1953) was already working along Expressionist lines before he was aware of European trends, and when he did discover them, they merely confirmed a direction already taken. Born in New Jersey, he had trained as an architect and studied painting with Anshutz at the Pennsylvania Academy, as had Henri and others of The Eight. In New York he felt the "warring, pushing, pulling forces" of the city, and he began to paint it as if it were vibrating to the rhythm of the times—its skyscrapers thrusting upward explosively, its streets full of motion. Then he discovered the coast of Maine. Wearing old sneakers and disreputable clothes, he wandered the beaches and the rocky shore, with keen and innocent eyes peering out from beneath a shock of unshorn hair. As crusty an individualist as

John Marin: *Sea Piece*,
1951, 22 x 28
(Collection Whitney Museum of
American Art, New York)

421

Thoreau, he shared the same delight in what he called "the big things, earth and sea and sky," not in their appearances, but in their dynamics. He spent the rest of his life rejoicing in the free movement of clouds, the sparkling and heaving of the waves, the blowing of pines, and the soaring of gulls. He painted first in water color and then also in oil, in an inventive harmony of energies as restless and as fresh as an ocean breeze. His water-color technique was a swift calligraphy, the strokes as surely applied as those of Winslow Homer, but with a totally different purpose and with vivid visual impact. His oils are less spontaneous because of the difference in the quality of the medium, but they have as much authority and originality, and they convey the same joyous excitement.

Marsden Hartley (1877–1943) was born in Lewiston, but it was almost a lifetime before he proudly identified himself as "the painter from Maine." A reserved New Englander, he developed his natural feeling for color studying with Chase at the Art Students League before going abroad. From 1912 to 1915 he painted and exhibited in Berlin with the group of German Expressionists who called themselves the Blaue Reiter (Blue Rider). Where Marin's response was immediate and intense,

Marsden Hartley: *Portrait of a Sea Dove*, 1935, 9¾ x 13¾
(Courtesy of The Art Institute of Chicago, Alfred Stieglitz Collection)

Hartley's was restrained and unsure. It was only after much wandering and experiment that Hartley returned to Maine, late in life, to develop the simple, solid style whose monumentality is his tribute to Ryder, whom he knew and admired. He painted a portrait of Ryder with the stocking cap the older artist used to wear while walking the streets at night and watching the reflection of the lights in the dark waters of the harbor. Something of the simple dignity of spirit of the older artist gives strength to Hartley's scenes of the mountains and the shore. A pile of lobster pots and buoys suggests the harshness and danger of a living wrested from the ocean; a dead black duck takes on finality and pathos; and a wave about to break is a silent symbol of the elemental power of nature. Perhaps most impressive of all are Hartley's portraits of his fisherman friends, shown seated around a table, as if at a last supper, with stars over the heads of those who had gone off on voyages from which they never returned. For Hartley and Marin, as for Homer and Ryder, and for Melville and Whitman, the sea provided a continuing theme to which they reacted and which they interpreted with a deep emotional response.

Georgia O'Keeffe (1887–   ) expressed the individualistic spirit of many of the artists of her generation when in 1923 she recalled that, years earlier, she had suddenly come face to face with the fact that "Schools and things that painters have taught me . . . keep me from painting as I want to." She decided that she "was a pretty stupid fool not to at least paint as I wanted to and say what I wanted to when I painted as that seemed to be the only thing I could do that didn't concern anybody but myself." After studying at the Chicago Art Institute and in New York at the Art Students League and Columbia University Teachers College, she taught in Texas and South Carolina. In 1915 she made a series of drawings and sent them to a friend in New York who showed them to Alfred Stieglitz. He presented the first show of her work the following year, and thereafter she became a mainstay of his gallery. Eight years later they were married. Despite her husband's strong interest in the various aspects of European art which he showed, along with the more advanced American work, in his galleries, she continued on her independent way. Like Marin, she responded to the grandeur of the skyscrapers of New York, though she painted them coolly, as she painted everything, but with an underlying intensity that somehow expressed both femininity and passion. She found a similar clean geometry in Canadian barns and adobe missions, and she revealed the sensuality of gigantic

Georgia O'Keeffe:
Black Cross, New Mexico,
1929, 39 x 30
(Courtesy of The Art Institute of Chicago)

flowers painted in enlarged close-up to dramatize their lushness.

She finally found her spiritual home in the Southwest, in the austere beauty of the desert, "the same big wonderful thing that oceans and the highest mountains are." She reveals the magic and timeless symbolism of the abstract forms of bleached bones scoured by windblown sands, of red mesas against a hard, clear sky, and of cloud formations in fierce storms sweeping down from the distant ranges.

Homer and Sargent had established water color as a major medium in American art and had used it with a sweep and boldness unknown in Europe. Marin found it ideally suited to his breezy, staccato style. Edward Hopper (1882–1967) employed it with the same solidity as his oils, and Charles Burchfield (1893–1967) used it, sometimes at the scale of oil, for his own personal interpretations of nature.

Burchfield, who spent his early years in a little Ohio town and who later lived in a small suburb of Buffalo, remained, from boyhood, acutely conscious of the change of the seasons, the cycle of growth and decay, and the skyscape and the landscape, with an intensity to match that of Homer or Marin. But he worked in a mood perhaps closer to that of Dove, though the two are entirely different in style. Burchfield felt a mysterious animation in everything, which led him to interpret the familiar things of earth and field and woods in patterns that show the measure of his empathic identification with natural forces. The pealing of bells in a church tower become visible in a vibrant expression of the brush. Old houses weep in the rain of a cold fall evening, and the crisp, repetitive motive of the ripe tops of weeds and grasses in a summer field echoes the chirping of the crickets. Swamps are haunted with shapes that are natural but seem endowed with more than natural forces. Old houses have the aura of years of human habitation, with unknown hopes and fears, sufferings and triumphs, suggested by mood. The stars swing low in his night skies, plants and trees are caught as if in a dance of life, while great sphinx moths gleam phosphorescently in the moonlight. Marin, Hartley, Dove, O'Keeffe, and Burchfield were leaders in the period among the more subjective artists, those inward searchers in the tradition to which Ryder, Blakelock, and Prendergast belonged, those whose "solitary voices," in Emerson's phrase, make up such a significant part of the great chorus of American art.

Just as Impressionism influenced a number of artists toward a fresher, lighter palette and a more immediate touch, so Cubism

Charles Burchfield:
Sphinx and the Milky Way,
1946, water color, 52⅝ x 44¾
(Munson-Williams-Proctor Institute,
Utica, N.Y.)

helped to bring about a formal clarification in the work of a group which has been called the Immaculates or Precisionists. Like O'Keeffe, they relished the spare lines of modern architecture, and went on to discover the abstract beauty of the machine. But they showed none of the self-conscious violence of the Italian Futurists, who took the machine as their compelling image and indulged their emotions in wordy manifestoes about destroying the old to make way for the new, which in their case was to be the doubtful benefit of Mussolini's gangsterish attempt at reincarnation of the Roman Empire. Nor did they show a terror of the machine, inherent in such European conceptions as that of the robot, or a confusion of its technology with humanity, as in the Bolshevist ideal of remaking men into cogs in a well-oiled mechanism of gigantic proportion to be controlled by an elite performing the function of a sociological and ideological engineer.

Americans had early turned to the machine to solve problems of labor shortage and other such immediate necessities in a rapidly growing and dynamically expanding society. As a nation of tinkerers and mechanics, without the strict social and economic structure of older parts of the world, they took it in stride. Progress was their pattern of life, and change its continuity. When American artists turned their attention to the technological aspects of the age, they brought similarly pragmatic attitudes to their investigation. They recognized in the modern machine the same qualities that their fathers and grandfathers had admired in the great Corliss engine at the Centennial Exposition of 1876—its precision, its accurately machined surfaces, and its essence lying in its function, whether it was moving or static, which preordains its forms. They also recognized that such particular requirements, dictated by function as essential elements, had an aesthetic application. Thus it is logical that their vision should share something of the camera's impersonal objectivity, and their compositions something of the calculated control of architectural renderings and mechanical drawings.

Charles Demuth (1883–1935) was one of a group of artists influenced by such ideas. He came of a family long resident in Lancaster, Pennsylvania, and studied at the Pennsylvania Academy with Chase and Anshutz in 1905, before going to Europe and working, like so many Americans, at several of the Paris studios, including the Académie Julian. Witty, elegant, and shy, "he had a curious smile," Marcel Duchamp remembered, "reflecting an incessant curiosity for every manifestation life offered." But perhaps because his was the sheltered life of a

Charles Demuth:
I Saw the Figure Five in Gold,
1928, oil on composition board,
36 x 29¾
(The Metropolitan Museum of Art,
Alfred Stieglitz Collection, 1949)

man who was both lame and a victim of diabetes, he was ever
the observer and never the participant. He looked on from a
distance, eliminating his own feelings in a cool analysis, formally influenced by Cézanne and by Cubism, which he recorded
with immaculate discipline in water color, tempera, and oil.

Like Everett Shinn, he was interested in the world of entertainment, the circus, and the stage, but he interpreted scenes of
acrobats and vaudeville acts with aristocratic reserve and fluent
line. There is the same remoteness combined with inner tension
in the effective illustrations he did for his own amusement of
Zola's *Nana,* Wedekind's *Der Erdgeist,* and Henry James's *The
Turn of the Screw,* which are rendered with a dandyism similar
to that of the mannered, decadent drawings of Aubrey Beardsley
in *The Yellow Book.* In a similar spirit he turned such bleak,
industrial elements as factory chimneys, grain elevators, and
storage bins into forms that are pure and prismatic, and gave
them such ironically enigmatic titles as *End of Paradise: Coates-
ville, Pa.* (private collection), *My Egypt* (Whitney), . . . and
the Home of the Brave (Chicago), and *Waiting* (Chicago).

426

Demuth developed a kind of painted symbolic portrait, related to Dove's collages, but more intellectualized and less humorous. Perhaps the best of these is that of the poet William Carlos Williams, which he titled *I Saw the Figure Five in Gold*. He had known Williams ever since the two met as students "over a dish of prunes at Mrs. Chain's boardinghouse on Locust Street" in Philadelphia, and, as the poet recalled, "formed a lifelong friendship on the spot. . . ." The title of the portrait is taken from Williams' poem called "The Great Figure," and the picture matches the concentration and the mood of the verses. The repeated five in the painting seems both to come clangorously forward and to recede, and the whole is unified by the slanting lines, suggesting both rain and light, but remaining basic elements of its tightly ordered design. Its relevance as a portrait is strengthened by the fragments of names which are a part of the compositional as well as the conceptual entity, the symbolic approach of the painter matching that of the poet's terse lines:

> Among the rain
> and lights
> I saw the figure 5
> in gold
> on a red
> firetruck
> moving
> tense
> unheeded
> to gong clangs
> siren howls
> and wheels rumbling
> through the dark city.

Another aspect of modern technology provided the theme for the paintings of Joseph Stella (1879–1946), who arrived in New York in 1902 fresh from Italy, where he had come under the influence of the Futurists. He found the city "rich with so many new motives to be translated into a new art. Steel and electricity had created a new world. A new drama had surged . . . a new polyphony was ringing all around with the scintillating, highly-colored lights. The steel had leaped to hyperbolic altitudes and expanded to vast latitudes with the skyscrapers and with bridges made for the conjunction of worlds." A painting of 1922, composed with the tense geometry of modern engineering, might be a visualization of Hart Crane's images in "The Bridge" (1930):

> Through the bound cable strands, the arching path
> Upward, veering with light, the flight of strings—
> Taut miles of shuttling moonlight syncopate
> The whispered rush, telepathy of wires . . .

427

Charles Sheeler: *American Landscape*, 1930, 24 x 31
(Collection, The Museum of Modern Art, New York, gift of Abby Aldrich Rockefeller)

Stella also painted his visions of Coney Island, with its garish, colored lights reflected in the murky, suffused atmosphere of a summer sky in a kaleidoscope of color like stained glass.

There is none of Demuth's ironic reserve or of Stella's dynamism in the cool perspectives of the paintings of Charles Sheeler (1883–1965). He was an outstanding photographer, and the monocular vision of the camera is reflected in the finite clarity of the forms of industrial architecture and engineering which were his favorite subjects, yet they frequently reveal the underlying romanticism which is a consistent current in American art. This is especially clear in his paintings of skyscrapers, which reach upward with the aspiration of cathedral towers, like the soaring structure of *Golden Gate*. He deliberately left out

428

the word "bridge" from its title because he wanted it to be "an opening to wherever the spectator feels desirable."

Born in Philadelphia, Sheeler also studied at the Pennsylvania Academy. He came in touch with the School of Paris on a trip abroad in 1909. He took up photography as a profession, and experimented with Cubist analysis of form. He discovered the ascetic beauty of the barns and community buildings of the Shakers, and of their furniture, which he began to collect, admiring not only its design but also its craftsmanship and construction. He recognized painting and photography as two different approaches, which can complement each other rather than compete, since the painting is constructed and synthetic, and the photograph momentary and inclusive. He admired the forms of both ancient Pennsylvania barns and modern industrial architecture. In a series of photographs and paintings of the colossal River Rouge plant of the Ford Motor Company, made between 1927 and 1930, he created a milestone in the new vision in America, showing the aesthetic qualities and epic scale of modern man's technological achievement in engineering that becomes architecture, and science that becomes art.

Photography had revolutionized the arts before it had come to be recognized as one of them. It made possible a superb accuracy and completeness of record, and created visual history,

Lewis W. Hine: *Carrying-in Boy in a Glass Factory, Alexandria, Va.*, 1909-13, photograph (George Eastman House Collection)

such as Mathew Brady's camera epic of the Civil War, and, starting just after the turn of the century, Lewis W. Hine's life-work of documenting with deep concern the lives of the immigrant, the miner, the factory worker, the tenement dweller, and the other underdogs in rich, teeming America. Improvement in equipment increased the camera's mobility and scope. It recorded the strikes and bloody battles of the growing labor movement, the rowdy clamor of politicking, wars and natural disasters, horse races, first nights at the opera, athletic events, gangsters' funerals, and society weddings; and it showed men and women, great and small, from J. P. Morgan with a midget on his lap to the latest movie star or visiting celebrity.

The immediacy of the camera image often influenced the vision of the painter, and the painter's eye as often directed the camera's use. Stieglitz explored new dimensions in photography with what he called his "equivalents"—studies that isolated certain details or visions of nature and thereby intensified their meaning. Edward Steichen also brought an artist's eye to the camera, having studied in Paris, where he picked out the water colors of the unknown John Marin to recommend to Stieglitz for showing in his gallery as "just about the best thing of the kind being done."

Sheeler and Paul Strand both shared a Whitmanesque vision of New York:

> . . . an island sixteen miles long, solid-founded,
> Numberless crowded streets, high growths of iron, slender, strong,
> light, splendidly uprising toward clear skies . . .

They used the technique of the documentary with a commentary consisting of quotations from Whitman to express the sights, scenes, and rhythms of "Mannahatta" in 1921. Berenice Abbott's camera recorded the five boroughs of the city with significant selectivity to create an urban portrait unique in complexity and power. In the same spirit Walker Evans photographed the face of America, revealing its ugliness and pathos in the record of the relentless course of obsolescence and change, with implications of the bleak loneliness of life, which is also a favorite theme of Edward Hopper's paintings. The perspective distortion and arbitrarily fragmenting field of the camera's monocular vision, which give force to so many of the photographs he made for the Farm Security Administration in the 1930's, provided Ben Shahn with telling expressive means which he richly exploited in his other art of painting.

As had been the case during an earlier wave of visual rediscovery, there were those who roamed yet farther afield. Paul Strand photographed weather-beaten trees in the Rockies, where Bierstadt had painted, and the battered buildings in Western ghost towns. Edward Weston explored the vast emptiness of Death Valley, the Great Plains loved by Teddy Roosevelt and Frederic Remington, and the wonders of the West Coast. Ansel Adams celebrated the timeless life of the pueblos and the incomparable grandeurs of the high Sierras, whose majesty had so captured the heart and the pen of John Muir.

Others, like Heade and Church earlier, pushed farther still. Robert Flaherty enlarged the documentary possibilities of the motion picture with his studies of primitive peoples from the Far North to the equatorial zone. "The River," produced in 1937 by Pare Lorenz for the Farm Security Administration, with a score by Virgil Thompson, achieved the epic quality so eagerly but vainly sought by the panorama painters of an earlier generation. Walt Disney turned the medium of the cinema cartoon into a world of fantasy related to Burchfield's animated landscapes. He revealed the beauty of animal life in the wild with superb nature photography that would have captivated Audubon, and he created a new mythology so successfully that a six-foot portrait of Mickey Mouse joined the Valhalla of national heroes shown by the United States government at the Moscow Fair in 1959.

The camera had dealt a deadly blow to the arts in America in the first half of the nineteenth century, when the rapid spread of the newly invented daguerreotype made the local portrait painter obsolete within a generation. But in the first half of the twentieth century it compensated by becoming an instrument of artistic exploration which not only established photography as a valid and significant art form, but which also contributed a new sharpness and immediacy to vision. It influenced the way of seeing of an era and had a profound and constructive effect on the development of painting.

Steichen pointed out that photography's success had invalidated the "look alike" ideal in painting. The painter Man Ray developed his "Rayographs," still lifes by indirection, as the record of objects placed on paper sensitized to light. Sheeler, Strand, and others experimented with photographic abstraction, while Stuart Davis (1894–1964) was one of the first and the best of the painters to illumine the character of modern life with abstract geometric elements related to Sheeler's industrial forms.

Davis' clear, bright color owed something to Matisse's cut-out designs, and, like Demuth, he used words and fragments of words. But it was the often tawdry, man-made world discovered by the relentlessly objective eye of the camera which supplied him with a vocabulary of motives transmuted in his paintings into both pictorial elements and symbols of the times. As robust and forthright as the neon signs and billboards, the gasoline stations, store fronts, and kitchen hardware which are some of the components of his pictures, they are always dynamic and often humorous. Though far more urbane than the later Pop Art, they suggest something of the Pop artist's preoccupation with the vulgar image, and bring to mind the cult of the found object. The angular formality in Davis' style, as in that of the other painters of this group, continued in the work of the hard-edged abstractionists of mid-century and later, who still show the characteristics of the machine-made in metallic shapes and surfaces. "All of my pictures," Davis wrote, ". . . have their originating impulse in the impact of the contemporary American environment." Few have equaled him in reflecting the tempo of modern life. His compositions bounce and blare, with echoes of New Orleans and Harlem, of the hot trumpet of Louis Armstrong and of Earl Hines' classic piano, in the insistent and restless rhythms of the jazz he knew and loved.

Stuart Davis: *Owh! In San Pao*, 1951, 52¼ x 41¾ (Collection Whitney Museum of American Art, New York)

432

THE COURSE OF AMERICAN SCULPTURE

There was another significant art exhibition held in 1908 besides that of The Eight at the Macbeth Gallery. Comfortingly free of any taint of the controversial, the other exhibition was universally acceptable because it was a memorial to Augustus Saint-Gaudens, who had died the year before. He was considered by his contemporaries as the giant of the age in the field of sculpture, and upward of a hundred of the many works produced during a busy lifetime were shown at the Corcoran Gallery in Washington. The exhibit marked the passing of a man but not of a style, because his numerous heirs continued a pedestrian classicism which was all that resulted from their borrowing of the more obvious externals of his complex and accomplished style. They missed the subtlety of his vision and his mastery of means, and they lacked the powers of observation and human sympathy which gave substance to his works. Daniel Chester French was to outlive him by twenty-four years, and though his most monumental work, the *Lincoln* of the Washington Memorial, was yet to come, he never surpassed him. But in the meantime a younger sculptor, George Grey Barnard, was working along lines that were to prove more fruitful for the future.

Barnard (1863–1938) occupied a transitional position in sculpture similar to that of his contemporary Maurice Prendergast in painting. Barnard's career links the generation of Saint-Gaudens and French with that of those who emerged between the world wars. A strong individualist, he would have none of the pallid eclecticism which remained dominant from the time of the Columbian Exposition. When he was only twenty-one, he began his heroic-sized *Struggle of Two Natures in Man*, to be cut directly from an immense block of stone, at a time when not even Rodin was attempting figures at this monumental scale. In the 1880's there was hardly a sculptor on either side of the Atlantic who could undertake such a task, so completely did most of them leave the actual execution of their work to professional assistants. And if Barnard's *Two Natures in Man* recalls the works of Rimmer in its power, his head of *Lincoln* suggests them also in its tragic intensity. Like Rodin, Barnard was fascinated with medieval art; at a time when few shared his interest, he had the foresight to collect superb Romanesque and

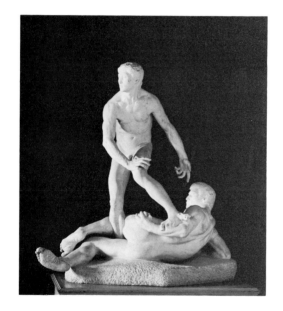

George Grey Barnard:
Struggle of Two Natures in Man,
1893, marble, h. 101½
(The Metropolitan Museum of Art,
gift of Alfred Corning Clark, 1896)

433

Gothic sculptures, which crowded his picturesque studio near the northern tip of Manhattan until John D. Rockefeller bought them as the nucleus of the remarkable collection now assembled at The Cloisters in nearby Fort Tryon Park. Barnard studied in Europe and was well aware what was going on there, but he chose to pursue his own course, returning to Michelangelo and the great sculptors of the past rather than being influenced, as were so many of the following generation, either by contemporary experiments or by the deadening continuity of the Classical tradition.

As was the case in painting, after the Armory Show sculpture displayed a strong strand of continuing realism, along with various degrees and directions of abstraction, from the mannered stylizations of Paul Manship (1885–1966), who often worked in an archaizing mood, to the Cubist experiments of Max Weber (1881–1961) and Robert Laurent (1890–   ), first carried out during the war years. None of the sculptural abstractions of the Americans had the dramatic power of the work of such Europeans as Brancusi, Duchamp-Villon, Picasso, and Matisse, whose work had so shocked the visitors at the Armory Show, or of Lipchitz and Archipenko, both of whom were later to settle in America. Some, like William Zorach (1887–1966), who turned from painting to sculpture in the 1920's, went through a phase of experimental abstraction before returning to the figure cut directly into the stone, in the tradition continued by such older artists as José de Creeft (1884–   ) and such younger men as Leonard Baskin (1922–   ), whose immobile wooden forms have a tragic dignity and moving presence. Also as in painting, the experiment of the avant-garde has had an invigorating effect. The influence of the radical simplifications of Brancusi's, Archipenko's, and Arp's abstractionism has been strong and continuing. Expressionism is represented among the older generation by Jacques Lipchitz (1891–   ), whose powerful forms based on nature are often manipulated with a Picasso-like brutality, as in his monumental bronze *Prayer* (Museum of Modern Art), a gesture of anguished despair which can also be read as the massive head of a bull, thus adding to its impact through its ambiguity. Among younger sculptors, the influence of Expressionism has been more largely abstract, as in the work of Seymour Lipton and Theodore Roszak. As a result of avant-garde experiment, the same spectrum of approach from extreme realism to the totally nonobjective continues in sculpture as in painting.

By its very nature, however, sculpture, being three-dimensional, can share less of the accidental, and because it exists in

Seymour Lipton: *Sorcerer*, 1957, nickel-silver on monel metal, h. 60¾
(Collection Whitney Museum of American Art, New York)

space, it must deal more emphatically with form, and material and technique play an even larger part than in painting. Kinetic experiments have introduced a new dimension which relates sculpture to both the momentary and the automatic aspects of much modern painting. The use of new materials—such as the plastics introduced by the Constructivists Naum Gabo and Antoine Pevsner—continues, and the application of industrial techniques such as welding, and the use of found objects and incorporation of fragments (innovations introduced by Duchamp, Picasso, and others) have immensely broadened its scope. Metals are used in many ways, from the traditional casting of bronze to the welded assemblage of fragments from the junk yard. Sometimes the metals are finished with the accuracy and polish of an essential part of a space-age mechanism, as in the immaculate convoluted forms of José de Rivera (1904–   ), or their surfaces are patinated as richly as Renaissance bronzes, as in the figures of Elbert Weinberg (1928–   ). Iron, steel, aluminum, and even concrete have been added to the materials employed by contemporary sculptors, while wood continues to be a basic material which has been proven capable of lending itself to new concepts through such treatment as lamination. Thus the variety in style of contemporary sculpture is reinforced by the variety of materials and techniques available.

Among the Realists was a group which specialized in the picturesque subject matter of the Old West, following the lead of Barnard's contemporary Frederic Remington (1861–1909), whose keen observation, from firsthand experience, is reflected in his lively bronzes, as well as in his paintings and illustrations. Two of these sculptors of Western subjects were the Borglum brothers, Gutzon and Solon, who produced horse-opera themes in a frenzied style which recalls the violence and action of a rodeo. But it was Gutzon Borglum (1867–1941) who carried out the most spectacular sculpture ever done by an American. With a furious energy that matched his ambition, he attacked with dynamite the sheer face of Mount Rushmore in the Black Hills of South Dakota, and blasted away hundreds of tons of rock to rough out the gigantic heads of Washington, Jefferson, Theodore Roosevelt, and Lincoln, which he then proceeded to complete from a swinging scaffold with a pneumatic drill. He then similarly assaulted the bald face of Stone Mountain in Georgia to produce the colossal likeness of Robert E. Lee, a project which would undoubtedly have dismayed the modest Virginian could he have known of it.

Perhaps nothing in American art better suggests the curious

Frederic Remington: *Bronco Buster*, 1905, bronze, h. 32¾
(Courtesy of The Art Institute of Chicago, gift of Mr. Burr L. Robbins)

436

Gutzon Borglum: Mount Rushmore
(United States Department of the
Interior; National Park Service photograph)

identification of size with grandeur—a notion that runs through our history—than these colossal undertakings of Gutzon Borglum, an idea sufficiently current so that the first image from America transmitted to Europe via the Early Bird satellite was a view of Mount Rushmore. As much as such works would have appalled Andrew Jackson Downing as blatant examples of tasteless exhibitionism, they would have delighted P. T. Barnum and filled the heart of John Banvard with admiration perhaps not untinged with envy, since they dwarf even his "Great Panorama of the Mississippi."

There were others who clung to a traditional realism, among them Malvina Hoffman (1887–1966), whose greatest achievement is the series of bronzes of the various racial types of the world, made during years of travel and research, for the Hall of Man in the Chicago Natural History Museum. In their combination of scientific and artistic aims, with a scrupulous accuracy of representation enlivened by a vivid sense of the spirit of man, they realize with unusual completeness the factual ideal which has been dominant throughout so much of American art from Colonial times, and which still influences the approach to art and provides the standard of judgment for many Americans.

Another interpretation of realism appears in the work of Jo Davidson (1883–1952). Davidson, who had shown at the Whit-

Jo Davidson: *Gertrude Stein*,
bronze, h. 7⅓
(Gertrude Stein Collection,
Yale University Library)

ney Studio Club and had been a member of The Association of
American Painters and Sculptors—the group which put on the
Armory Show, where he exhibited several sculptures and drawings—became something of an official portraitist of his era, since
many of the world's great personages sat for him. The ruggedness of the surfaces of his unsparingly observed busts owes
much to Rodin. His technique is similar in this respect to that
of Jacob Epstein, his contemporary from the Lower East Side
of New York, who became Britain's leading sculptor of his
generation. But the factualism which Davidson also shares with
Epstein is wholly in the American tradition; when combined
with vigorous simplification and massing, as in his seated *Gertrude Stein*, it produced memorable results.

Gaston Lachaise (1882–1935) had shown at the Armory
also. Born in France, he received his early training there before
coming to America as a very young man. During the time he
was an assistant to Paul Manship, he carved the latter's Morgan
relief for the Metropolitan Museum before setting out on his
own to devote himself to the variations on the theme of the
female nude which occupied him for the rest of his life. Delicate
poise and a frequent sense of weightlessness lend an enigmatic
quality to his figures, whose voluminous amplitude gives them
the great dignity and something of the mysterious symbolic
aspect of the Earth Mother. Stieglitz had early appreciated his
work and had given him a showing, as he did a young Polish-
American named Elie Nadelman (1882–1946), who carved
marble like a Renaissance master and made some of the best

Gaston Lachaise: *Standing Woman*,
1932, bronze, h. 88
(Collection, The Museum of Modern Art,
New York,
Mrs. Simon Guggenheim Fund)

438

portrait busts in the century. Nadelman's witty commentaries on the types of the day—such as *The Conductor* (private collection), *The Jazz Pianist, Dancing Couple,* and *Man in the Open Air* (all three, Museum of Modern Art)—are more than amusing satires on the age of the flapper and *The Great Gatsby* in their masterly simplification of form and the brevity with which they achieve their lively significance.

Nadelman had known the Steins in Paris and played a part in Cubism and other aspects of modernism before coming to America in 1914. At a time when almost no one was even aware of its existence, he began collecting American folk art, which inspired him to seek a solution to the problem that had preoccupied John Rogers more than a half-century earlier—the production of sculpture in quantity while maintaining quality. He collected heads of china dolls, studied the style of Tanagra figurines from Greece, and experimented with reproductive techniques in papier-mâché and plaster. His large collection of folk art later became a major part of the Abby Aldrich Rockefeller Collection at Williamsburg.

With an attitude toward nature similar to that of Dove and Burchfield, John Flannagan (1895–1942) sought to liberate natural form from boulders in "sculpture with such ease, freedom, and simplicity that it hardly seems carved but rather to have endured so always," as he expressed his aim in *The Image in the Rock.* He came from North Dakota and served in the merchant marine before Arthur B. Davies' encouragement turned him to sculpture. Though he had none of the urbane wit and virtuoso technique of Nadelman, he was not untrained, since he had managed a period of study at the Minneapolis Institute of Arts. But his style is very much his own. His animal forms—a monkey, an elephant, a fledgling (as in *The Triumph of the Egg;* Museum of Modern Art)—like his rare human figures, are so well understood that they are full of life, yet they still suggest the contours of the glacial boulders from which they were carved with a skill that is belied by their simplicity.

Like the painters Mark Tobey and Morris Graves, Flannagan felt "the deep pantheistic urge of kinship with all living things and fundamental unity of life, a unity so complete it can see a figure of dignity even in the form of a goat." Other sculptors carried organic abstraction into the nonobjective. Isamu Noguchi (1904–   ), who studied in Paris with Brancusi, cuts shapes suggestive of natural forms in marble slabs with immaculate craftsmanship, and carves monumental forms with cleanly worked surfaces to create totemlike images of primeval dignity.

Elie Nadelman: *Man in the Open Air,* c. 1915, bronze, h. 54½ (Collection, The Museum of Modern Art, New York)

John Flannagan: *Crouching Figure,* c. 1935, granite, h. 10¾ (The Collection of The University of Michigan Museum of Art)

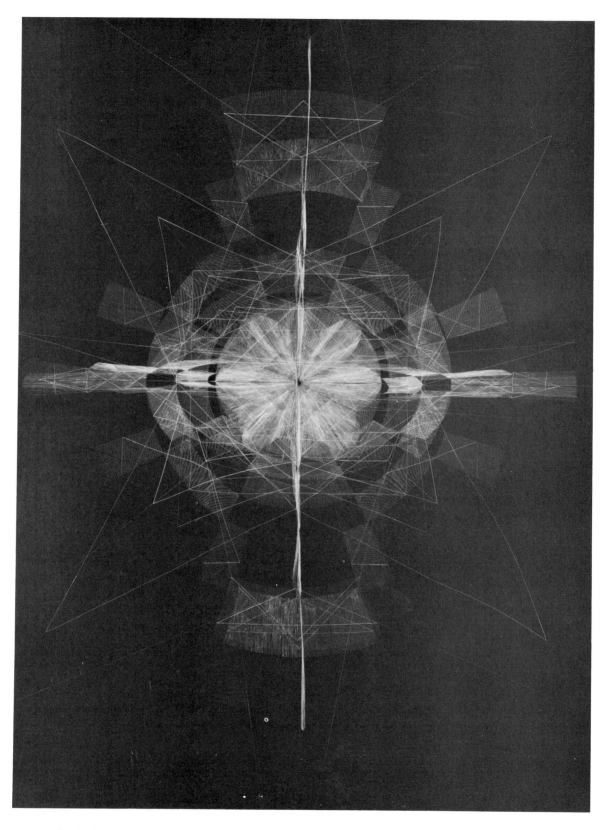

Richard Lippold: *Variation Within a Sphere, No. 10: The Sun,*
1956, gold-filled wire, 132 x 264 x 66 (The Metropolitan Museum of Art,
Fletcher Fund, 1956)

A style of organic abstraction is carried on in metal by Theodore Roszak (1907–   ) and Seymour Lipton (1903–   ). Roszak designs open, jagged forms and tortured surfaces, as in his compelling *Spectre of Kitty Hawk*. Lipton works with enclosed volumes with carefully studied and wrought textures, as in his ominous *Sorcerer*. The inventive work of David Smith (1906-65) placed him among the most powerful of the sculptors who exploited the brutality of metal in the big image. Richard Lippold (1915–   ) adds movement to the extreme delicacy of his wire construction of *The Sun*, with its glistening gold filaments.

Though many other sculptors are experimenting with the addition of motion, and the exploitation of such modern scientific techniques as electromagnetism and powering with transistors points new directions, Alexander Calder (1898–   ) was the pioneer in this field with his mobiles. There are echoes of Miró and Arp in his vocabulary of simple forms, and the floating compositions are so delightful in imaginative playfulness that one tends to overlook the deftness of their execution. Calder belongs to the third generation of a family of sculptors. His grandfather did the immense *William Penn* that surveys Philadelphia from the top of the City Hall, and his father produced a number of the figures that adorn Fairmount Park, but Alexander turned from the academic to experiment in a style of organic abstraction, both enlivened with motion in his mobiles and sturdily unyielding in his stabiles. The large black forms of the latter gesture angularly and have a contrastingly forthright power that makes them among the most effective large-scale sculptures of the period.

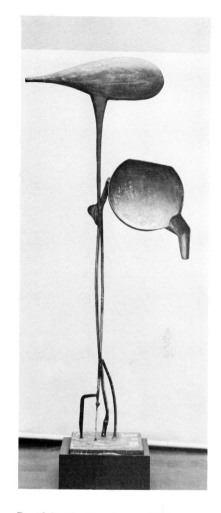

David Smith: *Tanktotem #1*, 1963, steel, h. 90 (Courtesy of The Art Institute of Chicago, gift of Mr. and Mrs. Joseph Z. Steinberg)

Theodore Roszak: *Spectre of Kitty Hawk*, 1946-47, welded and hammered steel brazed with bronze, h. 40¼ (Collection, The Museum of Modern Art, New York)

441

Andrew Wyeth: *Mother Archie's Church*, 1945, tempera on canvas, 25 x 48
(Addison Gallery of American Art, Phillips Academy, Andover, Mass.)

NEW ROADS AND FRESH VISIONS

Successive disruptions in Europe drove countless artists to seek refuge in America from the brutalities of Bolsheviks, Nazis, and Fascists, to accomplish a further internationalization of the world of art. The independent Surrealist Pavel Tchelitchew became as much at home in New York as in his native Moscow. The brothers Gabo and Pevsner brought from Russia their Constructivist sculptures of metal, plastic, glass, and wire. The Lithuanian Jacques Lipchitz brought from Paris his monumental Expressionism in bronze, and the Spaniard José de Creeft the vigorous technique of direct carving, which he shared with Zorach. After the Nazis forced the closing of the famous German school of design called the Bauhaus in 1934, Miës van der Rohe (1886–   ) came to the United States to plan buildings which illustrate his philosophy that "less is more," while Walter Gropius (1883–   ), who brought his purist conceptions of composing structure in space blocks, became head of the architectural school at Harvard. Josef Albers (1888–   ) continued at Yale the immaculate color explorations of squares within squares which were to develop into Optical Art. Moholy-Nagy (1895–1946) taught Chicago students his dynamic concepts of design. After a half-century spent mostly in Germany, Lyonel Feininger (1871–1956) returned to the land of his birth to develop new formulations of his evocatively colored linearism. The savagely satiric style with which George Grosz (1893–1959) had castigated German Nazism and militarism mellowed into a lyric celebration of the beauties of nature and of the female nude in the more sympathetic atmosphere of the New World until it was again mobilized by the Second World War. And Hans Hofmann (1880–1966) brought his genius for eliciting from his pupils their utmost in personal growth to influence the development of a generation of American painters.

Reawakened interest in the experimental led to the foundation of the Society of Abstract Artists in 1936 and to a renewal of the influence of Picasso, Miró, Braque, Arp, and other leading European masters. The Second World War encouraged another turning away from realism and an increasing exploration of various kinds and degrees of abstraction, which reached a climax in the 1940's and during the middle years of the century in the

443

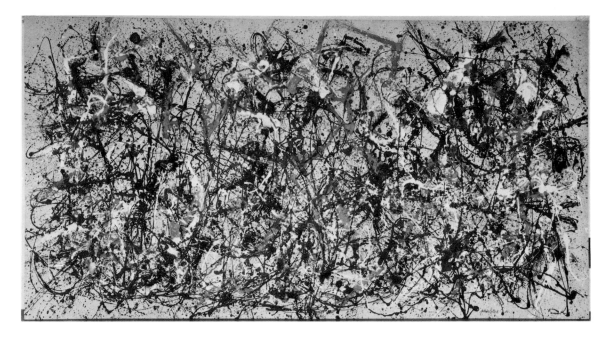

Jackson Pollock: *Autumn Rhythm*, 1950, 105 x 207
(The Metropolitan Museum of Art, George A. Hearn Fund, 1957)

emergence of the painting of Willem de Kooning (1904–),
Jackson Pollock (1912-56), and Franz Kline (1910-62) in
what has been called Action Painting or Abstract Expressionism.
These three painters were the leaders of the New York School,
along with such other artists as Arshile Gorky (1904-48), with
his delicate compositions of biomorphic forms in a personal
interpretation of Surrealism; Robert Motherwell (1915–),
with his obtrusively hard shapes of simple contour; Mark
Rothko (1903–), whose soft-edged rectangles are suffused in
color; Bradley Walker Tomlin (1899–1953), who composed
his interlacing bars of soft tones with calligraphic flourishes;
and Adolph Gottlieb (1903–), with his balancing of planetary
and bursting shapes. With Abstract Expressionism, America
took the lead in painting in the Western world that it had
partially assumed in architecture with the development of the
skyscraper in Chicago during the latter part of the nineteenth
century and the international influence of Frank Lloyd Wright
in the early years of the twentieth.

The half-century of experiment also tended to invigorate the
development of those who maintained a primarily objective
approach. It provided "a medicine for the disease of representing appearances," as John Sloan put it. As a result, artists
continued to work in almost every area within the same broad
spectrum that had appeared so shocking at the Armory Show,

444

from the descriptive realism of the old academy to the nonobjectivity of the new. Because of the immense variety and confusion of styles that resulted, only the major areas can be outlined here and only a few of the leading artists mentioned to illustrate some of the various tendencies.

The long career of Edward Hopper (1882–1967) provides a link in painting between the period of The Eight and the Armory Show, in which he exhibited, and today. He studied commercial art and illustration before working with Henri and going to Europe in his twenties. A tall, gaunt, quiet man of great presence, he believed that "originality is a matter neither of inventiveness nor of method—in particular a fashionable method. It is far deeper than that, and is the essence of personality." His long life was undeviatingly dedicated to painting, and his career showed a slow but constant growth which led him to the forefront of American art.

Edward Hopper: *The Nighthawks*, 1942, 33³⁄₁₆ x 60⅛ (Courtesy of The Art Institute of Chicago, Friends of American Art Collection)

Hopper handled both water color and oil as firmly and unostentatiously as Homer, with a similarly direct, masculine approach, and a spare, controlled style. His central theme is similar to Homer's also, in that it deals with the relation of the individual to his environment in America. However, Hopper does not show man alone with nature, but reveals his loneliness in the modern world, noisy and crowded though it may be. It is expressed in the mood of mansard-roofed houses in the glaring sun beyond the railroad tracks that isolate them; of a solitary nude, her face shadowed by her hair, sitting quietly in a shabby room while an August breeze blows the curtains; of the interior of a moving-picture palace upholstered in red plush, with the audience lost in the dream-world of the cinema, and a girl usher deep in her own thoughts; of an all-night lunch counter under the glare of fluorescent lights, which shine out on an empty street; of a gas station that could be anywhere in America. The attack is uncompromising, the human relevance never obtrusive but always clear. Hopper's pictures are pervaded with silence. Painted with intense concentration, his ordinary images become unforgettable, and rise from genre to symbol, from the commonplace to the memorable.

There are many painters working in a style which is basically expressionistic—that is, which reveals not only the artist's feelings about what he is painting, but also his emotional attitude toward himself and his world. Of this group, Ben Shahn (1898–   ) has perhaps won the most universal acclaim. The spirit of the social commitment of the Depression years and the WPA still lingers on in his art, which has been matured and enriched by time, but which remains dedicated to a purpose in which human values predominate. Like a number of other artists of his generation, he, too, was a photographer. In the late 1920's he turned to tempera in a palette suggestive of that of Renaissance frescoes to paint in the early 1930's the bitter pictures on the fate of Sacco and Vanzetti, and to comment on the growing pains of the labor movement. His children playing in a littered vacant lot say more than a tract about the life of the underprivileged in the great city. His *Pacific Landscape* (Museum of Modern Art) is eloquent in its expanse of pebbly beach, so minutely detailed that it acquires an obsessive tension as a setting for the body of a Marine sprawled at the water's edge in the distance. In his *Italian Landscape* (Whitney) he made his own poignant commentary on man's cruelty to man in terms of allegory, which he has increasingly employed to add depth and resonance to his work by raising it above the incidental or anecdotal. There are no screaming horses and heads as in Picasso's *Guernica*, but a landscape of rubble from buildings, destroyed except for a shattered remnant with a sign lettered "Europa," toward which a woman, in the black of mourning, gropes through the ruins.

Shahn is especially effective in black and white, perhaps because of his boyhood years as a lithographer's apprentice. In prints and drawings he makes maximum effect of his edgy, nervous line, possibly ultimately derived from Paul Klee but made very much his own. It has been turned with striking success to various purposes, in posters, such as that called *Hunger*, done for the State Department in 1946, in imaginative illustration, often accompanied by his personal printing style,

Ivan Albright: *"That Which I Should Have Done I Did Not Do,"*
1931-41, 97 x 36
(Courtesy of The Art Institute of Chicago)

and in separate prints, such as *Orchestra,* which shows a group of chairs and music racks humorously suggesting tuning up before a performance. It is typical of his work in line in the simplicity of means by which it achieves a maximum effect.

A more tragic view of man pervades the art of Ivan Le Lorraine Albright (1897–   ), and is shared by a number of other artists, including many of a younger generation who were involved with what has been called the restoration of the figure shortly after mid-century. Ivan and his twin brother Malvin, who took the name of Zsissly to avoid confusion, were the sons of a well-known portraitist. In the First World War Ivan was attached to the medical corps on the Western Front, and had to record with meticulous care the wounds, the mutilations, and their treatment. It was a traumatic and enlightening experience which not only disciplined his style, but also deepened his perception of man's mortality and physical frailty, of the contrast between his aspirations and achievements, of the depth and the variety of the human spirit, enduring despite intense suffering. Every fold and seam of the sou'wester in his painting of a *Fisherman* (Chicago) is as expressive of the hardship of the fisherman's life as are the minutely detailed wrinkles in his weather-beaten face. There is no ease, but there is the dignity of the man—stoic, independent, and close to nature like Homer's seafarers—who does his work, no matter how hard.

Albright's most memorable work is *"That Which I Should Have Done I Did Not Do,"* completed after almost a decade in 1941. It is a painting of a tall, battered door on which hangs a funeral wreath, and with one hand appearing at the left to relate the painting to the observer. As one critic has pointed out, the door is shut with the finality of a coffin lid. Every mar and scratch on the aged wood becomes a wound; every detail, almost surrealistically handled at minute scale, the record of an experience.

The vein of fantasy which runs through American art continues with great diversity to include a variety of artists of distinctly personal vision. Morris Graves (1910–   ) grew up and lived most of his life in the Northwest, where the Orient often seems closer than the East Coast and Europe. Study in Japan confirmed the sureness as well as the accent of his skillful brush as it analyzes "the phenomena of the external world . . . to make notations of its essences with which to verify the inner eye." Inspired by the art of the ancient Far East, Graves envisions birds and animals transformed with his own personal poetry of line into fragile but persistent images.

Morris Graves: *Blind Bird,*
1940, gouache and water color, 30⅛ x 27
(Collection, The Museum of Modern
Art, New York)

447

Because of the intensity of realization of surfaces in Albright's painting, he, too, is related to the trend of fantasy, as is Andrew Wyeth (1917–   ), who, like Albright, has been called a Magic Realist, since there is obviously more than the merely descriptive in both their styles. Wyeth was also the son of an artist, N. C. Wyeth, best known for his illustrations for such children's classics as *Treasure Island* and *Scottish Chiefs*. The younger Wyeth grew up in his father's studio and absorbed art and technique from boyhood. He lives in Pennsylvania, and spends summers in Maine, finding a limitless world for his painting in these two familiar places. He very early developed an extraordinary control of water color, handling it with Homer's sureness, but with a palette based on the earth tones and muted harmonies that prevail throughout his work, including the larger temperas with which he has become almost exclusively involved.

Wyeth is as aware as was Homer of the changing of the seasons, the direction of the wind, and the hour of the day. Many of his pictures are without figures—a laundry basket in a slanting ray of sunlight, a grain barrel in an old shed, a beached dory, the interior of *Mother Archie's Church*, with cracked plaster and a dove flying through the broken window like a descent of the Holy Spirit. But always "the trace of man" is there, the record of human habitation, of long use, and the stillness of a moment which is about to change. Underlying all Wyeth's painting is the theme he shares with other American artists—the solitariness of man, his relation to the natural world—expressed with a sense of wonder and of time's passing, of death and renewal, and of the irrevocability of the past that both haunts and creates our present and points on to our future.

Many artists have followed Dove's approach to abstraction, using elements derived from nature in a way that retains their organic qualities in the finished work, and they represent many stages from the recognizable to the nonrepresentational. All, however, retain a relevance to the natural world through their very organic quality. The influence of Mondrian and Albers, on the other hand, has led from the angular geometry seen in the painting of Sheeler into the nonobjective, without any such reference to nature. The latter are compositions on a flat plane or with a third dimension suggested by color relations or achieved through the use of collage and assemblage techniques that tend toward sculpture. The sharply delineated, flat forms derived from commonplace objects and the bright colors of Davis have been borrowed by Pop Art. Following the example of Marcel Duchamp with his Dadaist "ready-mades"—who in

1917 entered a urinal entitled *Fountain,* with the signature "R. Mutt," in a sculpture exhibition—food cans and cartons, pieces of pie, and other objects from the neighborhood store, sometimes greatly enlarged, appear as sculpture, while the comic strip, a form in which George Luks, Walt Kuhn, and Lyonel Feininger once excelled, has reappeared in blown-up scale as painting. Taking its elements from everyday life, Pop Art continued the trend established by the Ash Can School and carried on by Davis, with the added implication of the social commentary which informed so much of the art of the Depression years. For what is more effective in calling attention to the supermarket aspects of the aims and patterns of modern life than presenting as art, not the apotheosis of a saint, as in the Baroque period, but the apotheosis of a hamburger or a beer can? And enlarging to mural proportions, not episodes from the Bible or from national history, but a section of a comic strip of relentless banality?

Surrealism is characterized by a meticulously realized embodiment of imaginary forms or of forms unreally distorted, as in a dream, and, by automatism, the deliberate diminishing of conscious control to give free rein to the unconscious and the accidental, and then the exploiting of the results of chance. Albright has sometimes been called a Surrealist because of his minutely detailed surfaces, but his is an exaggerated naturalism used for Expressionistic purposes without the hallucinatory qualities of Surrealism. But it is the other aspect of the movement—its automatism—that has made the greatest impact on American art in recent times. Its form-making process appears in Arshile Gorky's works, which suggest visions of an internal landscape, with their visceral shapes and membranous connections painted in tones often dominated by red.

In its automatism and stress of the accidental Surrealism provided a basis for Action Painting. "The canvas began to appear," the critic Harold Rosenberg noted, "as an arena in which to act," and the painter became an actor creating "private myths" in an arena that often reached colossal size. The automatic approach produced de Kooning's brutal slashing with the brush, Kline's bold figure, and Pollock's compulsive interlace. It also produced Tomlin's more disciplined patterns of interweaving verticals and horizontals, Rothko's gradual simplification into rectangles with blurred edges floating against a related background color, and the many other forms of reduction of means. Its influence in technique was to produce all sorts of experiment with the handling of paint—splashing, dripping, blotting from one surface to another, mixing with other substances, and using various implements other than brushes—in an attempt to demolish traditional methods as well as attitudes.

The artists who have been grouped as the New York School came from many different parts of the United States and from other nations as well. Their association in New York has coincided with the emergence of that city as a leading artistic center in the completion of the internationalization of the world of art. But it is not the only artistically significant area in America, since there are flourishing regional centers—no longer provincial—from New England to the Pacific Northwest, where artists have won world-wide recognition. Mark Tobey (1890–) followed a development through figure painting, which he has never entirely abandoned, to the calligraphic style for which he is perhaps even better known and more highly respected in Europe than in this country. Inspired by the mystic approach to nature of Zen Buddhism and the one-world idealism of Bahai, he moved from abstract interpretations of city scenes to what he calls his "white writing," an interweaving and delicately controlled linearism of oriental flavor that suggests the trace of lights or the paths of stars. For him, its flowing continuity stands for the constant movement that he sees everywhere, a movement in and out of space and of time. Small in scale, delicate and cobweblike—but, like the cobweb, less fragile than may at first appear—his style has none of the ritual compulsion of Pollock's, which it has been thought to resemble. Tobey's style, in fact, preceded Pollock's in time and is of totally independent origin and purpose. Instead of tending to diminish or eliminate craftsmanship, as in the case of many artists of the New York School, Tobey has refined it and uses it so expertly that it is scarcely apparent. His scale is microscopic, but the implications of his work are universal.

The painting of the New York School and related nonobjective sculpture were the logical results of the experiment that had started in Europe during the early years of the century. As nature receded and subject disappeared, there came to be a compensating preoccupation with means and technique, until, as in all romantic periods—and the recent decades, with their emphasis on the self, the irrational, the expressive, the accidental, the compulsive, have been a romantic period in the arts in America—the act tended to become more important than the result, which maintained its significance largely as a record of that act. Means became an end instead of merely means. There was a mingling of categories and blurring of lines of demarca-

Adolph Gottlieb: *Blue at Night*, 1957, 42 x 60 (Virginia Museum of Fine Arts, Richmond, John Barter Payne Fund, 1958)

450

tion between the arts, as there had been in the earlier Romantic period before the Civil War, which progressed through emphasis on texture until paintings became as much reliefs as paintings. Assemblage grew increasingly three-dimensional, until it became sculpture; while sculpture added color and, finally, motion, to become appropriately kinetic. And, eventually, art merged with the theatrical, until the synthesis of the happening resulted.

In this process there seemed to take place a peeling away of traditional aspects of art, of proving the potential of each by isolating it as if in a laboratory, and pursuing it to its ultimate extreme. Thus de Kooning pushed bravura brush handling to the limit of automatic, compulsive slashing. Kline made the bold gesture the single subject and expression of his painting in a direction carried yet farther by that branch of sculpture concerned with what has been called minimal and primary structure. Pollock made the inner-directed ritual of creation the totality of his pictures; his large canvases are the record of the swirling, swinging, repetitive balletlike movements that became the purpose and end of the work. Kline and Gottlieb pursue in differing directions the significance of form which occupied David Smith in such sculptures as his series of brutal *Tank-totems*, and which appears more subtly in the work of Roszak and Lipton. Richard Lippold has concentrated on the straight line to evolve a sculpture of taut wire ordered in a Euclidian complexity.

Others have further reduced painting to vast and enveloping surfaces—to stripes, chevrons, and other flat figures, to shaped canvases, to panels of a single color. Sculpture has become an open or solid cube, a plastic tent, a clicking box, an undulation of pipe, a compressed automobile body, a transistorized mechanism executed in a deadpan Rube Goldberg manner. The object may look like a machine, or it may look as though a machine had produced it.

The urge to experiment has led to a reawakening of interest in print techniques, and the revival of lithography has attracted many by its flexibility and range. The potentialities of other traditional methods have been tested in graphic workshops. Silk screening has vastly enlarged the possibilities of scale. New materials and means, with stress on color and texture, have resulted in a similar diversity of style and approach in the graphic field as in the other arts.

Abstract Expressionism was an art of transition. As a movement it was soon over. A younger generation is leading other waves of experiment in other directions, in both painting and sculpture: to a different use of the image, to a reinterpretation of the figure in the light of Abstract Expressionist experience, to Pop Art, to Optical Art, to "painting" with light, as was envisioned by Thomas Cole, and to a "sculpture" of environment, even to the point of including sound, smell, and constantly shifting forms. But those who based their work, however abstract, on an organic relation to nature, as had Dove and Hartley in an earlier generation, and those who continued the representational tradition, whether infused with fantasy or stubbornly objective, also found new roads and fresh visions. With the exception of Surrealism, which proved important in American art chiefly through its influence on the development of Abstract Expressionism, art has continued to range throughout the entire spectrum, from the most experimental, through all stages of abstraction, to the strongly representational. And so deeply imbued is the American consciousness with the theory of progress that the energies of a majority of artists seem to be expended in a continuing search for novelty rather than for maturity or for truth.

Sculpture has become even more clamorous for attention than painting, and it is as exclusively purist in its elimination and reduction to ultimate form. Yet the old-fashioned notion that art must have a moral basis still exists by implication in such movements as Pop Art, in the assemblages of all sorts of objects of everyday use and consumption, and in the creation of environments with strange figures which point up the nightmarish qualities of life today.

Despite the hectic aspects of contemporary art, its diversity seems an index of its vitality and a measure of its capacity to express the various aspects of modern life, disturbing though they may be. In the midst of the gigantic happening which many consider the world of contemporary art to be, there is, nevertheless, a substantial number of artists whose careers have followed an organic evolution, independent of fashion, in the pattern of such older men as Hopper and Burchfield, and of Albright, Tobey, and Calder, who continue to grow as they tread their chosen paths with a constancy which is a measure of their strength.

X

The American Tradition

O. H. Ammonn, engineer: Verrazano-Narrows Bridge, 1959-64 (Triborough Bridge and Tunnel Authority)

THE AMERICAN TRADITION

We are a nation of immigrants. Unless we are pure-blooded American Indians, behind each of us lies an ultimate experience of the sea, of a pulling up of roots and a venturing forth into the unknown. As migrants we came and migrants we have remained, pushing the frontier westward and populating a continent, exploring the ocean and the air, and beginning to cross the threshold into space—always searching, always moving. Those who came brought bits and pieces of many traditions and ideals, which became a part of an American tradition and produced its most obvious characteristic, the diversity that is an expression of the pluralism and regionalism of our society.

Looking back on the three and a half centuries of our history, at the beginning we see fragments of the Middle Ages, and then, as beachheads grow into settlements and settlements into towns and cities, we hear echoes of the Baroque and the Rococo. With the achievement of independence, the Georgian shifts into the Classic as the new sense of nationality develops. The Classic is in turn replaced by the Romantic in a movement in which Americans play a greater part on both sides of an ocean which has become a highroad instead of the dangerous barrier of early years. As the traffic on that highroad increases, contacts and influences of Europe become stronger and closer. The Old World's constant troubles swell the stream of refugees which has continued into our own times, to the incalculable enrichment of the New World.

The dreadful split of the Civil War necessarily changed the emphasis and purpose of American efforts, turning energies into business and industry. The nation lapsed into cultural provincialism and was unprepared when, in the early years of this century, the full impact of European experimentation in the arts burst upon an unsuspecting America, smugly pursuing its materialist aims. But out of the wars and disruptions of this century came the dynamic artistic developments during which the New World captured the lead and carried the half-century of European experiment to its logical conclusion. At the same time, those native tendencies which cling to an essentially realist and naturalist tradition maintained a vigorous evolution, thus producing the almost chaotic variety we now see. Such a variety is not only a part of that tradition and an expression of

455

the energies which made the country grow, but also an index of the nation's vitality and of that of the arts today.

Though the extremes of Puritan austerity had noticeably relaxed by 1800, much of the Puritan heritage had been absorbed into the American tradition. It appeared in the sense of mission with which so many Americans viewed their country's growth, in the natural conservatism in clinging to older ways despite the attractions of the latest fashion, in the frequent preference for the useful over the ornamental, in a tendency toward the functional and toward pragmatic standards of judgment, and in the idea that the arts should embody some sort of lesson and have a higher purpose. The strain of austerity that runs through the arts in America is also a part of the same heritage, and the greater dignity and power of our utilitarian architecture and engineering—the bridges, skyscrapers, airplanes, dams, and grain elevators, which express greater creative force than our churches—is a continuation of the idea that the arts should be essentially utilitarian.

The Puritan's haunted world reappears in the "power of blackness" in Hawthorne's romances, in the doomed searching of Melville's heroes across the oceans of the world, in Allston's melancholy, in the macabre paintings of Quidor, in Ryder's visions, in Eakins' tormented inwardness, and in the brooding recognition of sinister and destructive forces in man and in nature in so much of the artistic expression of our own times.

Art has almost always been either more or less than art in America. In the early days it was a craft which had a recognized social function—creating a painted likeness, building a good house, or making a handsome and serviceable tankard or teapot. It was—and, no doubt, always will be—a matter of status and position, especially sought after in a society whose fluidity invites the meteoric rise that has come to be accepted as an American phenomenon. It was status to have fine plate and mahogany furniture and colorful and accurate portraits. The American way of life started early. With independence came an increasing desire to create a national art, again as a matter of prestige. Some saw it realized in the great panoramas of the Mississippi, but the Classic Revival in architecture and the rediscovery of the American scene by Thomas Cole provided a better answer.

Imbued with the attitudes of Romanticism, nineteenth-century Americans saw their country as a land of promise, with artists and writers alike sharing a sense of purpose to match the nation's sense of destiny. Thus their work frequently contains a moral ingredient derived from the Puritan tradition, considered essential in its day but foreign to ours. In 1836 Emerson wrote that "the world proceeds from the same spirit as the body of man. It is a remoter and inferior incarnation of God, a projection of God in the unconscious. . . . Its serene order is inviolable by us. It is, therefore, to us, the present expositor of the divine mind." This was also Cole's feeling and was widely shared by his contemporaries; it was expressed by Cooper through the natural piety and love of the wilds of Natty Bumppo, and it pervades the landscape of Hawthorne, still deeply shadowed with the Puritan past. A similarly empathic view of nature appears in the scenes of the Adirondack woods and of the sea by Winslow Homer, and, more subjectively, in Ryder's mysterious night pieces, which might be illustrations for the works of Melville, for whom the endless ocean was time or eternity, its depths and inhabitants symbols of nature's manifold power.

A response to nature similar to that which led Thomas Cole to wander the rugged slopes of the Catskills caused Albert Bierstadt to explore the distant valleys of the Rockies and beyond, and impelled Frederic Church to search out the remote peaks of the Andes and the icebergs off the wastes of Labrador. It inspired Audubon's lifelong quest and persuaded George Catlin and Seth Eastman to devote their careers to recording the vanishing folkways of the Indians. It summoned Martin Johnson Heade into the jungles of the Isthmus and the rain forests of South America in pursuit of the orchid and the hummingbird.

Art became an expression of national fulfillment, and there grew an increasing desire to promote and to share the arts, as vehicles of edification and education, which reached a crest around the middle of the nineteenth century in the Lyceum movement and, later, the Chautauquas, through whose programs even the inhabitants of remote villages attended lectures by such celebrated figures as Emerson, Dickens, Mark Twain, and, unlikely though it may seem, Oscar Wilde. Through the American Art-Union, art bulletins, engravings after good artists, and thousands of original works of art entered American homes. Gift books and annuals brought poetry, fiction, history, and belles-lettres to thousands of parlor tables in homes across the land, from town houses on the East Coast to frontier cabins in the West. American artists were busy and respected; their works sold, and a steady process of democratization of the arts seemed under way.

But the Civil War changed all that. An industrial and social revolution resulted. Only during the Depression years of the 1930's was the ideal revived, and art became a vehicle for social comment. Today it is again flourishing, with all the contradictions and also the press-agentry, a heritage of P. T. Barnum, which seem the inevitable accompaniment of things in this lively age. A movement that had been sidetracked a hundred years ago is now rolling again, but with an added power, because when America emerged as a leader in the arts around mid-century, the internationalization of the world of art was complete, and the last vestiges of the provincialism of the previous centuries were dispersed.

Again, art is many things to many people. It is collected by individuals and corporations, the new patrons. Led by the State of New York, government has re-entered the domain of the arts. Arts councils are everywhere, and museums have proliferated until there are thousands. An exhibition, "Art Across America," organized in 1960 for the opening of the Museum in Utica, New York, could illustrate the entire history of American art with works borrowed only from institutions open to the public in communities of a population of 100,000 or less, proving how far the geographical distribution of the sharing of the national artistic wealth had gone. More people attend museums than sports events, and art centers are sprouting across the land like mushrooms. Yet scarcely a symphony orchestra, resident theater, or ballet group in the country has adequate financial basis, and most museums are short-staffed and underfinanced. For a variety of reasons, art is still more than art in America. But again it has become a part of the ideal of the good life which men have been pursuing here since the first adventurers landed on Atlantic shores.

Looking back, we can see that certain qualities and tendencies are recurrent. The early settlers and those who followed the frontier found themselves in a new and alien environment with which the skills and knowledge they brought were not enough to enable them to cope. They were thrown on their own resources to experiment and improvise, and their sense of individualism grew with their self-reliance. It appeared early in the uncompromising Colonial portraits by unknown artisans, like the Freake and Pollard Limners, whose vernacular approach was continued by the countless itinerants and professionals without academic training. It comes out strongly in Copley, who learned a style that could compete with any academician, but whose vision had been sharpened by his New World

458

heritage, so that he could produce his incisive and telling likenesses of men and women of the Revolutionary generation. A
profound individualism underlay both the independent careers
and the insight of Homer, Eakins, and Ryder, and today it appears in the abundant diversity of the artistic scene.

Americans reacted to the vastness of the New World with an
extravagance that matched its extremes of size, of heat and cold,
of height of mountain, and breadth of desert and plain. The
violence of untamed nature became a part of the existence of
the pioneer and has remained a current in American life ever
since. It appears in the traditional tall tale, in the wildness of
frontier humor, in the brutal comedy of paintings by David
Gilmour Blythe, and in the ranting of the riverboatman, half
man, half alligator, "the old original iron-jawed, brass-mounted,
copper-bellied corpse-maker from the wilds of Arkansaw, who
scratched his head with the lightning, and purred himself to
sleep with the thunder." The same extravagance with its tendencies to violence and brutality lives on in American popular humor, which regards nothing so funny as to see someone
run over by a steamroller or so laughable as the clubbing and
pie-throwing of the old motion-picture comedy. Violence is a
part of current literature, television, and cinema, and it appears
in art, less in subject than in approach, in a handling of paint
that is almost savage, and in brutality of material and form in
sculpture.

Among contemporary artists there are many who show an
extravagance in the indulgence of individualism in the drastic
limitation of aims and means, in reducing the work to a single motive, form, or color; in cultivating the untasteful and the
unpainterly, the abrasive and hostile texture, for impact; and
in spurning any attempt to control or direct the character of an
observer's response to the work, which is reduced almost to the
equivalent of a found object. Yet, paradoxically, this extreme
reduction and abnegation grants greater freedom to the observer
to bring more of himself to the contemplation of the work, which
may then become the point of departure for a personal voyage
of discovery, and so to emphasize his own individuality all the
more.

Experiment and improvisation became habitual in America
and led men to develop all sorts of unexpected skills. It produced our Morses, Fultons, Fords, and Wright brothers, and became an approach to life. Improvisation is the basis of jazz,
an art form which is uniquely American. Jazz is the result of
the combination of skill and adventure, which creates a pattern

Ford Model T touring car, 1910
(Owned by the Henry Ford Museum
& Greenfield Village)

Mark Tobey: *Head*,
1957, sumi ink, 20¼ x 14¼
(Collection of Mrs. Wesley Hunner;
photograph by Earl Fields,
Seattle Art Museum)

of momentary syntheses in a swift duration of time, in a situation in which the act is more important than the result, because the art, as the philosopher John Dewey observed, "is in a quality of doing and of what is done." The parallel with much of recent painting is obvious, and its course of development gives evidence of a similar attitude.

In the impermanence and vastness of the New World the American grasped at what was palpable and clung to the finite and the factual. The light is hard and harsh in America. Objects appear clear-cut and with sharp edges, like motives in Sheeler's, O'Keeffe's, or Davis' paintings. The American sought and admired the factual in art, the realism of clearly defined objects—accurate, understandable, and specific. Fitz Hugh Lane's New England coast is as faithfully rendered as the rigging of his ships, which bore the critical scrutiny of mariners. James Hope, a minor nineteenth-century landscape painter, delighted in Professor Agassiz's certification of geological accuracy in the stratification of his painted rocks. And John Bard boasted that shipwrights had assured him that they could lay down the lines of the vessel appearing in any one of his steamship portraits. Accuracy was truth, and truth was the aim, whether in a portrait by Copley or Eakins, a still life by Harnett, frontier politicking by Bingham, or city scenes by members of the Ash Can School. Curiously, another aspect of factuality is represented by the modern artist's conviction that the painted canvas or the piece of sculpture is all—the thing itself, existing and finite, entirely apart from what it may or may not represent. And the less objective it is, the more it remains the single inescapable fact.

Man has always been more solitary in the New World than in the Old. He stood alone on an empty earth beneath an endless sky, and his feeling of solitariness kept recurring in his art. The American hero is a loner. He is Natty Bumppo or Daniel Boone in the wilderness, Remington's cowboy, Homer's Adirondack guide, or Gary Cooper stalking down an empty Western street at *High Noon*.

Man's relation to nature and to the extent of the New World has provided a theme which appears in the paintings of Fitz Hugh Lane and is central to the art of Winslow Homer. It runs through American literature from Melville, Whitman, and Mark Twain to Hemingway, Faulkner, and Steinbeck. It is reflected in the loneliness of the individual in the great city—the prevailing mood of the art of Edward Hopper—in the empty urban vistas of Ben Shahn's painting, and in the numinous still-

460

ness of Andrew Wyeth's landscapes. It has been and continues to be perhaps the central preoccupation of the American imagination as it constantly explores and seeks to come to grips with the problem of identity amidst the constant flux of a disturbing modern world, but always with the overtones of the earlier experience of the sea, of the limitless horizons of an unknown continent.

Since the American is a migrant and a wanderer, life becomes a search in time and space, Ahab's fated quest, or a voyage, as Thomas Cole saw and so explicitly symbolized it in the most famous series of paintings in American art. In the loneliness of the voyage, the American turns inward upon himself, to a world of fantasy and dream, which runs through his art as strongly as the opposing strain of factuality. It emerges in the reveries of Allston, in the Gothic novels of Charles Brockden Brown, in the nightmare paintings of Quidor, in the hallucinatory writings of Poe, in the romantic visions of Cole, Inness, and Blakelock, in the powerful symbolism of Ryder, and in the poetry of Wallace Stevens. It continues in the approach of many artists of today who look inward and seek to free the inner resources of the secret self and to liberate them in images and forms which have no objective existence in outward life.

In the constant moving and change, nothing is permanent, and the American looks back with the nostalgia that is another recurring theme in his art. It is the yearning for a home left long ago, for lost childhood, for times that seemed simpler and more carefree. It is in the homely farm scenes of William Sidney Mount and Eastman Johnson, in the prints of Currier & Ives, in the refrain of the folk song, in the ballads of Stephen Foster, and in the blues. And because life is motion and change, the American feels a compulsion to act, that action is a virtue in itself. So preoccupied is he with motion that he has streamlined his toaster and refrigerator, and the automobile has become a symbol of his acceptance of movement as a constant factor in his life. The theme of many American books and moving pictures is that of the chase—an expression of the cult of action—from the deadly *Flight and Pursuit* of Rimmer's strange painting to the mad rushing back and forth of the Keystone cops and the Marx brothers. Movement has become a function of life, and thus art has become increasingly an action, a means of carrying on a search, as in the laboratory of the scientist or in the workshop of the inventor. Change has become a continuity, and since progress is the recognized aim of life, and progress demands change, change has come to be confused with

Alexander Calder:
Lobster Trap and Fish Tail,
1939, painted metal, h. 114
(Collection, The Museum of Modern Art,
New York,
gift of the Advisory Committee)

461

progress, and novelty with originality. Thus fashion has entered the art world to demand the latest in painting and sculpture, as if it were a matter of hemlines and hairdos, to add further confusion to an already extreme variety. But the arts are undeniably back in the center of things.

The American's inheritance of frontier egalitarianism makes him suspicious of the thinker and instinctively prefer the doer to the egghead. Americans have not been notable for creating theories of art, and those artists who have carried European experiment to its present state have done so more by adventurous action, by experiment and improvisation, than by cerebration. Our arts have been predominantly romantic in their emphasis on the emotional, on identification with the natural world, over the theoretical. And in their experiment they have tended to merge old forms and create new. Thus Hawthorne invented something he called the romance because the traditional form of the novel suited neither his purposes nor his gifts. *Moby Dick*, America's greatest prose work, is part symbolic epic and part treatise, with an adventure story thrown in. And Whitman invented a new form, appropriately involving aspects of journalism, for his celebration of man in America. Robert Frost reconstructed everyday speech in verses that express far more than the parochial and are devoid of the self-consciousness of regionalism. Similarly, there has been a blurring of the traditional distinctions between the visual and even the performing arts in the process of recent creative experiment.

The freedom in the New World, its absence of history, and the fluidity of society encouraged men to act to satisfy immediate needs in the immediately practical way. In such a situation the artificiality of the usual categories of art history becomes apparent, for the true history of art is not merely a history of styles, but the story of the creative in man. Imagination often ran to the practical in America. Brought up with a tradition of experiment as the method, and pragmatism as the basis of judgment, Robert Fulton did not think twice about turning from painting to invention, and back to painting again to finance the invention. Like Morse, he was as creative in the one field as in the other.

Bulfinch was an engineer as well as an architect, and his India Wharf was as monumental as his Boston State House, yet without a detail suggesting any other than its specific function. Willard, Parris, Town, and Strickland were also imaginative engineers, as was Loammi Baldwin, an architect who developed the apple that bears his name. And whoever invented the bal-

Concord coach "The Kearsarge," c. 1865
(Owned by the Henry Ford Museum
& Greenfield Village)

462

Wadsworth Atheneum, 25 Atheneum Square N., *Hartford*, Conn. Among many other collections, an important group of American paintings and decorative arts objects.

Fogg Art Museum of *Harvard* University, Quincy Street and Broadway, Cambridge, Mass. Among many other important collections, distinguished American arts.

The *Henry Ford Museum* and Greenfield Village, Dearborn, Mich. Restored American period houses, furnishings, arts and objects of all kinds. A major collection of American art, history, and technology.

Historical Society of Pennsylvania, 1300 Locust Street, Philadelphia, Pa. State historical collection with portraits from Colonial times to the Civil War and a large manuscript collection.

William Rockhill Nelson Gallery of Art and Mary Atkins Museum of Fine Arts, 4525 Oak Street, *Kansas City*, Mo. Among diverse collections, fine examples of American painting and decorative arts.

Maryland Historical Society, 201 West Monument Street, Baltimore, Md. An historical museum and house with paintings, furniture, and other material pertaining to the area.

Massachusetts Historical Society, 1154 Boylston Street, Boston, Mass. An extraordinary collection of documents of American history, and a number of important colonial portraits and other objects.

The *Metropolitan* Museum of Art, Fifth Avenue and 82nd Street, New York, N.Y. One of the great museums of the world, which has remarkable and extensive collections of American arts from earliest days to the present.

University of *Michigan* Museum of Art, Ann Arbor, Mich. Collections include Western art from the 6th to the 19th centuries and contemporary American and European paintings, sculptures, drawings, and prints.

The *Minneapolis* Institute of Arts, 201 East 24th Street, Minneapolis, Minn. Among varied collections of all periods, fine examples of American painting.

The Pierpont *Morgan* Library, 33 East 36th Street, New York, N.Y. One of the great collections of manuscripts and rare books, including some American material.

Museum of the City of New York, 1220 Fifth Avenue, New York, N.Y. The history museum of the city with outstanding collections in all pertinent fields.

The *Museum of Modern Art*, 11 West 53rd Street, New York, N.Y. The leading institution in its field; its collections include a very large representation of American painting, sculpture, decorative arts, and design of the 20th century.

National Academy of Design, 1083 Fifth Avenue, New York, N.Y. An art museum whose collections are made up of the work of members, including self-portraits, since its foundation in 1825.

National Collection of Fine Arts, Smithsonian Institution, Constitution Avenue at Tenth Street, N.W., Washington, D.C. A varied collection including some fine American paintings, especially of the 19th century.

National Gallery of Art, Sixth Street and Constitution Avenue, Washington 25, D.C. Among large and varied collections, fine American paintings from Colonial times through the 19th century, including the Garbisch collection of American primitive paintings.

University of *Nebraska* Art Galleries, Lincoln, Neb. Collections include examples of 20th-century American paintings.

The *Newark* Museum, 43–49 Washington Street, Newark, N.J. A museum with varied artistic and scientific collections, and with fine examples of American paintings, sculpture, and decorative arts.

Newport Historical Society, 82 Touro Street, Newport, R.I. Maintains several historic houses and buildings, and historical collections pertaining to the area.

The *New-York Historical* Society, 170 Central Park West, New York, N.Y. Outstanding historical and art collections, including Audubon originals.

The *North Carolina Museum* of Art, 107 East Morgan Street, Raleigh, N.C. General arts collections, including examples of American art.

Old Salem Inc., 600 South Main Street, Winston-Salem, N.C. A preservation and restoration project, with art and historical collections, of the Moravian settlement of the 18th and early 19th centuries.

The National Gallery of Canada, Elgin and Albert Streets, *Ottawa*, Ontario, Canada. One of the great museums of North America, with outstanding English and Canadian paintings.

Peabody Museum of Salem, 161 Essex Street, Salem, Mass. An historical museum with one of the outstanding maritime collections in the United States.

The *Peale Museum*, 225 North Holliday Street, Baltimore, Md. An history museum of Baltimore and vicinity, with a collection of works by the Peale family.

The *Pennsylvania Academy* of the Fine Arts, Broad and Cherry Streets, Philadelphia, Pa. An historic art school with an outstanding collection of American paintings.

Pennsylvania Farm Museum of Landis Valley, 2451 Kissel Hill Road, Lancaster, Pa. Historical collections of Pennsylvania agriculture and of folk arts of the region.

Philadelphia Museum of Art, Benjamin Franklin Parkway at 26th Street, Philadelphia, Pa. One of the great museums of America containing extraordinary collections of American arts.

The *Phillips Collection*, 1600 Twenty-first Street, N.W., Washington, D.C. A distinctive collection of modern art and its sources, including fine American paintings.

Pilgrim Hall, Court Street, Plymouth, Mass. The Plymouth Historical Society's collection of material pertaining to the Pilgrims.

Plimoth Plantation, Inc., Warren Avenue, Plymouth, Mass. Re-creation of the early Pilgrim settlement, with historical collections.

The Art Museum, *Princeton* University, Princeton, N.J. A distinguished collection of works of art of virtually all media, schools, and periods.

Reading Public Museum and Art Gallery, 500 Museum Road, *Reading, Pa.* A small collection including excellent American paintings.

Remington Art *Memorial,* 303 Washington Street, Ogdensburg, N.Y. A large collection of paintings and bronzes by Frederic Remington.

The Morse Gallery of Art, *Rollins College,* Winter Park, Fla. An outstanding collection of Tiffany glass.

City Art Museum of *St. Louis,* Forest Park, St. Louis, Mo. Among many collections in various fields, fine examples of American painting and decorative arts.

M. H. De Young Memorial Museum, Golden Gate Park, *San Francisco,* Cal. Among varied collections, good examples of American paintings and decorative arts.

Seattle Art Museum, Volunteer Park, Seattle, Wash. Collections are particularly strong in Far Eastern art and West Coast American art.

Shelburne Museum, Inc., Shelburne, Vt. An history museum with period houses and other buildings, a Lake Champlain steamer and lighthouse, and a fine collection of American arts and crafts.

Museum of Fine Arts, 49 Chestnut Street, *Springfield,* Mass. Among general collections, excellent examples of American painting and other arts.

Old *Sturbridge* Village, Sturbridge, Mass. A preservation project including arts, crafts, and restored New England buildings.

Joe and Emily Lowe Art Center of *Syracuse* University, 309 University Place, Syracuse, N.Y. Largely a collection of recent American art.

The *Toledo* Museum of Art, Monroe Street and Scottwood Avenue, Toledo, O. Among various collections, excellent American arts, including glass.

Munson-Williams-Proctor Institute, 310 Genesee Street, *Utica,* N.Y. A collection primarily of American paintings and sculpture, with a restoration of an 1850 house, Fountain Elms.

Virginia Museum of Fine Arts, Boulevard and Grove Avenue, Richmond, Va. Among varied collections, fine examples of American art, including decorative arts, from Colonial times.

Old Dartmouth Historical Society *Whaling Museum,* 18 Johnny Cake Hill, New Bedford, Mass. A marine museum whose collections emphasize the history of whaling.

Whitney Museum of American Art, Madison Avenue and 75th Street, New York, N.Y. A large collection of American art of the 20th century.

Wichita Art Museum, 619 Stackman Drive, Wichita, Kan. Collections include American art from Colonial times to the present.

Colonial *Williamsburg,* Inc., Williamsburg, Va. An extraordinary recreation and restoration project of a Colonial capital, with rich collections of American and English arts of the 18th century.

The Henry Francis du Pont *Winterthur* Museum, Winterthur, Del. An extraordinary collection of American arts from earliest Colonial times until mid-19th century; a center of research in the American field.

Worcester Art Museum, 55 Salisbury Street, Worcester, Mass. An important and select collection of American arts.

Yale University Art Gallery, 1111 Chapel Street, New Haven, Conn.
Varied collections including fine American painting, silver, furniture, and glass.

Butler Institute of American Art, 524 Wick Avenue, *Youngstown*, O.
A museum devoted to American painting.

BIBLIOGRAPHY

Out of the staggering number of works written about the arts in America, the following have been chosen as being among the most useful for the general reader wishing to pursue various subjects in greater detail. Many of the books, which are listed in the general order in which their subjects occur in the text, contain more specialized bibliographies. An asterisk denotes those available in paperback.

The Art Index, *which may be consulted in any library, is an invaluable reference to articles in various periodicals on all aspects of the arts. A file of the magazine* Antiques, *also available in many libraries, is a gold mine of information, while* Old-Time New England, *the publication of the Society for the Preservation of New England Antiquities, also has much useful material. Winterthur's scholarly publications on furniture and related subjects are important sources of information, as are the publications of such significant collections of American art as Colonial Williamsburg, Shelburne Museum, Old Sturbridge Village, the New York State Historical Association at Cooperstown, the Henry Ford Museum and Greenfield Village in Dearborn, Old Deerfield, Plimoth Plantation, The Detroit Institute of Arts, The Art Institute of Chicago, The Metropolitan Museum of Art in New York, the Boston Museum of Fine Arts, The Corcoran Gallery in Washington, and of a number of other museums, historical societies, and other institutions, many of which are included in the list of sources for illustrations. The Whitney Museum of American Art, The Museum of Modern Art, and The Fine Arts Federation—all in New York City—have also published many catalogues, essays, and monographs, primarily on American painting and sculpture, which are of consistently high quality. The Archives of American Art in Detroit, The Index of American Design in Washington, and the Frick Art Reference Library in New York are major sources of information concerning the arts in America.*

EARLIER WORKS

William Dunlap: *A History of the Rise and Progress of the Arts of Design in the United States.* 3 vols. Boston: Goodspeed, 1918. A new edition, with notes, of the original two-volume work of 1834, the first of its kind.

Henry T. Tuckerman: *Book of the Artists: American Artist Life.* New York: Putnam, 1867. Another pioneering work by a sympathetic critic who was a contemporary of many about whom he wrote.

Samuel Isham: *The History of American Painting.* New York: Macmillan, 1905. A pioneering work still of value though superseded by Richardson and Barker.

Loredo Taft: *The History of American Sculpture,* new edition, 2 vols. New York: Macmillan, 1930. Seriously outdated but still the only general book on the subject.

Bibliography

CURRENT WORKS

Oliver W. Larkin: *Art and Life in America*, revised and enlarged edition. New York: Holt, 1960. The best general survey of the subject, with a detailed bibliography.

Hugh Morrison: *Early American Architecture from the First Colonial Settlements to the National Period*. New York: Oxford University, 1952. The best treatment of the subject.

Wayne Andrews: *Architecture, Ambition, and Americans*. New York: Harper, 1955. A lively history of American architecture from Colonial times, presented in terms of outstanding buildings, architects, and clients.

Edgar P. Richardson: *Painting in America: The Story of 450 Years*. New York: Crowell, 1956. The best survey of American painting, with a useful bibliography.

Virgil Barker: *American Painting, History and Interpretation*. New York: Macmillan, 1950. A thoughtful work on the course of American painting from earliest times through the period of Homer, Eakins, and Ryder, with a detailed bibliography.

*James T. Flexner: *The Pocket History of American Painting*. New York: Washington Square, 1962. A very brief popular treatment.

American Processional, 1492–1900, catalogue of an exhibition at The Corcoran Gallery of Art, Washington, D.C., 1950. An illustrated survey, with good text, tracing the development of American history and art.

Helen Comstock: *American Furniture, Seventeenth, Eighteenth, and Nineteenth Century Styles*. New York: Viking, 1962. An invaluable and generously illustrated survey.

Wolfgang Born: *Still Life Painting in America*. New York: Oxford University, 1947.

—— *American Landscape Painting, An Interpretation*. New Haven: Yale University, 1948. Both are useful books.

*Christopher Tunnard and Henry Hope Reed: *American Skyline, The Growth and Form of Our Cities and Towns*. New York: Mentor, 1956.

George S. and Helen McKearin: *American Glass*. New York: Crown, 1941. Still the most complete study.

Kathryn C. Buhler: *American Silver*. Cleveland: World, 1950. A brief book and the best general account.

C. Louise Avery: *Early American Silver*. New York: Century, 1930. Still the best detailed treatment of the subject.

*Alice Winchester: *How to Know American Antiques*. New York: Mentor, 1952. A brief but comprehensive guide.

*John W. McCoubry: *American Art 1700–1960: Sources and Documents*. Englewood Cliffs: Prentice-Hall, 1965. An anthology of letters, newspaper and magazine articles, etc., pertaining to major artistic developments, but primarily concerned with painting.

Aline B. Saarinen: *The Proud Possessors: The Lives, Times, and Tastes of Some Adventurous American Art Collectors.* New York: Random House, 1958. The story of major 19th- and 20th-century collectors.

George C. Groce and David H. Wallace: *The New-York Historical Society's Dictionary of Artists in America, 1564–1860.* New Haven: Yale University, 1957. A valuable reference.

BY CHAPTERS

Introduction

Rexford Newcomb: *Spanish Colonial Architecture in the United States.* New York: J. J. Augustin, 1937. A pictorial survey.

Trent Sanford: *Architecture of the Southwest.* New York: Norton, 1950.

Mitchell A. Wilder and Edgar Breitenbach: *Santos: The Religious Folk Art of New Mexico.* Colorado Springs: Taylor Museum, 1943.

Paul L. Grigaut: *The French in America, 1570–1763.* Detroit: Detroit Institute of Arts, 1951.

I. Colonial Enterprise

*Louis B. Wright: *The Cultural Life of the American Colonies, 1607–1763.* New York: Harper Torchbooks, 1957. Excellent general cultural background.

James T. Flexner: *First Flowers of Our Wilderness.* Boston: Houghton, Mifflin, 1947. Early Colonial painting.

Allen I. Ludwig: *Graven Images.* Middletown, Conn.: Wesleyan University, 1966. A beautifully illustrated essay on early gravestones, the first native school of sculpture.

Meyric R. Rogers: *American Interior Design.* New York: Norton, 1947. An illustrated survey from earliest times.

Marshall B. Davidson: *Colonial Antiques.* New York: Viking, 1967. A generously illustrated and handsomely presented survey.

II. Georgian America

Fiske Kimball: *Domestic Architecture of the American Colonies and of the Early Republic.* New York: Scribner, 1922. A pioneering work and a classic in the field.

Carl Bridenbaugh: *Peter Harrison, First American Architect.* Chapel Hill: University of North Carolina, 1961.

*—— *The Colonial Craftsman.* Chicago: University of Chicago (Phoenix Books), 1961. The best general work.

Joseph Downs: *American Furniture: Queen Anne and Chippendale Periods, 1725–1788.* New York: Viking, 1967 (rev. ed.). Scholarly, complete, well illustrated.

Henry Wilder Foote: *Robert Feke, Colonial Portrait Painter.* Cambridge: Harvard University, 1930.

—— *John Smibert, Painter.* Cambridge: Harvard University, 1950.

James T. Flexner: *America's Old Masters.* New York: Viking, 1939. An account of the most important of the Colonial painters.

Jules David Prown: *John Singleton Copley,* 2 vols. New Haven: Yale University, 1966. The most complete treatment of Copley's work, both in America and England.

III. The New Republic

*Russell Blaine Nye: *The Cultural Life of the New Nation, 1776–1830.* New York: Harper Torchbooks, 1960. Excellent background.

Grose Evans: *Benjamin West and the Taste of His Times.* Carbondale: Southern Illinois University, 1959.

Edgar P. Richardson: *Washington Allston, A Study of the Romantic Artist in America.* Chicago: University of Chicago, 1948.

Charles Coleman Sellers: *Charles Willson Peale,* 2 vols. New York: American Philosophical Society, 1934. A complete and scholarly account.

James T. Flexner: *Gilbert Stuart.* New York: Knopf, 1955. A lively account of a lively personality.

Ihna T. Frary: *Thomas Jefferson, Architect and Builder.* Richmond: Garrett and Massie, 1931.

Fiske Kimball: *Mr. Samuel McIntire, Carver, The Architect of Salem,* Portland, Me.: The Essex Institute, 1940.

Charles A. Place: *Charles Bulfinch, Architect and Citizen.* Boston: Houghton Mifflin, 1925.

Talbot Hamlin: *Greek Revival Architecture in America.* New York: Oxford University, 1944. The most complete treatment of the subject.

—— *Benjamin Henry Latrobe.* New York: Oxford University, 1955.

Agnes Addison Gilchrist: *William Strickland, Architect and Engineer, 1788–1854.* Philadelphia: University of Pennsylvania, 1950. Both Latrobe and his pupil Strickland were important Greek Revival architects and also imaginative engineers.

Classical America 1815–1845, catalogue of an exhibition at The Newark Museum, 1963. Well written and well illustrated, it deals with painting, sculpture, and decorative arts of Classic style.

IV. From the Greek Revival to the Gothic

Roger Hale Newton: *Town & Davis, Architects.* New York: Columbia University, 1942.

Everard M. Upjohn: *Richard Upjohn, Architect and Churchman (1802–1878).* New York: Columbia University, 1939.

Carl W. Conduit: *American Building Art, The Nineteenth Century.* New York: Oxford University, 1960. An excellent account of the progress of engineering and construction.

Clay Lancaster: *Architectural Follies in America*. Rutland, Vt.: Tuttle, 1960. An amusing treatment of an amusing subject.

Albert TenEyck Gardner: *Yankee Stonecutters: The First American School of Sculpture, 1800–1850*. New York: Columbia University, 1944. The only work in the field to date.

V. America Rediscovered

James T. Flexner: *That Wilder Image: The Painting of America's Native School from Thomas Cole to Winslow Homer*. Boston: Little, Brown, 1962.

*Helen G. Cruickshank, ed.: *John and William Bartram's America*. New York: Doubleday (Anchor Books), 1961. A generous sampling of the writings of America's pioneer naturalists.

Alexander B. Adams: *John James Audubon*. New York: Putnam, 1966.

Alice Ford: *John James Audubon*. Norman: University of Oklahoma, 1964.

*John James Audubon: *Audubon and His Journals*, ed. by Maria Audubon, 2 vols. New York: Dover, 1960. A collection of the artist-naturalist's own lively writings; the biographical material is entirely obsolete, however.

Esther I. Seaver: *Thomas Cole*, catalogue of an exhibition at the Wadsworth Atheneum, Hartford, 1949. The best treatment of the subject.

Frederick A. Sweet: *The Hudson River School and the Early American Landscape Tradition*, catalogue of an exhibition at the Chicago Art Institute and the Whitney Museum, 1931. An excellent summary of the subject.

VI. Democracy and the Arts

Jean Lipman and Mary C. Black: *American Folk Decoration*. New York: Oxford University, 1967. Excellent and well illustrated.

Jean Lipman and Alice Winchester: *Primitive Painting in America*. New York: Dodd, Mead, 1950. Excellent and well illustrated.

Nina Fletcher Little: *American Decorative Wall Painting, 1700–1850*. New York: Old Sturbridge Village and Studio, 1952. The best treatment of the subject.

—— *The Abby Aldrich Rockefeller Folk Art Collection, Colonial Williamsburg*. Boston: Little, Brown, 1957. An outstanding catalogue of an outstanding collection with an excellent introductory essay; that of the Edgar William and Bernice Chrysler Collection in the National Gallery, Washington, is also excellent.

Edwin O. Christensen: *The Index of American Design*. New York: Macmillan, 1950. Based on the tremendous record developed during the massive research undertaken under the WPA, it presents an extraordinary record.

Marion V. Brewington: *Shipcarvers of North America*. Barre, Mass.:

Barre Publishing Company, 1962. The authoritative work in the field.

Henri Marceau: *William Rush, 1756–1833, The First Native American Sculpture.* Philadelphia: Philadelphia Museum of Art, 1937.

*Russell Lynes: *The Tastemakers.* New York: Grosset & Dunlap (Universal Library), 1954. A highly interesting account of the progress of popular taste.

John Francis McDermott: *The Lost Panoramas of the Mississippi.* Chicago: University of Chicago, 1958. An entertaining account.

Lloyd Goodrich: *American Genre.* New York: The Whitney Museum of American Art, 1935.

VII. A World Changed

Denys Sutton: *Nocturne: The Art of James McNeill Whistler.* Philadelphia: Lippincott, 1964.

Frederick A. Sweet: *Sargent, Whistler, and Mary Cassatt,* catalogue of an exhibition at the Chicago Art Institute, 1954. An excellent presentation of three leading expatriate painters of the period. David McKibbin, author of *Sargent's Boston,* is preparing the definitive work on that artist.

Albert Ten Eyck Gardner: *Winslow Homer.* New York: C. N. Potter, 1961.

Lloyd Goodrich: *Thomas Eakins, His Life and Work.* New York: Whitney Museum of American Art, 1933.

Alfred Frankenstein: *After the Hunt: William Harnett and Other American Still Life Painters, 1870–1900.* Berkeley: University of California Press, 1953. An interesting account of scholarly detective work.

*Lloyd Goodrich: *Albert P. Ryder.* New York: Braziller, 1959.

Edgar P. Richardson: *American Romantic Painting.* New York: Weyhe, 1944. A thoughtful essay, well illustrated.

VIII. Architecture and Sculpture after the Civil War

Lewis Mumford, ed.: *Roots of Contemporary American Architecture.* New York: Reinhold, 1952. An important work by a leading authority in architecture and urban design.

*Nikolaus Pevsner: *Pioneers of Modern Design.* New York: Penguin Books, 1964. An excellent illustrated survey including European and American examples.

Henry-Russell Hitchcock: *The Architecture of H. H. Richardson and His Times.* New York: Museum of Modern Art, 1936. A solid work by one of the outstanding architectural historians of today.

Hugh Morrison: *Louis Sullivan, Prophet of Modern Architecture.* 1935. Excellent treatment of a very significant figure.

Wayne Andrews: *Battle for Chicago.* New York: Harper, 1946. A lively account of the development of the skyscraper.

Henry-Russell Hitchcock and Arthur Drexler: *Built in U.S.A.: Post-War Architecture*. New York: Museum of Modern Art, 1952. An excellent survey based on an outstanding exhibition.

—— *Architecture, Nineteenth and Twentieth Centuries*. A thoughtful and complete treatment of the emergence of modern architecture.

Frederick Gutheim, ed.: *Frank Lloyd Wright on Architecture: 1894–1940*. New York: Duell, Sloan, 1941. A selection of Wright's always lively opinions on architecture. Most of his books are now available in paperback.

Henry-Russell Hitchcock and Philip Johnson: *The International Style*. New York: Norton, 1932. Based upon the important exhibition of the same title shown at the Museum of Modern Art, organized by Johnson.

IX. A World Divided

Milton W. Brown: *American Painting from the Armory Show to the Depression*. Princeton: Princeton University, 1955. A good survey.

*Ira Glackens: *William Glackens and the Ash Can Group*. New York: Grosset & Dunlap (Universal Library), 1957. A delightful and highly readable account.

Milton W. Brown: *The Story of the Armory Show*. New York: Joseph H. Hirschhorn Foundation, New York Graphic Society, 1963. A lively narrative of an important event and its background.

John I. H. Baur: *Revolution and Tradition in American Art*. Cambridge: Harvard University, 1951.

Lloyd Goodrich: *Pioneers of Modern Art in America*, catalogue of an exhibition at the Whitney Museum of American Art, 1956. A useful survey.

Andrew C. Ritchie: *Abstract Painting and Sculpture in America*. New York: Museum of Modern Art, 1951. One of the many important and useful publications of the Museum.

X. The American Tradition

Constance Rourke: *The Roots of American Culture*. New York: Harcourt, 1942. A collection of perceptive essays on various aspects of American culture.

John Dos Passos: *Prospects of a Golden Age*. Englewood Cliffs: Prentice-Hall, 1959. An interpretive history.

Henri Dorra: *The American Muse,* New York: Viking, 1961. A generously illustrated interpretation.

*John A. Kouwenhoven: *Made in America: The Arts in Modern Civilization*. New York: Doubleday (Anchor Books), 1962. An analysis of what the author identifies as the "vernacular tradition" in America.

Oskar Hagen: *The Birth of the American Tradition of Art*. New York: Scribner, 1940. An interpretation of the artistic developments from the later 17th century to the Revolution.

Bibliography

Howard Mumford Jones: *O Strange New World: American Culture, The Formative Years.* New York: Viking, 1964. A fascinating study of American cultural backgrounds and developments from the earliest period of colonization to the early 19th century.

John W. McCoubrey: *American Tradition in Painting.* New York: Braziller, 1963.

INDEX